VOLUME 2
LONDON WALKS

25 WALKS BY
LONDON WRITERS

Time Out Guides Limited
Universal House
251 Tottenham Court Road
London W1T 7AB
Tel + 44 (0)20 7813 3000
Fax + 44 (0)20 7813 6001
Email guides@timeout.com
www.timeout.com

Editorial

Editor Sarah Guy
Deputy Editors Adam Barnes, Simon Cropper
Listings Checker Cathy Limb
Researchers Helen Babbs, Catherine Blake, Christina Dee, Andrew Kenny, Sarah Mackie, James Miller, Amy Nelson, Rob Norman, Holly Pick, Victoria Redclift, Helen Scott, Alan Simeoni, Zoe Strimpel
Indexer Jonathan Cox

Editorial/Managing Director Peter Fiennes
Series Editor Sarah Guy
Deputy Series Editor Cath Phillips
Business Manager Gareth Garner
Guides Co-ordinator Holly Pick
Accountant Kemi Olufuwa

Design

Art Director Scott Moore
Art Editor Tracey Ridgewell
Designer Josephine Spencer
Digital Imaging Dan Conway

Picture Desk

Picture Editor Jael Marschner
Deputy Picture Editor Tracey Kerrigan
Picture Researchers Monica Roche, Helen McFarland

Marketing

Marketing Director Mandy Martinez
Marketing & Publicity Manager, US Rosella Albanese

Production

Production Director Mark Lamond
Production Controller Marie Howell

Time Out Group

Chairman Tony Elliott
Managing Director Mike Hardwick
Group Financial Director Richard Waterlow
Group Commercial Director Lesley Gill
Group Marketing Director John Luck
Group General Manager Nichola Coulthard
Group Circulation Director Jim Heinemann
Group Art Director John Oakey
Online Managing Director David Pepper
Group Production Director Steve Proctor
Group IT Director Simon Chappell

Maps JS Graphics (john@jsgraphics.co.uk).

Photography Matt Carr, except: pages 3, 7, 13, 23, 30, 46, 68, 81, 107, 220, 246 Amanda C Edwards; pages 5, 12, 78, 150, 185, 201, 203, 264, 268, 285 Mockford & Bonetti; pages 33, 273, 307 Getty Images; pages 34, 48, 82, 90, 134, 135, 200, 223, 278, 289, 290 Hadley Kincade; pages 41, 73, 85, 91, 124, 127, 178, 185, 196, 224, 242, 244, 250, 252, 282, 283, 289, 299, 300, 303, Jonathan Perugia; pages 43, 57 Michael Franke; pages 52, 53, 101 Francesca Yorke; page 56 Mark Read; pages 74, 243 Heloise Bergman; page 83 Lukas Birk; page 98 Oliver Knight; pages 107, 182 Dominic Dibbs; pages 108, 116, 117 Suzy Del Campo; page 117 James Winspear; page 171 Alys Tomlinson; page 188 Natalie Pecht; page 211 Sarah Blee; page 212 Kerry Miles; pages 229, 255, 262 Tricia de Courcy Ling; page 235 Britta Jaschinski; page 251 Rex Features; pages 280, 293 Andrew Brackenbury.

The Editor would like to thank Andrew White for editing the first edition of the guide.

© Copyright Time Out Group Ltd
All rights reserved

Published by Time Out Guides Ltd, a wholly owned subsidiary of Time Out Group Ltd.
Time Out and the Time Out logo are trademarks of Time Out Group Ltd.

© **Time Out Group Ltd 2005**
Previous edition 2001.

10 9 8 7 6 5 4 3 2

This edition first published in Great Britain in 2005 by Ebury
Ebury is a division of The Random House Group Ltd,
20 Vauxhall Bridge Road, London SW1V 2SA

Random House Australia Pty Limited, 20 Alfred Street, Milsons Point, Sydney, New South Wales 2061, Australia

Random House New Zealand Limited, 18 Poland Road, Glenfield, Auckland 10, New Zealand

Random House South Africa (Pty) Limited, Endulini, 5A Jubilee Road, Parktown 2193, South Africa

Random House UK Limited Reg. No. 954009

Distributed in USA by Publishers Group West
1700 Fourth Street, Berkeley, California 94710

Distributed in Canada by Penguin Canada Ltd
10 Alcorn Avenue, Toronto, Ontario, Canada M4V 3B2

For further distribution details, see www.timeout.com

ISBN 978-1-904978-879

A CIP catalogue record for this book is available from the British Library

Colour reprographics by Icon, Crowne House, 56-58 Southwark Street, London SE1 1UN

Printed and bound in Germany by Appl
Papers used by Ebury Press are natural, recyclable products made from wood grown in sustainable forests

Contents

Contents

About the guide

We recommend that you read the entire text of any walk before setting out. Not only should this serve to whet your appetite for the journey ahead, it will also help you to plan stopping-off points according to opening times provided in the listings. Indeed, for the longer walks, it'll give you a chance to decide at which point you want to abandon the walk and stagger to the nearest café or pub.

In the interests of not interfering with the flow of the prose, we have avoided endless directions in the text. The text and the maps should be used alongside each other, so if one seems unclear, consult the other. That said, every one of the routes has been walked and scrupulously checked, so we hope you'll find it very hard to get lost…

Maps

The route is marked in red, including short diversions, while a dotted line marks an alternative route. Some, but not all, of the sites highlighted in the walk are marked on the maps. We have included all the Underground stations on the maps – apologies to bus travellers. To find out the best route to any location by bus, tube or train, call London Travel Information on 7222 1234, or access their website at www.tfl.gov.uk.

For an overview of central London, see the London by Area map on pages 314-5.

Distance

The distances given in the notes are to the nearest half-mile or half-kilometre.

Time

The timing of the walks obviously depends on the speed of your stride, and the length and frequency of any stops you might make. The times given in the notes are, therefore, approximate and assume that there are no lengthy stops

en route (though, of course, these are highly recommended), and that a healthy, though not frenetic, pace is maintained.

Notes

The notes at the start of each text are largely self-explanatory and merely aim to help walkers plan the timing of the walk, and forewarn them of any peculiar features. Geographical overlaps with other walks in the collection are also mentioned.

Listings

We have listed virtually every café, bar, pub, restaurant, shop, museum, gallery, church, park and relevant organisation mentioned in the text of the walk that is open to the public. They are arranged by category and alphabetically, not following the chronology of the walk. All the listings were accurate at the time of writing.

For the eating and drinking sections at the end of each walk, we have listed the opening hours of the establishment and, where we can, included a brief summary of the venue. Those included that are not mentioned in the walks are taken from Time Out's *Bars, Pubs & Clubs* or *Eating & Drinking* guides. In some cases we have added venues that are on the route (but not mentioned in the text), and are also recommended by Time Out's guides. For museums and galleries, no 'Admission' listing means that admission is free.

All the remaining listings are taken from the text, and are divided, sometimes somewhat crudely, into categories. The final 'Others' category, where it occurs, may list organisations that readers might wish to contact should the walk inspire further investigation.

Disabled

As a city that evolved long before the needs of disabled people were considered, London is a difficult city for disabled

visitors, although legislation is gradually improving access and general facilities. For advice about getting across London or information on provisions for the disabled on the tube, phone 7222 1234 or see www.tfl.gov.uk. All DLR stations have wheelchair access.

We thoroughly recommend *Access in London* by Gordon Couch, William Forrester and David McGaughey (Bloomsbury, 2003), which includes detailed maps of step-free routes and accessible tube stations alongside a guide to adapted toilets. The guide is available at some bookshops, or free of charge (although a £10 donation is appreciated) from Access Project, 39 Bradley Gardens, W13 8HE (www.accessproject-phsp.org). The organisations below offer help to disabled visitors to London:

Artsline
54 Chalton Street, Somers Town, NW1 1HS (tel/minicom 7388 2227/www.artslineonline.com). **Open** 9.30am-5.30pm Mon-Fri. Information on disabled access to arts and entertainment events in London and on adapted facilities in cinemas, art galleries, theatres and so on.

William Forrester
1 Belvedere Close, Guildford, Surrey, GU2 6NP (01483 575401). William Forrester is a London Registered Guide and, as he's a wheelchair user himself, has extensive experience in leading tours in the capital for disabled individuals and groups. He also contributed a walk to Volume 1 of the *Time Out Book of London Walks.* Book early.

Greater London Action on Disability (GLAD)
336 Brixton Road, Brixton, SW9 7AA (7346 5800/ information line 7346 5808/ minicom 7346 5811). **Open** *Phone enquiries* 9am-5pm Mon-Fri. *Information* 1.30-4.30pm Mon, Wed, Fri. GLAD is a voluntary organisation providing, via local associations, valuable information for disabled visitors and residents.

Tourist information

Visit London (7234 5800, www.visit london.co.uk) is the city's official tourist information company. You could also look at www.londontown.com for a different perspective.

Britain & London Visitor Centre
1 Lower Regent Street, SW1Y 4XT (8846 9000/www.visitbritain.com). **Open** 9.30am-6.30pm Mon; 9am-6.30pm Tue-Fri; 10am-4pm Sat, Sun.

London Information Centre
Leicester Square, WC2H 7BP (7292 2333/ www.londontown.com). **Open** 8am-midnight daily.

London Visitor Centre
Arrivals Hall, Waterloo International Terminal, SE1 7LT. **Open** 8.30am-10.30pm daily.

There are also tourist information offices in Greenwich, next to St Paul's, in Richmond and on the south side of London Bridge.

THESE BOOKS ARE MADE FOR WALKING

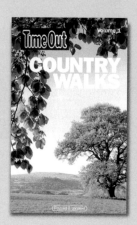

Introduction

When the Lord Mayor of London was summoned to check on a small fire in Pudding Lane in early September 1666, he casually dismissed it: 'Pish! A woman might piss it out'. By the time the flames had taken hold some hours later, however, only the Earth Mother herself would have had any chance of fulfilling his suggestion. Four-fifths of the City burned down over the next three days, spilling the people from their homes to watch the blaze from the higher ground of Highgate or from boats on the Thames.

As the embers cooled, London had an opportunity to engage in some city planning. Since the medieval street-plan had emerged largely on the lines of its Roman and Saxon predecessors, now was the time, surely, for grand boulevards, like those that emerged in Haussmann's Paris, or a grid pattern such as developed in Manhattan. Plans were proposed, most notably by Sir Christopher Wren and John Evelyn, but, characteristically, they never came to pass. The merchants and traders in the City could not wait for the planners to resolve their differences, and so, with some concessions to safety (more brick buildings, fewer overhanging shop signs), the old medieval street plan reemerged, as Londoners set to work rebuilding their lives.

London had missed its chance to reinvent itself, to bring some order and coherence to its layout, and the city continued to grow in a haphazard way. Grand Regency designs were only half completed; new developments such as St James's or Pimlico, while suggesting some coherence in themselves, were never part of an overall plan; outlying villages were swallowed up; even grand constructions such as the Crystal Palace couldn't settle, being moved from Hyde Park to the suburbs, only to later burn down. There was, and still is, no real coherence to the growth, and the survival, of the capital.

This second collection of London walks reflects the city's arbitrary nature. By inviting an assortment of novelists, historians, journalists, cartoonists and comedians to contribute their view of the city, we've sought to ensure a range of perspectives. There are biographical walks, retracing the paths of former distinguished residents: Claire Tomalin's journey to Greenwich with Samuel Pepys, dropping in on John Evelyn en route; a prowl through central London in the shadow of occultist Aleister Crowley; and a chance to conjure up the medieval city as Dick Whittington found it, in all its bawdy magnificence. Other walks sing personal praises of the city: Arthur Smith's hymn to Balham; Frances Morgan's tour of villagey Stoke Newington; and Robert Elms's fond memories of Holborn in the 1970s. Nick Barlay takes us on a 16-mile hike through history along what is now the A5, but which has been a main road out of the city since Roman times; Courttia Newland reminds us that genteel Notting Hill was once the scene of a racist backlash against post-war immigration; and David Aaronovitch discovers the canals, rivers and creeks of east London.

In all there are 25 walks around the capital, taking in everything from hospitals, churches and temples to courts and places of execution. Whether you find yourself chasing mushrooms among the deer in Richmond Park, memorising a Coleridgian digression in a rural lane on Hampstead Heath or eyeing up a Masonic vestment in a shop off Drury Lane, you should expect the unexpected. And don't dismiss, as the noble Lord Mayor did, your aroused curiosity as merely a flickering flame. It could grow out of control.

Andrew White

Old Holborn

Robert Elms

From Ye Old White Horse to the stations of the Cross, via doughty Georgian terraces and the bad-tempered peacock of Coram's Fields.

> **Start:** London School of Economics, Portugal Street
> **Finish:** King's Cross tube/rail
> **Time:** 2-3 hours
> **Distance:** 2 miles/3km
> **Getting there:** District or Circle lines to Temple (closed Sunday) or Central or Piccadilly lines to Holborn
> **Getting back:** Victoria, Piccadilly, Northern, Circle, Metropolitan or Hammersmith & City lines from King's Cross
> **Note:** there are two small parks suitable for children.

There are no dreamy spires here. Start your journey – as I did as an 18-year-old spiky, springy undergraduate back when the two sevens clashed – outside the main entrance of the London School of Economics (LSE) on Portugal Street and you have begun in a thoroughly urban place. The City, the Law Courts and the Strand are your neighbours in academia, and this notorious bastion of red radicalism has always really been a thought-factory for the metropolis. Back in my day there were Maoists in every coffee bar and occupations in every semester, but most of those fiery radicals went on to become pillars of the nearby establishment.

Today the atmosphere has changed and the chattering young throng milling around the school any term-time lunch break know they're going to leave here to head east to the banks or west to Westminster. My favourite walk, though,

and one I did time and again as a student, was north through one of London's last lost neighbourhoods to the true home of its lost souls – the London School of Economics to London King's Cross.

If you have any interest in the minutiae of power, it's worth stopping off at Waterstone's Economists' Bookshop on Portugal Street to browse the ranks of tomes on quasi-non-governmental institutions in developing democracies. But if all this intense intellectualism gets too much, salvation is close at hand just around the corner – and what a corner it is. St Clement's Lane is a tiny, twisting, cobbled reminder that this was once one of London's most cramped and claustrophobic rookeries, all but blown away when Kingsway and Aldwych were driven through the slums by Edwardian improvers. But St Clement's remains crooked and traditional, as does its tiny pub, Ye Old White Horse. It may be a little early for a drink, as you've only travelled 100 yards or so, but it's hard to resist a boozer, slap in the middle of the sprawling LSE site, that boasts a handwritten sign on the door proclaiming testily, 'NO STUDENTS'. There's no music or flashing lights or funky Mediterranean cuisine, either – just lots of red flock wallpaper and middle-aged men, who are definitely not students, drinking and talking quietly. It's great.

Next you go past the curious Old Curiosity Shop on Portsmouth Street, which is probably the oldest shop in London, and was last seen open some

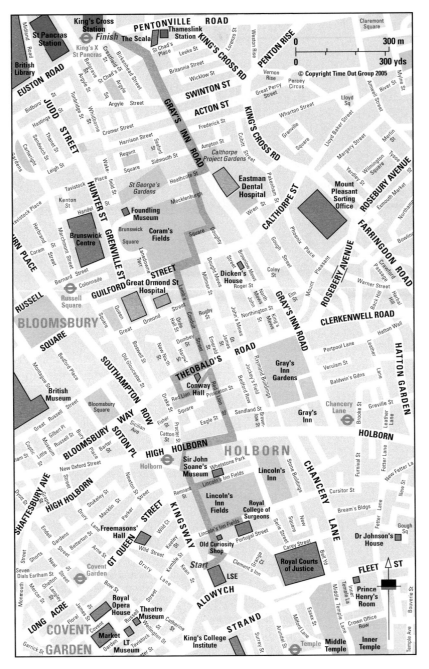

Lincoln's Inn Fields

time in 1864. It's currently a truly bizarre cobblers selling what appears to be footwear for overgrown elves, but quite when it does its business is anybody's guess. Certainly the bemused Americans who stand outside looking for Charles Dickens are confused. They should come with us; we're heading deep into Charlie's London.

Lincoln's Inn Fields still has the sombre air of legal London at its most Pecksniffian, even though it's actually a rather lovely green oasis flanked by some grand Georgian architecture. None grander than the home of Sir John Soane, rightly esteemed architect of this parish. His house is now a wonderfully wayward museum reflecting his fine eye and his jackdaw collecting tastes, with everything from Egyptian sarcophagi to Hogarth's *Rake's Progress* crowded together within the Tardis-like space. It's all unutterably mad and undoubtedly gratis, which makes it the best free entertainment around here. Unless, of course, you count the collection of things in jars in the museum of the Royal College of Surgeons on the other side of the square,

or the office girls playing netball in the middle of the fields, or (through the grand archway) the walled warren of the Inns of Court where the wiggy ones play legal eagle.

Keep north, though, and you go through the splendidly named Little Turnstile, passing the popular Polish vodka bar, Na Zdrowie. Little Turnstile is another serpentine reminder of the once depraved, cheek-by-jowl nature of this area when it was a true London neighbourhood. Cross the teeming yet dull office-worker thoroughfare of High Holborn and it still is, although hidden away to your right is the new American-owned Chancery Court Hotel, an expensively subdued riot of marble and brass aimed at expense-account visitors. Be sure to visit the elegant little inner courtyard, reminiscent of Somerset House.

You don't want to spend too long on this bland blustery high road, though – just enough time to cross it and get to Red Lion Street, where the character changes instantly and you start to enter Holborn proper. You are now in what may well be inner London's last great unreconstructed, ungentrified, unsung enclave. It isn't pretty or arty or chic, thankfully, but it is powerfully charismatic.

You might not notice it, of course. You could trawl these streets daily, as thousands of suited salarymen and women do, and not see all the signs. But if you know where to look, you'll know you've entered a truly beguiling part of town, steeped in stories. Red Lion Street was once the fringe of London's Little Italy, as evidenced by a couple of deeply old-style trattorias and Caradell's excellent deli, but most intriguingly by the mysterious Mazzini and Garibaldi Club. Word has it that during World War II the entire membership of this dark and perpetually closed Italian drinking den, named after Italy's two most famed patriots, was interred for suspected pro-Mussolini sympathies. Perhaps that's why, after more than 20 years of looking at it, I've never ever seen anybody go in or out. The windows are dark so you can't see in, but if you peer through the letter box, as I've done many times in the hope of clocking some camel-coated Dons, you can just about make out a few chairs and an authentic old Gaggia machine in the corner. As the once enormous Italian community has almost completely left the area, I always dread reaching 51 Red Lion Street and seeing that the Mazzini has followed them, to be replaced by a coffee chain. But, thankfully, it's still there, still apparently closed. A Marie Celeste of a club.

Close by on the left is Lamb's Conduit Passage. This is a slight diversion west, 50 yards perhaps, along another bent little alleyway, but you have to take it for two reasons. The first is that it suddenly reveals what up to now has been hidden – that Holborn is actually a densely populated part of town. There may not be many Italians left, but there are scores of old working-class families in the many almost hidden council flats, Peabody Buildings and slightly shabby

Lamb's Conduit Street

mansion blocks. Traditionally working as printers on Fleet Street, scene shifters in Covent Garden, barrow boys on Oxford Street and bumarees in Smithfield, these became my neighbours when I settled near here, not long after leaving the LSE. Then I became fascinated by their tales of playing run-outs in the nearby British Museum as kids or playing hookey from hugely overpaid jobs on the print, when Fleet Street was still number-one stop for the gravy train.

Most of the traditional trades have also left now, but somehow the families cling on. I met a local guy recently who had reluctantly quit the area. In fact, as he put it with a sadly resigned air, 'I've moved out of London.' 'Where to?' I asked, genuinely amazed that a Holborn boy could commit such apostasy. 'I've gone to Fulham,' he said, as if it were somewhere near Swindon. Holborn, you see, is real London.

The second reason for heading on to Red Lion Square is that it's where you'll find Conway Hall. Again, you could miss it, and even if you went inside to see nothing but a shabby old hall, hosting perhaps a weight-watchers' do or some such frippery, you would not know. But the fact that there's a Fenner Brockway Room and a Bertrand Russell Hall would surely tell you that you've stumbled into the home of British radicalism. Everybody – from the then new Labour party to CND and the anarcho-anti-capitalists with dogs on strings – has held major rallies and meetings here, plotting the overthrow of the state, probably before nipping out for fish and chips at the Fryer's Delight just around the corner on Theobald's Road. Many cab drivers will tell you the Fryer's is arguably the best in all London (and, believe me, cab drivers like an argument), but if any vegan class warriors from Conway Hall feel like a bag of chips, they should be warned that this is one of the last places that still use beef dripping to fry them.

Crossing Theobald's Road, possibly with chips in hand, you should pick Lamb's Conduit Street to carry you towards the Cross, as it's one of the highlights of the walk. Part pedestrianised, it's the kind of quirky street that keeps threatening to become horribly hip yet never quite makes it. At the moment, though, there are a couple of genuinely cool places interspersed with the traditional ones. The best restaurant on the entire route is Cigala, attempting to do for Spanish food what the River Café in Fulham did for Italian, but without the ludicrous west London prices. It sits handsomely on the corner of Rugby Street, which has a wonderful terrace of early Georgian architecture of the kind that gives this area its character. Opposite is A France & Sons, funeral directors who boast a model of HMS *Victory* in the window, because they organised bringing Nelson's body from the ship to his lying-in-state, the funeral and procession. If they were good enough for Horatio…

Another famous name here is that of Dombey. It's actually a street off Lamb's

Dickens' House

Conduit, which provided Charles Dickens with inspiration when he needed a name for a character in a book he was writing around the corner. For just east of here is Doughty Street, where Dickens lived and where his museum is to this day. Our American friends can perhaps go there, unless of course they'd like to join us for a drink. For the Lamb, at the very northern end of the street, is one of the finest traditional old drinking houses in London, complete with snugs and engraved screens, and the feeling that it's changed little since it was built in the 18th century.

should dally for a while in Coram's Fields. If, that is, you have any children with you. Formerly known as the Foundling Hospital and still always 'the Foundlings' to locals, Coram's Fields has to be one of the few places that can boast a synthetic football pitch, a paddling pond, two sheep, six goats, a bad-tempered peacock, a fat pig that once tried to eat my son Alfie, and a sign proclaiming, 'Adults Only Admitted if Accompanied by Children'. Today it's a lovely little city farm and all-round playground to entertain urban urchins for a few hours. Originally it was a place where unwanted children, or foundlings, could be left for ever. Established by the philanthropic Captain Coram in the 18th century, it was home to generations of London's street kids, orphans, bastards and mistakes. Someone recently told me that their father-in-law had been placed there in the 1930s as a small boy, and, like all Coram's kids, had undergone an instant name change, becoming Mr Faraday, because everybody that year was named after scientists.

We'll actually walk round the side of the fields, along Mecklenburgh Place, past the posh new gym full of sweaty City types and into the sedate grandeur of Mecklenburgh Square, where one of the finest rows of stuccoed High Georgian terraces protects us from the madness that lies on the other side. This is a quiet, elegant, gracious spot, just a matter of yards from the Gray's Inn Road, which isn't.

It's hard to love the Gray's Inn Road, a dirty, pock-marked mess that's perpetually clogged with traffic, rank with fumes and heavy with the air of badness. So, of course, I've worked hard and now love it. My kids like the Calthorpe Project, a slightly bonkers bit of Camden Council-led groovy urban greening, where you can go on slug hunts in an eco-friendly wilderness while the lorries rush past. I like the Water Rats, the pub where you can go and see noisy bands nobody has ever heard of play their first gigs, as

The only negative aspect of the Lamb is that a few members of the interminably dreary Bloomsbury Group used to gather there to talk pretentious twaddle and decide who would sleep with whom next. Indeed, we are now on the borders of Bloomsbury, and should you head west you would be deep in its leafy squares and literary connections. So I would far rather walk in the opposite direction towards the least celebrated and cultured bit of London, but one of the most fascinating. But before we descend into the grubby, track-marked arms of the Cross (you will notice that we are now going gently down into a valley, or perhaps a pit), we

Oasis and the Pogues did not that long ago. You have to like the Scala, the only former music hall, cinema and snooker club that is now a nightclub and was once a Primatarium, where you could see holograms of monkeys in a mock jungle.

In the past, by the time you got to the Scala you'd arrived at the signs of the Cross: a few bad folk hanging out doing no good whatsoever, ragged, harsh-eyed souls without strings who mooched slowly around milking these streets for their sad motherload. Such characters handsomely fed the dubious but undeniable pleasure of urban voyeurism, and the feeling that there are a million tales interwoven into this sump of a place. (Best of all, perhaps, is the one that Boudicca is buried under platform 19 of the architectural triumph that is our terminal destination.) But the long-mooted plans to regenerate raggedy old King's Cross, with a view to attracting a better class of punter and, more specifically, tourist, are finally coming to fruition. From 2007, a Norman Foster glass extension to St Pancras will shelter the new Eurostar international terminal, while King's Cross underground will be refurbished and the old train depot will be opened up for state-of-the-art concourses, waiting areas, shops and restaurants. The surrounding area, too, is undergoing a £37.5 million makeover.

Talking of money, the very fact that there are two major stations in front of you is a pleasingly insane product of the Victorian capitalist free market at its most competitive. One of these buildings has long been thought of as a masterpiece, the other largely ignored. Of course, it should have been the other way round: St Pancras is an overblown, downright silly neo-Gothic monstrosity; whereas King's Cross is a genuine masterpiece of pared-down, no-nonsense industrial design, a mighty fortress of a building that is the perfect place to end a little London journey. Or start another one.

Eating & drinking

Cigala
54 Lamb's Conduit Street, WC1N 3LW (7405 1717). **Open** 12.30-2.45pm, 6.30-10.45pm Mon-Fri.

Fryer's Delight
19 Theobalds Road, WC1X 8SL (7405 4114). **Open** noon-11pm Mon-Sat. Quality fish & chips.

Lamb
94 Lamb's Conduit Street, WC1N 3LZ (7405 0713). **Open** 11am-11pm Mon-Sat; noon-10.30pm Sun. Food served.

Na Zdrowie
6 Little Turnstile, WC1V 7DX (7831 9679). **Open** noon-11pm Mon-Fri; 6-11pm Sat.

Ye Old White Horse
2 St Clement's Lane, WC2A 2HA (7242 5518). **Open** 11am-8pm (varies) Mon-Fri. Food served.

River Café
Thames Wharf, Rainville Road, W6 9HA (7381 8824). **Open** 12.30-3pm, 7-9.30pm Mon-Sat; 12.30-3pm Sun. Modern northern Italian cuisine.

Clubs

Mazzini & Garibaldi Club
51 Red Lion Street, WC1 4PF (7242 3972). **Open** *Members only* 7pm-midnight Tue, Thur.

Scala
275 Pentonville Road, N1 9NL (7833 2022/ www.scala-london.co.uk). **Open** phone for times Mon-Thur; 10pm-5am Fri; 10pm-6am Sat.

Water Rats
328 Grays Inn Road, WC1X 8BZ (7837 7269). **Open** 8am-3pm, 8pm-midnight Mon-Sat.

Museums

British Museum
Great Russell Street, WC1B 3DG (7636 1555/ www.thebritishmuseum.ac.uk). **Open** *Galleries* 10am-5.30pm Mon-Wed, Sat, Sun; 10am-8.30pm Thur, Fri. *Great Court* 9am-6pm Mon-Wed, Sun; 9am-11pm Thur-Sat. *Highlights tours* 10.30am, 1pm, 3pm daily. **Admission** free. *Temporary exhibitions* prices vary. *Tours* £8; £5 concessions.

Dickens' House
48 Doughty Street, WC1N 2LX (7405 2127/ www.dickensmuseum.com). **Open** 10am-5pm Mon-Sat; 11am-5pm Sun. **Admission** £5; £3-£4 concessions; free under-5s; £14 family.

Kids rule at **Coram's Fields**.

Hunterian Museum

Royal College of Surgeons, 35-43 Lincoln's Inn Fields, WC2A 3PE (7869 6560/www.rcseng. ac.uk/services/museums). **Open** 10am-5pm Tue-Sat. **Admission** free.

Sir John Soane's Museum

13 Lincoln's Inn Fields, WC2A 3BP (7405 2107/ www.soane.org). **Open** 10am-5pm Tue-Sat; 6-9pm first Tue of the month. **Tours** 2.30pm Sat. **Admission** free; donations appreciated. **Tours** £3; free concessions.

Parks

Calthorpe Project

258-74 Gray's Inn Road, WC1X 8LH (7837 8019). **Open** *Summer* 10am-6pm Mon-Fri; noon-6pm Sat. *Winter* 9am-5pm Mon-Fri; 11am-5pm Sat.

Coram's Fields & Harmsworth Memorial Playground

93 Guilford Street, WC1N 1DN (office 7837 6138/nursery 7833 0198/play centre 7837 0255). **Open** *Park* 9am-dusk daily. *Play centre* Term time 3.30-6pm Mon-Fri; holidays 9am-6pm Mon-Fri.

Shopping

Caradell

58 Red Lion Street, WC1R 4PD (7405 2301). **Open** 8am-5pm Mon-Fri.

Waterstone's Economists' Bookshop

Clare Market, Portugal Street, WC2A 2AB (7405 5531/www.waterstones.co.uk). **Open** 9.30am-7pm Mon, Wed-Fri; 10am-7pm Tue; 9.30am-6pm Sat.

Others

A France & Sons

45 Lamb's Conduit Street, WC1N 3NH (7405 4901/france@ukonline.co.uk). Phone for details.

Chancery Court Hotel

252 High Holborn, WC1V 7EN (7829 9888/ www.renaissancechancerycourt.com).

Conway Hall

25 Red Lion Square, WC1R 4RL (7242 8037/ www.conwayhall.org.uk). **Open** *Office* 2-6pm daily. Phone for details.

Suffragette city

Maureen Freely

March with the suffragettes as they campaign for 'The Vote, the Whole Vote and Nothing but the Vote'.

Start: Royal Albert Hall, Kensington
Finish: Victoria Tower Gardens, Westminster
Time: 4-5 hours
Distance: 7 miles/11.5km
Getting there: Circle, District or Piccadilly lines to South Kensington; take third exit, and go left on Exhibition Road, then left again on Kensington Gore (ten-minute walk).
Getting back: short walk to Westminster tube (Circle, District or Jubilee lines)
Note: this is a long walk, often with quite lengthy stretches between specific sites prominent in suffragette history. There is some overlap with the walks of Liza Picard, Gareth Evans and Bonnie Greer.

I'd heard they were daring and dashing and righteous. I knew they'd pestered politicians, and chained themselves to iron grilles, and ended up in prison, where they were forcibly fed. I was only too aware I owed them everything, but for most of my life I've been happy to thank them without bothering with the details. There was something about the word 'suffragette' that made me think of an improving lecture in a large hall packed with stern-faced women wearing brown sandals with matching socks.

I found out how wrong I was almost by accident. It was one of those rare Sundays when I had done the dishes and put the children to bed ahead of schedule and was not feeling haunted by the usual five-volume list of long-avoided chores. To fill the time, I picked up a book that had been sitting in my study for many months – the *Virago Book of Suffragettes*, an anthology of first-hand accounts of the almost 100-year campaign to win women the vote.

The first thing I read was a newspaper account of two suffragettes who'd taken advantage of a loophole in the law to post themselves to 10 Downing Street as 'human letters'. The next item was about 20 suffragettes who'd managed to get inside the Palace of Westminster concealed in a furniture van. Then I read about another contingent that rented a boat and 'buzzed' the River Terrace, disturbing MPs and their ladies on a warm and sunny June afternoon, as they ate their strawberries and cream. Standing on the prow was 'General' Flora Drummond, who gave a speech, and then ad-libbed, 'I see you have lady waiters, but are you not afraid some of them might be suffragettes?'

There was also an excerpt from the memoirs of leading suffragette and celebrated actress Lillah McCarthy. During the worst days of the agitation, she recalled, she'd found herself alone in the Cabinet Room at Number Ten. 'Fervour for the cause took hold of me. I opened up my box of grease paints, took out the reddest sticks I could find and wrote across the blotting paper, "Votes for Women". I went out of the room exultant.'

Next to these were accounts of the humiliations they faced when campaigning in public, and the appalling way they were treated by prison wardens and the police.

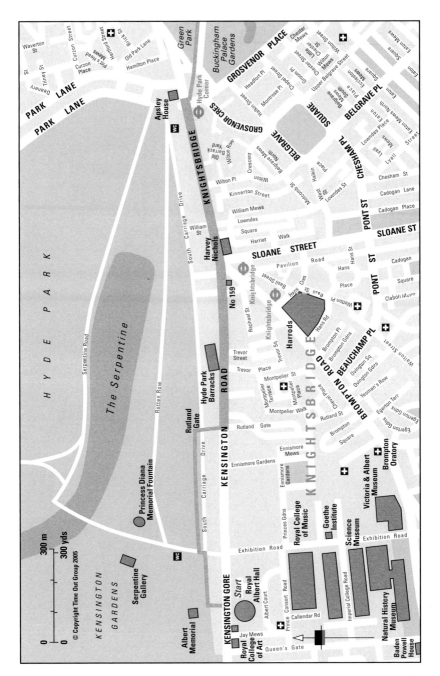

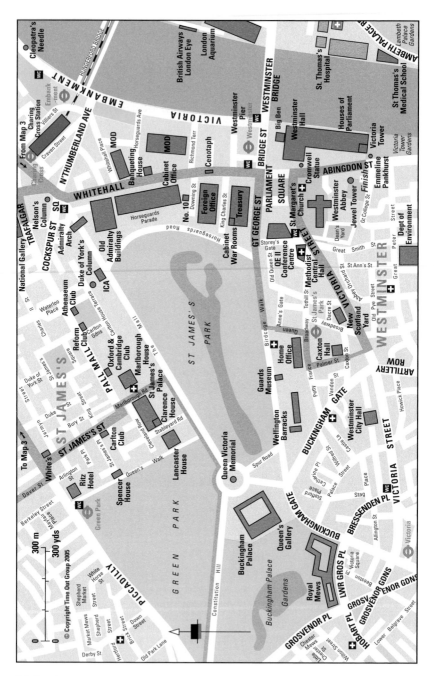

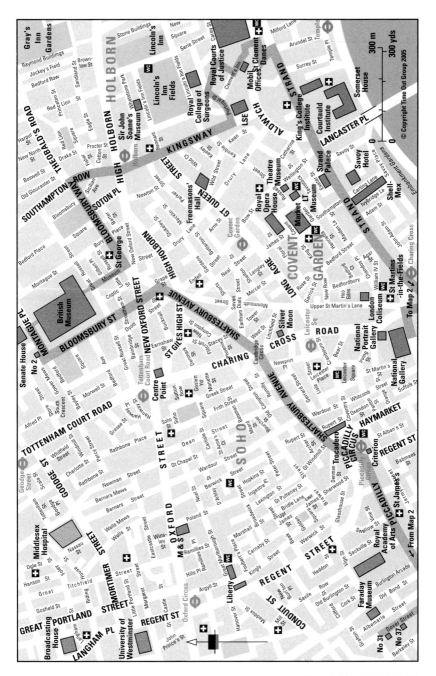

This was more familiar territory to me. Why, I wondered, did we prefer to remember them just as martyrs, not as women with nerve and flair?

I was also intrigued by the propaganda generated by the 'antis'. 'Shall we make a holocaust of maidens, wives, and mothers on the bronze altars of party? Shall we part with our birthright of simple womanliness for a mess of political potage?' That was the novelist Marie Corelli, writing in 1909. Change a word here and there, but it could be any number of high-profile women, repudiating the F word in the *Daily Mail* today.

The same goes for this sublime anti 'recipe': 'Cabinet Pudding and How to Make It: Take a fresh young suffragette, add a large slice of her own importance, and as much young sauce as you like, allow to stand on a Cabinet Minister's doorstep in a white heat, mix freely with one or two policemen, well roll in mud, and while hot run into a Police Court, allow to simmer, garnish with a sauce of martyrdom. A popular dish always in season. Cost: a little self-respect.'

This recipe was first circulated in 1909, by which time many suffragettes had come to a full boil. Their leader, Mrs Pankhurst, encouraged them to make their displeasure known. 'The smashing of windows,' she said pointedly, 'is a time-honoured method of showing displeasure in a political situation.' They went on to develop other, even more ingenious methods. Some of them take my breath away. It's impossible to condone them all. But the more I read about the suffragettes, the more convinced I am that they were braver, tougher and brighter than we could ever be – not just more resourceful, but also more fun. I'd like to use this walk to pass on my enthusiasm.

I have to warn you, though. You're going to have to make heavy use of your imagination. There is only a handful of plaques to commemorate the heroes and heroines of the suffrage movement. Most of the buildings from which they launched

their daring campaign have disappeared, while the objects of their political desires are mostly still standing in all their glory. If I gave you the itinerary of this walk and asked you to guess my reasons for choosing it, you'd probably say I was taking you on a tour of the Monuments of Empire. This was, in effect, what the suffragettes were doing: knocking on the doors of the Establishment, sometimes becoming so enraged that they knocked them down.

Today we'll retrace the route along which they walked and marched and demonstrated and caused havoc during the worst years of the 'agitation'. We'll take it as far as they did, to the Palace of Westminster. We'll begin beneath the imposing Royal Albert Hall, but women's suffrage graduated from the parlour to become a matter for serious discussion at 44 Phillimore Gardens, in the refined and leafy middle-class neighbourhood of Holland Park a mile or so to the west of here. This was the former headquarters of the Kensington Society.

The Kensington Society was founded in the 1860s. Its honorary secretary was Emily Davies, the great educational reformer. When she was still a young woman, she is said to have paid a visit to her friend Elizabeth Garrett, who (under her married name of Anderson) went on to become Britain's first woman doctor. As they sat by the fire, discussing the great causes of the day, a moment arrived when Emily turned to Elizabeth and said, 'Well, it's clear what has to be done. I must devote myself to securing higher education, while you must open up the medical profession. After these things are done, we must see about getting the vote.' Here there was a pause. Then, turning to Elizabeth's little sister, she said, 'You are younger than we are, Millie, so you must attend to that.'

Millie is better known by her married name, Millicent Garrett Fawcett. She led the constitutionalist wing of the suffragist movement from the late 19th century right through to victory in 1928. She was still a

Hyde Park

young woman in the spring of 1865, when she helped the Kensington Society collect 1,499 signatures for a petition asking for women to be given the vote. When she and Emily Davies took their roll over to the House of Commons, they suffered a loss of nerve. So they asked the apple lady if she would hide the petition under her skirts. When their sponsor, John Stuart Mill, came into the lobby, he was perplexed to find the women empty-handed. But when Emily and Millicent retrieved the huge roll from its hiding place, he said, 'Ah, this I can brandish with effect.' It all came to nothing, but this time (the first time since Mary Wollstonecraft introduced the daring thought 70 years earlier) the issue wouldn't go away.

Suffrage societies proliferated all over the country. The most famous was in Manchester, headed by the dynamic Lydia Becker. During the next 30 years, these societies submitted petition after petition to parliament. Few got beyond the second reading; most died long before that. In 1897, 20 leading suffrage societies joined to form the National Union of Women's Suffrage Societies (NUWSS) and elected

Millicent Garrett Fawcett president. In 1902, Emmeline Pankhurst founded the Women's Social and Political Union (WSPU) in Manchester. In the beginning, there was harmony between the two acronyms. Then in 1906 the WSPU went militant. Fawcett's NUWSS refused to follow suit. There was great bitterness between the two wings of the movement, but from time to time they managed to put on magnificent shows of solidarity.

One such show was here, at the Royal Albert Hall. Tear your eyes from the gleaming gold statues on the Albert Memorial opposite to admire this stately dome. Until the WSPU was banned from it in 1913, the Royal Albert Hall was the suffragettes' favourite venue for uplifting events. The most impressive of these was the Pageant of Women's Trades and Professions on 29 April 1909, held in honour of a delegation from the International Women's Suffrage Alliance. All the female professions and trades then open to women were represented that evening. Each had its own emblem. For the Weavers it was a golden spider and a web for Arachne. The Glassworkers had shields of stained glass, each featuring a

Buckingham Palace

Rose of England, while the Secretaries displayed red and silver secretary birds, red tape and sealed documents. 'It was a black and stormy night,' wrote the reporter for *Common Cause*. 'This was a pity, but if it had been lighter you would have been unable to see the procession gemmed and ablaze with countless old-fashioned watchmen's lanterns, swung aloft, winding its way along the skirt of Hyde Park. The entry into the Albert Hall from five approaches was affected amid a scene of warm enthusiasm, our foreign visitors and many of the general audience rising and waving their handkerchiefs.'

Such events were considered essential for raising funds as well as morale. But they were not just for the converted: great thought went into projecting the right sort of image to the general public. One of the WSPU's most successful publicity coups was its Exhibition in May of the same year. Walk east, either through the park, or along Kensington Road towards Knightsbridge. It is, alas, no longer with us, but it was held at the Prince's Skating Rink, on the west corner of Trevor Place, Knightsbridge, which is a five-minute

walk from the Royal Albert Hall. To maximise coverage, they arranged for it to be 'opened' every day by a different prominent woman. One day it was Her Highness the Ranee of Sarawak, Malaysia.

By 1909 the suffragettes were deep into a merchandising offensive. At the Exhibition you could buy suffragette postcards, suffragette games, suffragette jewellery, badges, bags, belts, scarves and hatpins. The embroidery on the bunting and the banners was every bit as good as anything ever produced by a god-fearing wife. Also on sale were 'dignified' photographs of suffragette leaders – to counteract the ones that always ended up in the papers, in which their clothes were in disarray and their hats askew.

Suffragette photographers also recorded the WSPU's 'monster rallies' – most of them held across the street in Hyde Park. The biggest one was 1908 when specially chartered trains bringing women in from all over the country, and 30,000 people dressed in white, green and purple (the suffragette colours) marched into the park in seven separate processions. One was headed by a suffragette named Elsie

Howie, dressed as Joan of Arc on a white horse. Inside the park there were 20 platforms, 70 speakers and between 300,000 and 500,000 spectators. The crowds were a tribute to the suffragettes' brilliant promotional efforts – not only had they gone on citywide 'chalking parties', they'd also sent out a 'suffragette cavalry' to distribute leaflets. Not all in attendance were committed to the cause. Some, like Kitty Marion, began the day in a spirit of ambivalence. 'I joined the ranks to the stirring music of "La Marsaillaise" mostly, and marched,' she later wrote. 'I had thought it quite funny, like a pantomime Grand March, but when I listened to the speakers, I became serious.' The event generated admiring copy in Fleet Street. No one was surprised when it had zero effect on Asquith.

There were higher hopes for the Women's Coronation Procession, on 17 June 1911. The suffragists were at this point still hopeful that the new king would support them. In pursuit of this end, they invested in acres of embroidered, appliqued banners, the most extraordinary floats representing women from all over the British Isles and the Empire, and a lavish Historical Pageant of Women. Again, the wish was to counteract the drab images put forward by the 'antis' and thus to show the world how wrong it was to portray suffragettes as mewing kittens, crying babies or badly dressed butch women. The procession, which skirted Hyde Park to end at the Royal Albert Hall, was again headed by a suffragette, Marjorie Annan Brice this time, doing Joan of Arc on the horse. Behind her marched the almost 700 women who had survived prison sentences, hunger strikes and forcible feeding. They all carried silver pennants that defined them as militant martyrs. The slogan on their banner was 'From Prison to Citizenship'.

Their anthem (music by Ethyl Smith, words by Cicely Hamilton) was all the more shocking for the way it kept to the conventions of the moment: 'Shout, shout, up with your song!/Cry with the wind for the dawn is breaking./March, march, swing you along,/Wide blows our banner and hope is waking…' Imagine what the soldiers must have thought of these singing marchers as they peered out at them from the Hyde Park Barracks to your left – or what they made of 'Drum Major' Mary Leigh's Women's drum and fife band when it took to the streets to advertise the Women's Exhibition. The symbolism was deliberate, according to Sylvia Pankhurst. With their precision, their regalia, their marshals and captains, suffragette processions 'had a decided military flavour'. A number of leading suffragettes such as 'General' Flora Drummond and the WSPU chauffeur, Vera 'Jack' Holmes (who once charged a mounted police officer while on horseback and snatched away his bridle), went so far as to wear mock military uniforms.

Still walking east along Knightsbridge, pause for a moment outside No.159. This is where Mrs Pankhurst was living in 1913 when she was arrested in connection with an explosion in a house in Walton Heath. Now it's a hotel, and its owners know nothing about the building's history. Continuing along Knightsbridge, and crossing over to the other side of the main artery at Harvey Nichols, we come to Hyde Park Corner and Constitution Arch. This was an important landmark for the suffragettes, who routed many of their processions around it. It was the starting point for a very large 1907 demonstration organised by Fawcett's NUWSS. It later became known as the Mud March, due to the inclement weather.

As we cross over to Constitution Hill (take exit 2 in the first subway, Green Park in the second), we are also following the route taken by the militants on 21 May 1914, when they 'rushed' Buckingham Palace. They were feeling frustrated by the lack of parliamentary progress. Off they went, some armed with clubs, Emmeline Pankurst to the fore. When she was stopped, she said, 'Arrested at the Gates of the palace! Tell the king!' No one did. But behind her there were between 20 and 30,000 persons backed up on to Constitution Hill and the Mall and Buckingham Palace Yard. And so the agitation continued. Some women rushed at the gate and railings and climbed on to the crossbars. Others attacked or were attacked by police. Some were on foot, others were mounted. There were charges of brutality, and some stirring photographs that support these claims.

Carrying on along the Mall, until we're standing across from Marlborough House, we arrive at the point from which two suffragettes, Marie Brackenbury and Dorothy Smith, came close to handing a petition to the King in 1913. He was on his way to the opening of parliament. The Mall was lined with two rows of soldiers and one line of police. When the soldiers raised their muskets, the two women ducked underneath them. Coming face to face with a row of flabbergasted

One of the 'still grand clubs', the **Carlton**.

flunkeys, they asked the big question. 'Will your Majesty mention Votes for Women in your opening speech and put an end to the torturing of women in your prisons?' But the windows were closed, and so the conversation ended there. Off they went on their separate ways, the King to Parliament, the suffragettes to Cannon Street Police Station.

Our route takes us left into Marlborough Road. Just before we come to Cleveland Row, we can see the Chapel Royal on our right. Here, in 1912, a suffragette named Una Dugdale married Mr Victor Duval, member of the Men's Political Union for Women's Enfranchisement, in a ceremony that caused a national scandal, because the bride made a point of not promising to obey her husband.

Before we turn left on Cleveland Row and right into St James Street, I'd ask you to stop for a moment to glance down Pall Mall, at the still grand clubs that are only just slightly more welcoming to women than they were in the early 20th century. You pass still more as you climb up St James's Street – the Carlton Club on your left (Mrs Thatcher needed honorary male status to become a full member in this, the Conservative Party's second home), and White's towards the top, the oldest and still exclusively male. So it's not too hard to imagine the day when two suffragettes dressed as orange sellers threw a bottle of ginger beer at the Prime Minister as he left the Reform Club. The prank earned them both headlines and prison sentences.

But there were slower, less dramatic, but still very important changes that they and other suffragettes were making during the same years. For example, they decided that women like themselves needed clubs every bit as much as men did – and acted accordingly. In the 1860s, when the first women's clubs began to open, mostly around the Strand and in the Oxford Street area, there was widespread derision. Upon hearing that one had a reading room, a writer in the *Saturday Review* wondered why its female members 'would want to read anything but cookery books'. But by 1898 there were more than 50 ladies' clubs in the West End.

According to Amy Levy, they were often the only place a woman could write letters and read 'undisturbed by the importunities of a family circle, which can never bring itself to regard feminine leisure and family solitude as things to be respected'. One of the grandest (and the first to be located in the heart of male clubland) was the Lyceum. Founded in 1904 by Constance Smedley, it was for ladies engaged with literature, journalism, art, science, and medicine in need of 'a substantial and dignified milieu where [they] could meet editors and other employers and discuss matters as men did in professional clubs all in surroundings that did not suggest poverty'. It had a library, an art gallery, 35 bedrooms, sewing maids and an American expert on chafing dish suppers. At its height, it had branches in Berlin, Paris, Rome and Florence. It had monthly concerts for new music, a book gallery where works by members were displayed, and a weekly club dinner. Its first address was 128 Piccadilly. Later on, it moved to No.138. Both would have been in the area of the large office buildings that you can see on your left, beyond the Ritz, overlooking the traffic and Green Park. You can get a better sense of these clubs and what they had to offer if you cross Piccadilly, to take a quick right into Dover Street, once the home of the Empress Club, the Sesame Club, the Ladies' Athenaeum (at No.31) and the Albemarle Club (at No.37). The best preserved of these is the last. It's now home to a financial services business. If you're nice to the security guard, he might let you take a peek at its long and beautiful, highly polished foyer.

Ladies' clubs catered to a wide range of tastes. Some were most concerned with 'tea and shopping', and quite a few were open only to ladies who could be presented at court. Others were stern, high-minded and radical, aiming to improve members' minds as well as offering them a safe haven. The most famous of these was the Pioneer Club, at 180 Regent Street – it may not surprise you to hear that there is nothing left of it now. But never mind.

Carry on down Piccadilly, past the Royal Academy and into Piccadilly Circus, another favourite suffragette haunt. When Kitty Marion joined the suffragettes, her first assignment was to go to Piccadilly Circus and sell the WSPU newspaper, *Votes for Women*. This, she said, was the 'acid test'. 'What a lesson in self-denial, self-abnegation, self-discipline. The first time I took my place on the "island" in Piccadilly Circus, near the flower sellers, I felt as if every eye that looked at me was a dagger piercing me through, and I wished the ground would open up and swallow me. However, that feeling wore off and I developed into quite a champion paper-seller.'

Crossing over to the statue, Eros, we come to the splendid Criterion Brasserie.

The **Reform Club**, where a PM was soaked.

The WSPU held rallies at the **Royal Albert Hall** until they were banned from entry in 1913.

Restored by Rocco Forte in 1995, and owned by the chef Marco Pierre White, it is as famous for its golden neo-Byzantine mosaic walls as it is for its food. The potted history it hands out to its customers goes back as far as 1685 but neglects to mention that this is where the Actresses' Franchise League gave its monthly At Homes in the years before World War I. Actresses played a very important role in the suffrage movement. Their plays and entertainments were thought to be of a very high standard even by those who thought little of the ideals they sought to express. Many of the most admired actresses of the day – Ellen Terry, Lillah McCarthy and Lily Langtry to name just three – were active members. Our next stop was to have been 156 Charing Cross Road, the most central of the suffragette stores. This was also home of the Women's Press, and the office of the suffragette newspaper, *Votes for Women*. There is nothing left of it now but an underpass overshadowed by Centre Point.

So I'll spare you the depression and sweep you past the many theatres of Shaftesbury Avenue to where it joins up with New Oxford Street and Bloomsbury Way. At Cambridge Circus, a short hop to the left up Charing Cross Road lands at Foyles bookshop, whose top floor holds the Silver Moon Women's Bookshop, the largest such shop in Europe. At the junction with Bloomsbury Street, go north through Bedford Square into Gower Street, where you will find yourself in front of 2 Gower Street, home of Millicent Garrett Fawcett. Here, finally, we see a plaque. The building itself is dusty and rather sad, so after you've paid your respects, you might want to turn left into Montague Place and take a stroll through the British Museum's Great Court.

Leave via Great Russell Street, take Museum Street and then turn left on to Bloomsbury Way. Here we arrive at St George Bloomsbury (closed for renovations until Autumn 2005), the early 18th-century Hawksmoor church where the funeral of Emily Wilding Davison was held on 14 June 1913. Davison was a teacher before becoming a 'career militant' in 1909. During the last four years of her life, she served nine prison sentences for offences including stone-throwing, obstruction, window-breaking, setting fire to pillar boxes and assaulting a Baptist minister she mistook for Lloyd George. Like so many others, she went on many hunger strikes while in prison and was forcibly fed on many occasions: to protest the treatment of suffragettes in Holloway, she once threw herself down a flight of stairs. Her last heroic act was to try to stop Amner, the king's horse, at Epsom. He didn't, and she died of head injuries.

Tens of thousands came to watch her funeral procession, which was marched to the sound of drums and Chopin's 'Funeral March'. At the front was Charlotte Marsh, blonde and bareheaded, followed by 12 girls in white with laurel wreaths, and a banner that read 'Fight On and God Will Give the Victory'. After them came a crowd of women in black carrying purple irises, followed by others in purple, carrying red peonies, and still others in white with Madonna lilies. The coffin was on a low open bier and held three laurel wreaths from the WSPU. Each was draped with the same words: 'She Died for Women'.

If we turn left outside the church and carry on past Bloomsbury Square to Theobald's Road, we come to a place that has happier associations for suffragettes. This was where the 20 suffragettes piled into that furniture van for what they later referred to as the pantechnicon raid. The press preferred to remember it as the suffragettes' Trojan Horse. Their final destination was the same as always. Whenever possible, they marked the ends of their prison sentences in style.

After we've turned right into Southampton Row, and before crossing over into Kingsway, we can look to our left down Holborn and imagine the Inns of Court Hotel, where the WSPU was in the custom of holding rather grand breakfasts to celebrate the release of its members from Holloway. One of the grandest was on 22 December 1908, following the release of Emmeline

Pankhurst and her daughter Christabel. We'll move on now to see what remains of the WSPU HQ.

Walk down Kingsway, pausing at Portugal Street, where a suffragette café restaurant called the Tea Cup Inn was once located on the corner. Turn left, and then right into Clements Lane, which will take you, via Grange Court, through a gate and down some steps into a narrow alley running alongside the Royal Court of Justice. This is Clements Inn. No.2 was the home of the Pankhursts' closest allies, the wealthy socialist Pethick-Lawrences. Here the WSPU had its headquarters from 1907 to 1912. The building was destroyed during the Blitz. In its place is a grey office building owned by Mobil Oil. (If the gate is locked, you can still see the building that has replaced No.2 – it's the huge grey block on your right.)

But after we turn right into Aldwych, we have to fall back on our imaginations once again. Aldwych is where the WSPU held its all-night skating event on 3 April 1911 to celebrate No Vote No Census! Night. It began at five in the evening and went on for nine hours. Skaters were entertained by a Spanish singer, and by the glamorous Decima Moore reciting suffragist poetry. There were also rousing renditions of the suffragette anthem, 'The March of the Women'. But it was still too much for the writer from the *Evening Standard* and *St James Gazette*, who wrote, 'The interminable circling has made me think and blink in circles.'

Now we come to the Strand, another important road on the suffragist map, where we bear right. It was at Exeter Hall (which stood where the Strand Palace Hotel stands now) that Israel Zangwill gave his famous One Plus One speech at the end of the Mud March. ('Our case is so simple, that it is like having to prove that one and one is two. Indeed, this is precisely what the opposition denies.') It was across the street at the Savoy where Millicent Garrett Fawcett was guest of honour at a suffragist banquet on 11 December 1906, to celebrate the release from Holloway of her friend Anne Cobden Sanderson. It was a splendid evening: the music was by the Aeolian Ladies Orchestra. Next door, at what was then the Hotel Cecil, and now is the Shell-Mex building, the Tax Resistance League (slogan: 'No Vote No Tax') and the Actresses' Franchise League gave a very grand Costume Dinner on 29 June 1914. It was the last such event before the war.

The Strand was also a favourite place for other activities, as Charlie Marsh recalled in her unpublished memoirs. There was the day she and friends went to a beach at Southsea, where they collected pebbles, 'great big stones you could call them'. Then she took the train into London, equipped not just with pebbles but with a hammer. 'I was given the top of Villiers Street.' (This is the last left off the Strand before we reach Charing Cross station.) Stopping to buy violets and the evening paper, she waited until 5.45pm. 'That was my moment.' Out came the hammer. After smashing up a jeweller's, she went on to the Strand, where she did 'at least nine windows'. 'It was as though I was playing hockey.'

Pausing at Trafalgar Square, we have another chance to consider both sides of the suffragette coin. No.27 was the headquarters of the Artists' Franchise League. They are the ones who, with the help of Sylvia Pankhurst, did all the wonderful postcards and posters. My favourite is: 'What's Sauce for the Gander is Sauce for the Goose'. My next favourite features a Mrs John Bull saying, 'Now you greedy boys. I shall not give you any more until I have helped myself.'

Trafalgar Square was also where Millicent Garrett Fawcett and the law-abiding constitutionalists held their Equal Political Rights Rally, on 16 June 1927. But it was at the National Gallery on the north side of the square that 'Slasher' Mary Richardson attacked the *Rokeby Venus* (attributed to Velázquez, incorrectly, according to Sylvia

Criterion Brasserie

Pankhurst) in May 1914. Richardson later confessed that her dislike of the painting made it 'easier for me to do what was in my mind'. She hid her axe inside her left sleeve, and held it in place with safety pins. She waited until the guard was behind a newspaper and then hacked at the painting five times. Then she was subdued by two German tourists wielding Baedeker guides. And off she went to Holloway. 'The one-time castle of the Warwick family seemed to have become my home.' The painting is restored and now hangs in Room 30.

After this and related events, the Royal Academy and the Tate closed to the public altogether. Others refused entrance to women unaccompanied by gentlemen. The police sent photographs of the suffragettes deemed most dangerous to works of art to all leading museums and galleries. Not even in the most violent days of the agitation did the suffragettes cause loss of life. Neither did they lose their sense of middle-class entitlement.

As we turn our backs on Nelson's Column to walk down Whitehall, past government office after government office and finally past the gates and guards that protect Downing Street, think what would happen today if two protesters had themselves posted to Number Ten as 'human letters'. Or if anti-capitalist protestors chained themselves to the grille outside, as a group led by 'General' Flora Drummond did in 1909 – or pelted Number Ten with stones and broke four windows, as Mrs Pankhurst and friends did in 1912.

And so to the next-to-last stop on our walk, Caxton Hall, where the WSPU held its famous 'Women's Parliaments'. To reach it, we turn right on to Great George Street and then follow along the edge of St James's Park. Take a left through a passage at Queen Anne's Gate, right at Petty France, and left again on to Palmer Street. On the left-hand side just as Palmer Street meets Caxton Street is a large, ailing brick building that has been covered with green tarpaulin for some time now. There are signs on the door warning us not to enter. To the right is a plaque to tell us that this is Caxton Hall, and that Churchill spoke here during World War II.

Before the war, during the days when Churchill was just another pestered and suffragette-hating politician, Caxton Hall was much better known as the base from which the WSPU liked to 'rush' the House of Commons. The most notorious rush was on what came to be known as Black Friday, 18 November 1910. Their slogans of the moment describe the mood that day: 'The Bill, the Whole Bill and Nothing But the Bill'. And 'Who Would Be Free Must Themselves Strike the Blow'. Furious at the machinations

of Asquith over the Conciliation Bill, they marched to Westminster to find an army of police waiting for them.

One witness stated: 'For hours I was beaten about the body, thrown backwards out of the crowd, only to be pushed helplessly along in front of one's tormentor into a side street…while he beat one up and down over the spine until cramp seized one's legs… What I complain about on behalf of us all is the long drawn out agony of the delayed arrest and the continuous beating and pinching.'

The suffragettes took many different routes from Caxton Hall to Parliament Square. Or, to quote the press and the police, they arrived by 'devious courses'. Our route today will take us across Caxton Street into Christchurch Gardens to look at the statue put there by the Suffragette Fellowship. It's in the shape of a scroll and pays tribute to the 'men and women' who faced 'derision, opposition and ostracism' and endured 'physical violence and suffering' during the long battle to win women the vote. It also makes its claim on Caxton Hall.

As we leave Christchurch Gardens and turn left into Victoria Street, we are within sight of our final destination. Once we've skirted Westminster Abbey and are walking along the western side of Parliament Square past St Margaret's church, we can look across the street to take stock of the queue outside the Palace of Westminster. If it reaches beyond the statue of Cromwell, you are looking at a two-hour wait, if not longer.

If that seems too long to make someone wait out in the cold, just think how much longer it was for the suffragettes. Think about almost 100 years of failed petitions. Think about the 100 women who were ejected in 1906, screaming and shrieking as the police beat them back, leaving behind them a trail of hatpins and bonnets. Over the next eight years, there were at least another dozen failed rushes. Think about these, but don't forget those other, more 'devious courses'. Spare a moment for Muriel Matters and Helen Fox, who chained themselves to the grille of the Ladies' Gallery in 1908, so that Matters could address the House on votes for women without immediate interruption. They were both removed 'with ironwork still chained to their bodies'. Think about Marion Wallace-Dunlop, who chartered an airship in Hendon in 1909: when it was directly over the Palace of Westminster, she dropped 56 pounds of leaflets. In the same year, the same woman sneaked into St Stephen's Hall with a male sympathiser and stamped an extract of the Bill of Rights on its walls in red ink. In 1911, Emily Wilding Davison also managed to sneak into the Palace of Westminster. She hid inside a cupboard for 46 hours, winning the headline 'Guy Fawkes in Petticoats'. And yet another stint in Holloway.

What changed the suffragettes' luck? Many believe it was the truce they called in 1914, and the fine work they did for the war effort. Others say nonsense, that it was law-abiding constitutionalists who won the argument, and that it might have been sooner had the militants not caused so much trouble. Still others say that, thanks to support inside the Labour Party, women's suffrage was going to happen sooner or later and that after the war its time had come. Whatever – in 1918, the Representation of the People Bill gave the vote to women over 30 with household credentials, and in 1928, the franchise was extended to women on the same terms as men.

Mrs Pankhurst was dead by then. The third reading of the bill coincided with her funeral, which took place at Westminster and went from there to Brompton Cemetery. Millicent Garrett Fawcett was a very old lady by then. But she was sitting in the gallery of the House of Lords to hear the King's Assent. Imagine how she felt as she walked down St Stephen's Hall, thinking of all that had passed in the 60 years since the day she hid her first suffrage petition under the

apple lady's skirts. She died just a year and a half later. Her memorial service was held in Westminster Abbey, which we can see again as we leave through the Stranger's Entrance and turn left to walk past the House of Lords.

Just beyond the Sovereign's Entrance is Victoria Tower Gardens. Here we find the most generous tribute to the suffragettes: a shiny black statue of Emmeline Pankhurst, and, underneath it, a replica of a medallion given to 1,000 people during the agitation and another replica of a medallion showing Christabel in profile.

According to Rachel Ferguson in *We Were Amused*, when news went out that a statue of Mrs Pankhurst was to stand within spitting distance of the House of Lords, something strange happened. A police band volunteered to come and play at the unveiling. It must have been a shock for the organisers, but they decided to accept this generous and forgiving offer. You can imagine what the mood was like that day, how the surviving suffragettes must have laughed as they thought about the ironies. After all those skirmishes and beatings and arrests and hunger strikes and forcible feedings, to see Mrs Pankhurst turned to stone, and the police transformed into her fondest admirers.

My own first visit was very much in the same vein. I had missed the statue when I took the walk for the first time with two very patient students. I finally tracked it down on 1 May 2001. I was with my daughter that day: it was her 18th birthday. As irony would have it, it was also the day the Met put 6,000 police into Westminster and the West End, to exercise 'zero tolerance' against an estimated 2,000 anti-capitalist marchers, some of whom had given an indication that they were thinking of smashing a few windows along the way. Their well-advertised route was not to take them through Parliament Square, but as they had wreaked havoc there only a year earlier, the Met was not willing to take any chances. My daughter and I arrived

Emmeline Pankhurst and daughter **Christabel** on their release from Holloway in 1908.

to find four police vans parked on the street opposite the entrance to Victoria Tower Gardens. When we tried to enter the park by what turned out to be the Sovereign's Entrance to the House of Lords, the policeman in the box sprang to his feet and rushed outside to stop us. From his expression it was clear that he thought we were about to hatch a devious and violent plot. When we told him we were only looking for the statue of Mrs Pankhurst, he relaxed and smiled. I almost asked him: did he have any idea what that name would have done to him, if we'd turned the clock back 90 years?

But he was a kind and decent man, who only wanted to help us. The park was closed for the afternoon, he explained, 'because of the marchers'. But we were in luck, because if we went back on to the street, and turned left, and walked ten or 20 paces, we'd be able to look into the park and see her perfectly. And so we did. And here's what we found: a gracious and most elegant Mrs P, her arms outstretched, her famously tragic

eyes turned away from the House of Lords. Almost smiling at the police who surrounded her. And still behind bars.

Eating & drinking

Atrium
4 Millbank, SW1P 3JA (7233 0032/www.atrium restaurant.com). **Open** 8am-11pm Mon-Fri. *Restaurant* noon-3pm, 6-10pm Mon-Fri. Much favoured by politicos. Fine food in a light setting.

Coffee Gallery
23 Museum Street, WC1A 1JL (7436 0455). **Open** 9am-5.30pm Mon-Sat; 11am-5.30pm Sun. Cakes and pastries.

Criterion Brasserie
224 Piccadilly, W1J 9HP (7930 0488/ www.whitestarline.org.uk). **Open** noon-2.30pm, 5.30-11.30pm Mon-Sat. Grand French dishes in opulent surroundings.

Fortnum & Mason
181 Piccadilly, W1A 1ER (7734 8040/ www.fortnumandmason.com). **Open** *Shop* 10am-6.30pm Mon-Sat. *Fountain Tea Room* 8.30am-7.45pm Mon-Sat. *St James's Restaurant* 10am-5.30pm Mon-Sat. Opt for the slightly formal restaurant or afternoon tea.

India Club

Second Floor, Strand Continental Hotel, 143 Strand, WC2R 1JA (7836 0650). **Open** noon-2.30pm, 6-10.50pm Mon-Sat. Inexpensive curries.

Point 101

101 New Oxford Street, WC1A 1DD (7379 3112). **Open/food served** 4pm-2am Mon-Sat; 4pm-midnight Sun.

Buildings & churches

Buckingham Palace & Royal Mews

SW1A 1AA (7766 7300/Royal Mews). **Open** *6 Aug-30 Sept* 9.30am-4.15pm daily. *Royal Mews* Oct-July noon-4pm (last entry 3.30pm); Aug-Sept 10.30am-4.30pm (last entry 4pm) Mon-Thur. **Admission** £11; £5.50 5-16s; £9 OAPs; £27.50 family. *Royal Mews* £4.60; £2.70 5-16s; £3.60 OAPs; £11.80 family.

Caxton Hall

Caxton Street, SW1 (no phone).

Chapel Royal, St James's Palace

Cleveland Row, SW1A 1BL (7930 4832). **Open** *Services* Oct-Good Friday 8.30am, 11.15am Sun; 12.30pm on Holy Days as announced. Easter Day-31 July services take place in the *Queen's Chapel, Marlborough Road, SW1,* times as above.

Houses of Parliament

Parliament Square, SW1A 0AA (Commons information 7219 4272/Lords information 7219 3107/tours information 0870 906 3773/www.parliament.uk). **Open** (when in session; always phone to check) *House of Commons Visitors' Gallery* 2.30-10.30pm Mon; 11.30am-7.30pm Tue-Thur; 9.30am-3pm Fri. *House of Lords Visitors' Gallery* from 2.30pm Mon-Wed; from 11am Thur, Fri. Phone to check times. *Tours* summer recess only; phone for details. **Admission** *Visitors' Gallery* free. *Tours* £7; £5 concessions; free under-5s; £22 family.

Royal Albert Hall

Kensington Gore, SW7 2AP (information 7589 3203/box office 7589 8212/www.royalalberthall.com). **Open** *Box office* 9am-9pm daily. **Tickets** £3-£100.

St George Bloomsbury

Bloomsbury Way, WC1 (7405 3044). Closed for renovations until Autumn 2005. After that, phone for opening times.

Westminster Abbey

Dean's Yard, SW1P 3PA (7222 5152/tours 7654 4900/www.westminster-abbey.org). **Open** *Chapter House, Nave & Royal Chapels* 9.30am-3.45pm Mon, Tue, Thur,

Houses of Parliament

Fri; 9.30am-7pm Wed; 9.30am-1.45pm Sat. *Abbey Museum* 10.30am-4pm Mon-Sat. *Cloisters* 8am-6pm Mon-Sat. *College Garden* Apr-Sept 10am-6pm Tue-Thur; Oct-Mar 10am-4pm Tue-Thur. **Admission** £7.50; £5 concessions; free under-11s with paying adult; £15 family.

Hotels & clubs

Carlton Club
69 St James's Street, SW1A 1PJ (7493 1164/ www.carltonclub.co.uk).

Knightsbridge Green Hotel
159 Knightsbridge, SW1X 7PD (7584 6274/ www.thekghotel.com).

Reform Club
104 Pall Mall, SW1Y 5EW (7930 9374).

Ritz
150 Piccadilly, W1J 9BR (7493 8181/ www.theritzlondon.com).

Savoy
The Strand, WC2R 0EU (7836 4343/ www.fairmont.com).

Strand Palace Hotel
372 The Strand, WC2R 0JJ (0870 400 8702/ www.strandpalacehotel.co.uk).

White's Club
37 St James's Street, SW1A 1JG (7493 6671).

Literature

Millicent Garrett Fawcett
Ray Strachey (1931)
The Suffragettes in Pictures
Diane Atkinson (1997)
The Suffragette Movement
Sylvia Pankhurst (1931)
Unshackled: The Story of How We Won the Vote Christabel Pankhurst (1959)
Votes for Women: The Virago Book of Suffragettes ed Joyce Marlow (2001)
We Were Amused Rachel Ferguson (1958)
The Women's Suffrage Movement: A Reference Guide 1886-1928
Elizabeth Crawford (1999)

Museums & galleries

British Museum
Great Russell Street, WC1B 3DG (7636 1555/ www.thebritishmuseum.ac.uk). **Open** *Galleries* 10am-5.30pm Mon-Wed, Sat, Sun; 10am-8.30pm Thur, Fri. *Great Court* 9am-6pm Mon-Wed, Sun; 9am-11pm Thur-Sat. *Highlights tours* (90mins) 10.30am, 1pm, 3pm daily. **Admission** free; donations appreciated. *Temporary exhibitions* prices vary. *Highlights tours* £8; £5 concessions.

National Gallery
Trafalgar Square, WC2N 5DN (7747 2885/ www.nationalgallery.org.uk). **Open** 10am-6pm Mon, Tue, Thur-Sun; 10am-9pm Wed. *Tours* 11.30am, 2.30pm Mon, Tue, Thur, Fri, Sun; 11.30am, 2.30pm, 6pm, 6.30pm Wed; 11.30am, 12.30pm, 2.30pm, 3.30pm. **Admission** free. *Special exhibitions* prices vary.

Royal Academy of Arts
Burlington House, Piccadilly, W1J 0BD (7300 8000/www.royalacademy.org.uk). **Open** *Temporary exhibitions* 10am-6pm Mon-Thur, Sat, Sun; 10am-10pm Fri. *John Madejski Fine Rooms* 1-4.30pm Tue-Fri; 10am-6pm Sat, Sun. **Admission** *Fine Rooms* free. *Exhibitions* prices vary.

Tate Britain
Millbank, SW1P 4RG (7887 8000/ www.tate.org.uk). **Open** 10am-5.50pm daily. *Tours* 11am, noon, 2pm, 3pm Mon-Fri; noon, 3pm Sat. Sun. **Admission** free. *Special exhibitions* prices vary.

Others

Fawcett Society
1-3 Berry Street, EC1V 0AA (7253 2598/ www.fawcettsociety.org.uk). Organisation campaigning for equality between men and women in the UK.

Harvey Nichols
109-125 Knightsbridge, SW1X 7RJ (7235 5000/www.harveynichols.com). **Open** 10am-8pm Mon-Fri; 10am-7pm Sat; noon-6pm Sun.

Holloway Prison
1 Parkhurst Road, N7 0NU (7979 4400/ www.hmprisonservice.gov.uk).

Silver Moon Women's Bookshop
Foyles, 113-119 Charing Cross Road, WC2H 0EB (7440 1562/www.foyles.co.uk). **Open** 9.30am-9pm Mon-Sat; noon-6pm Sun.

Women's Library
Old Castle Street, E1 7NT (7320 2222/ www.thewomenslibrary.ac.uk). **Open** *Reading Room* 9.30am-5pm Tue, Wed, Fri; 9.30am-8pm Thur; 10am-4pm Sat.

The hanging gardens of Balham

Arthur Smith

Strike out across Tooting and Wandsworth Commons and dive into Tooting Bec Lido in the company of the self-proclaimed Mayor of Balham.

Start: Balham tube/rail
Finish: Balham tube/rail
or Wandsworth Town rail
Time: 2-3 hours
Distance: 4 miles/6km
Getting there: Northern line
or rail to Balham
Getting back: Northern line or
rail from Balham, or rail from
Wandsworth Town to Victoria
or London Bridge
Note: the walk goes through
two parks, and can be muddy,
but also passes by the Tooting
Bec Lido, so bring a swimming
costume (check listings for
opening times).

The following walk can be cut in half by returning to Balham tube at the appropriate moment. It is not a route that passes by grand houses or museums or historic monuments. Rather it carves its way through the leafier sections of a fairly typical inner-city suburb. The places and amenities along the way are used on a day-to-day basis by its residents. Only the most determined tourists pass this way (I have never yet seen Balham or Tooting mentioned in any guidebook to London – *Time Out* excepted, of course – but that is part of its charm). To north Londoners, and the world at large, south London is a strange, mysterious place inhabited by monsters and bad food. But for those of us who live here it has

an unpretentious urban charm that grounds you in reality after the more overt attractions to be found in the West End and points north. In north London, goes the joke, they have little blue plaques commemorating famous people. In south London we have big yellow signs saying, 'Did you see this murder?' You won't see any murders, but you will hear about the violence, pain and good humour of Balham during the war – the most serious event in this area's history.

With its broad boulevards and its pulsating nightlife, Balham is like a cross between Paris and Rio de Janeiro. This line usually raises a laugh among London audiences because, of course, Balham is a bit of a joke. It always has been. In the Domesday Book it is written in the margins as an afterthought to Clapham. In the 18th and 19th centuries it was known as a brothel on the way to Brighton. These days it is the only place in London with its own catchphrase, 'Gateway to the South', from the Muir and Norden sketch, made famous by Peter Sellers and repeated ad nauseam by all black-cab drivers since.

Our walk begins on the platforms at Balham tube station. On the night of 14 October 1940, 680 people were sheltering here from German bombs. They were ill advised to do so, since this is the shallowest of London Underground stations, only 12 yards below the surface of the pavement. In this 12 yards lies a network of water, gas and sewage pipes. Out on the street at 8pm the blackout was

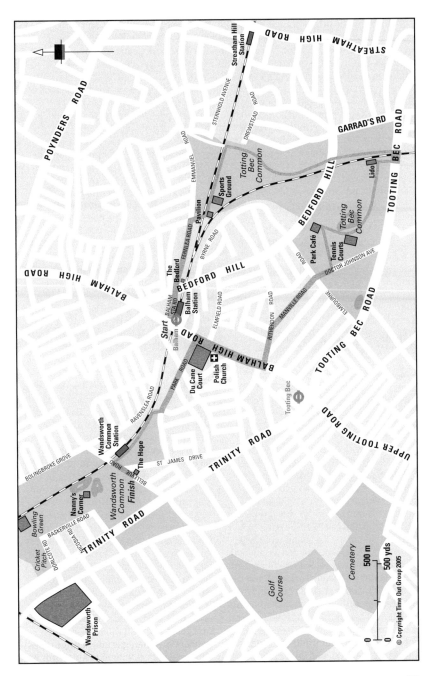

punctured by the bright orange light of flares that presaged an imminent cascade of bombs. The one that hit just outside the tube caused the deaths of 68 of the people huddling below. Accounts of this tragedy are coy, perhaps because it would seem the poor souls drowned in the sewage and gas of the ruptured pipes.

But let's get on with the promenade. Stride purposefully down Balham Station Road, keeping Sainsbury's car park to your left. When you get to a crossroads, go straight over into Fernlea Road with the Bedford pub to your right, or go into the Bedford for a pre-ramble livener. It is an established comedy venue in London and one of the most distinctive, too, with its circular auditorium and gallery. On weekends, after the shows, it turns into what was known in my day as a disco. Oh yes, because, despite all the jokes, Balham is getting a bit groovy – my local hardware shop is now a cappuccino bar. I resent the gentrification a bit because, well, it's not meant to be Kensington, but I like to applaud modern initiatives, especially in my capacity as Mayor of Balham (self-proclaimed. And only night Mayor: I don't do days). Fifty years ago, according to my father, the Bedford was a den of iniquity, where prostitutes would earn their money in dark corners. (It wasn't long ago that Bedford Hill was dotted with prostitutes; I think they've moved on to Streatham now.)

At the point where Fernlea Road becomes Emmanuel Road and a strip of common appears, turn right and go under a railway bridge. Behold the glory that is the Northern Frontier of Tooting Common. The common is large enough that I once persuaded a Canadian girlfriend that an escaped lion lived there. It is not manicured or glamorous, but it has a rufty charm and several points of interest, some of which we shall now visit.

After the bridge, turn left following the wall of the railway embankment. Gaps in the overgrowth permitting, you'll see that the bricks are decorated with classic examples of graffiti art, and when it reaches another railway bridge you might remark a pink 'AS' that I have sprayed there especially for you. This bridge was guarded for a few evenings in 1940 by my father, who was a schoolboy member of the Home Guard. His job was to challenge passers-by, who would laugh at him and walk on.

As shall we. Turn right following the second side of this triangular bit of the common. You could follow the tarmac path or the bridleway. You are unlikely to be trampled on, since in all the times I have walked down here I have never once seen a horse. The path arrives at the railway line that forms the third side of the triangle and continues its short leafy way to the road. An old unrepealed by-law states that all walkers should hop this section. It would be impolite to ignore this. If you pass anyone who is not hopping, you should remonstrate loudly with them.

Stop hopping, cross the road (Bedford Hill) and plunge into the dark woods ahead of you. If you haven't managed it already, this is an excellent opportunity to get your shoes muddy, and, if you are wearing shorts, to get your legs scratched. As you make your way through the trees, you will catch a glimpse, across the other side of the railway line, of some coloured squares. These are the doors to the cubicles at the shallow end of the glorious monument that is Tooting Bec Lido.

Continue through the wood (again alongside the railway) until you reach another road (Tooting Bec Road). Turn right over the bridge and take some steps down immediately on your right that lead towards the entrance to the Lido. Gaze at its blue, tatty, inviting carapace. If it is open (mid May to mid September), pay the small fee, go in and plunge into the electric blue shock of the cold water.

On warm summer days Tooting Lido is the best place to be in London. In 1910, four years after it opened, a journalist wrote: 'We know all the London suburbs and we cannot call to mind any swimming

The new generation of young British artists show their skills on **Tooting Common**.

lake like this, three hundred feet long, one hundred feet wide and seven feet deep.' It is still true today. It is one of the biggest pools in Europe and on a hot weekend, even if it's hard to find a spot poolside, there's always plenty of room in the water. A certain prime minister did her best to close down open-air pools and Tooting survived by the skin of the teeth of the wiry people who run the swimming club. They kept it open and several of them swim every morning of the year, with a big splash on Christmas Day.

One of the greatest pleasures of my life is to sit in the sun in the Lido with a cup of tea, a smoke and drying hair and then glance up from my novel to observe the Gatwick Express rattling by. Look at those fools, flying off to sit by a pool or on some scuzzy beach when, here, beneath their speeding noses, lies the finest bathing experience on earth.

From the Lido (what a great word that is), strike off across the common about 100 yards from and parallel to the road. After 300 yards you come to

some clumpy bushes, which shelter a pond. Mallards, Aylesbury, Barbary – these are all types of duck and, who knows, some of them may be represented here. Ducks are benign birds, beloved by children, comical and beautiful. Or are they? It is not unknown for female ducks to be gangbanged to death by hordes of male ducks. You can feed the ducks, but beware: you may be giving sustenance to rapists and murderers.

Beyond the duck pond is a path where you turn right and pass some tennis courts and a playground before you see an unpretentious café. If it is open, go in and drink a cup of tea. Have it on me. I have deposited enough money for the first 40 people who pass by to get a free cuppa. If you are following this walk in the year 2070, then the offer, if not the café and the world, may well have expired.

Refreshed, turn right immediately out of the café and head towards a wooden car barrier. You have arrived at the road that bisects this part of the common. It bears the unlikely name of Doctor

Wandsworth Common – a 'very attractive chunk of greenery', says the Mayor of Balham.

Johnson Avenue. It seems that Dr Johnson was a frequent visitor to Streatham and came this way perhaps in pursuit of Cynthia Payne's ancestors in nearby Ambleside Avenue. It was Dr Johnson who coined the phrase 'when a man is tired of London he's tired of life; when a man is tired of Colliers Wood, he's been there about ten minutes'.

Stride the few yards to the end of the avenue, continue straight over into Manville Road, which leads to Ritherdon Road, where you turn left, passing the Blue Pumpkin restaurant. Turn right at a T-junction and you will find yourself enjoying the sumptuousness of Balham High Road. After not very long you arrive at the church of Christ the King, a solid redbrick building that was bought in 1978 for use by Polish Catholics.

There is a large Polish community in Balham, which sprang up after the war when dispossessed (and disillusioned) Poles wisely chose this leafy corner of London to settle in. It is one of two churches between here and the tube, the other being St Mary and St John. William Wilberforce attended its opening in 1808 when it was known invitingly as a Chapel of Ease. These days the vicar, Dorothy Stephenson, tells me the church works with the local community: 'We don't bother too much with the spiritual stuff.' There certainly wasn't much spiritual stuff going on when I opened the first Balham festival here in 1998. Speaking through a megaphone to a handful of worthies and sniggering friends of mine, I announced that it was the greatest moment of my life.

Just past the Polish church an enormous ocean liner of a building hoves up on your left. This is Du Cane Court, a sort of south London Dolphin Square, which opened to much brouhaha in 1934. It boasted its own restaurant, shop and roof terrace, and had a lobby so modern that they still film Agatha Christie adaptations there. It rapidly acquired a racy reputation with the arrival of showbiz types including, apparently, most of the Tiller Girls. It was known briefly as Cocaine Court, but then, here it comes again, the war.

Du Cane Court has an odd association with the Nazis. It was never bombed during the Blitz and it was rumoured that the Luftwaffe used it as a navigational aid. 'Turn right at the big building.' This gave rise to theories that there were German spies living on the top floor, that from the air the flats resemble a swastika or the German eagle, and that

Hitler was planning to live there after the invasion. I first heard this assertion when I was eight and even then it seemed unlikely, but I have heard it from so many different people that I wonder what the truth is. Hitler had extensive plans for London and certain Londoners. Perhaps Du Cane Court, with its size and security, would have made a good HQ and it's probable the Panzers would have chosen the A24 into town thus taking them straight past the big block.

There's nothing to prevent you looking briefly at the foyer of Du Cane Court, which still exudes a certain pre-war glamour. You may spot me there on the way to the shop.

If you have had enough of this walk, you can go straight up Balham High Road to the tube. If, however, you're still game, then off we go to Wandsworth Common, turning left down Balham Park Road just after Du Cane Court. Carry straight on at the junction for 250 yards to where the road bends left. You will see an alleyway between houses on your right. Follow this and, after a short distance, you reach the southern extremity of Wandsworth Common. Continue along by the side of the railway, passing Wandsworth Common station, until you come to a junction with traffic lights. To your left is Bellevue Road, a strip of upmarket shops and restaurants that is one of the most fashionable roads in south London.

If Balham is up and coming, then Bellevue Road has already done the business and is enjoying a post-coital fag. Twenty yards up Bellevue Road, Chez Bruce is not, as it sounds, a pretentious Australian joint, but a top-class restaurant with a Michelin star. It used to be called Harvey's and was where Marco Pierre White first got a foothold in the London restaurant scene.

Unless you require sustenance, ignore Bellevue Road and cross over at the lights on to the main body of Wandsworth Common. It is a very attractive chunk of greenery, less scrubby than Tooting Common, and less featureless, treeless and boring than nearby Clapham Common.

I've decided to allow you to use your own initiative to follow your own grassy dreams at this point. You need eventually to return to this place (by the Hope pub), but you are invited to roam freely around the common, exploring its pastoral delights. Here are a few highlights you might like to investigate. The common is not so big that you won't find most of them.

1. The Bowling Green. As I have advanced further into middle age, I have felt an increasing affinity with the elderly people in white, bent over their big, heavy, shiny balls. There is a wooden hut round the back of the green where you can rent the appropriate equipment and practise for your dotage.

2. The Pond. A big one. Ducks. Bread. A dinky little bridge, observation platforms.

Common sophistication at **Chez Bruce**.

3. The Cricket Pitches. In summer the not very good grass strips entertain the not very good players. I am one of them. My team, the Dusty Fleming International Hairstylists' XI play here. Watch out for Ainsley Harriott rushing in to bowl like some out-of-control steam engine, all arms and legs and pistons.

From some of the pitches you can look across at Wandsworth Prison and shudder at its grim Victorian solidity. Oscar Wilde was kept here before being transferred to Reading Gaol. When he waited at Clapham Junction station, just up the line, he was spat upon. Another celebrity inmate was 'Mad' Frankie Fraser, who reports that after his release some years ago he attempted to hang the then governor and his dog from a tree on the common.

4. Nanny's Corner. A small children's play area. During the week it is encircled by bored and beautiful foreign au pairs keeping an eye on their playful nippers. At weekends, bored and beautiful mums take over.

5. The Trim Trail. This comprises a series of odd wooden constructs dotted around one triangle of the common. You could look at them as objets d'art or, if you're feeling more energetic, you could hop over them, climb them, or generally follow the instructions given on plates of wood next to each apparatus.

Having ticked all or some of these off your list, you now return to the Hope. This is your opportunity to nose up Bellevue Road and back again. Cakes, art, cappuccino, fish, clothes and a parrot all invite your attention. Or maybe just go into the pub.

From here you return whence you came to Balham High Road and go left to the tube. If you tell one of the people in blue working there that you have just completed Arthur Smith's *Time Out* Trail Round Tooting and Wandsworth Commons, he will issue you with a gold embossed certificate signed by the Mayor of Balham. Or possibly not.

Eating & drinking

Bedford
77 Bedford Hill, SW12 9HD (8682 8940). **Open** 11am-11pm Mon-Wed; 11am-midnight Thur; 11am-2am Fri, Sat; noon-10.30pm Sun. **Food served** noon-2.45pm, 7-10pm Mon-Fri; noon-4pm, 7-10pm Sat; noon-5pm, 7-9.45pm Sun.

Blue Pumpkin
16-18 Ritherdon Road, SW17 (8767 2660). **Open** 10am-11pm Mon-Sat; 10am-10.30am Sun.

Chez Bruce
2 Bellevue Road, SW17 7EG (8672 0114/www. chezbruce.co.uk). **Lunch served** noon-2pm Mon-Fri; 12.30-2.30pm Sat; noon-3pm Sun. **Dinner served** 6.30-10.30pm Mon-Sat, 7-10pm Sun.

Hope
1 Bellevue Road, SW17 (8672 8717). **Open** noon-11pm Mon-Sat; noon-10.30pm Sun. Food served.

Park Café
Tooting Common, Bedford Hill, SW12. **Open** 9am-5pm daily. Breakfasts, sandwiches and ices.

Churches

Christ the King
232-4 Balham High Road, SW17 7AW (8672 5070). **Services** 9.30am, 10.45am, noon Sun.

St Mary & St John
Balham High Road, SW12 9BS (8675 3278/ 1188). **Open** 10am-noon Mon, Wed, Thur, Sat.

Parks

Bowling Green
Wandsworth Common, Bolingbroke Grove, SW18 (8876 7685/www.wandsworth.gov.uk). **Open** *23 April-14 Aug* phone for details. **Admission** *casual play* £1.65. **Membership** £53/yr.

Tooting Bec Common
Tooting Bec Road, SW16 (8871 8688/ www.wandsworth.gov.uk).

Tooting Bec Lido
Tooting Bec Road, SW16 1RU (8871 7198/ www.wandsworth.gov.uk). **Open** *late May-late Aug* 6am-8pm daily. *Sept* 6am-5pm daily. *Oct-Mar* 7am-2pm daily (club members only). **Admission** phone to check.

Wandsworth Common
Bolingbroke Grove, SW18 (8871 8688/ www.wandsworth.gov.uk).

Tooting Bec Lido

The village of visionaries

Frances Morgan

Stoke Newington retains more than a trace of its literary and radical heritage, not least in the tranquil surroundings of Abney Park Cemetery.

> **Start:** Abney Park Cemetery, Stoke Newington High Street entrance
> **Finish:** Clissold Park, 141 bus stop
> **Time:** 1-2 hours
> **Distance:** 2 miles/3km
> **Getting there:** rail to Stoke Newington, 73 bus from Angel tube or 149 bus from Liverpool Street tube/rail
> **Getting back:** 141 or 341 bus to Manor House (Piccadilly line)
> **Note:** this is a short walk from a cemetery to a park, and so is ideal for children.

Before I moved to London, if I heard the name Stoke Newington at all, I thought it must be a little village you drive through on the way somewhere else, like Stansted Mountfichet or Much Hadham. In fact, it wasn't until I lived there that I could actually tell you where it was, although I'd been in London a good three years. Because it has no tube station, and is sandwiched between a nice but dull part of Islington and a bit of east London that people have only recently decided not to avoid, it's hard for non-inhabitants to place Stoke Newington. But despite its reputation as a sleepy hollow on the edge of town – or maybe because of this – radical urban ideas have flowered in this secret suburb for over 300 years.

It's still not the easiest place to get to: whether you brave the overground train

and walk down Stamford Hill or take the bus from Islington, first glimpses of Stoke Newington High Street may disappoint. Look out for the big cemetery gates, as your real journey starts here. If you've visited any of the other big London cemeteries, as you approach the gates of Abney Park you may think you know what to expect. After all, the entrance is a classic example of Victorian funerary exotica, with its Egyptian pillars flanked by two 'temples'. There are even some hieroglyphics, still legible on the lintels: composed by Joseph Bonomi, Egyptologist and former curator of Sir John Soane's Museum, they translate as 'The gates of the abode of the mortal part of man'.

But, once inside, you won't find the crazy colonial sarcophagi of Kensal Green, nor the elegant bohemianism of Highgate. Abney Park, founded in 1840 with the initial purpose of containing the overflow from Bunhill Fields, Moorgate's dissenters' cemetery, is a memorial to another Victorian state of mind, of the drive to reform, to help, and to quietly and simply rebel. It's also the least urban of all the city graveyards: its lush wilderness isn't just because of neglect by Hackney Council; an original intention of the founders was to create a haven for trees and wildlife.

Looking straight ahead, take the path on your right, and walk down to the chapel. Along the way are some typically Stoke Newingtonian graves, including, on your left, that of Samuel Robinson, who founded a refuge for the widows of Calvinist ministers. A little further

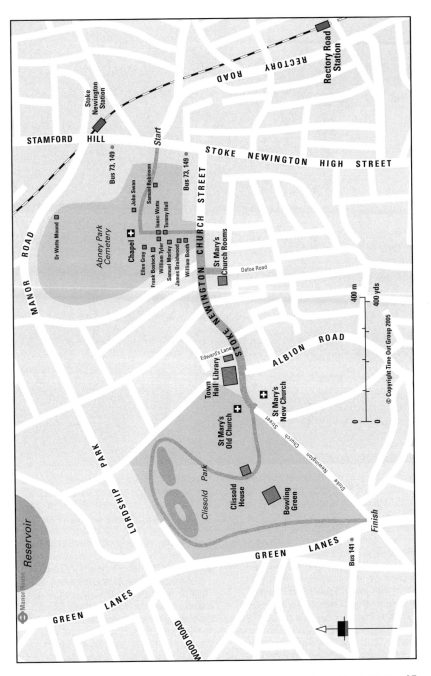

Abney Park Cemetery

on, look to your right for the grave of John Swan (1787-1869), engineer and inventor of the steamship's screw propeller and the self-acting chain messenger. The dense epitaph explains that he was never rewarded for his innovations, his employer getting the credit for both. His daughter, who erected the monument to try to redress the balance, sums up philosophically that 'Some men labour and others enter into their labours', and tries not to sound too bitter.

The chapel in the centre of the cemetery is an eccentric, medieval-style creation, one of those ruins you can imagine seeing as a folly in the grounds of a stately home. But it was widely used up until the 1950s. It's built in the shape of a Maltese cross (with all sides the same length) rather than the traditional crucifix, providing the interior with just one space to be used for funerals of all denominations, in keeping with the cemetery's principles.

A few feet away, facing the main door of the chapel, is the war memorial and the entrance to the cemetery's only catacomb, which has been sealed off due to vandalism. Set on a plinth past the memorial is a nine-foot statue of Isaac Watts, put up just after the

cemetery opened, and as much of a focal point as the chapel. We'll come to him later. Instead, head towards him, but take the path on his right. You'll see – in crumbling stone – the uniform of PC William Tyler, a victim of what local history people call the 'Tottenham Outrage' of 1909. The story goes that Russian anarchists hijacked a tram carrying wages and sparked off a full-on chase through the streets of Tottenham and over the Walthamstow marshes, ending in a shoot-out in which PC Tyler was killed – and, apparently, the anarchists ended by shooting themselves.

Head down this path, and you start to appreciate the wilderness of Abney Park. In the summer, it can be almost impossible to find your way around, as the trees block your view of the chapel, and each stone path, flanked by bluebells, looks the same. The ivy is rich and rampant, rendering monuments unrecognisable, and it seems a shame to guide you around the graves, when there is so much else to see – not least squawking jays and the occasional tapping woodpecker. But if London wildlife isn't enough for you, turn right at the end of this path and on your right you'll see a huge, sleepy stone lion, a

Bookish delights in **Church Street**.

You should be walking down a long and relatively clear path now, with the chapel to your right. As you follow it, other little paths on your right-hand side beckon you back towards the centre. Any of these are great to explore, passing the tombs of a colourful mix of past residents: Emily Gosse, seashore naturalist and mother of Sir Edmund Gosse; Mary Hillum, 105-year-old resident of Stoke Newington who never travelled by railway or omnibus, and never went more than 15 miles from home; and WG Hunt, a music hall songwriter credited with bringing the word 'jingoistic' into popular use.

Whether you take some diversions or not, keep following the big path round to a little winding woodchip path on your left. Follow this and you'll come to Dr Watts's mound. This, says the inscription, is where Isaac Watts (1674-1748) used to come to meditate upon and compose his famous hymns and less famous poems and philosophical writings. He was the first well-known writer of hymns: up until then, only psalms were sung in church. He wrote over 600 hymns, many of which are based on the psalms, but some are original. This was quite a radical step, as it was really one of the first instances of people publicly worshipping God 'in their own words' rather than those prescribed by the religious establishment. His two most famous hymns are probably 'O God, our help in ages past' and 'When I survey the wondrous cross'. This is what he is chiefly remembered for, especially by Victorian nonconformists; however, in his lifetime, he was also well known as a preacher and poet, and writer of academic works on geography, astronomy and philosophy, as well as religion.

Looking at the mound from the front, it's hard to ignore the modern houses beyond the (very old) wall, but turn your back to these, sit down on the mound and look out at the cemetery for inspiration. Of course, when Watts sat here, he would have seen Abney House, where he lived and taught for a number of years, and its

memorial to Frank Bostock, a Victorian menagerist. Those with a taste for the surreal will also like the angel statue on the grave of Ellen Gray, a few feet away: you'll see that, rather than classical features and flowing hair, this heavenly body has the face – and hairstyle – of a middle-aged, 1940s lady, earrings and all.

grounds. But I like to think that the birds and trees he might have also seen haven't changed much. A Victorian legend states that this mound is also the real resting place of Oliver Cromwell's body – a nice story, but completely false.

Come down from the mound and take the little path on your left back on to the main path you were on before. Keep following this, and take any of the paths you like to lead you back to the chapel and a proper look at the Watts monument. It's not hard to see why he was a hero to the Victorian dissenters who founded this cemetery: in his hymns, especially, they found their nonconformist ideals beautifully articulated. To be buried in the walk that leads directly up from his statue was a mark of great honour. Although the little grave (complete with 1930s racing bike) of Tommy Hall, record-breaking cyclist, is a bit incongruous, the stately and rather forbidding Victorian tombs on this walk are Protestant pomp personified. There's Samuel Morley, founder of Morley College, and, if you follow the path round to the right when it forks, James Braidwood, the superintendent who revolutionised British fire-fighting but died in the Tooley Street fire of 1861. There's also Conrad Loddiges, of the famous Hackney gardening family, who were responsible for the beautiful woodland design of the cemetery, as well as supplying rare plants to Kew Gardens and, back in the 18th century, introducing rhubarb to London.

As the path bends round again to the left, you soon come out by a collection of Abney Park's most ostentatious memorials – those to the founding family of the Salvation Army. If you've any doubt about the importance and sheer scale of the Sally Army in the late 19th and early 20th centuries, these graves say it all. The huge shields that commemorate the Booth family and other leading lights are well maintained: the gold lettering marking not only births and deaths (otherwise known as being 'promoted

to glory' or being 'called home') but also the date of being 'born again of the spirit' still shines brightly. If you look out from the Booth graves over to the other side of Church Street, you'll see the neon sign of a more ironic tribute to the strictly teetotal general: Booth's Pizzeria, offering cocktails and bar food.

Although you could easily spend some more time in the cemetery, here is a good place to leave it behind and explore Stoke Newington. You should now be facing the Church Street gates, which are the original gates of Abney House, the manor house upon whose grounds Abney Park Cemetery was built. The history of Stoke Newington's great houses is a convoluted one. Fleetwood House, which preceded Abney House, established Stoke Newington as one of the 17th century's first centres of religious dissent, owned as it was by Charles Fleetwood, son-in-law to Oliver Cromwell. After Fleetwood's death in 1692, Thomas Gunston redeveloped the

St Mary's New Church, built in 1858.

land, planning and building a new manor house. He died after it was completed, in 1700, having first arranged his sister's marriage to Sir Thomas Abney (who was gently mocked by Daniel Defoe, among others, for his establishment links, including a stint as Lord Mayor of London. As Defoe refused even to be a local churchwarden, this isn't surprising). And it's through this link that Isaac Watts – friend to the Abneys and the Gunstons – came to live at Abney House.

Turn right as you come out of the cemetery onto Stoke Newington Church Street. You are about to approach Defoe Road, which leads off Church Street to your left. Defoe's links with Stoke Newington are important. As a schoolboy in Newington Green (where he later tried his hand – unsuccessfully – at civet farming), he had a classmate named Crusoe, who, according to legend, gave him the title of his most famous book. Whether this is true or not, Defoe ended up here again in 1710, after his years of brick-making, spying, pamphleteering and imprisonment, to settle down and write *Robinson Crusoe*, published in 1719.

His house is gone, but he is commemorated by a plaque and a pub. On Defoe Road is the ruin of St Mary's Church Rooms, which are a great example of the nonconformist assembly rooms of the 19th century. See them before they become fashionable live-work spaces.

Stoke Newington Church Street was described in the 1890s by local historian Dr Benjamin Clarke as 'somewhat like those long, serpentine roads that take you through a small country town'. At least until you reach Clissold Park, this is remarkably still the case. It's notable for being a street of independence: despite its increasing fashionability, not a single chain store, café or restaurant seems to have appeared, unless you count the Post Office and a branch of Oddbins. Instead, signs on shop doors say 'We open 11ish', and all manner of enthusiasms are catered for, from organic food and health products (Fresh & Wild, at Nos.32-40), to violin repairs and supplies (Bridgewood & Neitzert, at No.146). It's in keeping with Church Street's literary reputation that there are a couple of excellent second-hand bookshops – Ocean Books and

Clissold Park

Church Street Bookshop – that are worth a look as you head towards the churches and the park.

Unconventional beliefs still get a look-in, in the form of alternative medicine – it's a Stoke Newington cliché, but if the number of health-food shops and homeopathic clinics is anything to go by, it's not inaccurate. Perhaps the nonconformist spirit has turned inwards, to Reiki, yoga and kinesiology, but at least it's still there – and there are enough ads up for writers' groups and classes to keep up the image of Stoke Newington as a village of ideas.

Defoe wasn't the only famous storyteller of Stoke Newington. The young Edgar Allan Poe, sent to Manor House School in 1817, was enchanted by the village. He later wrote of its 'deeply-shadowed avenues… the fragrance of its thousand shrubberies… the stillness of the dusky atmosphere in which the fretted Gothic steeple lay imbedded and asleep'; the school in his story 'William Wilson' is a (much-exaggerated) version of Manor House School. You'll pass a Poe plaque next door to the Fox Reformed Wine Bar; the school itself was in Edward's Lane, which is the road that runs by the side of the library. With a bit of imagination you can see how these little side streets would have been shadowy avenues, but the reference to a Gothic steeple is a bit puzzling, as even the little spire on the old church wasn't added until 1829. Incidentally, if the library is open, it's worth popping in to see Defoe's original gravestone, stolen from Bunhill Fields, found in Southampton and finally returned to Stoke Newington.

These literary back alleys are rudely interrupted as you come to the town hall, a grandiose and strangely stylish 1930s thing that dwarfs the old church and the little shops around it. It was built on top of Church Row, which, if it were still standing, might have blue plaques to Isaac Disraeli, father of Benjamin and author of *Curiosities of Literature*, FM Evans, proprietor of *Punch*, and visitors

Charles Dickens and Wilkie Collins. In their absence, walk a few more steps and you're at St Mary's Old Church.

Although there's been a church on this site since Anglo-Saxon times, what you see now was mainly built in 1563 by William Patten, whose motto 'ab alto' (from above) is still above the door. One drawback is that it's hard to go inside: the church is usually only opened for services. But a quick detour around the churchyard is worth doing. You won't find famous names now, although members of the anti-slavery Wilberforce family, and Anna Laetita Barbauld, Romantic poet and author, were buried here. You do, however, get a sense of Stoke Newington in the late 18th and early 19th centuries, from the occupations given on the graves to the doom-laden inscriptions. This is the sleepy, Gothic Stoke Newington as romanticised by Poe, right down to the headstone with two stone skulls on either post. At least, it looks sleepy. On some Sundays the church is used by an African Christian group whose services go on all day, with drumming and singing, making the churchyard a good place to stop and listen as well as to look around.

The church across the road is St Mary's New Church, built in 1858 to a design by George Gilbert Scott, and supposed to look like a mini-Salisbury Cathedral.

As you stand between the two defiantly non-urban churches, it's time to enter Clissold Park, where you'll immediately notice Clissold House, built in 1790 for James Hoare, a Quaker banker, by another local botanist and exotic plant enthusiast, Joseph Woods, and named after its last owner, Augustus Clissold. The grounds became a public park in 1889 after plans to build houses on the area met with fierce local opposition.

Clissold House is now a proper park café, where people stop for fry-ups, tea and ice-cream on the terrace and lawn. If you've gone this far without a break, then you should perhaps stop here for a while. It's never very relaxing, as it's almost always busy with families and dogs, but after all that poking about in the past, it's good to feel part of the real world again. If other parts of Stoke Newington are like the countryside, Clissold Park has a streak of small-town eccentricity in its park wildlife. If you look across the river from the house, you'll see an enclosure full of deer, and one full of very fat goats. There's been a deer enclosure in Clissold Park since Victorian times – I'm not sure about the goats.

The water that separates you from the animals is an ornamental canal that originated as part of the New River, which provided much of London's drinking water. The formidable turrets you should be able to see on the horizon beyond the park belong to a mock-medieval castle, built by the Victorians as a novel way of housing part of the waterworks, and now used as a climbing centre.

Following the river around to the left, you can take a closer look at the animals, including some haughty-looking swans that glide around ignoring the ducks. There's also a small aviary and a 'butterfly tunnel', which, along with the bowling green and tennis courts, make this a model municipal park. Clissold Park isn't a wild area by any means, and, because it's so flat, you're always aware of the traffic passing by. But, as London's rare green patches go, this is a particularly bright and spacious one, as well as being another haven for rare and old trees. A wander around the two lakes and back across the park past the paddling pool brings you out at the top of Church Street where it meets busy Green Lanes.

While you still have one foot (kind of) in the tranquil and green side of Stoke Newington, I'd advise you to get on the 141 bus and head back towards Manor House tube. It's shocking how quickly the scenery turns back into grimy north London, and may be a little depressing – but only because you've just spent a few hours in one of London's time-slips, where reminders of the past are neither

rigorously preserved, nor insensitively trampled upon. The ideas and ideals that have helped Stoke Newington thrive throughout its long history mean that, although it may no longer be Poe's 'misty village of old England', buzzing with anti-establishment voices, it's still much more than just another suburb.

Eating & drinking

Blue Legume
101 Stoke Newington Church Street, N16 0UD (7923 1303). **Open** 9.30am-6.30pm daily. Good breakfasts and decent, mainly veggie food.

Booth's Pizzeria
71-73 Stoke Newington Church Street, N16 0AS (7275 9809). **Open** *Bar* 11am-11pm Mon-Sat; noon-10.30pm Sun. *Restaurant* 5-11pm Mon-Fri; noon-11pm Sat, Sun. Pizzas, salads, pasta and baked potatoes in the restaurant.

Clissold House Café
Clissold Park, N16 (no phone). **Open** 10am-4pm daily.

Daniel Defoe
102 Stoke Newington Church Street, N16 0LA (7254 2906). **Open** 1-11pm Mon-Fri; noon-11pm Sat; noon-10.30pm Sun. **Food served** 1-10pm Mon-Fri; noon-6pm Sat, Sun.

Rasa

Fox Reformed

*176 Stoke Newington Church Street, N16 0JL
(7254 5975/www.fox-reformed.co.uk).* **Open**
5-11pm Mon-Fri; noon-11pm Sat, Sun. **Food
served** 6.30-10.30pm Mon-Fri; noon-3pm, 6.30-
10.30pm Sat, Sun. Bar snacks all day Sat, Sun.
Brasserie food with excellent own-baked bread.

Rasa

*55 Stoke Newington Church Street, N16 0AR
(7249 0344/www.rasarestaurants.com).* **Lunch
served** noon-3pm Sat, Sun. **Dinner served** 6-
10.45pm Mon-Thur, Sun; 6-11.30pm Fri, Sat.
Home of exemplary Keralan (South Indian)
vegetarian cooking.

Rasa Travangore

*56 Stoke Newington Church Street, N16 0AR
(7249 1340/www.rasarestaurants.com).* **Meals
served** 6-10.45pm Mon-Thur; 6-11.30pm Fri, Sat;
12.30-3pm, 6-10.45pm Sun. Sister restaurant to
Rasa serving meat, seafood and vegetarian meals.

Shopping

Bridgewood & Neitzert

*146 Stoke Newington Church Street, N16 0JU
(7249 9398/www.londonviolins.com).* **Open**
10am-6pm Mon-Fri; 10am-4pm Sat.

Church Street Bookshop

*142 Stoke Newington Church Street, N16 0JU
(7241 5411).* **Open** 11.30am-6pm daily.

Fresh & Wild

*32-40 Stoke Newington Church Street, N16 0LU
(7254 2332/www.freshandwild.com).*
Open 8am-9pm Mon-Sat; 9am-8.30pm Sun.

Ocean Books

*127 Stoke Newington Church Street, N16 0UH
(7502 6319).* **Open** 11.30am-6pm Mon-Fri;
11am-6pm Sat; noon-6pm Sun.

Two Wheels Good

*165 Stoke Newington Church Street, N16 0UH
(7249 2200/www.twowheelsgood.co.uk).*
Open 8.30am-6pm Mon-Sat.

Others

Abney Park Cemetery

*South Lodge, Stoke Newington High Street,
N16 0LN (7275 7557/www.abney-park.org.uk).*
Open 8am-dusk daily.

St Mary's

*Stoke Newington Church Street, N16
(7254 6072/www.stmaryn16.org.uk).*
Open *by appointment.* **Services** 9.30am,
6.30pm Sun.

Stoke Newington Library

*Stoke Newington Church Street, N16 0JS
(8356 5231/www.hackney.gov.uk).* **Open**
9am-8pm Mon, Tue, Thur; 9am-6pm Wed;
10am-8pm Fri; 9am-5pm Sat.

Passport to Pimlico

Nick Wyke

A journey through Thomas Cubitt's Stuccoville, past the homes
of politicians, actors and artists.

Start: Pimlico tube
Finish: Pimlico tube
Time: 1-2 hours
Distance: 2.5 miles/4km
Getting there: Victoria line
to Pimlico
Getting back: Victoria line
from Pimlico
Note: pleasantly quiet on
a Sunday.

'Pimlico is anonymous. You need no
passport to get into it. Pimlico is No Man's
Land. And from No Man's Land you can
move in any direction.' Glenys Roberts,
Metropolitan Myths

Out on a limb to the south of the
multicoloured tangle of central
London's inner circle, Pimlico is one
of Zone One's outsiders. Like its position
on the Underground map, this low-key
tranche of central London, shaped like
a melted Dairylea and wedged into a
bend on the Thames, is a detached,
almost forgotten place with a faint
aura of suburbia.

Mention Pimlico to most people
and those without blank faces recall
the art gallery or the film. Both are
local anomalies. Tate Britain is
situated at Millbank, way beyond
the boundaries of Pimlico proper;
and *Passport to Pimlico*, the Ealing
comedy that promised 'French goings-
on in the heart of London', was filmed
across the Thames in Lambeth. Perhaps,
then, it was alliteration that led the
film's producers to choose Pimlico.

The other typical response is 'Pimlico,
oh, very posh' – usually made by people
who have never actually been to SW1's
most modest quarter, but who knew some
snooty aunt or college chums who used
to live here. I confess that I thought it
was grand before moving here. After all,
one shares a postcode, or at least part of
it, with royalty. But the truth is, though
actually north of the river, it is where
'sarf London' meets south Belgravia.
And the one sort of neutralises the other.

So many of London's neighbourhoods
are loaded with lifestyles. Think Notting
Hill, Hampstead, Chelsea, Fulham, Soho,
Islington, Clerkenwell, Stoke Newington
or Clapham and, rightly or wrongly,
each area readily delivers a type of
person to match. Pimlico eludes such
pigeon-hole identity. It is a place to live
or work, not one to be seen in, for no
one will notice you here.

The benefits of its proximity to the
centre are twofold: it is close enough
to indulge in the glamour of the capital
and then, once bloated or dazzled, easily
to escape its insufferable crowds and
pretence. A walk home won't tax the
legs and a taxi won't break the bank.
And, as a bonus, at the relative still
of midnight – not that you're likely to
be doing this walk then – you can hear
the chimes of Big Ben roll out through
the amber dark.

The walk begins at Pimlico Underground
station, which would never have been built
but for the Tate Gallery (now Tate Britain).
For a taste of the Tate, without putting in
the legwork with the shoals of weekend
art lovers, take the left-hand subway at
the station past the splendid spread of

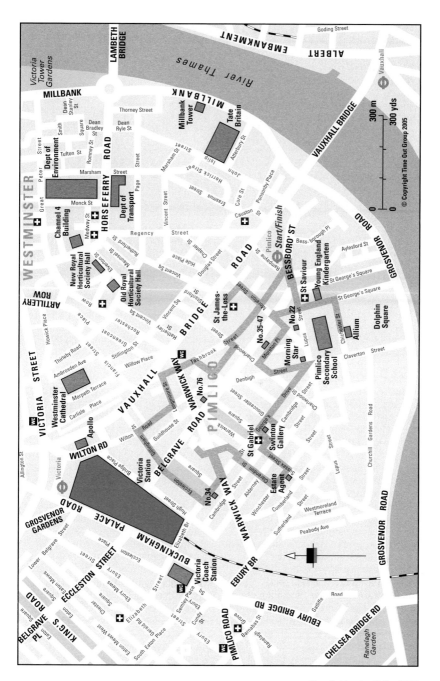

Tate Britain

the flower-seller. The subway is lined with eight tawdry murals of masterpieces (some of which are now held downriver at Tate Modern). The copies are blistered and graffitied and seeing them before a trip to the gallery is the artistic equivalent of going to KFC before a meal at Allium, a fine restaurant just around the corner. The Degas and the Singer Sargent are truly dismal, the latter reminiscent of the manically depressed artist from the *Fast Show* who unfailingly sees black and doom. My favourite is the Henry Wallis with its scratched pale face of a prostrate poet and its background window opening on to another London.

Now climb the stairs for some authentic art: a sculpture by Sir Eduardo Paolozzi. Born of Italian parents in Edinburgh in 1924, Paolozzi was part of the Independent Group credited with introducing Pop Art to these shores in the 1950s. He had a one-man show at the Tate in 1971 and was responsible for the colourful mosaics at Tottenham Court Road Underground station. His tube air vent has to be London's coolest – a sort of silver Futurist ensemble with divers and butterflies among the tools and cogs branded on its side. Beside it

rises the robust National Statistics office shaped like a Panettone box with smooth eyebrow-style windows. It seems a shame that on weekdays its modern-meets-medieval frame is full of stattos.

Cross the road and head towards the steeple. Pause to look at the award-winning photo of a teenage Diana Spencer in the corner of the Top Curry Centre window – intriguingly the place bills itself as an 'English and Continental Restaurant'. Caught mid-stride outside the restaurant, both feet off the ground, she looks startled as she hurries through the rain to her job at the nearby kinder-garten. One of the press's first, it's a truly beautiful photograph of her but, arguably, in retrospect there's a fateful eeriness about the wary look she's giving the camera. Though I swear she had a Mini Metro, the curry house owner tells me how back in the good old days she used to emerge from the tube station daily in her pinafore. Maybe William and Harry's brides-to-be are out there somewhere riding the District and Circle lines.

On the corner of St George's Square and Belgrave Road, which if you walk its length will take you to Hyde Park, is

a blue plaque commemorating Major Walter Clopton Wingfield. Who? The 'father of lawn tennis', of course, and a reminder of what silly names people used to have. Wingfield, an army officer from Wales, called his version of tennis Sphairistike ('playing ball'), after an ancient Greek game. But in his quest for a livelier sport than croquet for the leisured classes he combined ideas from court tennis, squash racquets and badminton, too. Like the catchy name, his patented lawn tennis kits (1874) and hourglass-shaped court were soon to be replaced, but the foundations of the modern game had been laid.

Cross to the green cabmen's shelter, and, if it's open, pop your head around the door to look at the bite-size canteen and the day's menu on the blackboard – it reads like a wartime cookbook. I couldn't persuade Pam, one of the shelter's cooks, who has a Gypsy Rose glint about her, to make me a cuppa, but you might fare better. The shelter is one of a dozen or so still standing in the capital. It was built for £200 as part of a philanthropic drive by newspaper proprietor Sir George Armstrong to offer

taxi drivers an alternative pitstop to the pub. In 1894 the Cabmen's Shelter Fund reported that in the more exclusive areas cabbies were 'extremely particular' about their food; it claimed, 'they are quite as ready to complain as members of West End clubs if things are not right'. The building in the triangular garden behind the shelter is a less aesthetically pleasing air duct from the Underground.

The church opposite, St Saviour's, would not look out of place in a country parish. Built in 1864, it has a 170-foot tower and houses a copy of Michelangelo's *Madonna and Child* (the original is to be found in Onze Lieve Vrouwkerk in Bruges, Belgium).

The actor Laurence Olivier, whose family moved to Lupus Street in 1912, was a choir boy and altar server here. If you look at the plaque on the World War I memorial outside the church, you can see his family name.

Tucked behind the church in St George's Square gardens – where the beautiful people of Pimlico sunbathe and an exotic coloured parrot holds court at the church end of the gardens – is Lady Di's last employer. It was here that a shy but radiant kindergarten teacher newly in love with a prince posed for that now notorious picture holding a child in each arm and, oops, wearing a see-through dress. 'Halfway through the picture session the sun came out for the first time and I saw for the first time what beautiful legs she had,' said a paparazzo. 'Diana, when I told her later that afternoon what the picture showed, blushed and said, "I'd hate to be known as the girl who didn't wear a petticoat".'

Partially blotted out by the bunker-like Pimlico School is the equally bulky Dolphin Square. This vast 1930s community of apartments – once the largest of its kind in Europe – is a residential powerhouse second to none. Home to dozens of MPs and Lords, as well as various generals, admirals and an African tribal chief, it is where Oswald Mosley and the Admiralty spy John Vassal were arrested, where Christine Keeler and Mandy Rice-Davis entertained clients, and where Conservative MP Iain Mills met his lonely end from alcohol poisoning in 1997. To this day, some of the privileged residents are reported to pay peppercorn rents that are less than those paid by struggling families on the nearby Churchill Gardens Estate.

Have a peek at the carefully tended gardens complete with palm trees; you can even rent a room here if you have your own dangerous liaisons in mind.

They used to say that you either married or lived in Dolphin Square. William Hague, however, is an exception to the rule. He lives here in his former bachelor pad with his wife Ffion. But Tory style gurus tried to persuade Hague to move out. They felt that the secretive, institutional character of Dolphin Square, which had already begun to fray at the edges 15 years ago when the Princess Royal took rooms here briefly, was at odds with a young wannabe Prime Minister. After all, Pimlico never really boosted anyone's profile.

On a brighter note, few Londoners know that the often empty art deco pool that once featured in a 1970s Levi's ad is open to the paying public and that in 1944, in his Dolphin Square flat, Hubert Gregg wrote 'Maybe It's Because I'm a Londoner' in just 20 minutes. So, plenty to mull over during lunch at Anton Edelmann's excellent restaurant, Allium, on the ground floor, then.

Back at the school wall, look up at the top window of 22 Lupus Street, the one with the blue door. It was behind the curtains of this nursery window that the young Olivier first took to the stage. Stood upon a wooden chest surrounded by footlights – candles set in tobacco tins by his father – he proclaimed the Hubert and Arthur scene

from *King John*. 'I never played to an empty house as long as my mother was at home,' Sir Larry later wrote.

Walk past the grassy triangle behind the cabbies' shelter and admire the stylish homogeneity of the 'Italianate-Westminster' porticoes along Belgrave Road, conceived as middle-class family homes, although many are hotels today. You are now entering what estate agents puff as the Moreton triangle, one of Pimlico's prettier village hubs, dotted with art galleries and beauty salons. From the junction with Moreton Place you can see three of Battersea Power Station's mighty chimneys rising up in the distance.

In elegant Moreton Place you pass the birthplace of Billy Hughes, who sounds like a nifty-'50s footballer but was in fact Australian Prime Minister from 1915 to 1923, and not the only PM to have lived in Pimlico. By all accounts, Hughes, a partially deaf misogynist with gnomish features, didn't beat about the bush. As the representative of Australia at the Versailles Peace Conference he struck a hard line for his country, much to the annoyance of Woodrow Wilson, who called him a 'pestiferous varmint'. When Wilson tried to gain the upper hand by mentioning to Hughes that he represented a nation of 100 million people, Hughes, who was aware that the Australians killed in action exceeded the US fatalities, retorted that he spoke for 60,000 dead.

A little further along, note the faded craftsmen's signs on the wall that leads down to Moreton Terrace Mews. The water-level marker is there to warn against such calamities as when the Thames burst its bank in 1928 and flooded the area. The Tate lost valuable works, and firemen had to rescue people trapped by the railings on the windows of their basement flats. One dreads to think what would happen to Pimlico School if the same accident were to occur today, especially on a weekday.

Sir Eduardo Paolozzi's tube air vent.

In this tranquil, glaring-white slice of Pimlico are the first of many varied examples of in-fills – post-war homes plugging gaps in the original terraces caused by the bombs of the Blitz. No.22 is a very functional in-fill, as is the block with spidery iron balconies where Nos.35-47 once stood, though amazingly the tall iron lamp standard outside survived the blast. Pimlico's proximity to Victoria station and Parliament, and its munition factories on the riverbank, ensured that it was the hardest hit area in Westminster. Bombing raids included parachute mines and V1 flying bombs. Rows of the barely century-old terraced houses were razed to the ground causing scores of casualties, and, in one particularly bad night in 1941, in nearby Lillington Street (now Lillington Gardens), 41 fatalities.

Where Denbigh Street traverses Charlwood Street is a good place to get a 360-degree take on Stuccoville, a nickname picked up by Pimlico for its plaster-covered genteel houses. At the top of Denbigh Street you can meet the man – or at least a noble representation of him – responsible for transforming Pimlico from marshy gardens riddled with highwaymen to its current grid layout.

Long overdue, a statue of Thomas Cubitt was unveiled in 1995 by the Duke of Westminster, a fairly down-to-earth chap considering that he owns 300 of central London's most desirable acres, and a descendant of the 1st Marquess of Westminster on whose land Cubitt laid out his *grand projet*.

A model of Victorian industry, Cubitt was a prolific master builder – a world apart from the sort of tea-swilling cowboy of today who may or may not show up next Tuesday. After building houses in Bloomsbury and much of Belgravia in the 1820s and '30s, he turned his hand to South Belgravia, as Pimlico was then known. A conscientious employer – the first thing he always built was a pub – he became a personal friend of Queen Victoria and Prince Albert, who referred to him as 'Our Mr Cubitt'. In fact, his family's royal connections continue to this day – one of his great-great-granddaughters is Camilla Parker-Bowles.

Continue down the generous swathe that is St George's Drive, pausing at the junction with Charlwood Street for a distant view north, through the treetops, of the towers of Westminster Abbey. The steeple at the end of St George's Drive belongs to St Michael's of Chester Square.

A rare Victorian deviation from Cubitt's wedding-cake style within the Pimlico grid is 33 Warwick Square. Built in 1860 for £6,610 as a live-in studio for the popular portrait painter James Swinton, it was distinguished by its tartan brick scheme, vast window and unconventional form that upset the neighbours. Swinton,

Dolphin Square swimming pool.

a regular on the Grand Tour circuit, wanted a stately villa reminiscent of Renaissance Rome. After he died, in 1888, the house was inhabited by a series of tenants including Isadora Duncan, a serious American art collector, and Sir Charles Ross, who had patented the Eton rifle while still at school and unwittingly inspired Paul Weller to write a hit with the Jam. Today, after incarnations as the Grosvenor School of Art, a dancing school, the local ARP centre in World War II and a temporary role as a Roman Catholic Church, it is the Swinton Gallery, home to a first-class collection of modern art that includes works by Jack B Yeats and John Hoyland. It is stumbling upon such secrets that makes cities worth living in, although, regrettably, the gallery is not open to the public.

Warwick Square is the second of Pimlico's three green spaces, though unlike St George's it is not open to the public. The so-called Fifth Man of the Cambridge ring of spies, John Cairncross, lived at No.76, at the far end of the square, when he first entered the Foreign Office in 1936. Although MI5 were soon on his trail, when handwritten notes found at Guy Burgess's flat went by chance to an officer whose secretary recognised the writing (she had previously been Cairncross's secretary), it took the authorities another 40 years of sleuthing to get around to finally arresting Cairncross.

We pick up the art theme behind St Gabriel's Church at 114 Cambridge Street, home to Pimlico's most avant-garde resident, Aubrey Beardsley. In the naughty '90s, the enigmatic young insurance clerk, who had a face like a gargoyle and was parodied in *Punch* as Danbrey Beardless and Daubaway Weirdsley, was the art world's equivalent of his literary acquaintance Oscar Wilde. The explicit eroticism of his sinuous black-and-white graphic art sent shock-waves through the drawing rooms of the Victorian establishment of the sort Tracey Emin can only dream of achieving.

I wonder if any of his imaginative 'art-porn' was inspired by the looming presence of the church and its stained-glass windows directly opposite his front door. According to a recent biographer, Beardsley was still a virgin when he died from tuberculosis at 25, although fragments of gossip suggest that he may have slept with his sister, and a notorious London prostitute, Penny Plain. A drab block of flats on Tachbrook Street is named after him.

Hang a left into Sussex Street and walk down to the first estate agents on the right, where you can play Spot the House Valued At Under £1m. Through the window you can see an original poster for *Passport to Pimlico* (1949). The film is a cheeky look at what happens to a London community when they discover it belongs to Burgundy; apparently, it was based on a genuine news item. When Keith Vaz, the Minister for Europe embroiled in the passports-for-cash scandal, recently put in an offer of £900,000 for a Pimlico pad, thanks to the famous film the tabloids had a ready-made headline. Typically the papers didn't miss the chance to point out that at that price he could buy an entire street in his Leicester East constituency.

On the side of a house where Cambridge Street meets Clarendon Street is the less familiar site of a green plaque (English Heritage blue plaques are only awarded to people who have been dead for at least 20 years). It is in memory of Laura Ashley (who died in 1985), another hugely influential designer, albeit far more wholesome and less subversive than Beardsley. It was in a flat here, at the kitchen table, that the pregnant Ashley created her famous Victorian-inspired rustic prints on a handful of tea towels. 'I like things that last for ever, like the straw hat you're fond of and wear all your life,' she once said. Her legacy lasts in the high street of many a well-heeled town and in living rooms and wardrobes around the globe.

Across the road at 76-8 Cambridge Street is a good case of an in-fill adding character to a street. Follow the line of the view south-west along Clarendon Street, which ends with the Italianate tower of the Western Pumping Station built in 1875 by London sewer maestro Sir Joseph Bazalgette, proof that even functional buildings were constructed with care and ambition in the 19th century.

Continue along Clarendon Street, crossing over Warwick Way, the old willow-lined track that linked Westminster to Chelsea, and purely for diversionary purposes loop down and around the cobbled Eccleston Square Mews, where the cottages are considerably lower than the backs of the towering houses of Eccleston Square. It is one of Pimlico's quirkier traits that the basements of the houses are below ground at the front, but at ground level at the back, the result of Cubitt raising his streets by a whole storey before building.

Turn right back on to Warwick Way and right again into Eccleston Square. Although the square supposedly remains the most sought after of Pimlico's big three set-pieces, it is only just acceptable by Belgravia's aristocratic standards. In Anthony Trollope's novel *The Small House at Allington*, a friend warns the house-hunting Lady Alexandrina, who has a sketchy knowledge of Pimlico: "'For heaven's sake, my dear, on no account let him take you anywhere south of Eccleston Square!'"

At No.34, opposite the gate to the private garden, you can admire one of Sir Winston Churchill's (Pimlico's other PM) early London homes, acquired when he was a leading radical in Herbert Asquith's Liberal government. On spring days in these gardens his young wife, Clementine, would lie on her back and compose love letters to her busy husband. She addressed them to her Pug or Pig and signed them Cat, Kat or even Clem Pussy Bird, keeping him up to date on the domestic front and expressing her views on social and political affairs. Churchill replied with a candour and tenderness rarely seen in his public guise. The house actually became the headquarters of the Labour Party during the General Strike of 1926, by which time Churchill had long departed.

Walk down the west side of the square, where two of the houses were used as hospitals for the wounded of World War I stretchered straight off the trains from nearby Victoria station, known as the 'Western Front's back door'. The square continued to play a role in the war effort of World War II when railings were removed for melting down to make armaments and the gardens cultivated as allotments. Cross over Belgrave Road – which forms a less attractive fourth side to the square – into Gillingham Street and pause at the junction with Wilton Road. In contrast to the shiny new office blocks and housing projects that are changing the landscape almost daily, there is a shabbiness to the ageing buildings in Wilton Road.

Sadly one of the country's first cinemas, the Biograph, built in Wilton Road in 1905, was a casualty of such changes in 1983. But, if you look towards the station, you can just see, still standing in all its art deco glory, another of London's most magnificent former cinemas, the New Victoria. Now the Apollo Theatre, it seats a whopping 2,750, and has hosted the likes of Andrew Lloyd-Webber's rollerskating extravaganza *Starlight Express*. The area seems doomed when it comes to the big screen. Its previous closest cinema, the Minema near Hyde Park Corner, closed down in 2000.

The handful of titillating flyers stuck in the phone boxes around here are a wink to Pimlico's insalubrious past. The air of illicit liaisons is compounded by an excess of dated B&Bs. One hundred years ago, when Joseph Conrad lived across the street, prostitution thrived in Pimlico; a local rate payer counted 180 brothels. In between long sea voyages Conrad lived a solitary five years here plagued by bouts of melancholia, and one wonders if he ever succumbed to the local vice. Eventually he managed to complete his first published novel here, *Almayer's Folly*, for which he received £20 and rave reviews.

Walk up to Pimlico's slightly tatty commercial core via Longmoore Street. This end of Tachbrook Street has some tasty shops: try a hot slice of freshly baked pizza at Gastronomia Italia; Rippon Cheese Stores always has a blackboard special at giveaway prices; get hip at dressing-up-for-grown-ups boutique, Cornucopia. Among the locals' lifeline, Tesco Metro, and the junk-stuffed charity shops, there are several good delis. The area has no outstanding pub that I can

Moreton Place

recommend, but the Page (formerly the Slug & Lettuce and before that the Royal Gardener) is one of a handful of original Cubitt-built corner pubs. Its fine large windows make it a suitable place to watch the bustle of the 100-year-old street market, and it serves fairly decent Thai food, too.

Head up Tachbrook Street digressing briefly to wander around Churton Street and Charlwood Place. This is a pleasant place to stop for a bite. Chimes (traditional English food and cider) and the Mekong (good-value Vietnamese) are both agreeable, but Grumbles is the neighbourhood favourite. Back in the swinging '60s, when such restaurants were a novelty, the Beatles and Julie Christie were among the celebs who shelled out nine shillings for a fillet steak. Grumbles is also the home of a fashion first, according to its original owner, Jeremy Friend: 'For some reason Grumbles used to attract beautiful waitresses, often out-of-work actresses, and one of them would come to work in a skirt so short you could see the colour of her knickers. And so the miniskirt was invented here before

it even appeared on the King's Road.' It is not without irony, then, that the appeal today of this homely wood-clad bistro serving hearty Franco-fare is that it remains unfazed by central city fads.

Tachbrook Street traces the course of a tributary from the old Tyburn river, its splendid curve a welcome relief from the straight lines of the terraced grid. The two sides of the street create an interesting juxtaposition with the Victorian town-houses facing the sturdy layers of the continental-style Lillington Gardens Estate. The estate, complete with all its own amenities and green courtyards, was cleverly built around the red-brick Victorian church of St James the Less by Darbourne and Darke in the early 1970s. The church is the only one in the vicinity to be included in Simon Jenkins's recent *England's Thousand Best Churches*. When built in 1858-61 by GE Street, it was described by the *Illustrated London News* as a 'lily among weeds'. Its Italian Gothic exterior merits particular attention.

At the top of Tachbrook Street we are back at the tube station. From here you can follow the signs to Tate Britain or check out of Pimlico.

Victorian builder **Thomas Cubitt**.

Eating & drinking

Allium
Dolphin Square, Chichester Street, SW1V 3LX (7798 6888/www.allium.co.uk). **Open/food served** noon-3pm, 6-10.30pm Tue-Fri; 6-10.30pm Sat; noon-2.30pm Sun. Perfectly balanced, light, modern European fare. Well worth the passage.

Chimes
26 Churton Street, SW1V 2LP (7821 7456). **Open/food served** noon-2.30pm, 5.30-10.15pm Mon-Sat; noon-3pm, 5.30-10pm Sun. Traditional English food and drink, including cider.

Gastronomia Italia
8 Upper Tachbrook Street, SW1V 1SH (7834 2767). **Open** 9am-6pm Mon-Fri; 9am-5pm Sat. Selling all types of Italian delicacies.

Grumbles
35 Churton Street, SW1V 2LT (7834 0149/ www.grumblesrestaurant.co.uk). **Open** noon-2.30pm; 6-11pm Mon-Sat; noon-3pm, 6-10.30pm Sun. Popular and reasonably priced eaterie.

Mekong
46 Churton Street, SW1V 2LP (7834 6896). **Open** noon-2.30pm, 6-11.30pm daily. Vietnamese.

The Page
11 Warwick Way, SW1V 4LT (7834 3313). **Open** 11am-11pm Mon-Sat; noon-10.30pm Sun. **Food served** noon-3pm, 6-10pm Mon-Fri; noon-4pm, 6-10pm Sat; noon-4pm, 6-9.30pm Sun.

Pizza Express
46 Moreton Street, SW1V 2PB (7592 9488). **Open** 11.30am-11.30pm daily.

Rippon Cheese Stores
26 Upper Tachbrook Street, SW1V 1SW (7931 0668). **Open** 8am-5.15pm Mon-Sat.

Top Curry Centre
3 Lupus Street, SW1V 3AS (7821 7572). **Open** noon-3pm, 6pm-midnight daily. Indian food, of course, but also a selection of continental dishes.

Churches

St Gabriel's
Warwick Square, SW1V 2AD (Vicar 7834 7520). **Open** *Services* 8.15am, 10.30am Sun.

St James the Less
Thorndike Street, off Moreton Street, SW1V 2PT (7630 6282). **Open** noon-3pm Mon-Fri. *Services* 9.30am, 11am, 6pm Sun.

St Michael's
Chester Square, SW1W 9EF (7730 8889/www.st michaelschurch.org.uk). **Open** *Recital* 1.05pm Mon. *Services* 1.05pm Wed; 9.30am, 11am, 6.30pm Sun.

St Saviour
St George's Square, SW1 (7834 9520/7592 9733). **Open** phone for details.

Westminster Abbey
20 Dean's Yard, SW1P 3PA (7222 5152/www. westminster-abbey.org). **Open** *Chapterhouse, Nave & Royal Chapels* 9.30am-3.45pm Mon, Tue, Thur, Fri; 9.30am-7pm Wed; 9.30am-1.45pm Sat. *Museum* 10.30am-4pm Mon-Sat. *Cloisters* 8am-6pm Mon-Sat. *College Garden* Apr-Sept 10am-6pm Tue-Thur; Oct-Mar 10am-4pm Tue-Thur. **Admission** £8; £6 concessions; free under-11s; £18 family.

Entertainment

Apollo Victoria Theatre
Wilton Road, SW1V 1LG (0870 161 1977). **Open** *Box office* 9am-8pm Mon-Sat.

Dolphin Square Swimming Pool
Dolphin Square Hotel, Chichester Street, SW1V 3LX (7834 3800/www.dolphinsquarehotel.co.uk). **Open** noon-10pm Mon-Fri; 8am-8pm Sat, Sun. **Admission** £6; free under-5s.

Film & literature

Almayer's Folly Joseph Conrad (1895)
Metropolitan Myths Glenys Roberts (1982)
Passport to Pimlico (Henry Cornelius, 1949, GB)
The Small House at Allington Anthony Trollope (1864)

Museums & galleries

Tate Britain
Millbank, SW1P 4RG (7887 8000/www.tate. org.uk). **Open** 10am-5.50pm daily. *Tours* 11am, noon, 2pm, 3pm Mon-Fri; noon, 3pm Sat, Sun. **Admission** free. *Special exhibitions* prices vary.

Shopping

Cornucopia
12 Upper Tachbrook Street, SW1V 1SH (7828 5752). **Open** 11am-6pm Mon-Sat.

Others

National Statistics
Office for National Statistics, 1 Drummond Gate, SW1V 2QQ (7533 6262/www.statistics.gov.uk). **Open** by appointment only; phone 7533 6266.

Behind the façade

Sue Arnold

From quaint Chelsea terraces to the palatial pensioners' residence, what was once the village of palaces is still as fashionable as ever.

Start: Sloane Square
Finish: Peace Pagoda, Battersea Park
Time: 3-4 hours
Distance: 3.5 miles/5.5km
Getting there: District or Circle lines to Sloane Square
Getting back: walk or 137 bus (see map for bus stop) to Sloane Square
Note: the Chelsea Physic Garden is only open on Wednesday and Sunday afternoons.

Tell people you live in Chelsea and the reaction is always the same. Interest, speculation, envy flicker across their faces – I must be rich or famous or artistic, possibly all three. I'm not, I'm just lucky. I moved in at the end of the '60s, the swinging '60s that put modern Chelsea on the map and sent prices soaring. It was here that designer Mary Quant sold the world's first mini-skirt from her tiny shop in what was then little more than the local high street, lined with the usual neighbourhood shops, bakers, greengrocers, fishmongers, cafés, pubs, and art shops, of course, because Chelsea has always been associated with artists. It was called the King's Road. It still is – but the chances of your finding anything as humdrum or as useful as a butcher in its entire length from Eaton Square to Parson's Green are almost as thin as the supermodels, pop stars and wannabes who now stride its pavements in search of the latest fashion gear.

There is, thank heavens, more to Chelsea than designer labels. You have only to stray a few yards either side of the King's Road to appreciate why, over the last 500 years, writers, artists and eccentrics have come to live here. Chelsea is charming. In its time, it has charmed residents like Sir Thomas More, Jonathan Swift, Charles Dickens and Oscar Wilde, and the walk you are about to take, along some of its oldest streets, past some of its most famous buildings, will charm you, too.

Sloane Square, where we start, has never been quite the same since style guru Peter York published his *The Official Sloane Ranger Handbook* (co-written with Ann Barr) in 1982. Before that, it was merely a geographic location, the station you went to if you wanted to shop on the King's Road or go to the Royal Court theatre. Now it's the ersatz breeding ground of a social species called the 'Sloane Ranger' or simply 'Sloane' – best described as the female equivalent of the Hooray Henry. A Sloane is a well-heeled, upper-class, not especially intelligent, young woman, wearing expensive casual clothes and a Hermès head scarf knotted under her chin. She drives a shiny new Renault Clio that Daddy bought her and talks as if she is permanently accommodating half a dozen plums in her mouth. A Sloane doesn't say: 'Oh, hello', she says: 'Air, hair-lair'. If you cross the road from the station into Sloane Square, you will see hordes of them disappearing into Peter Jones, the department store opposite. PJ is the Sloanes' corner shop. It's the only place for miles to buy ordinary useful

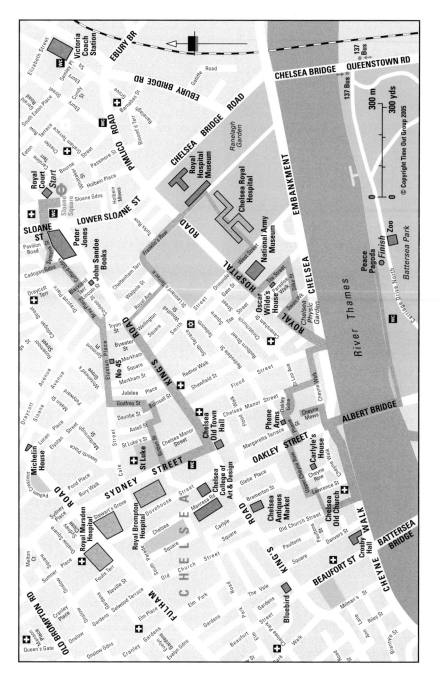

Royal Court

things, like a bath mat or a reel of cotton. It started as a small draper's shop in 1877 and flourished for 28 years until 1905 when Mr Jones sold it as a going concern to a Mr John Lewis who had a shop in Oxford Street. The story goes, Mr Lewis jumped on a 137 bus one lunchtime, got off in Sloane Square and paid for his new shop in cash from his pocket.

I wish at this early stage I could impress you with my knowledge of avant-garde theatre by telling you how many mould-breaking plays by Osborne, Pinter and Edward Bond I've seen at the Royal Court. Alas, I cannot. It's the old story; you never visit things on your doorstep and I wasn't around when *Look Back in Anger* had its première at the Court in 1956.

For politeness's sake, before leaving Sloane Square, you should spare a thought for Dr Hans Sloane (1660-1753), the genius who 'put the Sloane into Sloane Square, the milk into chocolate and the original museum collection into the British Museum'. It was when he was physician to the governor of Jamaica that he discovered the advantage of mixing milk with cocoa powder, a secret recipe that was later bought by the Cadbury brothers.

In normal circumstances I'd leave Sloane Square and head like a homing-pigeon straight down the King's Road to Flood Street, where we live, but this isn't a shopping spree. Instead, I'm cutting down Symons Street on the right of Peter Jones towards Cadogan Gardens. I know this area well. My landlord, the Earl of Cadogan, who owns most of Chelsea, has his estate office here and it's here that we send our quarterly rent. This might be the moment to tell you a bit about Chelsea rents. When we moved into our present flat 30 or so years ago, the rent was £9 a week. The current rate for a four-bedroom flat in Chelsea is upwards of £1,000 a week. We pay considerably more than £9 now but the only reason we can still afford to live here is that we're on the fourth floor without a lift and no one but us, it seems, wants to climb 82 stairs to their front door. As for buying somewhere in Chelsea, £1 million will just about get you a small terrace house with a tiny back yard. No wonder all the artists have moved to Hackney. Chelsea is where film directors, Swiss bankers and American lawyers live, and a few anomalies like me.

The other reason I know Cadogan Gardens so well is that years ago I used to come to soirées given by a glamorous Greek literary socialite called Arianna Stassinopoulos, famous, among other things, for her slick biographies of Maria Callas and Picasso. She was incredibly stylish. Her flat consisted of a salon the size of a ballroom and three broom cupboards in which she respectively cooked, slept and bathed. She used to hire 150 gilt chairs to seat her guests and after a little chamber music and a lecture about Indian mysticism, we ate stuffed vine leaves made by her mother, who shared one of the broom cupboards. Last time I heard of Arianna, she had married an American millionaire called Michael Huffington, who failed to become governor of California, and was giving her publishers a headache because Arianna Stassinopoulos Huffington is a long name to put on a paperback.

Talking of books, once you've crossed Cadogan Gardens into Culford Gardens, you'll reach Blacklands Terrace, home of John Sandoe Books, the best bookshop in London. Why? Because the people who work there actually read books themselves and can tell you just what biography to buy for a cat-loving maiden aunt, or whether last year's Booker Prize winner is worth taking on holiday. How can anyone, you wonder, possibly find what they're looking for among the piles of books on the stairs, window sills, landings and overflowing on to the floor of this Dickensian shop? They can and they do. John Sandoe's is the sort of bookshop where regular customers have a monthly standing order for six books – two biographies, two novels, a history

and a travel book – the choice to be left to John Sandoe's discretion. It is the antidote to buying books on the Internet.

If you keep glancing to the left as you walk down Bray Place, you'll catch glimpses of the King's Road and the multi-billion-pound shopping development built where the old Duke of York's barracks used to be. Chelsea needs new shops as much as a fish needs a bicycle, but business is business, I suppose. Crossing Sloane Avenue, you will see the Queen's Head (well-known gay pub) straight ahead, and then on into Elystan Place. Pause at No.45 – you can't miss it. The entire façade of this tiny house, which looks like a Gothic grotto, is famous for its eccentric owner, Lady Rusheen Wynne-Jones. Her neighbours complained that the ornamental birds, butterflies, garden gnomes and waterfall cascading down the front of the house were a traffic hazard. Motorists would jam on their brakes and stare in fascination at this replica of a Brothers Grimm fairy tale fantasy. Lady Rusheen refused to move a single toadstool.

The miniature triangular garden on your right called Chelsea Green is all that's left of Chelsea Common, where Cromwell's Puritan soldiers once exercised. At first glance, the small shops clustered round the green remind you of what Chelsea must have been like when it was a sleepy village ('as dead as Chelsea' was a common 18th-century saying) until you look more closely at their rarefied wares. French country antiques, hand-painted children's toys and Finns, an upmarket deli, where I once queued for a sandwich behind Martina Navratilova.

Left, off Chelsea Green, is my favourite London street, Godfrey Street. My children know that if they ever won the lottery, this is where Mummy would like to live. It's less a street than a lane, lined with tiny artisans' cottages painted ice-cream colours, each with a Porsche or a

Ferrari parked outside. Modern artisans work for Goldman Sachs. Godfrey Street leads into Burnsall Street, where again you can see the King's Road, but we're turning right into Astell Street, at the end of which looms the redbrick Victorian bulk of Sutton Dwellings, low-rent housing that's increasingly being taken over by canny middle-class folk who know how to fill in forms. Left into Britten Street past the Builders' Arms, which used to be a spit and sawdust pub with jazz on Sundays. Only the name remains. The Builders' Arms (shouldn't that be the Property Developers' Arms now?) has been tarted up and offers rush matting, scrubbed pine tables, modern European cuisine – and no jazz. Oh well, at least it's a pub (the Markham Arms on the King's Road, favourite haunt of gangsters like the Kray Twins in the 1950s, is now, depressingly, the Abbey National Bank).

This section of Britten Street I know considerably better than the back of my hand because at some stage every one of my six children trundled a bicycle along it to reach the park beside St Luke's church. This is where they all learnt to ride bicycles while I sat on a bench under a tree in the middle shouting advice like 'Brake now!' or 'Get back on and stop wailing. It's only a scratch.' On the right of the park gate is what we always call the smallest house in London. I'm not sure if it is, but it certainly looks that way. The only life-size feature is the front door. Turning left out of Britten Street into Sydney Street and seeing Chelsea Town Hall ahead brings back two vivid memories. The first was when, wheeling my pram, I went to vote in the local election in 1979 and my neighbour, Mrs Margaret Thatcher, who was also casting her vote, patted my new baby on the head. 'Another little Conservative, I hope,' she cooed. Fat chance, I thought, but became a little worried later when I heard a man describe how when he was a baby, Lloyd George had patted him on the head, after which he became

prematurely bald. My second vivid memory was of getting married second time round in Chelsea Register Office next door. The registrar said, 'You should have seen it last week. David Frost got married and there were people trying to climb in through the windows to get pictures.'

At some stage we're going to have to cross the King's Road, and since we're on it, we may as well stroll a little way past its glossy shopfronts and do a little celebrity spotting as we turn left out of Sydney Street and back towards Sloane Square. The novelist William Boyd must live locally. In his novel, *Armadillo*, he wrote about the Picasso café on your right, though it appears thinly disguised as the Matisse. The Picasso is one of the King's Road's oldest establishments, a coffee house that offers real coffee, not that insipid American junk that's all the rage these days. You might see Bob Geldof, another local resident, having his breakfast here. Next door is the Harley-Davidson shop, where every Saturday afternoon phalanxes of bikers in leathers, gauntlets and helmets converge. Once disrobed, some of them disconcertingly turn out to be elderly, balding, slightly wispy men, who flop on to chairs and ask the Picasso waitresses for a pot of Earl Grey tea and some buttered toast, please.

It's funny to think that if Hans Sloane hadn't organised a petition at the beginning of the 18th century, George I had it in mind to stop the public from using the King's Road and to keep it as his private royal carriageway through Chelsea. When I first arrived as a student here, every teenager's dream was to be taken for a drink at the Chelsea Potter pub, which you are about to pass on your right. It was always full of weird bohemian characters, but now, alas, after countless facelifts, no self-respecting revolutionary would be seen dead here, unless he were keen on Australian tourists and Chelsea football fans.

We're heading for Royal Avenue a few streets down on the right, so-called

Colourful **Godfrey Street**, the author's desired London address.

because Charles II intended it to be his route from the Royal Hospital to Kensington Palace. The money ran out and this short stretch between the King's Road and St Leonard's Terrace is all that's left, although the houses themselves are early 19th-century. If you saw the film The Servant, starring Dirk Bogarde and James Fox, you will remember Royal Avenue. Joseph Losey, who directed it, lived at No.29. Whatever you do, don't cross the sandy area in the centre, except when they have art exhibitions in the summer. It's a dogs' lavatory, and, though the dogs are expensive pedigrees in tartan coats and diamond collars, you walk over it at your peril. At the end of Royal Avenue on the left corner with St Leonard's Terrace, you will see the adjoining houses bought by architect Richard Rogers in the

1980s. Predictably he gutted the period interiors and installed stark steel gantries, just visible through the shuttered windows. This is my favourite view of the Royal Hospital and where you are most likely to see the famous Chelsea Pensioners in their red coats, strolling. I used to know one called Sergeant Tommy Cosgrove who told me endless stories of his World War II exploits. Once he moved to Chelsea he never had to buy himself another drink because the tourists, fascinated by his Gilbert and Sullivan get-up, always treated him. If you've got the time, go into the Royal Hospital, which, to me, is as much a Wren masterpiece as St Paul's Cathedral. The time to avoid this area is during the Chelsea Flower Show in May when you are likely to be stampeded

Here there be fairies – **Elystan Place**.

in Franklin's Row by droves of little old ladies in flowered dresses and hats racing to see the new rose called after the Countess of Wexford.

If you do visit the Royal Hospital, you will rejoin the Royal Hospital Road just before the National Army Museum, which contains among other things the Duke of Wellington's shaving mirror and Florence Nightingale's lamp. Turn left into Tite Street past Oscar Wilde's house at No.34 (formerly No.16) and the studios further down on the left where Augustus John used to paint and then right into Dilke Street, where at the end you'll see the brick walls of the Chelsea Physic Garden.

The cunning thing, friends tell me, is to become a member (it's not very expensive), so that you can come at any time and sit peacefully on a bench in the sun, surrounded by all those wonderful old-fashioned smells of rosemary, rue and meadowsweet. The Physic Garden was established in 1673 by the Worshipful Company of Apothecaries, a magical-sounding word that puts me in mind of love potions and cures for warts involving wormwood and slugs.

Cheyne Walk, which we're just turning into, conjures up shadowy pictures of Lady Dedlock in *Bleak House*. I like to think of Charles Dickens looking speculatively at these tall, imposing façades and choosing one as the residence of Sir Leicester and his mysterious wife. When my eldest daughter was small she was invited to tea at 10 Cheyne Walk and when she came home we questioned her narrowly about the house. 'Was it very grand?' we asked. 'Yes,' said Chloe. 'They had three sofas in their kitchen.' Another novelist, George Eliot, lived at No.4 – this is blue plaque country. And now we're turning right into Cheyne Gardens and Chelsea Manor Street, where somewhere on the left Henry VIII's manor house once stood. Usually when I walk this way, I'm heading for supper with my old friend John Ritchie, who lives in Oakley Gardens, but since his new status as Madonna's father-in-law, he's very often at glamorous parties or giving press interviews. The other reason to walk through Oakley Gardens is to have a reviving drink at the Phene Arms, my favourite Chelsea pub. I'm biased. I used to have secret romantic assignations with the man who eventually became my second husband here. They do very good burgers at the Phene and there's a large garden for summertime drinking.

Coming out of the Phene, turn right and continue into Upper Cheyne Row. This for me is pram-pushing territory. When they were small, my children went to Chelsea Open Air Nursery in Glebe Place, which we will pass, and when I collected them from school we would wind our way through the various Cheynes – Row, Gardens, Walk – on our way to Battersea Park for picnics. Where Upper Cheyne Row hits Laurence Street, the site of the old Chelsea potteries and the house where Tobias Smollett used to live, turn left and then right into Justice Walk, a highly desirable street because it is so quiet and carless. I used to now people who lived in Justice Walk. They had a child called Percy, which anywhere else would have been ridiculous but somehow suited this old-fashioned corner. Now we're in Old Church Street and heading towards the river. It was somewhere near here that Sir Thomas More (1478-1535), Chelsea's most famous resident, had his 'goodlie manor'. There's a black and gold statue of the martyr on the embankment next to Chelsea Old Church, favourite venue for fashionable weddings.

This is a good place to take stock. To your right you will see the lavish Chelsea Harbour development and the road leading to the Harbour Club where Princess Diana played tennis and worked out in the gym. To your left you'll see London's most beautiful bridge, Albert Bridge, especially at night when it's all lit up like fairyland. Take a moment just before you cross Albert Bridge and look on the corner of Cheyne Walk and Oakley Street at a small plaque at the entrance to the mews that says: 'King Henry VIII's

manor house stood here until 1753 when it was demolished after the death of its last occupant, Sir Hans Sloane.' The garden of the old manor house still lies beyond the end wall. Some of the mulberry trees are said to have been planted by Elizabeth I. This is where we leave Chelsea, and head across the river to Battersea Park, the nearest thing my town-bred children ever had to a garden.

Battersea Park is where, the story goes, the Romans crossed the Thames to attack the ancient Catuvellauni tribe. It is certainly where the infamous Colonel Blood took a pot shot at Charles II in 1671 when the king was bathing. Until Queen Victoria's day, the park was pretty much derelict marsh, criss-crossed by ditches

Chelsea Physic Garden

Battersea Park

that emptied into the river. But the queen commissioned Sir James Pennethorne to landscape it and now its 200 square acres are a haven for flat-dwelling, gardenless Londoners to play football, have picnics, listen to jazz and visit the children's zoo.

Sadly the famous Easter Bonnet Parade is no more, but every Thursday a fanatical bagpiper can be heard practising at dawn. My favourite monument in Battersea Park is the Japanese Buddhist Peace Pagoda, built in 1985, from whose steps you can look back across the river at Chelsea. Once I ran into a very small, very serene Buddhist monk tapping a miniature drum, who told me he was a Chelsea supporter; he particularly liked Jimmy Floyd Hasselbaink. You're the wrong side of the river, I said. He just smiled blissfully and went on tapping his drum.

Eating & drinking

Builders' Arms
13 Britten Street, SW3 3TY (7349 9040). **Open** 11am-11pm Mon-Sat; noon-10.30pm Sun. **Food served** noon-2.30pm, 7-9.30pm Mon-Sat; noon-4pm, 7-9pm Sun.

Chelsea Potter
119 King's Road, SW3 4PL (7352 9479). **Open** 11am-11pm Mon-Sat; noon-10.30pm Sun. **Food served** 11am-9pm daily.

Finn's
4 Elystan Street, Chelsea Green, SW3 3NS (7225 0733). **Open** 8.30am-6.30pm Mon-Fri; 8.30am-1pm Sat.

Phene Arms
9 Phene Street, SW3 5NY (7352 3294).
Open 11am-11pm Mon-Sat; noon-10.30pm Sun.
Food served noon-3pm, 6-10.30pm Mon-Sat;
noon-4pm, 6-10.30pm Sun.

Picasso
127 King's Road, SW3 4PW (7352 4921).
Open 7am-11pm Mon-Sat; 8am-11pm Sun.
One of the few remaining haunts of the
swinging '60s.

Queen's Head
25 Tryon Street, SW3 3LG (7589 0262). **Open**
11am-11pm Mon-Sat; noon-10.30pm Sun. **Food
served** noon-7pm Mon-Sat; 12.30-5pm Sun.

Buildings

Chelsea Open Air Nursery School
51 Glebe Place, SW3 5JE (7352 8374).

Chelsea Register Office
*Chelsea Old Town Hall, King's Road, SW3 5EE
(7361 4100/www.rbkc.gov.uk).*

Chelsea Town Hall
King's Road, SW3 5EE (bookings 7361 2220).

Harbour Club
*Watermeadow Lane, SW6 2RR (7371 7700/
www.harbourclub.co.uk).* **Open** 6.30am-11pm
Mon-Fri; 8am-11pm Sat, Sun.

Royal Hospital Chelsea
*Royal Hospital Road, SW3 4SR (7730 0161/
www.chelsea-pensioners.org.uk).* **Open**
Apr-Sept 10am-noon, 2-4pm daily. *Oct-Mar*
10am-noon, 2-4pm daily. **Admission** free.

Churches

Chelsea Old Church
*64 Cheyne Walk, SW3 (7795 1019/www.chelsea
oldchurch.org.uk).* **Open** 1.30-4.30pm Tue-Fri;
8am-1pm, 2-6pm Sun.

St Luke's Church
Sydney Street, SW3 6NH (7351 7365).
Open *Office* 9.30am-12.30pm Mon-Fri.
Services 10.30am, 6.30pm Sun.

Film & literature

Armadillo William Boyd (1998)
Bleak House Charles Dickens (1853)
Look Back in Anger John Osborne (1957)
**Maria Callas: The Woman Behind the
Legend** Arianna Stassinopoulos (1981)

The Official Sloane Ranger Handbook
Peter York & Ann Barr (1983)
Picasso: Creator and Destroyer Arianna
Stassinopoulos Huffington (1988)
The Servant (Joseph Losey, 1963, GB)

Museums

National Army Museum
*Royal Hospital Road, SW3 4HT (7730 0717/
www.national-army-museum.ac.uk).* **Open**
10am-5.30pm daily. **Admission** free.

Parks & gardens

Battersea Park
SW11 (8871 7530/www.wandsworth.gov.uk).
Open 7.30am-dusk daily. *Events Office* 8871
7534. **Open** 9am-5pm Mon-Fri.

Chelsea Flower Show
*Royal Hospital, SW3 (check website for details:
www.rhs.org.uk).* Usually held in May.

Chelsea Physic Garden
*66 Royal Hospital Road (entrance in Swan Walk),
SW3 4HS (7352 5646/www.chelseaphysicgarden.
co.uk).* **Open** *Apr-Nov* noon-5pm Wed; 2-6pm
Sun. **Admission** £5; £3 5-16s, concessions; free
under-5s.

Shopping

John Sandoe (Books) Ltd
*10 Blacklands Terrace, SW3 2SR (7589 9473/
www.johnsandoe.com).* **Open** 9.30am-5.30pm
Mon, Tue; 9.30am-7.30pm Wed; 9.30am-5.30pm
Thur-Sat.

Peter Jones
*Sloane Square, SW1W 8EL (7730 3434/
www.peterjones.co.uk).* **Open** 9.30am-7pm
Mon-Sat; 11am-5pm Sun.

Warr's Harley-Davidson
*Clothing & accessories: 125 King's Road,
SW3 4PW (7376 7084/www.warrs.com).*
Open 10am-6pm Mon-Sat; noon-5pm Sun.
*Bikes & accessories: 611 King's Road, SW6 2EL
(7736 2934/www.warrs.com).* **Open** 8am-6pm
Mon-Wed, Fri, Sat; 8am-8pm Thur.

Theatre

Royal Court
*Sloane Square, SW1W 8AS (7565 5000/
www.royalcourttheatre.com).* **Open** *Box office*
10am-6pm Mon-Sat. **Tickets** 10p-£24.50; all
tickets £5 Mon.

Cult following

Nicholas Royle

Watch your back as you trace film locations and explore hidden alleys through
Bloomsbury and Covent Garden to the South Bank.

Start: Cinema Bookshop,
Great Russell Street
Finish: National Film Theatre
Time: 1-2 hours
Distance: 1.5 miles/2.5km
Getting there: Central or Northern
lines to Tottenham Court Road
Getting back: short walk to
Waterloo station (Bakerloo,
Northern, Waterloo & City
lines or overground rail)
Note: if you set off at 5pm, you'll
find the Cinema Bookshop still
open, Detroit also open, and
you'll be in time to wrap up the
walk with an evening screening
at the NFT. There is some overlap
with Steven Appleby's walk.

No one has yet written a book about
the film director Christopher Nolan.
He's only made a handful of films, after
all. But when they do – as they inevitably
will – the place to get hold of a copy will
be the Cinema Bookshop. Fred Zentner
has been selling film books and other
movie paraphernalia out of these Great
Russell Street premises for more than
30 years. Just don't arrange to meet a
whole bunch of people here, because
Fred's stock has swelled to such an
extent that there's barely room to
execute a 360-degree panning shot
inside the tiny shop.

What form will it take, the first book
about Nolan? Will it be a somewhat dry,
film studies analysis of his output from
an academic point of view, or a fannish
retrospective of his career, published 25

years hence? Perhaps Chris Rodley will
do *Christopher Nolan on Christopher
Nolan* for Faber & Faber? Or the British
Film Institute may let Chris Darke
loose on Nolan's *noir* debut, *Following*
(1998), for its Modern Classics series.
Nolan's second film, *Memento*, made
in Hollywood and consequently
more widely distributed than his
British debut, is better known, as is
his third movie, a 2002 remake of Erik
Skjoldbjaerg's *Insomnia* (1997). However,
it is *Batman Begins*, starring Christian
Bale and Michael Caine, that should
thrust Nolan firmly into the premier
league of Hollywood film directors.

While there may not yet be any
studies of Nolan's work, the director
has contributed to a volume published
in April 2001 by Faber. *Memento &
Following* contains Nolan's screenplays
to those two films, plus interviews and
commentary by himself and brother
Jonathan Nolan, who wrote the original
story on which *Memento* was based.

Whether you browse or buy, the Cinema
Bookshop is our starting point on this
walk, which is a film walk generally, and
a Christopher Nolan walk in particular.
It may seem wilfully obscure, creating
a walk based on locations from a film
that was released for three weeks in
one London cinema (the Curzon Soho
on Shaftesbury Avenue), but *Following*
was an exciting and highly ambitious
first feature, shot cheaply over an
extended period in black and white,
while cast and crew juggled day jobs
and shooting schedules. The film has
since been shown on FilmFour and is
now available on DVD. As a result of

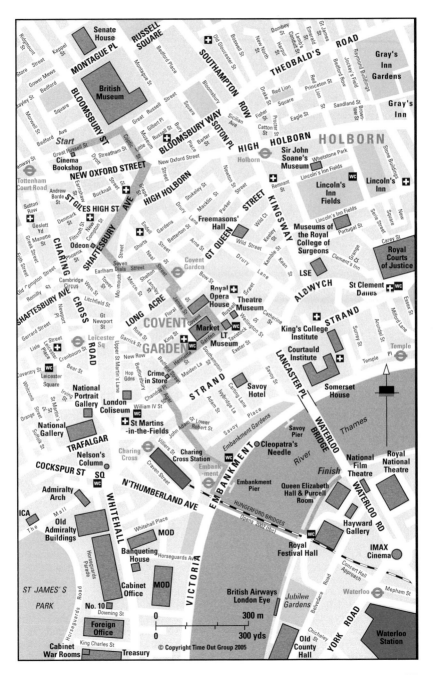

Slightly cheaper than the opera: street performers wow the tourists in **Covent Garden**.

its critical success, Nolan embarked upon a new day job as a fully fledged Hollywood film director.

Across the street from the bookshop are two very different refreshment points, should you need one this early in the walk. Eve's Sandwich Bar is run by friendly Italians, and, next door, Malabar Junction, an excellent Indian restaurant specialises in Keralan cuisine. Whether we stop for a bite or not, we go east along Great Russell Street, crossing at the junction with Bloomsbury Street. Once across, note a couple of bookshops on the right-hand side of Great Russell Street: Gosh!, which sells comics and so-called graphic novels, is a bookshop for people who don't like reading; and as for Arthur Probsthain Oriental and African Bookseller – well, take a wild guess.

When you reach the corner of Coptic Street, stop. Withdraw from the flow of pedestrian traffic at this point. Shrink into the background. We're looking for someone interesting to come along Great Russell Street, from either direction, and turn into Coptic Street. You may spot a *flâneur* and find your curiosity piqued. Or you may see someone who strides so purposefully you just have to know where they are going. Alternatively your eyes may alight on someone so pulchritudinous, so irresistible, you cannot, by definition, resist. The thing is, we're going to follow them. How far is up to you. But at least to the bottom of Coptic Street.

The premise of *Following*, as the title suggests, is that a young man, Bill (Jeremy Theobald, who also co-produced along with Nolan and Emma Thomas), follows people at random around central London. As he explains to the detective who later questions him, he's on the lookout for ideas, material for a novel he intends to write.

Many of the film's locations are unrecognisable, or they are interiors to which we would not have access in any case, but a few street shots do stand out. In one we see Bill walking along Great Russell Street close to the British Museum (the big building across the street with the crowds of tourists outside).

As soon as you've picked your subject, set off down Coptic Street. At this point, you could choose to abandon the rest of this text and strike out on your own, following whomever you have chosen to follow. In which case, farewell. But, you never know, the person you're following may also be doing this walk, and they could be following someone ahead of them who is also engaged on the same project, while in front of them… well, you get the idea. Or, you may, like me, find it virtually impossible to walk past a Pizza Express without going in, sitting down and ordering an American Hot with extra capers and extra peas. There's a very good branch halfway down Coptic Street on the left. It was one of the first to open, in 1965.

If you're still with us, plot a diagonal course across New Oxford Street and head into Shaftesbury Avenue. Keep going down, negotiating one or two sets of lights or dodging the traffic, according to your preference. Further down on the right-hand side, is the Odeon Covent Garden cinema. Formerly the excellent two-screen ABC Shaftesbury Avenue, it was converted into a four-screen multiplex by Odeon, whose 'Fanatical About Film' slogan surely invites some scrutiny. How exactly does carving up a two-screen cinema to make four screens demonstrate fanaticism about film? Would not an organisation that is truly fanatical about film present examples of the medium in the best possible surroundings?

Making the screens smaller in order to maximise revenue is hardly the act of such an outfit. Remember the Odeon Marble Arch, which once boasted the largest cinema screen in Europe? Now a multiplex. The Odeon Camden Town squeezes five screens into premises that held two when the Camden Parkway was still in business.

The ABC Shaftesbury Avenue was one of only two cinemas in the West End able to show David Cronenberg's adaptation of JG Ballard's novel *Crash* when it was released here in November 1997. The other was the ABC Tottenham Court Road. These two cinemas are outside the City of Westminster, which had banned the film. The ABC Tottenham Court Road is now, inevitably, an Odeon. Film-goers may remember the striking 50-foot neon display on an adjacent wall, drawing attention to the cinema; the Odeon chain has replaced this with its own drab sign complete with ubiquitous slogan.

Anyway, the ex-ABC Shaftesbury Avenue has since become the Odeon Covent Garden, which is stretching a geographical point. We're about to head into Covent Garden and no one who has glanced at a map recently would claim the district begins this side of Shaftesbury Avenue.

Head into Mercer Street. In a moment or two you'll hit Seven Dials, where you need to keep your wits about you, as traffic approaches from, yes, seven different directions. We want the third exit on the left, Earlham Street. Halfway down Earlham Street on the left is Detroit, a bar/restaurant that is the most significant location in *Following*.

Detroit doesn't open until 5pm, so if you've timed your walk right you'll be able to drop in for a beer – or more. And if you haven't, you can at least admire the distinctive doors from the outside. In the film, Bill ill-advisedly tries to chat up a character listed among the cast as simply the Blonde (Lucy Russell). He suggests he buy her a drink and she points out that her boyfriend, who is sitting not far away, might not like that. Her boyfriend, whom Bill christens the Bald Guy, is played by Dick Bradsell.

Dick Bradsell – in real life – is a maverick bartender and cocktail guru, mover and shaker on the London bar scene. No sooner has his involvement in the latest exciting new bar project been announced than he's off exploring the next underground car park ripe for transformation into a trendy nightspot (Hakkasan on Hanway Place is one of his more recent ventures). When *Following* was being made, Bradsell was managing Detroit. In a tense scene in the film, Bill empties the bar's safe in the middle of the night, frantically taping wads of banknotes to parts of his body, while in the gloom, unknown to Bill, a figure lurks.

We can lurk in the gloom as long as we like, grabbing a bite to eat or just enjoying a couple of drinks. Once you're back on Earlham Street, keep going in the same direction. Across the street is Belgo Centraal, the enormously successful restaurant chain specialising in Belgian food and beer (though these days the latter is a better bet than the former). When you hit Neal Street, head for Long Acre, but beware that you will be running the gauntlet of Hare Krishna lookalikes trying to 'give' you vegetarian cookbooks in return for your soul and a cash donation, and resting actors in charity bibs angling for covenants, direct debits and God knows what else to Help the Aged, Childline and Amnesty International. Long Acre offers you a zebra crossing and – relatively – safe passage over to James Street (Covent Garden tube station is on your right).

James Street, leading down to Covent Garden Piazza, is one of the most over-crowded streets in the whole of London, which is presumably why Nolan chose to get a shot of Bill standing there, the only still point in a blurry swell, just before James Street nudges into the Piazza.

The Piazza itself – and the whole central Covent Garden complex of expensive shops, overpriced bars and street entertainers – can be negotiated in any number of ways. Normally, in fact, the best advice would be to avoid it altogether. But you might be visiting the area for the first time and Covent Garden deserves to be seen at least once.

So, go left. Ahead of you, behind the colonnade of chainstores, is the rebuilt Royal Opera House. Turn right when the space opens out allowing you to do so. Ahead of you now, and slightly to the left, is the superb, if awkwardly named, London's Transport Museum; its shop, which you may enter for free, is worth a visit, even if you have only the slightest interest in how we move around this huge city, when not on foot.

With the museum behind you, walk towards Henrietta Street. On your right is Covent Garden Market, on your left Jubilee Market. As recently as the early 1970s, when Hitchcock directed *Frenzy*, all this was fruit and veg. Robert Rusk (Barry Foster) runs a stall in the market and has a flat on the first floor of a house at 3 Henrietta Street. On the ground floor of the same building are (or were, in the film) the offices of Duckworth publishers. Strangely, when Rusk is leading Babs Milligan (Anna Massey) up to his flat, he tells her it's located on the second floor, yet we can clearly see that it's actually on the first floor. This apparent concession to the American market slightly undermines the continuing and otherwise masterful long shot in which the camera recoils from the flat, once they have entered, retreats down the stairs and backs out of the house. As it emerges into the street, the volume on the soundtrack is turned up and only then do we realise how deathly quiet it had been inside the house.

While not one of Hitchcock's best films, *Frenzy* does have some bravura set pieces and excellent location work, mainly around Covent Garden, and the opening titles sequence, where the camera

A bit of breathing
space: **Tate Modern**.

The new **Hungerford Bridge**, whose predecessor Nolan used as a film location.

swoops upriver past the still smoking Bankside Power Station (now Tate Modern) and under Tower Bridge, is breathtaking. As the search for the 'necktie murderer' proceeds, the noose tightens around the wrong man's neck in typical Hitchcockian fashion. It's possible that the choice of Covent Garden for important locations in both *Frenzy* and *Following* is not coincidence. The way Nolan grabs hold of narrative and applies his own killer twist is not unlike the manner of his predecessor. 'Hitchcockian' is, of course, one of *the* most overused adjectives in film writing, but in the case of Nolan its use seems not entirely gratuitous.

It may be pushing it to compare Bill's interest in the Blonde to the obsession of Scottie (James Stewart) with Madeleine (Kim Novak) in *Vertigo*, but Bill's voyeuristic tendencies, especially when encouraged by his house-burglar associate Cobb (Alex Haw), recall those of Jeff (Stewart) in *Rear Window*.

Anyway, if we don't move on, the present occupants of Robert Rusk's flat will be calling the police. Keep walking to the bottom of Henrietta Street. If you turn left into Bedford Street and cross over, you'll find yourself outside Crime in Store, a lovely bookshop dedicated to crime, mystery and suspense. Should you need a rest, there's a comfy settee within and lots of good books, including a fine selection of second-hand titles and first editions.

We're rolling on down to the river now. One thing you could do on the way is pick up a copy of *Time Out* magazine and see what's showing tonight at the National Film Theatre, since that's ultimately where we're headed.

Turn right into Chandos Place, then left into Agar Street. As you saunter down Agar Street you get your first view of the London Eye, sandwiched between office buildings on the south side of the Strand. Cross the Strand and nip down the steps into George Court. Just after John Adam Street, when the street we're on becomes York Buildings, there's an atmospheric little street on your left (Lower Robert Street) that ducks sharply down under a building and curves away to the right.

You don't have to go down here. I wouldn't actually lead you down here, because it looks like *one of those places*. It may not be, but it has that definite look about it. One of those places where things happen. Don't you think? Doesn't it look spooky? A little dangerous? Obviously, I did have a look and you might be tempted to do so as well, but I can't be held responsible, OK? It's not my fault.

If you *do* venture down there – and we're off the map, remember – you'll find it eventually leads to the back entrance of some unknown building. It doesn't feel seedy as such, just, in a strange way, *blank*. It's a blank zone, an interzone. Alienating. Unsettling. This is a place where you *don't* want to hear footsteps behind you.

If you've got any sense, you're still hanging around on York Buildings. Keep going to the bottom and go right through the wrought-iron gate. Down the steps, with Victoria Embankment Gardens on your left behind the railings. We're almost there. Through the gardens – pause if you wish – up to you – right out on to Embankment and climb the steps to Hungerford Bridge (just past the entrance to the tube). The swish pedestrian half of this new Hungerford Bridge is all soaring white poles and cables. The river views to the left are much more inspiring than the disorienting latticework view of the trains and, beyond them, the London Eye on your right. You may be wondering: why on earth has this fool dragged us up here? Because Nolan dragged Bill up on to the old bridge, and got a neat little shot of him.

Off to the right, in the shadow of the London Eye, although some 20-odd years before its erection, is where Hitchcock makes his trademark cameo appearance in *Frenzy*, among a crowd of rubberneckers trying to get a glimpse of the necktie murderer's latest victim washed up on the foreshore outside County Hall.

Following, not stalking.

But we're heading left off the bridge, not right, along in front of the Royal Festival Hall. Refurbishment work will make one of the best views in London – from the terrace on the fifth floor – unavailable until early 2007, but in the meantime there's a newly landscaped riverfront, with shops and cafés, on which to take a breather. When you're ready, carry on past the Queen Elizabeth Hall and bear left, past the weird chrome sculpture and towards the steps that go down to the National Film Theatre (NFT), huddled underneath Waterloo Bridge. Outside you'll find a number of second-hand bookstalls, very good for paperbacks.

If it's after 7pm, the bookdealers may well have packed up and gone home, in which case get yourself a drink in the Film Café or see if you can get a ticket for whatever's showing in NFT1. There's probably something like a one-in-a-million chance that one of its three screens is showing *Following*, *Memento*, *Insomnia* or even *Batman Begins*. Or they might be running a Hitchcock season and be showing *Frenzy*. The NFT, although it has recently trimmed its programme, cutting out weekday matinées, remains the best place to see a film in London. Membership is cheap and simple to take out, or you can purchase instant day membership in the price of your ticket.

Do make the most of this opportunity to have a look around, for the NFT is considering a move to newly regenerated King's Cross if plans to create a new national film centre on the South Bank come to nought. It's impossible to count the number of key figures who have been interviewed on stage here as part of the *Guardian* Lectures and, later, *Guardian* Interviews series. The NFT is one of the prime venues for the internationally renowned London Film Festival. Even the location of the cinema itself is remarkable, wedged as it is beneath Waterloo Bridge. See it while you still can.

You may end this walk knowing little more about *Following* or Christopher Nolan as you did at the start. That's deliberate, really. The last thing I want to do is spoil your enjoyment of his work by telling you what happens in it. I can confidently leave that to film reviewers. The plot of *Following* twists and turns as this walk has done, involving numerous jump cuts and double-crosses. That's a journey you have to make yourself – either in the cinema or on video at home. But, really, as ever, inside your own head.

Eating & drinking

Belgo Centraal
50 Earlham Street, WC2H 9LJ (7813 2233/ www.belgo-restaurants.com). **Meals served** noon-11pm Mon-Thur; noon-11.30pm Fri, Sat; noon-10.30pm Sun. Subterranean beer hall, where pseudo-monks serve Low Country fare.

Detroit
35 Earlham Street, WC2H 9LD (7240 2662/ www.detroit-bar.com). **Open** 5pm-midnight Mon-Sat. **Food served** 5-10.30pm Mon-Sat. Cocktails and absinthe accompany smart snacks.

Eve's Sandwich Bar
108 Great Russell Street, WC1B 3NA (7636 9949). **Open** 6am-6pm Mon-Fri; 7am-4pm Sat.

Film Café
National Film Theatre, South Bank, SE1 8XT (7928 3535). **Open** *Bar* 11am-11pm Mon-Sat; noon-10.30pm Sun. **Food served** *Café* 9am-9pm Mon-Sat; 10am-9pm Sun. Salads, sandwiches etc.

Hakkasan
8 Hanway Place, W1T 1HD (7907 1888). *Bar* **Open** noon-12.30am Mon-Wed; noon-1.30am Thur-Sat; noon-midnight Sun. *Restaurant* **Lunch served** noon-2.45pm Mon-Fri; noon-4pm Sat, Sun. **Dinner served** 6-11pm Mon-Wed, Sun; 6pm-midnight Thur-Sat. Excellent Chinese cuisine in extravagant surroundings.

Malabar Junction
107 Great Russell Street, WC1B 3NA (7580 5230). **Open** noon-3pm, 6-11.30pm Mon-Sat; noon-3pm, 6-11pm Sun. Good Keralan fare.

Pizza Express
30 Coptic Street, WC1A 1NS (7636 3232/www. pizzaexpress.co.uk). **Open** 11.30am-midnight daily. Very good branch of the excellent chain.

The **British Airways London Eye** – an ideal location for any remake of *Vertigo*.

Cinemas

Curzon Soho
*93-107 Shaftesbury Avenue, W1D 5DY
(7734 2255).*

National Film Theatre
*Belvedere Road, South Bank, SE1 8XT (Box
Office 7928 3232/www.bfi.org.uk/showing/nft).*

Odeon Shaftesbury Avenue
*135 Shaftesbury Avenue, WC2H 2AH (0871
224 4007/www.odeon.co.uk).*

Shopping

Arthur Probsthain Oriental &
African Bookseller
*41 Great Russell Street, WC1B 3PE
(7636 1096/www.oriental-african-books.com).*
Open 9.30am-5.30pm Mon-Fri; 11am-4pm Sat.

Cinema Bookshop
*13-14 Great Russell Street, WC1B 3NH (7637
0206).* **Open** 10.30am-5.30pm Mon-Sat.

Gosh!
*39 Great Russell Street, WC1B 3NZ (7636 1011/
www.goshlondon.com).* **Open** 10am-6pm Mon-
Wed, Sat, Sun; 10am-7pm Thur, Fri.

Others

British Airways London Eye
*Riverside Building, next to County Hall,
Westminster Bridge Road, SE1 7PB (0870 500
0600/www.ba-londoneye.com).* **Open** *Oct-Apr*
9.30am-8pm daily. *May, June, Sept* 9.30am-9pm
daily. *July, Aug* 9.30am-10pm daily. **Admission**
£12.50; £10 concessions (not applicable weekends
or Jul, Aug); £6.50 5-15s; free under-5s.

British Museum
*Great Russell Street, WC1B 3DG (7636 1555/
www.thebritishmuseum.ac.uk).* **Open** *Galleries*
10am-5.30pm Mon-Wed, Sat, Sun; 10am-8.30pm
Thur, Fri. *Great Court* 9am-6pm Mon-Wed, Sun;
9am-11pm Thur-Sat. *Highlights tours* (90mins)
10.30am, 1pm, 3pm daily. **Admission** free;
donations appreciated. *Temporary exhibitions*
prices vary. *Highlights tours* £8; £5 concessions.

London's Transport Museum
*Covent Garden Piazza, WC2E 7BB (7379 6344/
www.ltmuseum.co.uk).* **Closed** summer 2005-Nov
2006 for major refurbishment.

South Bank Centre
*South Bank, Belvedere Road, SE1 8XX (08703
800400/www.rfh.org.uk).* **Open** *Box office* 9.30am-
8pm daily. Royal Festival Hall closed till Jan 2007;
Queen Elizabeth Hall, Purcell Room and Hayward
Gallery remain open.

Film & literature

Crash JG Ballard (1973)
Crash (David Cronenberg, 1996, Can)
Following (Christopher Nolan, 1998, GB)
Frenzy (Alfred Hitchcock, 1972, GB)
Insomnia (Erik Skjoldbjaerg, 1997, Nor)
Memento (Christopher Nolan, 2000, US)
Memento & Following Christopher Nolan (2001)
Rear Window (Alfred Hitchcock, 1954, US)
Vertigo (Alfred Hitchcock, 1958, US)

I will not tell you where the mushrooms are

Nigel Williams

Fear not the Wimbledon poisoner: poets, pubs, parks and Putney flavour this south-west London stroll.

Start: Putney Bridge tube
Finish: Putney Bridge tube
Time: 4-5 hours
Distance: 9 miles/14.5km
Getting there: District line to Putney Bridge
Getting back: District line from Putney Bridge
Note: plenty of parkland and plenty of mud. The walk is probably too long for children, and is best avoided during the Oxford & Cambridge Boat Race (March/April).

This walk has been carefully designed not to conflict with Liz Jensen's excellent trip through Wimbledon in *Time Out London Walks 1*, and though it includes a trip through Richmond Park, I have kept away from the area covered in Thomas Pakenham's man-sized excursion through Richmond Park in the same volume. You could, however, do it in conjunction with either journey. One of the things I like about it is that it is quintessentially suburban, offering you glimpses of tamed countryside and, at the same time, private glimpses of the lives of those who inhabit the suburbs.

Start at Putney Bridge station. Come out and go through the bus station and on to Putney Bridge. Cross over to the right-hand (west) side of the bridge, designed by Sir Joseph Bazalgette in 1884 to replace a previous wooden structure. He also designed Hammersmith Bridge, in case any of you are interested. Looking upriver is, to my mind, one of the finest river views in London. The Thames curves back north towards Hammersmith, offering you a skyscape almost empty of buildings, smudged with seagulls and suggestive, to me anyway, of a kind of inland estuary. (A stroll along the towpath towards Hammersmith will bring you to the Wetland Centre, which, if you like bird spotting, may well be the place for you. Over on the south bank, on your way to it, is Barn Elms Park, originally the home of Sir Francis Walsingham's mansion.) For those not minded to take the detour, on your left as you reach the south side of the bridge is the church of St Mary, where the victorious Cromwellian army held the Putney Debates – that crucial discussion about democracy, miraculously preserved in shorthand, which itself was only invented a few years before the debates took place. Don't bother to go into the church. It is heavily restored – rebuilt by Lapidge in 1837 – and, inside, about as 17th century as a Richard Clayderman album.

Putney Bridge, incidentally, is where both the Head of the River and the Oxford and Cambridge Boat Race start, so, unless you like drunken hoorays, avoid it at the end of March.

Just beyond are two pubs that face the river – Bar M (the words 'Star and Garter', denoting its previous incarnation, are still visible) and the Duke's Head. Gavin Ewart, one of the finest post-war

I will not tell you where the mushrooms are

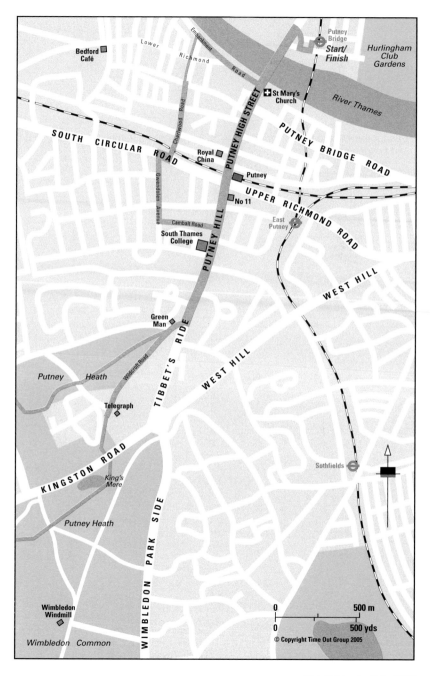

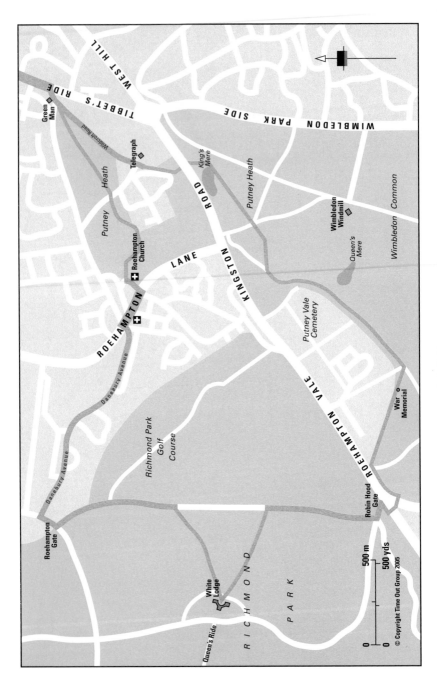

British poets, but now sadly dead, used to live in the redbrick mansion flats opposite. I had several drinks with him in the second pub, which is the one I would recommend (Young's beer, great view of the river). All those wishing to toast his memory should, at this point, recite his great quatrain:

> *Miss Twye was soaping her breasts in the bath*
> *When she heard behind her a meaning laugh*
> *She turned, and to her amazement discovered*
> *A wicked man in the bathroom cupboard.*

I am grateful to Roger Tagholm's excellent *Walking Literary London* for reminding me that JR Ackerley, author of the classic memoir *My Father and Myself*, used to walk his pet Alsatian, Tulip, on the embankment just outside the pub.

Follow up Putney High Street, a notorious traffic bottleneck, nearly always choked with cars and now lined with restaurants and bars. The La Mancha tapas bar and, in Chelverton Road just before the lights at the junction with the Upper Richmond Road, the Royal China are to my mind the ones to try. The Royal China serves the best dim sum outside Soho. Now cross over to the left-hand side of the road and start up Putney Hill. On your left, at No.11, just after the dry cleaners, is a big, grey-brick house in which Theodore Watts Dunton sheltered that late Victorian *enfant terrible* Algernon Charles Swinburne. Swinburne, a milk and water *poète maudit*, who nonetheless wrote some lovely lyrics in early life, never wrote anything decent when he was in the suburbs. He was, reportedly, only allowed a bottle of Guinness a day by the highly moral Watts Dunton.

Carry on up Putney Hill until you reach the second set of traffic lights. Take the road off to the right, past the Green Man, a Young's pub that Swinburne visited. Putney Heath was a great favourite with highwaymen, and the most famous of them, an individual named Tibbett, who was hanged for his crimes, has given his name to the stretch of dual carriageway that leads south on to the A3. He is commemorated in a weird piece of sculpture that was once a great favourite with a disturbed toddler of my acquaintance. Tibbett's Ride, however, is not your route. Now you must strike over to the south-west of the Green Man (if you want to drink here, use the bar on your right, the nearest thing to an old-style public bar I have found in this part of London) and head down Wildcroft Road, keeping the reservoir on your left.

When you reach the crossroads with Telegraph Road, visit the pub that, in its previous role (two centuries ago) as a telegraph station, gave the street its name. The Telegraph is an old-fashioned pub with regulars and some astonishingly comfortable chairs. Continue to the end of Wildcroft Road past a mock-Tudor block of mansion flats on your left called Wildcroft (straight out of *The Avengers*) and on to one of two paths leading into a patch of the heath that runs past the A3. Ahead of you, you will see a tunnel under the main road. Take this and, on the other side of the highway, you will find yourself on the edge of a large pond called King's Mere. It's a miniature gravel pit created when they dug the main road, but now, fringed by birch trees and dotted with swans and ducks, it can present a pleasant aspect. Bear round the southern end of King's Mere and follow the broad track that leads through the trees, with the road away to your right. This is called Stag Ride.

Superficially there is not a lot to recommend this end of Wimbledon Common. It may well be this bit of it that roused Virginia Woolf to describe it as 'bleak' and, as you push on down the

The **Wetland Centre** – worth the detour.

hill, fragments of semi-urban landscape loom through the trees. Here, behind iron railings, is Putney Vale Cemetery, one of the early examples of a non-consecrated burying ground, created by Wandsworth Council in the late 19th century, when the pressure on churchyard resting places simply became too much. I find the tangle of graves and paths rather beautiful. If, on the other hand, you have an urge to explore, strike off left into the trees. Within minutes you will lose all sight of strangers. If you have a dog, you can wander for hours, resurfacing on one of the main tracks that cross the common, often with no clear idea of where you are.

Continue along the track until you reach a couple of wooden posts that form an open gate, beyond which are playing fields. Head past the war memorial and straight across the fields towards the pavilion, and beyond, to the Robin Hood roundabout, where the A3 meets Kingston Hill. If there's too much activity on the fields, turn sharp right and rejoin the road before carrying on down to the Robin Hood entrance to Richmond Park.

The only way to cross the main A3 is by the iron footbridge, but, once you're inside the park, suburban London is quite forgotten. A friend of mine, Alan Franks, the *Times* journalist, once told me that Richmond Park was laid out on the medieval field system; certainly, if you look at the pattern of some of the oak trees, there is a curiously calming quality to them. Two thousand acres in area, the

park was first enclosed by Charles I, and stocked with deer that are still much in evidence. It made a favourite hunting ground until the 18th century.

As you strike off to your right, alongside the metalled road that leads to Roehampton Gate, watch out for the deer. Most of the year they don't give you any bother, but when, in May and June, the females have young (which they leave in the bracken) and you have the misfortune to go anywhere near them they will attack. I was once charged by an angry four-legged Mum when my lurcher got too close to one of her babies. The only thing that stopped her was a thwack on the nose from a handy stick.

When you are in line with the concrete bridge over the stream to your distant right, strike left onto a grass path rising steeply up through a line of trees. This is the haunt of mushroom pickers in early autumn; in fact, the whole of this walk may involve mushrooms, including the delicious *boletus edulis* or *porcino*. I am certainly not going to tell you where to find them but I will admit that I have had large quantities of parasol mushrooms, delicious fried with egg, out of this area.

Climb to the crest of the hill where you arrive at a flat expanse of rough grass. You are headed towards White Lodge. Thomas Pakenham, in *Time Out London Walks 1*, is not overly impressed by this 18th-century hunting lodge, built for George II in 1727. I beg to disagree. It is best seen not from the front – its slightly overly composed façade at the end of the ride that leads off from it (Queen's Ride) smacks to me so much of *trompe l'oeil* (I promise this is the last French expression I am going to use in this article) – but from the direction from which you are approaching it, the rear. If at the end of the plateau you are now crossing (a great view back towards Roehampton here by the way) you turn down right, you will see the arse end of the Royal Ballet School (the function now fulfilled by the building). Sometimes, in the early morning, with no one else about, I have watched mysterious vans waiting at the shrouded gates, their engines ticking, suggestively sinister. Sometimes, from within, you can hear strange music. George VI and the late Queen Mother lived here at the start of their married life and they didn't like it – mainly, as far as I can gather, because people like me peered in at them.

Descend to the metalled road you left at the bottom of the hill, and follow it left until you reach Roehampton Gate. On coming out of the park, you pass a stables and, after a few hundred yards, a roundabout with Danebury Avenue leading off to the right. Take this route, which leads you through the Roehampton Estate, listed in Pevsner's *The Englishness of English Art* as a deservedly famous attempt to create *rus in urbe*. It was designed in the 1950s by Sir Leslie Martin and its generous use of space around the (too high) blocks of flats gives it an open and pleasant feel. I am no middle-class Betjemanesque tourist of this area, but

can claim a more intimate relationship with it. Some years ago I was returning from a dinner party, by bicycle, when I noticed an elderly Volvo coming towards me. It was about ten yards away before I realised it was mine and that the person driving it was unknown to me. I gave chase but failed to catch it. Weeks later the police found it on the Roehampton Estate, and, armed with a spare key, I went down one morning and took it away, watched from some floors up by the enterprising youth who had stolen it.

When you reach the top of the estate, cross the road towards Roehampton Village, not a place to stop, as the best restaurant in it was forced to close a while ago. Bear right and past the petrol station, strike off left up Ponsonby Road past Holy Trinity church and a school into the field that runs back from the road. You are now back on Putney Heath. Follow the path leading up the slope; if you bear to the right, you will come to a circular depression and, ahead of you, a high fence marking the limits of the mansions of Putney Heath, in one of which lived Lord Hailsham.

Follow the path with the fence that backs on to the heath to your right and you will find yourself facing a cricket pitch. Cross over Telegraph Road and take the path that leads through the heath and back to the Green Man, or, if you are desperate for a pint, retrace your earlier route along Wildcroft Road. When you reach Putney Hill, head back down it and retrace your steps along the High Street. If you are energetic enough,

Wimbledon Common

Putney Vale Cemetery

you can take a left just past South Thames College and, subsequently, a right down Gwendolen Avenue, past some rather fine suburban housing.

Cross Upper Richmond Road to bring you back to the Lower Richmond Road, and then on to Embankment Road, from where you could follow the river back to the bridge. A few streets further west is the Bedford Café that inspired Gavin Ewart to write his memorable lyric *Breakfast All Day*. But by the time you read this, it will probably, like a lot of other things in this area, be an expensive coffee bar.

Eating & drinking

Bar M
4 Lower Richmond Road, SW15 1JN (8788 0345/www.barm.co.uk). **Open** 11am-11pm Mon-Sat; noon-10.30pm Sun. **Food served** noon-10pm daily.

Bedford Café
219 Lower Richmond Road, SW15 1HJ (8788 5060). **Open** 7am-2.30pm Mon-Sat. English fried breakfasts and sandwiches.

Duke's Head
8 Lower Richmond Road, SW15 1JN (8788 2552). **Open** 11am-11pm Mon-Sat; noon-10.30pm Sun. **Food served** noon-2.30pm, 6-10pm Mon-Fri; 11am-10pm Sat; noon-9pm Sun.

Green Man
Wildcroft Road, Putney Heath, SW15 3NG (8788 8096). **Open** 11am-11pm Mon-Sat; noon-10.30pm Sun. **Food served** noon-3pm, 6-9.30pm Mon-Fri; noon-9pm Sat; noon-5pm Sun.

La Mancha Tapas Bar
32 Putney High Street, SW15 1SQ (8780 1022/ www.lamancha.co.uk). **Open** noon-11pm Mon-Thur; noon-11.30pm Fri, Sat; noon-10.30pm Sun. Recommended tapas bar and restaurant.

Royal China
3 Chelverton Road, SW15 1RN (8788 0907). **Lunch served** noon-3.30pm Mon-Sat; noon-4pm Sun. **Dinner served** 6.30-11pm Mon-Sat; 6.30-10.30pm Sun. **Dim sum served** noon-3.30pm daily. Excellent dim sum, helpful staff.

Telegraph
Telegraph Road, SW15 3TU (8788 2011). **Open/food served** 11am-11pm Mon-Sat; noon-10.30pm Sun.

Churches

Holy Trinity Parish Church
Ponsonby Road, SW15 4LA (8788 9460). **Open** 8.30-10am Mon-Fri, Sun. *Services* 10am Sun.

St Mary's Church
Putney Bridge Southside, Putney High Street, SW15 1SN (8788 4414/www.parishofputney. co.uk). **Open** *Parish office* 9.30am-12.30pm Mon-Fri during term time. *Services* 10am Sun.

Literature

All My Little Ones Gavin Ewart (1978)
The Englishness of English Art Nikolaus Pevsner (1956)
Late Pickings Gavin Ewart (1987)
My Father and Myself JR Ackerley (1968)
Time Out London Walks 1 (revised and updated 2005)
Walking Literary London Roger Tagholm (2001)

Parks

Richmond Park
Richmond, Surrey (8948 3209/www.royalparks. gov.uk). **Open** *Mar-Sept* 7am-dusk daily. *Oct-Feb* 7.30am-dusk daily.

Wildfowl & Wetland Trust
Queen Elizabeth's Walk, SW13 9WT (8409 4400/www.wwt.org.uk).

Wimbledon Common & Putney Heath
Ranger's Office, Windmill Road, Wimbledon Common, SW19 (8788 7655/www.wpcc.org.uk).

Others

Putney Vale Cemetery
Stag Lane, SW15 3DZ (8788 2113/ www.wandsworth.gov.uk). **Open** *Jan, Feb, Nov, Dec* 8am-4pm Mon-Sat; 10am-4pm Sun; *Mar, Oct* 8am-5pm Mon-Sat; 10am-5pm Sun; *Apr, Sept* 8am-6pm Mon-Sat; 10am-6pm Sun; *May-Aug* 8am-7pm Mon-Sat; 10am-7pm Sun.

Royal Ballet School
White Lodge, Richmond Park, Richmond, Surrey TW10 5HR (8876 5547/www.royal-ballet-school.org.uk).

South Thames College
50-52 Putney Hill, SW15 6QX (8918 7000/ www.south-thames.ac.uk).

Obelisk to arch

Nick Barlay

Wildlife, factories, picture palaces and motorway junctions all feature on this walk
into the heart of London along the ancient Watling Street.

Start: Royal National Orthopaedic
Hospital, Brockley Hill
Finish: Marble Arch
Time: all day
Distance: 16 miles/25km
Getting there: Jubilee line
to Stanmore, then either the
hospital shuttle service (hourly,
at 40 minutes past the hour –
except the 8.50am) or the 142,
then 107 bus to the hospital.
There is also a car park by
Stanmore tube.
Getting back: Central line
from Marble Arch
Note: this is a very long walk
along a main road. Tube stations
are at regular intervals along
the route. Not all the places
mentioned in the text are
included in the listings, for
reasons of space. The last
half-mile or so overlaps with
Andrew Humphreys' walk.

Ancient tribes, modern vigilantes,
a hermit, a murderer, a Vorticist,
a poet, a pop star, a suicidal painter,
hidden streams, missing crosses, lost
stones, an Oriental city, a picture palace,
a trumpet factory, an aero works, bombs,
fires, robberies, ruddy ducks, cormorants,
reed warblers, a harmonious blacksmith,
a mattress king, five boroughs, one
gallows, relentless traffic, around 12
miles of pavement and Joan Collins:
welcome to the A5, one of Britain's
greatest arterial Roman roads originally
running from Richborough in Kent

via St Albans to Chester, and these days
on to Holyhead on the island of Anglesey.

The stretch described here runs
south from Brockley Hill to the heart
of town, and is itself the straightest,
longest and one of the oldest of London's
roads. Behind the perfection of the alpha-
numeric A5 lurk no fewer than 15 names,
some out of date, some disputed, some
cunningly repeated along its length.
Brockley Hill becomes Stonegrove,
then High Street Edgware, Burnt Oak
Broadway, Edgware Road, the Hyde,
West Hendon Broadway, Edgware Road,
Cricklewood Broadway, Shoot Up Hill,
Kilburn High Road, Maida Vale, then
Edgware Road once more. The A5 was
also known as the London Way up to the
end of the 16th century, occasionally as
the Roman Way and, much more often
than not, as Watling Street. But names
aside, put simply and symbolically, you
will be walking from an obelisk to an
arch on a 2,000-year-old route.

To get to the start point in the grounds
of the Royal National Orthopaedic
Hospital on Brockley Hill, take the Jubilee
line to its northern terminus at Stanmore.
On weekdays, a shuttle service runs to
the hospital. On weekends, turn right out
of Stanmore tube and either walk or take
the 142 bus to Canons Corner, and then
take the 107 bus up Brockley Hill. Enter
the sombre hospital through the main
entrance and cut along the main path
through the 112-acre grounds until you
get to the architectural afterbirth that is
the biomedical engineering department.

Among the trees beside this
department stands a tall stone obelisk.
Erected in 1750 by William Sharpe, a

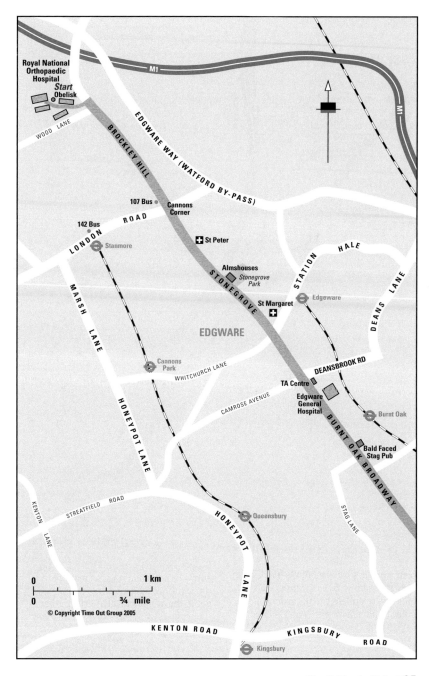

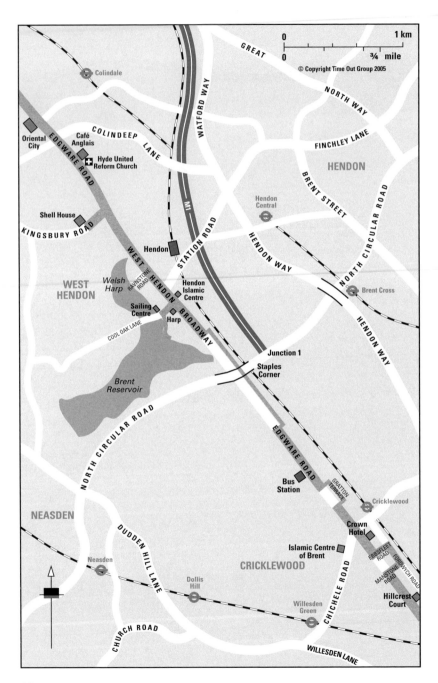

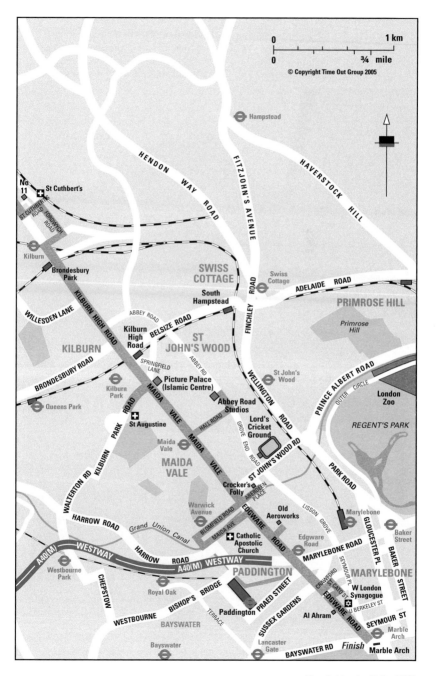

0 | 1 km
0 | ¾ mile
© Copyright Time Out Group 2005

Hampstead

HENDON WAY ROAD

FITZJOHN'S AVENUE

HAVERSTOCK HILL

No 11
St Cuthbert's
ST CUTHBERT'S ROAD
FORDWYCH ROAD

Kilburn

Brondesbury Park

SWISS COTTAGE

Swiss Cottage

ADELAIDE ROAD

PRIMROSE HILL

WILLESDEN LANE

South Hampstead

Primrose Hill

KILBURN HIGH ROAD

ABBEY ROAD
BELSIZE ROAD

Kilburn High Road

ST JOHN'S WOOD

FINCHLEY ROAD

KILBURN

BRONDESBURY ROAD

SPRINGFIELD LANE

ABBEY RD

St John's Wood

PRINCE ALBERT ROAD

OUTER CIRCLE

London Zoo

Kilburn Park

Picture Palace (Islamic Centre)

WELLINGTON ROAD

Queens Park

PARK ROAD

MAIDA VALE

St Augustine

Abbey Road Studios

HALL ROAD

Lord's Cricket Ground

GROVE END ROAD

REGENT'S PARK

WALTERTON RD

KILBURN PARK ROAD

Maida Vale

MAIDA VALE

ST JOHN'S WOOD RD

MAIDA VALE

Crocker's Folly

ABERDEEN PLACE

Old Aeroworks

LISSON GROVE

Marylebone

GLOUCESTER PL

Baker Street

Warwick Avenue

BLOMFIELD ROAD

EDGWARE ROAD

MAIDA AVE

HARROW ROAD

Grand Union Canal

Catholic Apostolic Church

Edgware Road

MARYLEBONE ROAD

BAKER STREET

A40(M) WESTWAY

Westbourne Park

HARROW ROAD

A40(M) WESTWAY

PADDINGTON

CRAWFORD ST

SEYMOUR PL

MARYLEBONE

CHEPSTOW

Royal Oak

BISHOP'S BRIDGE

PRAED STREET

SUSSEX GARDENS

CATO ST

W London Synagogue

U BERKELEY ST

SEYMOUR ST

WESTBOURNE

Paddington

TERRACE

Al Ahram

EDGWARE ROAD

Marble Arch

BAYSWATER

Bayswater

Lancaster Gate

BAYSWATER RD

Finish

Marble Arch

secretary to the second Duke of Chandos, it marks the midway point between Londinium, which once belonged to the Tribobantes tribe, and St Albans or Verulamium, the capital of the Cassi. Inscriptions on the four faces of the obelisk mark out the territory of the Suellani to the south, the stronghold of the Celtic Catuvellauni to the north, the ancient

Oriental City

Café du Liban and the Al Ahram bookshop at the lower end of the **Edgware Road**.

settlement of Cassi to the west, and the high ground of Brockley, 450 feet above sea level, to the east.

A major battle took place here between the Tribobantes and the Catuvellauni, the latter becoming the most powerful of the tribes by the time of Caesar's invasion in 55 BC. In another version, the obelisk could also mark the defeat by Caesar in 54 BC of the Catuvellauni, the scythed tribal war chariots succumbing to five legions and 2,000 cavalry. According to legend rather than established fact, it was near here that the uprising of Boudicca, Queen of the Iceni, was defeated by the Romans several years later. Four stone tablets used to lie around the base of the obelisk. One was apparently spotted in the 1930s being used as a doorstep in Stanmore. The other three are still missing.

Retrace the path, which is an ancient one originally linking Stanmore and Elstree, to the hospital entrance. On your right is the imposing main building, once known as Verulam House and subsequently a convalescent home established by Mary Wardell in 1884 for victims of scarlet fever. Since then the hospital has catered for children with ricketts sent here for country sun to combat Vitamin D deficiency, injured or disabled World War I soldiers, and further orthopaedic cases during World War II.

Leave the hospital and cross the road. Peering into the untended hedgerow a touch south will reveal a blue plaque that, despite a few buttercups, must surely be the loneliest blue plaque within spitting distance of the 1927 Watford Bypass. It denotes the presence of the Roman pottery of Sulloniacae, AD 65-165. No souvenir shop. No octogenarian Friend of the Pottery to welcome you. Still, just as an ice-age glacier once stopped in Finchley, so the Romans pottered here in the clay soil of what is now the London Borough of Barnet. Chances are the Celtic or Belgic Catuvellauni, with their Goddess Sulis, got here first. Although archaeological digs have

unearthed evidence of pottery kilns, ceramic materials and even a Roman folding knife, evidence of a settlement has yet to be found.

On your right as you go down the shaded hill is an enclosure of low derelict buildings, windows smashed, grass poking through stonework, marked only by a sign for a security company. The series of functional parallel blocks is owned by the MOD. Derelict? Maybe. But there are no loose words here. The security company only talks to the MOD on Thursdays. And the MOD is keeping shtum. Some say it was the Army pay office. Others say its proximity to Bletchley Park led to involvement in wartime code-breaking. But the Army wasn't here. Nuff said.

The Romans, however, were. Along the grass verge and in the car park of the golf course further down the hill, workmen laying pipes in the 1920s discovered rammed gravel with a foot of large, carefully laid, nodular flints set in lime grouting and kerbed with gravel concrete. This may have been Roman construction at its best but road building sooner or later leads to road repairing. The Romans often repaired it and, one way or another, so has everyone else ever since. Heavy traffic made the road 'ruinous and dangerous' in the Middle Ages with locals constantly struggling to keep silted, flooded and muddy parts of it passable through grants of pavage. These days the lower left side of Brockley Hill is well paved and well heeled with some sumptuous properties. In contrast to the drudgery of the Roman fixed-axle cart, the natives' power-steered Ferraris shout 'dolce vita'.

Cross the Canons Corner roundabout at the bottom of the hill. On your left is the first of five McDonald's restaurants strung strategically along the A5 from here to Marble Arch, today's corporate equivalent of wayfarers' inns. Between here and the mid 20th-century St Peter's mission church down on the left is a residential outfall of courts and blocks on the edge of what was the 18th-century estate of the Duke of Chandos. There are no roads or streets here but drives, groves, avenues and ways.

After the odd, grey St Peter's, with its unwieldy cross like an experimental telecommunications apparatus, note Watling Court on the right, not for its look but as the first 'Watling' on this route. The etymology of this key name is uncertain, but here are some 'true or bluff' options to exercise the mind: Watling originates in 'Atheling', Old English for 'noble'; Watling comes from Sara Gwyddelin, the Irish Highway pronounced by Romans as Weatlinga; Watling derives from Anglo-Saxon settlers who called old Verulamium Waetlingaceaster. Take your pick. Or phone a friend.

The Nagila Jewish nursery on the left indicates the presence of a sizeable Jewish community in the quietude of this almost provincial neighbourhood between Stanmore and Edgware. However, there are sinister stirrings. The nursery is also the site of my apprehension by the boys from CST, the self-styled card-carrying Jewish Community Security Service, who, having followed me, wish to know what I'm doing here and why I'm taking notes. 'It's because of the Middle East,' they tell me. 'We have to be careful.' I tell them I'm Jewish, that in my teens I was chased by Nazi skinheads along the forecourt of Stanmore tube. But they look at my head and it begins to dawn on me that, all these years later, I, too, am a skinhead. Then a topless Ferrari draws up. The young male driver aims a camera, takes a few snaps of me and speeds off. 'For the records,' they tell me. I'm a writer, I tell them, any publicity is good publicity.

Just beyond the besieged security zone on the left is Ailantus Court, ailanto or ailantus meaning 'tree of heaven'. In the forecourt, looking somewhat out of place, is a rare, tall Asiatic tree. Across the street on the right is Stonegrove

House, one of the original 18th-century buildings in this once part-wooded, part-agricultural territory. Continuing down on the left is the Bottle & Dragon, formerly a traveller's hostelry, the Leather Bottle. It existed in the 1750s, was 'silenced' in 1759 and in its latest incarnation has a Thai restaurant.

A hundred yards or so further are eight almshouses contained in a single-storey 19th-century Gothic building with a clock and slate roof. Charles Day built these in 1828 for specially selected alms folk from the local parish: those who did not sell anything; did not imbibe intoxicants; did not swear or break the Sabbath. And definitely did not take notes in note-free security zones. The one-acre plot of the almshouses backs on to Stonegrove Park, once the area's pound.

Edgware, which lends its name to intermittent segments of Watling Street, welcomes you after the Jet petrol station. Edgware, Ecgi's Weir or fishing pool, was in use as a road name from 1574. On the right are the twin columns of Canons Drive, the entrance to the Duke of Chandos's Canons Park estate, broken up and sold off after the family hit hard times. Opposite the Blacking Bottle pub is the unlikely insurance brokerage of Beard, Pipe & Benbow, clearly one man with two assets. The excellent Two Jays second-hand bookshop, the Flying Elephant and Zan Zi Bar provide Benbow with suitably surreal neighbours.

But by now you cannot fail to have spotted the small timbered Tudor-style building occupying the middle of the right-hand pavement. A monumental mason's today, this was a blacksmith's dating from 1492. Known to locals as Handel's Smithy, it was the inspiration for Handel's set of harpsichord variations, *The Harmonious Blacksmith*. Handel Close, Handel Way and Handel House are nearby reminders of the *kapellmeister*'s association with the Duke of Chandos, for whom he composed the 'Chandos Anthem' in 1718.

Marble Arch

Nice spot for a picnic – the **North Circular** flyover.

More or less behind the former smithy is the Victorian, still family-owned Stonebridge Funeral Service. This is in the same 16th-century building as the Vecchia Romagna (Roman Way) Italian restaurant beside it. The big stone cross of a World War I memorial, and the 1905 Caxton House opposite, further confuse the jumbled history of this conservation area.

At the junction ahead, turn left into Station Road. Immediately on your left is the Truth, a shed-like community café with a plaque commemorating one of the children killed when Tip 7 collapsed on to a school in the Welsh mining village of Aberfan in 1966. Overshadowing it is the tower of St Margaret built of 15th-century Reigate stone but incorporating 14th-century bricks. An earlier clock was replaced in 1756 by an 'eight-day ting tang clock'. By last century, locals were still so enamoured of the ting and the tang that they had it silenced. Look down Station Road to the vast Railway pub. Beyond it is the Edgware Branch Northern line terminus completed in 1924, although by then this outpost of

the metropolitan transport system had been served by coaches, stage coaches, omnibuses and electric trams.

Back on Watling Street, walk past the German supermarket Lidl to the Change of Hart pub. It changed its Hart in 1992. For over 300 years prior to that, it was the White Hart, a coaching inn that still features a covered entrance for coaches, a timbered door and a lantern at the rear. A curiosity attached to the White Hart is the empty office of a former 'communication, secrecy, surveillance' business.

A little way on comes the next local name change. Just beside Europcar is the point where High Street Edgware transforms imperceptibly into Burnt Oak Broadway. It is actually a bridge, site of the original 1370 Eggewere Brigge that carried Watling Street over Deans Brook. The bridge is marked by two stones: Barnet 1968; Hendon 1865. The brook beneath is marked by floating supermarket bags from 2005.

Stroll on along the pavement and Peugeot, the first of many major car dealerships, comes into view on the left followed by the Yamaha dealership on the right. The A5 is not about money for the car manufacturers. It's about prestige. One manufacturer, which failed to achieve main road frontage, is quietly smirked at by some of the big wheels of the motor trade. So a certain Gary tells me.

The junction of Deansbrook Road on the left is marked on the southern side by the cubic Territorial Army building. The stone moulding over the entrance says the Royal Engineers were here. Affixed to the Deansbrook Road side of the building is a blue plaque, site of the Edgware Turnpike between 1711 and 1872. A glance at the Ordnance Survey map for 1864 shows that the turnpike was not here at all but actually on the northern side of the road controlling the traffic along the seven-mile run to the Kilburn turnpike.

Having descended from 450 feet on Brockley Hill to around 150 feet in Edgware, a gentle climb begins. Within a few yards is the car park of Edgware Hospital. The main hospital building is set back from the street and topped with a clock. Opened in 1927 as Redhill Hospital by one Neville Chamberlain, Minister of Health, it was originally the grim Edgware workhouse.

Along the opposite side of the road are the pretty pastel semis of Lindsay Parade and beyond, part of the new housing reflecting rapid working class immigration in the 1920s. As you enter Burnt Oak, likely to be thus called because of the Roman custom of oak-burning at boundary points, the striking pre-Victorian Prince of Wales pub is on your left. A strange detritus of human activity – Irish theme pub and Barnet register office on the left, Jesus Lives in the Burnt Oak Christian Fellowship down Oakleigh Avenue on your right, and Victorian funeral director Sydney Hurry beside a shop blending African handicrafts with Internet services – bares the soul of Burnt Oak. A busy

grocer near the Highlands cross street caters for a heterogeneous Jewish, Indian, Irish and African community.

On the southern side of the junction with Watling Avenue is the Bald Faced Stag pub. Opposite is Stag Lane. A renowned travellers' haunt, the pub is also associated with stag hunting and the custom of exfoliating part of the stag's face as a trophy. Whether this operation was carried out dead or alive or in the pub is uncertain.

Laminate flooring and Allied Carpets lead the way on to Edgware Road and Colindale. The Citroën dealership on the right is followed by a grand former picture palace, now a bingo hall. This part of the A5, and the next three or four miles, took much Luftwaffe punishment. Over 600 high-explosive bombs were aimed at local industries, in particular aircraft manufacturing just to the east of the main road.

Survival along this stretch takes big bucks. Weather-beaten Montrose and Southbourne Courts on the left and the extravagantly named A5 Sauna opposite are dwarfed by the pompous cross-street face-off between, on the right, Mercedes, and on the left, Audi. Even Chrysler, further down on the left, looks insignificant. It takes an Oriental City to compete. Guarded by stone dragons, the almost ten-year-old Oriental City draws local Chinese, Bangladeshi and Japanese families as well as overseas executives. If you don't eat noodles there, at least pick up a pair of novelty chopsticks from the Toko £1+ Shop.

A Japanese bookshop, Carlito's Way café and the Beis Yaakov primary school stand in succession on the right opposite Colindale Avenue, once called Ancient Street. This avenue leads to the British Library Newspaper Library and the Hendon RAF museum. As you walk Edgware Road, take in the Café Anglais on the corner of Sheaveshill Avenue. It's a cheap local favourite with photos of film stars, and perfect for a fry-up. Continue past the Hyde United Reform Church, which includes the Chinese Church in London, until you get to the junction of Kingsbury Road.

The Red Lion stands on the corner, another travellers' choice dating from at least 1826. View its selection of chimneys, lantern and red lion moulding from its car park. A hundred feet or so along Kingsbury Road is Goldsmith Avenue on your left. The shuttered house facing it is known as Shell Cottage – the shell is just below the roof. This was where Oliver Goldsmith lived while he wrote *She Stoops to Conquer* from 1771 to 1774. His name is often confused with other parts of the Edgware Road and even led to a street, Goldsmith Place, being erroneously named after him in Kilburn. Opposite Kingsbury Road is the hideous '60s Hyde House office block, the name of which inspired fear in vagabonds – it was once a vagabond pound – the sight of which can still chill to the bone.

Continue along Watling Street, Edgware Road having become the Hyde. Note on the right the 1947 postal sorting office, outside which a bomb went off on 14 April 2001, and believed to be the work of the Real IRA. Just beyond is the Hendon courthouse. And just beyond that, turn right into a car park. In the bottom left-hand corner of Halfords you can see the automatic grabbing 'equiptment' (sic) for keeping the Silk Stream free of ordure. This ancient stream, which has been flowing secretly down the east side of Watling Street, now emerges and crosses to the west side before flowing into the Brent Reservoir just to the south-west.

Cross the Silk Bridge and on your left is Toyota. Although the glass frontage is typical of the dealerships, its understated structure belonged to the Schweppes factory. The sign for Schweppes Table Waters once illuminated the A5 as early 20th-century workers hand-bottled, corked and wired the liquid for loading on to horse-drawn vans and later steam wagons.

Proceed up the hill into West Hendon. The semi-dereliction of this strip is best seen in the context of Ravenstone Road, a half road on your right whose amputated demeanour is set against a sprawling estate. It was the unfortunate Ravenstone Road that bore the brunt of one of World War II's biggest bombs to fall on London, on 13 February 1941. The cross marking the event has disappeared and, in case you haven't been counting, you are down three stone tablets, one Roman settlement, one explanation for a derelict MOD building and now a wooden cross.

Look left with incredulity to the Welsh Harp Boating Centre. The wisdom of this family-owned business only becomes apparent after you've negotiated the Shree Gayatri Mandir on your right and the purple-and-gold Hendon Islamic Centre in Brent View Road to your left.

From the crest of the hill you can look down towards the Staples Corner interchange and the flyover of the North Circular. On your right is the Harp public house. Between 1850 and 1910 the Welsh Harp (taking its name from its shape) was a leisure resort boasting its own railway station. The original alehouse (the Harp is not it) became a big draw for Victorian holidaymakers wishing 'to bid London smoke adieu for the pleasures of a rural spot'. It was memorialised in the form of 'The Jolliest Place That's Out', a music-hall foot-stomper. Nature and Staples Corner make uneasy if not perverse neighbours but, before braving one of London's busiest pedestrian-terrorising interchanges and the biggest man-made entity on this walk, turn right into Cool Oak Lane.

On your left just past Woolmead Avenue, and before the narrow bridge that traverses the Welsh Harp and the mile-long Brent Reservoir, used by several sailing clubs, is a gateway. The path leads to an observation hide controlled by the Welsh Harp Conservation Group and, should you want to, you will need to 'buy' a key (*see listings*).

Otherwise, continue along the path until you get a view of the reservoir that was created in the 1830s by damming the Silk Stream and Brent River. Dollis Brook also flows into it. In the distance, across the placid water, is Wembley Stadium. Bull rushes, yellow flag irises and several species of orchids can be seen here, along with cormorants, great crested grebes, terns, a few herons, the occasional osprey and the more obvious Canada geese. Come in the summer and there are two dozen species of butterfly and a dozen different types of dragonfly. No surprise, therefore, that this is an SSSI, Site of Special Scientific Interest, and a designated nature reserve.

The battle between nature and the pollutants of the A5 is now also your battle. Take a lungful of this air and retrace the route to the main road. Cross towards the balconied houses opposite, once used by holidaymakers. At this point the A5 gets a central, and very unnatural, reservation. There is often a rose seller standing at the head of it, guaranteed proof of a bottleneck and long delays for motorists. It is the sort of road configuration that gives rise to the twisted cant of traffic police and traffic broadcasters alike: SWT or Sheer Weight of Traffic is a phrase only a rose seller can truly appreciate. Stay on the left side of the road because it's the best, and safest, way of crossing Staples Corner.

Descending into fume and gloom along what is now West Hendon Broadway, you will pass the bizarrely decorative façade of Philex House, whose current occupants make the equally bizarre claim that this was once a German embassy. Complete Scheiss. To the left along Brent Park Road is a rail bridge carrying freight towards Brent Sidings and passengers into Cricklewood. Crossing to the pavement below the A5 elevated section affords a glimpse of the Brent River (from the Celtic goddess Brigantia), which flows across Watling Street at this point,

ending up in the Brent Reservoir. Otherwise, just by Vauxhall Vans, ascend the pedestrian overpass.

From a vantage point above the central roundabout, you have the chance to examine your concrete surroundings. A few hundred feet to the east is the Brent Cross interchange and the first junction of the M1 motorway (Brockley Hill is close to Junction 4). Arcing above you exactly five miles from the centre of town is the A406 North Circular Road flyover, built in 1976 and carrying 100,000 vehicles each day. The combination of A5, M1 and A406 carries 400,000 vehicles each day. But to reduce this interchange to numbers is to belittle it. The North Circular flyover, 100-foot sections of which can cost over £1 million, is so much more. It is 'a multi-span, post-tensioned reinforced concrete structure with retained fill approach ramps' and a 'multi-cellular reinforced concrete box girder deck'. Yes, really. In fact, it is not such a far cry from the Roman road layers of statumen, rudus, nucleus and summum dorsum. Roads are ingenious, at least compared to the simplicity with which they can be flooded, pitted, rutted or otherwise disrupted. The massive IRA van bomb on 11 April 1992 shook glassware across north London, almost killed two policemen, structurally damaged the flyover and caused Sheer Weight of Traffic for over a year.

As you continue along the overpass, look diagonally across. All this post-tensioned reinforced complexity does not owe its name to the Staples Office Superstore at the spectacularly numbered 1000 North Circular Road, but to a mattress, a patent spiral spring mattress in fact, introduced to this location in 1926 by Ambrose Heal. Heal, who had bought the Staples bed patent from a New Yorker named Staples, sprung to fame by supplying the unique bed to King George V after a riding accident.

Descend the overpass on the southbound side. The slip road joins what is now Edgware Road and you are heading uphill towards Cricklewood. On your left is Geron Way, which may have some etymological connection to the Greek 'old' since it is on the edge of the major rail terminus of Brent Sidings and was almost certainly the route to and from the main road. Today Geron Way leads to a business park with, among others, PC World, Tempo, Courts and UGC cinema.

Continue up the hill. Over on the right is Humber Road, at the end of which the IRA detonated a small device in 1993 for obscure reasons. Here the eastern side of the A5 is heavily railtracked. Look out beyond the exit of Geron Way, just before Parcel Force, towards the railtrack and you will see the Shanks Hendon Waste Transfer Station. For over 25 years, two trains a day take 1,000 tonnes of bulked and compressed London waste to a landfill in Bedfordshire. Londoners from Barnet, Brent, Harrow and Camden generate a quarter of a million tonnes of waste a year, which in turn generates ten megawatts of electricity from landfill gas. The A5 is often called arterial, but venal is equally accurate.

The opposite western side is, by contrast, the edge of what was, until the early 20th century, the sparsely populated hamlet of Dollis Hill. Oxgate Lane, close to Staples Corner, and Oxgate Gardens, on the right, were exactly that, 13th-century gates to prevent livestock straying on to Watling Street. The next right is Dollis Hill Lane leading to Gladstone Park. Two streets on is Gladstone Park Gardens and after that Gladstone Park Parade, reminding us of Gladstone's association with the area. Between parliamentary sessions he used to stay in Dollis Hill House.

Still on the right, past Brent Tavern is the Cricklewood Bus Garage. The organised development of transport defines this part of the A5 and the long struggle against grim road conditions, dung heaps, road gravel shortages and highwaymen preying on unwary travellers. By 1728 there was a daily stage coach from Oxford Street to Edgware. 150 years later there were 45 omnibuses an hour to South Kilburn, 35 an hour to Kilburn and half a dozen to Cricklewood. By the 1950s, around 200 buses operated from the Cricklewood Garage, which still retains a Reg Varney *On the Buses* feel with its chugging engines, ill-lit corridors and forlorn main office.

On the left, opposite American-style supermarket Matalan and behind the trees, you will discover Cricklewood Cottages. Walking into Gratton Terrace reveals a unique series of five parallel terraced streets, named after railway officials and purpose-built for the workers of the Midland Railway and their families. Walk through the gardened terraces to emerge from this peaceful haven on Kara Way. Note the white-painted corner cottage with red trimmings.

Immediately on your right looking back north is the milestone telling you that you are now four miles from London and ten from Watford. Just past Ashford Road on the right is the Islamic Information Centre, where a question about the area is answered with a gifted book, *A Simple Call to One God*, and the words: 'If you ask me ABCD I can answer ABCD but if you really want to know ABCD you must go to the mosque.'

On the right, past Pedro's Café, is the 1890 Chichele Road corner. Look down along it to the church that is now both the mosque and the Islamic Centre of Brent. Opposite is Cricklewood Lane, which in 1913 led to a Handley Page factory with a nearby aerodrome. Now it is dominated by Ashtons Night Club and the Galtymore Dance Club to the south. The two clubs are landmarks for the local Irish population, which grew steadily from the 1830s, followed some 120 years later by West Indians and, in the intervening years, by working classes from the overcrowded inner London areas.

Further up on the left is the commanding Crown Hotel, catering since the 18th century for travellers,

Kilburn's **Tricycle Theatre**.

and after 1890 for the stabling of the London General Omnibus Company's horses. The huge sandstone edifice (Free Flemish Renaissance, no less) with three (there used to be four) cast-iron lamp standards, became a Cannon then Allied brewery. The Crown was known locally as the capital of Ireland. In the hardcore Republican-sympathising 1970s a hat would often be passed around for the boys and, when the singing began, you sang, too. It is also most likely the pub Frank McCourt refers to in *Angela's Ashes* when Paddy gets 'a grand job in a pub in Cricklewood', and, as everyone knows, 'one room in Cricklewood is better than ten' anywhere else you care to name.

Continue on the left side of the road where some of the first phone boxes on the A5 to advertise prostitutes offer a better indication of distance to the centre than a milestone. Also on the left is Calabash African Food. Look above it – this is the London Borough of Hampstead. Behind you is Barnet

Food and odd maps on **Kilburn High Road.**

and over the road is Brent. Step from one side to the other and back. Well, people do it at the equator, don't they?

Carry on along the left side past the blue-painted moulding of a head attached to the side of Gray's Tyres and Exhausts (note the gargoyled stonework), and after an apple crumble dessert from the Broadway Bagel Bakery, turn left by the St James Gate pub into Ebbsfleet Road.

Tiled porches, decorative mouldings, flowers and cherry blossom lead to Fordwych Road, which parallels Watling Street for the best part of a mile, running east of Shoot Up Hill, then down into Kilburn. Fordwych Road was the main road through the Powell-Cotton Estate, John Powell being the secretary to King George III, and Captain Henry Cotton of the Bengal Cavalry being the inheritor in 1883 of a huge tract of land covering Shoot Up Hill.

How the original 18th-century Powell and the 19th-century Cotton came together is a tedious affair of nephews and brothers and begetting and inheriting. But the name Fordwych derives from the Powell family seat in Kent and has always been a fashionable area to live, especially during the Edwardian era when it was home to portrait artists and flower painters. Skardu and Rondu Roads on your right are the names of Kashmiri places visited by Major Percy Powell-Cotton who was… oh don't ask, just enjoy the scenery.

Turn right off Fordwych into Manstone Road to rejoin the main road, which is now Shoot Up Hill. Shoot Up or Shotuppe or Shutt-up Hill, once part of the dense oak Forest of Middlesex, was the place King Henry VIII came to hunt game. The forest was also the typical hideout of all manner of Turpinite robber or 'footpad'. These days it's defoliated, residential and ill-served by game or by shop with not a lot to rob. Locals labour up and down this hill hunting and gathering in Cricklewood or in Kilburn as van and car drivers grind gears, weave the bus lanes and say 'cheese' through speed traps.

Until the 19th century, the junction with Mill Lane on the left was characterised by a windmill. Built for grinding corn, it stood on the right southern side of the hill from 1798. Diagonally opposite is a tasteful commemoration in the form of the high-rise Windmill Court. The Kilburn Mill itself, painted by Constable, burned down on 3 December 1863 with its 'sails blazing like a great Catherine Wheel', according to one eyewitness. The disaster led to the establishing of the Kilburn Voluntary Fire Brigade.

The first residential court on the left, on the crest of Shoot Up Hill, is the imaginatively named Hillcrest Court. Joan and Jackie Collins lived at No.20, Jackie having been born in a nursing home in Fordwych Road. Their parents – Dad Joe was a vaudeville agent – were most likely to have been the first occupants of the flat in 1936. The next left, with its silver birches, is Kingscroft Road where Doris Lessing used to live at No.11 until moving to Mill Lane. Opposite are the three concrete blocks they call Watling Gardens. Take in the view of Kilburn bridges down the hill.

Then turn left into St Cuthbert's Road. On your right is Templar House, opened in 1954 by Princess Anne after the original building was destroyed by a flying bomb. The name also connotes the Knights Templar, an order dissolved in the early 14th century but which then controlled large segments of Shoot Up Hill.

Facing you at the end of the road is St Cuthbert's church, again on Fordwych Road. The first church was opened in 1887 but subsequently had to make way for the Midland Railway just to the east. The second church was firebombed during World War II. This third-time-lucky 1988 resurrection sure ain't pretty no more but incorporates the 1906 bell, before you, as well as foundation stones from 1903 and 1987.

Turn right along Fordwych. No.10 is marked by a blue plaque for painter David Garsen Bomberg who lived and worked at this address between 1928 and 1934. When referred to at all these days, he is called a Vorticist or Cubist, but his paintings, at least those completed here, are sombre and poignant examinations of both himself and his second wife, Lilian Mendelson. Bomberg used a large mirror to scrutinise the mood and features of his subject. His uncompromising 1932 self-portrait suggests a dark and withdrawn individual. But his still life paintings of *Kilburn Bridges* are the perfect note on which to hang a right on Maygrove Road to emerge more or less beneath two Kilburn bridges and opposite Kilburn tube on what is now Kilburn High Road.

This special junction, if you can handle steel, oppression and darkness, is at the end of the road inhabited by Tax, the narrator of my first novel *Curvy Lovebox*. It is also the strip of Kilburn High Road along which Ian Dury journeyed many times, inspiration perhaps for his first band, Kilburn and the High Roads, whose pub circuit success is still talked about in these parts. Turn left and another paintable bridge confronts you, the main line between West Hampstead and Brondesbury.

This is the doorway to Kilburn or Kyle Bourne, Anglo-Saxon for the cold water of the ancient stream that ran parallel to the main route but is now culverted. Today Kilburn High Road is often choked with pedestrians and vehicles, and provides the most varied of Watling Street's modern populations in age and culture. As I walk, an old Irish man mutters, 'She's a runner to be sure,' to his equally old companion. A young West Indian shouts across the street, 'Just runnin' up Nathalie's. My wood's achin' innit.' Kilburn is also the area in which my parents settled soon after their arrival in England, having fled Hungary in 1956.

Before the bridge is Iverson Road, interesting only for its ghosts: a maker of Clarence and Brougham carriages; a manufacturer of lightning conductors and speaking tubes; an orderly room of the London Artillery Brigade; the all-night mooing emanating from the cattle trucks of the Midland Railway. All played their part in pissing off the long-suffering residents. In 1945, they had to suffer further when Iverson Road's railway embankment hosted the first V2 rocket in the area.

On the corner of Palmerston Road, second left, is a Nando's restaurant, once the Palmerston Hotel, later a terminus for horse buses, then the Roman Way pub. Cookies & Cream on the right side is much more relaxed. Sit in the window to watch the pedestrian world being squeezed along the narrow pavements, and to get away from the drum 'n' bass booming out of car stereos.

On the left, the 17th-century Black Lion pub, rebuilt in 1898, still has a fantastically ornate ceiling. Opposite is the popular Tricycle Theatre, which opened in 1980 in the hall of the Ancient Order of Foresters. Destroyed by fire, it reopened, plus a cinema and art gallery, in 1998 and has survived where others, such as the Grange across the road, have failed.

The domed – and doomed – Grange has been the National nightclub since 1976 but originally opened in 1914 as the biggest cinema of its day, seating 2,000. The first film shown here was *She Stoops to Conquer*, the influence of the same misguided Goldsmith fixation that led to the erroneous eponymous Goldsmith Place further down.

Immediately across, on the corner of Buckley Road, is the classic Victorian undertaker – or 'funeral furnisher' – James Crook, with its wrought-iron entrance arch. Walk along the right side to the junction with Willesden Lane. The Southern K, a 1861 pub, was bombed by the IRA in 1975 (when the boozer was called Biddy Mulligan's). Opposite is the 19th-century pawnbroker Thompson, now a jeweller. On the right,

but best viewed from the left side of the road, is the Kilburn State, another former cinema now squatted by bingo. Opened in 1937 and looking, yes, like the Empire State, this cinema was Europe's biggest, with over 4,000 seats, and massively popular. George Formby performed here, as did Jerry Lee Lewis in the 1950s.

On the right after Victoria Road is the 1486 Cock, one of Kilburn's oldest wayside hostelries, rebuilt in 1794 after burning down, and again in 1900. When Harrison Ainsworth wrote his very successful *Rookwood* in 1834, including a fictionalised account of Dick Turpin's ride to York, Turpin and his gang met at an inn based on the Cock. Turpin's connection to Kilburn is doubtful, as are many stories about him – note the 1925 film *Dick Turpin* in which star American cowboy Tom Mix plays the homegrown highwayman. Ainsworth's connection, however, is certain: he occupied Elm Lodge on the site of the Grange cinema and also wrote about Jack Sheppard, another highwayman we will meet again on Watling Street.

Beyond Kilburn Square on the right, now partly a covered market, is Brondesbury Villas, where Sean Connery lived in the 1950s. In 1957 he had a small part in *Hell Drivers*, an excellent film about an ex-con driving heavy loads over pitted roads, which sets the Watling Street connection in concrete.

On the left side of the road, pause at the junction with Belsize Road. This corner was once an often robbed bank but is now a Holland & Barrett. Look up to the first floor. The stone plaque marks the site of Kilburn Wells, once a producer of slightly bitter and saline water said to have had, after three slow pints, a purgative effect.

A few feet east is where the Kylebourne or Kelebourne stream flowed into a lake making all the purgation possible. Meadows beyond were used as pleasure grounds. It was most likely in these meadows that Keats composed his

'Ode to a Nightingale' in the summer of 1819. He recited the poem to his friend, the painter Benjamin Haydon, 'in low tremulous undertone' that, Haydon wrote, affected him greatly. They listened as the nightingale's

plaintive anthem fades
Past the near meadows, over the still stream,
Up the hill-side; and now 'tis buried deep
In the next valley glades.

Opposite is Kilburn Bookshop, whose plaintive but solitary 21-year crusade to bring the word to the people is unmatched along Watling Street. Around Kilburn High Road mainline station, look to the south-west and you should see the 250-foot tower of St Augustine's on Kilburn Park Road (considered by Simon Jenkins in his *England's Thousand Best Churches* to be in the top 50), a Gothic redbrick Victorian church with a vaulted interior, third in size only to St Paul's and Westminster Abbey. Visit it with the adjectives 'awesome', 'stunning' and 'breathtaking' forming on your lips.

Just before Kilburn Park Road, Oxford Road on the right was the home between 1893 and 1899 of Israel Zangwill, a leading Zionist and author of the very-apt-for-this-end-of-town *King of the Schnorrers* (beggars). He also wrote *Ghetto Tragedies* while living at No.24.

Beyond the junction of Kilburn Park Road on the right and Kilburn Priory on the left is Maida Vale. If you haven't liked Kilburn, blame it on a little guy called Godwyn. For it was Godwyn the Hermit who, in the early 12th century, built a cell for himself near the stream and started the rush. Three nuns by the names of Emma, Gunhilda and Christina took over in 1134, establishing the Kilburn Priory, which helped St Albans-bound pilgrims with food, lodgings and a haven from robbers on the wooded road for 400 years thereafter.

Which brings us, inevitably, to Allah and Charles Chaplin. Before you on the left are the unmistakeable twin, copper-domed towers of the Maida Vale Picture Palace, now home to an Islamic Centre. Chaplin's first full-length feature, *The Kid*, starring Jackie Coogan and Chaplin himself, opened here in 1921. The Palace itself started selling its 1,500 tickets in 1913. In the intervening years it has claimed the dubious privilege of being (what else?) the UK's first commercial bingo hall in 1961.

Maida Vale's dimensions contrast dramatically with anything else on the A5; its name is derived from the 1806 Battle of Maida in Italy in which the British defeated the French. In short, Maida Vale simply isn't British. At least, it represented a new Britishness, a luxurious urban Continentalism that became a part of metropolitan lifestyle from the 1830s on. This is how the other half intended to live: in apartment blocks with carriage drives rather than in houses, not railed, crowded or bespattered by passing traffic but as stylish boulevardiers, practitioners of the stroll.

At 136 Maida Vale (next to the Islamic Centre), a small 1990s council block cowers in the gap left after the demolition of William Friese-Greene's house. Remember that behind you is the Picture Palace, for Friese-Greene was a motion picture pioneer. He patented the first motion picture camera – two years before Edison's Kinetoscope in 1891 – and was the first to suggest that Edison's phonograph could be linked to it to create a talking picture. He once had a blue plaque. Buy some paper, cut a disc, colour it blue, stick the guy's name on it, date it 1855-1921 and superglue it to the council wall.

Stroll on. Carlton Hill to the left and Carlton Vale to the right take their names, and their prestige, from the baronial Carlton House in Pall Mall later associated with the lavish Prince Regent. The *Kilburn Times* was first published in Carlton Vale in 1868. On the right past the junction, a plaque on the St George's Catholic School commemorates Philip Lawrence, the headteacher who was stabbed on 8 December 1995 as he tried to help a pupil. Continue past townhouses on the left, some, like No.68, with wrought-iron and stained-glass porches, others warning of dangerous dogs.

On the right along Elgin Avenue is the beautifully preserved Maida Vale tube station. Charles Booth, who categorised Maida Vale's streets for his 1889 study *Life and Labour of the People*, found only those that were upper class and well-to-do, and none that were 'vicious, semi-criminal or in chronic want'. A commentator on Jewish affairs wrote in 1902: 'Jews who put down their bundles... rest not until they have given up the struggle or found social salvation in Maida Vale.' Even in 1972 the *Financial Times* described Maida Vale as 'middle aged, middle class, middle European'.

On the left is Wellesley Court and on the right is Hamilton Court on the corner of Abercorn Place, completed in 1836 and 1838 respectively. Note the Tudor-style Vale Close on the left with its timber doorway and wrought-iron tradesmen's entrance. Just past Vale Close is the junction of Hall Road to the left, Sutherland Avenue to the right. This pleasant junction is really about murder. And from it emerges an unlikely conjunction of fact, fiction and the A6.

Fact: on 28 December 1836, next door to the home of journalist George Augustus Sala in Pineapple Villas, a bricklayer called Bond discovered a blood-soaked package. It contained the remains – the trunk without head or legs – of a woman. Her head, part sawn, part broken, was later discovered in Ben Jonson Lock in Regent's Canal. An osier-cutter found her legs in February 1837 in a ditch in Cold Harbour Lane, Camberwell. The murderer, James Greenacre, used a canvas bag and public transport to get the bits about,

at one point suggesting to an omnibus conductor that he 'ought to pay for two passengers'. He was hanged on 2 May 1837.

Fiction: the streets of Maida Vale to the west of the main road are the rough setting for Hitchcock's 1954 *Dial M for Murder*. Although the action takes place exclusively inside a flat, it's the local telephone number, MAI 3499, that puts the 'M' into 'Murder'.

And finally, the A6: along Sutherland Avenue was the Hotel Vienna, where petty thief James Hanratty stayed on the night of the so-called A6 murder in which a man was shot dead and his girlfriend severely injured. A cartridge case from the gun was found in Hanratty's room. He was hanged on 17 February 1962, and his guilt is still being disputed despite recent DNA evidence that seemed to reconfirm it.

Turn left into Hall Road for a diversion that connects Hanratty to the Beatles to the origins of Kilburn to a song about a Maida Vale traffic warden. Hall Road – home to composer Sir Edward German as he completed Sullivan's opera *The Emerald Isle* in 1901 – takes you past the red-brick and stucco Hamilton Terrace and on to Grove End Road. Bear left on to Abbey Road, so-called because it leads to Kilburn Priory. On the left, at No.3, you will find the famous 1931 studios, that famous zebra crossing, and somewhat less famous Japanese tourists.

John Lennon, who accused the British state of murder following Hanratty's hanging, did his first recording session here with the Beatles on 6 June 1962. Paul McCartney, who tried to park his car around here many times in the early '60s, got to know local traffic warden Meta (not meter) Davis. It was for her that he wrote 'Lovely Rita' after she ticketed his car.

Back to Maida Vale, and a succession of courts: Florence to the left, Sandringham to the right, the timbered arch gateway of Clive Court also on the right, and the later Rodney Court of 1915 on the left opposite the fancy entrance mouldings of Alexandra Court, and Mackenzie Lodge.

Abbey Road

Beyond them to the left is St John's Wood Road, leading to Lord's Cricket Ground.

These monolithic, soulless but superior courts belie the decline of other parts of Maida Vale. By the 1930s the streets to the west, south of Kilburn Park, teemed with sleazy bedsits. Poet Stephen Spender, a sometime resident of these streets, said that Maida Vale 'almost rivals Berlin in its atmosphere of decay'. His friend, South African poet William Plomer, captured street life in the witty 'French Lisette: A Ballad of Maida Vale':

Who strolls so late, for mugs a bait,
In the mists of Maida Vale,
Sauntering past a stucco gate
Fallen, but hardly frail…?
… Now a meaning look conceals the hook
Some innocent fish will swallow,
Chirping 'Hullo, darling!' like a cheeky starling
She'll turn, and he will follow.

Plomer, who died in 1976, recalled seeing many French Lisettes with their 'winks and leerings and Woolworth earrings' standing along Maida Vale 'at regular intervals like lamp posts'.

Turn left on Aberdeen Place for the highly irregular interval of Crocker's Folly. This extraordinarily gaudy Victorian pub, at the end of the street on the left, was never meant to be so secluded. The brainchild of a speculator called Crocker, its combination of marbled bars, moulded ceilings and ample billiard room (now a restaurant) was intended to face Marylebone station. The interval we're talking about is between the completion of the building in 1898 and Crocker's realisation that the station was being built half a mile to the southeast. (He subsequently leapt to his death from an upstairs window.)

Opposite Aberdeen Place are Blomfield Road to the right and Maida Avenue to the left. The Café La Ville straddles the Maida Hill Tunnel over the Grand Union Canal. The canal is partly fed by the waters of the Brent Reservoir and its Paddington arm opened in 1801. Walk down leafy Blomfield Road to Warwick Avenue Bridge to catch a glimpse of tranquil houseboating folk in an urban setting. Meditate on the names they give their floating homes: *Gladstone, Quail, Geranium II.*

Cross the bridge. On the right is Little Venice, which has inspired no end of poetry. Byron compared it to Venice first and the name eventually stuck. And, while in prison in 1874 for shooting Rimbaud in the wrist, Verlaine recalled a visit to Maida Vale: '… a river in the street/Fantastically appeared… moving… without sound'. Maida Vale's part of the Grand Union Canal famously appears in *The Blue Lamp*, Basil Dearden's tense 1949 cop-killer yarn starring Dirk Bogarde.

Turn left, and walk back up Maida Avenue past the Catholic Apostolic church. On the right near the top is a plaque commemorating actor Arthur Lowe. Turn right on to what is now Edgware Road, the final name change before Marble Arch. The A40 Marylebone flyover should be in view ahead.

Turn left at Boscobel Street. Looking left into Hatton Street should give even houseboat folk an unexpected industrial thrill. The Palmer Tyre Company's resplendent, tiled Old Aeroworks, now residential, once built parts for Spitfires, Hurricanes and Lancasters. The plaque on the building completes the A5's association with aircraft manufacturing, from Hendon to Cricklewood to a tiny side street less than a mile from Hyde Park.

Return to Edgware Road. On your left is the Broadway Bagel Bakery, which completes the bagel tour of the A5, too. Diagonally opposite on the right, on the corner of Church Street, is a property developer's scenic board to help us bear the pain of the missing Wheatsheaf Tavern. Ben Jonson was a Wheatsheaf regular, composing *To Celia* here:

*Drink to me only with thine eyes
And I will pledge with mine.*

Perhaps it was one of Jonson's many acolytes who wrote *The Puritaine, or The Widow of Watling Street*, a 1607 comedy by an unknown. Perhaps it was one of the Fraternity of High Toby, a highway gang that went drinking and robbing along this route. Shakespeare, too, haunts this part of town, once a player in the Red Lion, now also demolished.

On the left hand, eastern, side of Church Street there is a cheap, popular pre-World War I weekend market.

Continue down to Edgware Road tube – tempting but you cannot cop out now. Instead, note the sign for the telephone and the classic interior. It was one of seven new stations built along the world's first underground system in 1863. You are now in the shadow of two not exactly sub-atomic realities: the 1973 Metropole Hotel (now the Hilton Metropole) and the 1967 flyover. The latter, a sign tells us, is an 'Air Quality Improvement Area'. The 350-yard slab of solid and vibrated concrete, which carries the A40 west, sits like a lid on the junction, physically and psychologically sealing the West End beyond.

Past it on the corner of Chapel Street is a 1959 Marks & Spencer. Poignantly for contemporary customers and business analysts, it stands on the site of a pre-World War I Penny Bazaar. Behind it is the 16-storey Foster Wheeler (now Capital) House. When it was built in 1967, *Private Eye* described the high-rise as being 'cleverly unrelated to its low-rise neighbour'. It still is.

On the left is the cleverly related paintwork of the 1885 King's Arms. Cross the road towards the striking façade of the 1797 Robertsons pawn-brokers. Its neighbour, on the corner of Star Street, is a Lloyds Bank whose window you should examine. In it, among the usual bankery, is the Tyburn Milestone. Or at least a half-a-milestone

since it marks half a mile from Tyburn Turnpike House, which in turn marked the junction of Oxford Street to the east, Bayswater Road to the west and Edgware Road to the north.

Cross to Crawford Street and walk down a few steps. On the left are the Christian Union Almshouses. On the right, beneath the arch of a 1939 block, is Cato Street. No walk would be complete without a conspiracy and this was the scene of one of London's finest. The radical Cato Street Conspirators plotted to murder the whole cabinet as they dined in Grosvenor Square. The Bow Street Runners (the cops) attacked on 23 February 1820 and put paid to their plan, arresting all of them eventually. A plaque on the right above a stable marks the event.

Continue to the end of Cato Street and turn right into Harrowby Street. At the end of Harrowby, as you glance back, is the glitzy stairway of the Victoria Casino. Cross the road. Directly opposite is Burwood Place, where Keats's painter friend Benjamin Haydon lived, although the precise address (Nos.4, then 12) no longer exists. It was also here that Haydon committed suicide aged 60 on 22 June 1846 in front of one of his colossal historical paintings. What connects him to this walk, even more than either his address or his Kilburn meadows nightingale experience, is his work. Haydon complained bitterly that his paintings were neglected, but one at least, on display at the Tate Britain, captures the times. The 1829 *Punch or May Day* shows us an intense London street scene, 'life' as Haydon described it, Dickensian in scope with its newly-weds, funeral hearse, fruitseller, pickpocket, black coachman and crowd entertainer.

Continue down Edgware Road past phone boxes by now plastered in prostitutes' cards. The Lebanese and Middle Eastern population is evident on the streets and in the many bars and restaurants. On the corner of George

Little Venice

Street on the left is Beirut Express with a good window in which to drink juice and gaze before the last quarter-mile. On the right further down is the Al Ahram Bookshop, the biggest Arab bookshop in London. Café du Liban, also on the right, is another place to smoke a narghile or sheesha and the Al-Dar Lebanese restaurant is a good place to eat. If day is turning to night, note the landmark pink, green and blue neon of a kebab restaurant on the right. Cross to the

corner of Stourcliffe Street. Looking to the end of the street you will see the stained glass of the 1840 West London Synagogue of British Jews. Its entrance is on Upper Berkeley Street.

The Harley-Davidson in the window of the Signor Marco Italian restaurant on the left is telling you that the A5 needs a Route 66-style song written about it. On the corner of Bryanston Street at No.20 is a bar that takes its name from the Tyburn gallows: the Tyburn Tree.

The more or less inaccessible stone disc marking the gallows itself is in the traffic island where the Edgware Road ends, opposite the Odeon cinema (which in 1928 showed the world's first talkie, *The Singing Fool* starring Al Jolson). They were in use for almost 600 years, the first recorded execution being in 1196, the last in 1783. Notorious 22-year-old highwayman Jack Sheppard, written about by Kilburn's Harrison Ainsworth, was hanged at Tyburn in 1724 watched by 200,000 Londoners. As Bill Naughton wrote in his classic story 'Late Night on Watling Street': 'He might have got one across the law, but he hadn't got one across Watling Street.'

Time now to turn your first real corner. With the Central line tube on your left, take a moment to ponder the confluence of two great routes. Watling Street from the north meets the Tyburn Way, now Oxford Street, in the form of Marble Arch. This is certainly the physical end of the walk and, after 12 or so miles, the meeting of obelisk and arch is surely some psycho-sexual comfort.

But Marble Arch is an appropriate end, too. You have navigated the uncertainties of approximate Roman settlements, missing stone tablets and columns, a wrongly placed plaque, a wrongly named street, a missing plaque, a disappeared cross and lamp post, and a virtually inaccessible stone disc. Well, Marble Arch is a displaced arch. It was designed by John Nash in 1828 to be the entrance to Buckingham Palace. Due to lack of space there, it was moved here in 1851.

Obelisks are erected and big arches get built, but a road is never really completed, its constant use, abuse and repair justifying its existence throughout the ages. Its runes and symbols appear and disappear but, in the end, it is pure and simple wayfaring that keeps Watling Street alive.

Eating & drinking

Al-Dar
61-63 Edgware Road, W2 2HZ (7402 2541/ www.aldar.co.uk). **Meals served** 8am-1am daily. Sheeshas, fruit juices, grills, meze and cakes.

Beirut Express
112-114 Edgware Road, W2 2DZ (7724 2700). **Open** 7am-2am daily. Lebanese food.

Blacking Bottle
122-126 High Street, Edgware, Middx HA8 7EL (8381 1485). **Open** 11am-11pm Mon-Sat; noon-10.30pm Sun. **Food served** noon-9pm daily.

Black Lion
274 Kilburn High Road, NW6 2BY (7624 1424/ www.blacklionguesthouse.com). **Open** noon-midnight Mon-Fri; 11am-midnight Sat; noon-11.30pm Sun. **Food served** noon-3pm, 6-10pm Mon-Fri; 11am-10pm Sat; noon-9.30pm Sun.

Broadway Bagel Bakery
394 Edgware Road, W2 1ED (7723 4481). **Open** 8am-7pm Mon-Sat; 9am-4pm Sun.

Café Anglais
1-2 Sheaveshill Parade, Edgware Road, NW9 6RS (8205 3720). **Open** 6.30am-6.30pm daily. Breakfasts galore and cheery staff.

Café du Liban
71 Edgware Road, W2 2HZ (7706 1534). **Open** 9am-midnight daily. Juices, cakes and full Lebanese menu, and, of course, sheeshas.

Café Laville
453 Edgware Road, W2 1TH (7706 2620). **Open** 10am-10.30pm Mon-Fri; 9am-10.30pm Sat, Sun. Café/restaurant hybrid, straddling the canal.

Change of Hart
21 High Street, Edgware, Middx HA8 7EE (8952 0039). **Open** 11am-11pm Mon-Sat; noon-10.30pm Sun. **Food served** noon-9pm daily.

Cock Tavern
125 Kilburn High Road, NW6 6JH (7624 1820). **Open** 11am-11pm Mon-Sat; noon-10.30pm Sun. **Food served** noon-7pm Mon-Sat; noon-6pm Sun.

Cookies & Cream
321-323 Kilburn High Road, NW6 7JR (7328 9262). **Open** 7am-11pm daily.

Crown Moran Hotel
152 Cricklewood Broadway, NW2 3ED (8452 4175). **Open** *Restaurant* 12.30-2.30pm, 5.30-10pm Mon-Fri, Sun; 5.30-10pm Sat.

Harp
117 Edgware Road, NW9 7BP (8202 6793). **Open** 11am-11pm Mon-Wed; 11am-midnight Thur; 11am-2am Fri, Sat; 11.30am-midnight Sun. **Food served** noon-3pm daily.

Nando's
308 Kilburn High Road, NW6 2DG (7372 1507/ www.nandos.co.uk). **Open** noon-11.30pm Mon-Thur, Sun; noon-midnight Fri, Sat.

Prince of Wales
218 Burnt Oak Broadway, HA8 0AP (8952 1510). **Open** 11am-11pm Mon-Sat; noon-10.30pm Sun. Food served.

Red Lion
95 Edgware Road, The Hyde, NW9 6LJ (8205 8430). **Open** noon-11pm Mon-Sat; noon-10.30pm Sun. **Food served** until 30mins before closing.

Southern K
205 Kilburn High Road, NW6 (7624 2066). **Open** noon-11pm Mon-Thur; noon-12am Fri, Sat; noon-10.30pm Sun. Food served.

Zan Zi Bar
113 High Street, Edgware, Middx HA8 7DB (8952 2986). **Open** noon-midnight daily. Indian food served.

Clubs

Ashtons Night Club
194 Cricklewood Broadway, NW2 3EB (8450 5390/www.galtymore.co.uk). **Open** 9pm-2am last Fri of mth. **Admission** £6. Dress smart casual.

Galtymore Dance Club
194 Cricklewood Broadway, NW2 3EB (8450 5390/www.galtymore.co.uk). **Open** 9pm-2am Sat. **Admission** £7 members; £9 non-members. **Membership** free. Dress smart casual.

Film & literature

The Blue Lamp (Basil Dearden, 1949, GB)
Dial M For Murder (Alfred Hitchcock, 1953, US)
Dick Turpin (John G Blystone, 1925, US)
England's Thousand Best Churches Simon Jenkins (2000)
Ghetto Tragedies Israel Zangwill (1893)
Hell Drivers (Cy Endfield, 1957, GB)
The Kid (Charles Chaplin, 1921, US)
King of the Schnorrers Israel Zangwill (1894)
Late Night on Watling Street Bill Naughton (1959)
Rookwood Harrison Ainsworth (1834)
The Singing Fool (Lloyd Bacon, 1928, US)
She Stoops to Conquer (George Loane Tucker, 1914, GB)

Shopping

Al Ahram Bookshop
73 Edgware Road, W2 2HZ (7706 4333). **Open** *Summer* 9am-10pm daily. *Winter* 9am-9.30pm daily.

Kilburn Bookshop
8 Kilburn Bridge, Kilburn High Road, NW6 6HT (7328 7071). **Open** 10am-6pm Mon-Sat.

Oriental City Food Court
399 Edgware Road, NW9 0JJ (8200 0009). **Meals served** 10.30am-9.30pm Mon-Sat; 10am-8.30pm Sun. Various oriental food stalls.

Two Jays Bookshop
119 High Street, Edgware, Middx HA8 7DB (8952 1349). **Open** 9am-5pm Tue-Sat.

Others

British Library Newspaper Library
Colindale Avenue, NW9 5HE (7412 7353/www.bl.uk). **Open** 10am-5pm Mon-Sat. Last requests at 4.15pm. Readers must be over 18; ID required.

London Orthopaedic Hospital
Royal National Orthopaedic Trust, Brockley Hill, Stanmore, Middx HA7 (8954 2300).

MCC Lord's Cricket Ground
St John's Wood Road, NW8 8QN (7289 1611/ www.lords.org).

Royal Air Force Museum Hendon
Grahame Park Way, NW9 5LL (8205 2266/ www.rafmuseum.org). **Open** 10am-6pm daily. Last entry 5.30pm. **Admission** free.

Tricycle Theatre & Cinema
269 Kilburn High Road, NW6 7JR (7328 1000/ www.tricycle.co.uk). **Open** *Box office* 10am-9pm Mon-Sat; 2-9pm Sun.

Welsh Harp Conservation Group
(Roy Bedd 8447 1810/John Colmans 8446 4029). Guided walks 10am one Sunday per month.

Religion

Chinese Church
Varley Parade, Edgware Road, NW9 6RR (7602 9092). **Service** 2pm Sun.

Hyde United Reform Church
Varley Parade, Edgware Road, NW9 6RR (8200 9123). **Services** 1.15pm Wed; 10am Sun.

Hendon Islamic Centre
Brent View Road, West Hendon, NW9 7EL (8202 3236). **Open** *Summer* 4-4.30am, 1-2pm, 6.30-7.30pm, 8.30-9.30pm, 10-10.30pm daily; *Winter* 6.30-7am, 1-2pm, 2.30-3.30pm, 4-6.30pm, 7-8pm daily.

Islamic Centre England
140 Maida Vale, W9 1QB (7604 5500). **Open** 9am-5pm Mon-Fri.

St Augustine's
Kilburn Park Road, NW6 5XB (7624 1637/ 7328 9301). **Open** 7.30-8.30am, 5.30-6pm Mon, Wed-Fri, Sun; 9.30am-noon Tue, Sat.

St Cuthbert's
Fordwych Road, NW2 3TG (8452 1913). **Services** 10.30am, 6.30pm Sun.

St Margaret's
1 Station Road, Edgware, Middx HA8 7JE (8952 4066). **Services** 11am Sun.

Shree Gayatri Mandir
201 The Broadway, West Hendon, NW9 7DE (8202 1000). **Open** 9am-7.30pm daily.

Done Roman

Rick Jones

Follow the course of the old Roman wall that surrounded Londinium and the later medieval city.

Start: Tower Hill tube
Finish: Blackfriars tube/rail
Time: 1-2 hours
Distance: 3 miles/4.5km
Getting there: District or Circle lines to Tower Hill or DLR to Tower Gateway
Getting back: District or Circle lines or Thameslink from Blackfriars
Note: it is worth planning this walk to coincide with as many open churches as possible; therefore, it is probably best to avoid weekends. There is some overlap with Joy Wotton's walk.

London was built by Italians, of course. They settled here only a decade after the execution of the upstart Jesus in another province of the Roman Empire and stayed for nearly 400 years, which shows how much they liked Britannia. They had villas in the Cotswolds. Londinium prospered and attracted the attention of marauding and possibly bogus asylum-seeking Saxons from across the North Sea, which necessitated the erection of a defensive wall in AD 200. It ran in an arc from Tower Bridge round to Blackfriars enclosing an area of 330 acres. The Roman sentries who marched round the top, therefore, paced out the first official walk in the history of the city. Some of the wall still stands. Walker, don your boots! It is the Roman sentry's beat we follow.

Start at Tower Hill tube. Walk the short underpass towards the Tower of London. Stop at the iron railing. Here is the first bit of rubble to be identified

as part of the ancient wall. A handsome blue-and-white-tiled panel nearby to the left reveals that the ancient stones are all that is left of a medieval postern gate into the city. It was built around 1300 on top of the much older Roman wall. This is how it was before the heavily regulated era of council planning permission. Londoners just built on to what was there before. No one removed Londinium. It is still there underneath the present city. Dig that, Tony Robinson! The only surprising thing about finding old coins in the mud is how careless people were with their money in previous centuries. If nothing else, the walk shows by how much the level of the city streets has risen with layer upon layer of earth, cobbles, asphalt, tarmacadam and general rubbish.

The tiled panel is marked with the number 1. Retrace your steps back through the underpass to find number 2. In all there are 21 of these panels marking out the course of the London Wall Walk, although some have gone missing over the years since they were established at a cost of £30,000 in 1984. This is unhelpful, as each panel tells you where the next is to be found. The Roman Department at the Museum of London is seeking a sponsor to pay for replacements. If you are a millionaire in search of a little publicity, you could be the benefactor they are looking for.

The wall is very tall at panel number 2 by Tower Hill tube. It is Roman to 14 feet and medieval above that. The Roman part is marked by layers of red tiles, which were put in to bond and strengthen the wall. The later addition is not so well

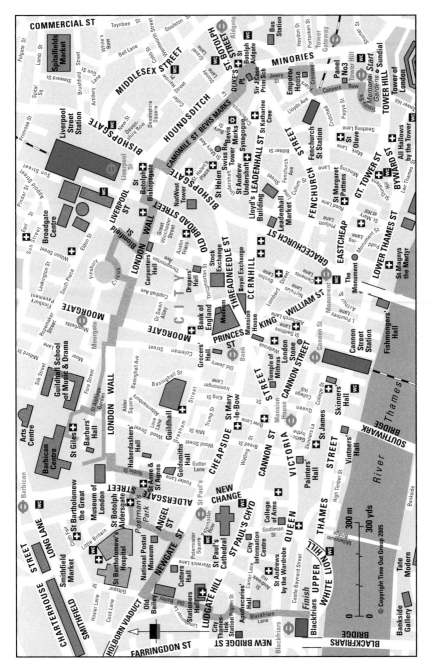

built. It is one thing to have building regulations but quite another to live with shoddy practices. Civilisations regress after the disappearance of an empire. The British are experiencing their own decline now. Nothing works like it used to. All we can do is slow the descent and hope for a soft landing.

There is a bench nearby and a 19th-century bronze statue believed to be of Trajan, Emperor of Rome from AD 98 to 117. Not even the donor, the late Reverend 'Tubby' Clayton of the nearby church of All Hallows-by-the-Tower, was sure of its provenance. More relevant is the slab with the Roman inscription. It is a replica of one found during excavations and commemorates the provincial procurator (tax collector) Julius Classicianus who by contemporary accounts made a good job of getting the province back on its feet after the murderous revolt in AD 60 by Boadicea, the first feminist and queen of the Norfolk-based Iceni tribe. The original stone is the oldest piece of writing in the country and now lies in the British Museum.

Walk back along Trinity Place. Visit the giant sundial on the mound where public executions took place until 1747. There was a time when people thought it edifying to watch summary justice in action. They took their children. The encircling beds have not been well maintained and are full of stinging nettles. By comparison the memorial gardens a little further on in Trinity Square are beautifully kept. The names of the tens of thousands of merchant seamen and fishermen who lost their lives in the two world wars are inscribed here. It is the most peaceful spot in the City. Rest a while if you have no appointment to keep. The duration of the walk is not set in stone, unlike the names of the drowned.

Continue along Cooper's Row. Panel number 3 is missing, but the Roman wall is still there, on the piazza behind the spectacular five-star Grange City Hotel. Coopers are barrel-makers. Appropriately the ancient street is full of pubs – Pepys

Bar, Pitcher & Piano, the Cheshire Cheese. Walk under the railway bridge on top of which is Fenchurch Street station, the most obscure of the Monopoly board stations. Turn right into Crosswall. Pass an elegant neo-art deco office block labelled One America Square. Not all the City's buildings are drab and grey. Turn left at the Angel pub into Vine Street. Panel number 4 is on the left at the Emperor House office block, which is drab and brown. Nod to addictive office workers who have been sent outside to smoke. Enter through the tradesmen's gate. The Roman wall, which includes part of a catapult tower, is in the cellar but visible from the outside through windows. The Romans walked around at basement level. London has risen like a cake.

At the end of Vine Street, turn left into India Street and right into Jewry Street. Pass the entrance to London Metropolitan University. The students have a section of the Roman wall in their basement, too, but it is inaccessible unless you enrol. If you cannot spare three years for any of the many bachelor courses offered by the university, continue to the end of Jewry Street, cross Aldgate and you will find panel number 5 fixed to the wall of the Sir John Cass Foundation Primary School. The panel has a picture of the Roman gate that straddled the long straight road from Colchester or Camulodonum, an even older Roman settlement. It fed straight into the road (now Leadenhall Street) to the forum (at Cornhill), the great open market and business square on the north side of which the sentry could see the basilica, the headquarters of the judiciary and the grandest building in Londinium. When the Romans left, the Saxons viewed the spooky Roman capital as a 'city of giants' and left it largely uninhabited. It was only in the medieval period that people returned in numbers and made use of what was there. The panel also displays a picture of the poet Geoffrey Chaucer who lived in the gate when he worked as a customs official. Opposite is the church of St Botolph-without-Aldgate, where Daniel Defoe, the author of *Robinson Crusoe*, was married. A number of genuine London alcoholics waste the day in the peaceful garden.

But of the Roman wall there is no sign. It lies below the street. The pedestrian underpass leading to Duke's Place cuts through it but a mosaicist has marked its course in the subterranean wall. Descend to see. Follow the subway through towards exit 1, and here you will find panel number 6 and a further illustration of how we are walking around on the heads of our ancestors.

Emerge out of exit 1, and continue to panel number 7 on the south-west side of Bevis Marks, which was where the Abbot of Bury St Edmunds lived – Bevis being a corruption of Burics. Houndsditch, which runs parallel, was the accepted dump for dead dogs. The Sha Hasha Ma'im or Gate of Heaven or, indeed, Bevis Marks Synagogue, replaced the abbot's house in 1700, the first to be built in London since Oliver Cromwell invited the Jews

back in 1657. Puritanism had a positive side. It is also known as the Spanish and Portuguese Synagogue because many of the first members were refugees from persecution by the Inquisition. Benjamin Disraeli was a member of the congregation in the 19th century. Step inside and breathe the calmness but don't forget to put on a skullcap if you are a man. There is a tray of them by the door.

Proceed to the end of Bevis Marks and stroll into Camomile Street. In 1993, an Irish terrorist bomb in Bishopsgate blew up panel number 8 along with the wall it was fixed to, a hapless freelance journalist, an entire medieval church, a parade of shops and a very large number of windows. The Roman wall was already rubble. It ran through the beautiful churchyard of St Botolph-without-Bishopsgate where Edward Alleyn the Shakespearean actor and John Keats the poet were baptised and where panel 9 should be. There is no sign of it. No worry. Sit here awhile. If it is lunchtime, there may be girls on the netball court.

A statue, believed to represent **Emperor Trajan**, holds forth in front of the Roman wall.

Panel 20 of the **London Wall** walk looks down on a corner of the Roman fort.

Up you get. Walk out through the west end of the churchyard past Cina's Italian Restaurant and out into London Wall. The church of All Hallows-on-the-Wall is built against the ancient brickwork. You can see where the Roman tower was in the vestry. The upper parts of the wall in the churchyard are medieval. In those days, people constructed their houses around it. It was like Delhi. Panel number 10 would explain all this if it were there. But it is not.

Make a slight detour into Finsbury Circus, where there are some very tall plane trees and the bowling green is the pride of the City. Sometimes there is music in the bandstand. Complete a circuit and return to London Wall. Stay on the north side and cross Moorgate where panel number 11 should be. Look for it in vain. That £30,000 is starting to look like a poor investment.

Climb the steps to the flying pedestrian walkway and march along St Alphage Highwalk, which runs parallel to London Wall; this will make you feel even more like the Roman sentry. After a short distance – just after St Alphage House, behind the shops – descend by steps into St Alphage Garden, where the ancient wall is long, high and sturdy. The medieval brickwork

is geometrically decorated and the flower beds are full of seasonal plants and shrubs. The garden is a haven and was once part of the yard around St Alphage church, of which only half a wall and a couple of Gothic windows remain. Panel number 12 is here. Water has seeped under the grouting and frost has burst the tiles.

Before the Romans built the wall, they maintained a fort at Londinium. The garrison housed the governor of Britannia's official guard, which consisted of about 1,000 infantry men and cavalry officers, or somewhat less than a full legion. The governor's palatial residence is buried beneath Cannon Street station half a mile away. Daily changes of guard would march from the fort and back. Centurions practised marching, sword-fighting and chariot-racing. Everyone spoke Latin. '*Caesar ad sum iam forte. Et cetera*'.[1] The ghosts of gladiators pass by on their way to the 11,000-seat amphitheatre that lies beneath the new Guildhall Art Gallery off Gresham Street. The floor inside the entrance there shows part of the perimeter of the arena. Plans are afoot to allow public access to the excavated ruins, but no date has yet been given. For now you will have to imagine the muscular athletes marching off to box, run or throw the discus in civilised competition. You are sitting inside the fort looking at the north wall, which, along with the west one, eventually became part of the two-mile city wall.

When you have explored the garden and sat down for a breather, walk on to the corner with Wood Street, where you will find panel number 13. It marks the site of Cripplegate, which was the northern entrance to the Roman fort. The road ran straight to Islington, which was just a peasant village on a hill in Roman times. Nowadays, Islington likes to go to peasant villages near Rome. A barbican, or fortified watch-tower, projected from the gate. It gave its name to the area outside it, Barbican, and eventually the exclusive residence, botanical garden, library and arts centre that was opened in 1982 and is home to, among others, the Royal Shakespeare Company. You are entering its peaceful environs now. Pop along to the box office and buy a ticket to see *Julius Caesar* if it is on. Beware the Ides of March.

From Wood Street turn left into the pedestrian precinct around the church of St Giles Cripplegate next to the City of London Girls' School and the Guildhall School of Music and Drama. Hear the brass players practising and a soprano or two trying to shatter the windows. Ducks swim peacefully on the artificial lakes. Over by the fountains are the cafés outside the Barbican. Shakespeare visited St Giles. His brother's bastard child was baptised, Oliver Cromwell married and the blind poet John Milton buried in it.

Panel 14 is attached to railings. The crumbling wall here relishes its salubrious environment. *O mure felix!*[2] It squats in its young surroundings like a much loved grandparent. A swan swims by. There are ruined turrets in the wall across the lake. One of them secretes a park bench but it is only accessible to the residents of the expensive Barbican apartments. You can see into their rooms. Some of them are judges who are sensitive about their security and do not want their

peace disturbed by noisy tourists such as yourself tramping through. This is why further progress is barred by locked gates and you may only continue to follow the wall by doubling back on yourself.

Pass by panel 13 again and ascend the steps at the western end of St Alphage Garden. If you have not eaten, you may find the presence of Pizza Express, El Vino's wine bar or the lowly City News fortuitous.

Just before you emerge from the covered shopping area, descend by steps to the gardens by Barber Surgeons' Hall where you can already see the medieval turrets and uneven outline of the continuing city wall. Follow the path across the grass and along the side of the pond until you can go no further. From here you will be able to see St Giles church again and, better still, the actual north-west corner of the Roman fort (which we glimpsed earlier from St Giles). A World War II bomb and the Barbican redevelopment together excavated the area and lowered the ground level to reveal the ruins. Panel number 15 has escaped the attention of Vandals, Visigoths, Saxons and those who still have an interest in destroying the evidence of the Roman occupation.

Not so panels 16 and 17, which once recorded the history of the two west wall towers standing in this surprisingly spacious park. They are nowhere to be seen. Barber Surgeons' Tower was built on to the Roman wall in the 13th century. The ruins now enclose a discreet herb garden – how pungent the prunella vulgaris! – which is appropriate to the members' calling. Medieval barbers assisted monks in practising surgery but were always the senior partners even until 1800. 'Short back and sides and remove my appendix while you're at it, barber!'

Panel number 18 lies by the entrance to the underground car park opposite the medieval tower. It tells of the western gate into the Roman fort, the ruins of which are visible in a separate room within the car park under London Wall. For viewing times ring the Museum of London, says the panel. No need! We have done it for you. They are on the second Tuesday of every month at 11am and again at midday. All you have to do is turn up at either of those times at the reception desk of the Museum of London at the western end of London Wall. Staff will, however, arrange separate group visits if you ask nicely.

Cross London Wall and enter Noble Street alongside, which runs with the last and longest visible section of the Roman wall. Panel 19 at the northern end of the wall has disappeared, but panel 20 at the southern end is intact. It looks down on to the ruined south-west corner of the fort. Access down to the Roman street level is difficult, but the Lutheran church of St Anne and St Agnes is here and it has a lovely garden and lunchtime concerts in its resonant interior on most weekdays.

Continue to the end of Noble Street, turn right into Gresham Street and right again into Aldersgate. The gate itself has gone but panel 21 is there (opposite the entrance into Postman's Park) to reveal that it once faced north and gave on to the livestock market at Smithfield. The sequence of panels ends here because the Museum of London, which established them, is just nearby and would like you to visit. However, you are following *Time Out*'s wall walk to Blackfriars and must cross Aldersgate and enter Postman's Park beside the church of St Botolph-without-Aldersgate, where John Wesley converted to a more methodical and disciplined form of Christianity, later known as Methodism by his followers who now number millions. Postman's Park is famous for its Heroes' Wall, which has nothing to do with the Roman one buried beneath, but which commemorates fatal acts of bravery usually involving rescuing children from burning buildings at the end of the 19th century.

Exit the park by its west gate, turn left into King Edward Street, where you may have a more or less unimpeded view of the north side of St Paul's Cathedral depending on how far the Paternoster Square development has progressed. The Roman sentry would have gazed upon a Temple of Diana, which was there first.

Turn right into Newgate and after a short distance left into Warwick Lane. Admire the carved stonework on the face of the Royal College of Physicians. Turn right into Warwick Square and pass a small garden furnished with a set of Doric columns. Though you have seen nothing of the wall for a while, they will remind you that it and the sentry once passed this way. Descend a flight of steps into a tiled tunnel under the Old Bailey law courts (8am-6pm, Mon-Fri), which occupy the site of the former Newgate Prison. The Roman wall runs through the Old Bailey's cellar and has been preserved behind glass. The general public cannot, unfortunately, see it but they can visit the courts and watch British justice in action. It can still be edifying even without the death sentence. The Romans, of course, were used to much bloodier retribution. Crucifixion was popular. How different the world would have been if Jesus had been served only with life imprisonment.

If the tunnel is shut, retrace your steps to Newgate Street, turn left, walk on a short way and turn left again into the street called Old Bailey; if the tunnel is open, it will bring you to Old Bailey about halfway down. A notice by the front door of the law courts provides details of the trials taking place on any given day. Continue to the bottom of Old Bailey past a sandwich bar, a Thai restaurant and, at the end, a branch of All Bar One. Cross Ludgate Hill when it is safe to do so. Take no risks. Look to the left and feel small and insignificant before the imposing mass of St Paul's Cathedral at the top of the hill. But for the executed Christ we would still be worshipping Diana, goddess of the moon and of the hunt. The tourist gift shops think we still are, with their Lady Di postcards in spinning pavement racks. Post one home to your friends and tell them how London is sending you up the wall.

The sombre mood of Heroes' Wall is not shared by all visitors to **Postman's Park**.

Enter Pageantmaster Court, walk through into Ludgate Broadway and straight on into Blackfriars Lane, which is narrow and Dickensian. At least, by the author of *Hard Times*' day, most offences were rewarded with imprisonment.

Cross Queen Victoria Street and turn into Puddle Dock, where the Romans lined the embankment with wharves and left a boat in the mud for us to discover, which we did in MDCCCCLXII along with some coins, carelessly dropped, from the reign of the Emperor Domitian (AD 81-96), which are now in the Museum of London.

Here the Roman wall met the Thames and the sentry the end of his watch. Here you meet Blackfriars railway station and the end of this chapter. Think of the city that time has buried as you wait to catch a train, chariot or omnibus[3] home. *O tempora, O mores, O lector, vale!*[4]

[1] Caesar had some jam for tea. And the rest.
[2] O happy wall!
[3] For all
[4] O Time, O Customs, Oh Reader, farewell!

Eating & drinking

All Bar One
44 Ludgate Hill, EC4M 7DE (7653 9901/ www.allbarone.co.uk). **Open** 11.30am-11pm Mon-Fri; 11am-5pm Sat. **Food served** noon-10pm Mon-Fri; noon-4pm Sat.

Angel
14 Crosswall, EC3N 2LJ (7702 9751). **Open** 11am-11pm Mon-Fri. **Food served** noon-3pm Mon-Fri.

Cheshire Cheese
48 Crutched Friars, EC3N 2AP (7265 5141). **Open** noon-11pm Mon-Fri. **Food served** noon-8pm Mon-Fri.

Ciro's Pizza Pomodoro
7-8 Bishopsgate Churchyard, EC2M 3TJ (7920 9207/www.pomodoro.co.uk). **Open** noon-midnight Mon-Fri. This listed building, built in 1894 was originally an Ottoman hamam.

City News
1 Bastion High Walk, 125 London Wall, EC2Y 5AS (7600 7979). **Open** 7am-7pm Mon-Fri.

Pepys Bar
Novotel Hotel, 10 Pepys Street, EC3N 2NR (7265 6029/www.accorhotels.com). **Open** noon-11pm Mon-Fri; noon-10.30pm Sat, Sun. **Food served** 7am-11pm Mon-Fri; 9am-10.30pm Sat, Sun.

Pitcher & Piano
The Arches, 9 Crutched Friars, EC3N 2AU (7480 6818/www.pitcherandpiano.com). **Open** 11am-11pm Mon-Fri. **Food served** 11am-10pm Mon-Fri.

Pizza Express
125 Alban Gate, London Wall, EC2Y 5AS (7600 8880/www.pizzaexpress.co.uk). **Open** 11.30am-11pm Mon-Fri; 11.30am-10pm Sat; 11.30am-8pm Sun. Sit astride London Wall at this glass and chrome branch of the reliable chain.

Thai 33
33 Old Bailey, EC4M 7HS (7236 2440/ www.thai33.co.uk). **Open** noon-3.30pm, 6-10pm Mon-Fri.

El Vino
125 London Wall, EC2Y 5AP (7600 6377). **Open/food served** 8.30am-9pm Mon; 8.30am-10pm Tue-Fri.

Museums & galleries

Barbican Art Gallery
Level 3, Barbican Centre, Silk Street, EC2Y 8DS (box office 7638 8891/www.barbican.org.uk). **Open** 10am-6pm Mon, Wed, Fri, Sat; 11am-6pm Tue, Thur, Sun. **Admission** £8; £6 concessions; free under-12s.

Guildhall Art Gallery
Guildhall Yard, off Gresham Street, EC2P 2EJ (7332 3700/www.guildhall-art-gallery.org.uk). **Open** 10am-5pm Mon-Sat (last entry 4.30pm); noon-4pm Sun (last entry 3.45pm). **Admission** £2.50; £1 concessions; free under-16s. Free to all after 3.30pm daily; all day Fri.

Museum of London
150 London Wall, EC2Y 5HN (0870 444 3852/ www.museumoflondon.org.uk). **Open** 10am-5.50pm Mon-Sat; noon-5.50pm Sun. **Admission** free. *Exhibitions* £5; £3 concessions.

Religion

All Hallows-by-the-Tower
Byward Street, EC3R 5BJ (7481 2928). **Open** 9am-6pm Mon-Fri; 10am-5pm Sat, Sun. *Services* 11am Sun.

Bevis Marks Synagogue
*Bevis Marks, EC3A 5DQ (7626 1274/www.bevis
marks.org).* **Open** 11am-1pm Mon-Wed, Fri;
10.30am-12.30pm Sun.

St Anne & St Agnes
*Gresham Street, EC2V 4BX (7606 4986/www.
stanneslutheranchurch.org).* **Open** 10am-6pm Mon-
Fri; 10am-8pm Sun. *Services* 11am, 2pm, 6pm Sun.

St Botolph-without-Aldgate
*Aldgate, EC3N 1AB (7283 1670/
www.stbotolphs.org.uk).* **Open** 10am-3pm Mon-
Fri. *Services* 1pm Mon, Thur; 10.30am Sun.

St Botolph-without-Bishopsgate
Bishopsgate, EC2M 3TL (7588 3388).
Open 8am-5.30pm Mon-Fri. *Services* 1.10pm
Wed; 12.10pm Thur.

St Giles Cripplegate
*Fore Street, Barbican, EC2Y 8DA (7638 1997/
www.stgilescripplegate.com).* **Open** 11am-4pm
Mon-Fri. *Services* 8am, 10am, 4pm Sun.

St Paul's Cathedral
*Ludgate Hill, EC4M 8AD (7246 4128/www.st
pauls.co.uk).* **Open** 8.30am-4pm Mon-Sat. *Crypt,
galleries & ambulatory* 9.30am-4pm Mon-Sat.
Phone to check. *Tours* 11am, 11.30am, 1.30pm,
2pm Mon-Sat. **Admission** *Cathedral, crypt &
gallery* £8; £3.50 6-16s; £7 concs; free under-6s;
£19.50 family. **Audio guide** £3.50; £3 concs.

Others

City Bowling Club
Finsbury Circus, EC2M 7AB (no phone). **Open**
members only.

City Information Centre
St Paul's Churchyard, EC4M 8BX (7332 1456).
Open *Easter-Sept* 9.30am-5pm daily; *Oct-Easter*
9.30am-5pm Mon-Fri; 9.30am-12.30pm Sat.

City Parks & Gardens Office
7374 4127/www.cityoflondon.gov.uk.

Grange City Hotel
*8-10 Cooper's Row, EC3N 2BD, (7863 3700/
www.grangehotels.com).*

London Metropolitan University
*31 Jewry Street, EC3N 2EY (7320 1616/
www.londonmet.ac.uk).*

Postman's Park
*between King Edward Street & Aldersgate Street,
EC2 (7332 1456).* **Open** 8am-dusk daily.

Reflect on your walk at the **Barbican**.

Tales of the riverbank

Simon Hoggart

A feast of Ham House, Eel Pie Island and Marble Hill, all along the merry Thames.

> **Start:** Richmond tube/rail
> **Finish:** Richmond tube/rail
> **Time:** 5-6 hours
> **Distance:** 9 miles/15km
> **Getting there:** District line or rail to Richmond
> **Getting back:** District line or rail from Richmond
> **Note:** although this is a long walk, it can be truncated by a journey on Hammerton's Ferry.

This walk takes in part of Richmond, but is mainly about Twickenham. These days Twickenham is often seen as just another suburb, half an hour from Waterloo, but a couple of centuries ago it was regarded by some as a rural paradise – as peaceful and charming as anywhere in the English countryside, but with the advantage of being just a couple of hours' ride from London. Alexander Pope lived here, as did Alfred Lord Tennyson and JMW Turner. More recently it was a cradle of British rhythm and blues; bands that played their earliest gigs here went on to conquer the world. This walk will take you past some of the finest houses in the London area, by superb riverside vistas, into near wilderness, and also through perfectly ordinary suburbia that could have been transplanted from the North Circular.

Leave Richmond station by its main entrance, cross the road opposite, the Quadrant, and turn left. Shortly after, turn right down Duke Street, which brings you to the east corner of Richmond Green. This is the start of a brief trail in which you hunt for rock, film and TV stars,

many of whom live in the massive houses now surrounding you. Cross the Green diagonally towards the west, where you'll come to what remains of Richmond Palace, occupied by Henry VII, Henry VIII and Elizabeth I, but largely demolished after the execution of Charles I. Now it's a mishmash of original buildings, plus numerous additions. It still exerts a powerful charm. Follow signs to the river, which will take you down Old Palace Lane. This leads to the towpath where you begin the main part of the walk.

Turn left and walk upstream along the Surrey bank. There are two pubs within a short distance: the White Cross and Slug & Lettuce, both with space for alfresco drinking, both tending to be crowded at weekends. Next you pass the impressive Quinlan Terry development facing Corporation Island, one of the many small islets (or 'eyots') in this stretch of the Thames. This part of the river is bustling with pleasure boats and launches, and the bank is dotted with bars, cafés, little shops, tearooms and restaurants.

Pass under Richmond Bridge and follow the path round the first of many great bends in the river. Above you is Richmond Hill (worth a detour if you're feeling energetic), lined with homes even more expensive, in some cases, than those on the Green. It's not enough to be a rock star to live here; you need to be a superstar, or a megastar if you're lucky. Mick Jagger and Pete Townsend are among those who have homes here. If they're not in, they might be dining in Canyon, the restaurant on the riverside just below the Hill. You could always

Tales of the riverbank

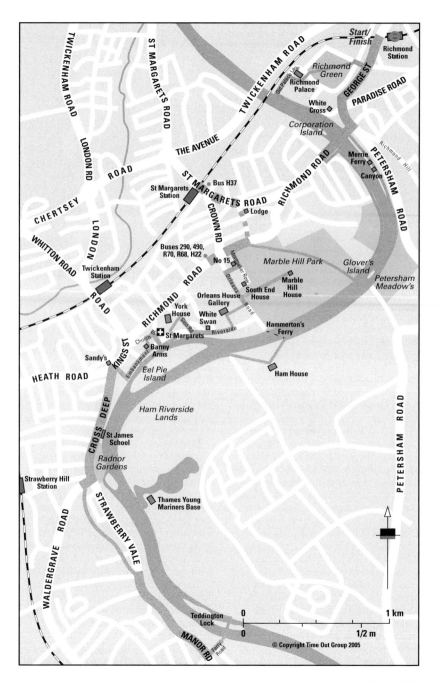

The Thames at **Richmond**, much favoured by rock stars and their acolytes.

glance in and try to spot them (Sunday brunch is very popular), though the prices may well drive you out to the cheaper tea room and snack bars also found nearby.

It's unlikely, but possible, that the towpath will be flooded. If it is, you can wait a short while – it's rarely under water for long – or alternatively climb on board the Merrie Thames launch, which for £4 will take you on a 45-minute round trip to Teddington Lock and back, almost exactly covering the route of this walk.

Assuming you can walk, head down the towpath. You first go past Petersham meadows, usually dotted with livestock and surrounded by trees. It's an almost perfect sylvan scene. You are also now part of the celebrated view from Richmond Hill and may well be under observation by the rock stars as they sip the day's first glass of Roederer Cristal.

As you continue upstream, you'll soon see a handsome Palladian villa, Marble Hill House, and its park on the Middlesex bank. Then on your side you'll quickly reach Ham House.

This was built in 1610 and has recently been refurbished by the National Trust. It's well worth a visit; even if it happens to be closed, the beautifully kept gardens are usually open. On summer weekends you may find a polo match going on behind the house; follow the booming amplified commentary to get there. Anyone can stand and watch, and although the game is almost impossible for most of us to follow, the spectacle is certainly worth a look, and it might give rise to a moment's contemplation on the continued existence of the class system in Britain.

(If you want a much shorter walk, it's possible to take Hammerton's Ferry over to the landing stage at Marble Hill on the Middlesex side.)

Rejoin the river at a point where some idiot has decided that a large and busy car park would enhance the landscape. There are views of riverside Twickenham and some splendid houses of which you'll see more later. Then you reach Eel Pie Island, a strange village marooned in the middle of the river, which looks as if it might float off towards Kent at any moment. There is no connection to the Surrey bank.

On your left you'll pass Ham Lands. Before the war this area was all quarries. Then it was filled in with rubble from the Blitz, and is now left as a sort of managed

wilderness, if such a thing is possible,
dotted with artificial lagoons, and
a nature reserve that is home to a
remarkable variety of wildlife and rare
plants. Foxes, tawny owls, weasels,
woodpeckers, doves, kingfishers and
pheasant have all been seen here. It's
worth drifting off the path for a while,
provided it's not too wet underfoot, to get
a sense of this mysterious, undeveloped
territory, so close to some of the more
expensive suburbia in the country.

On the other bank, in the elbow of
a bend in the river, you'll see St James
independent school, which occupies the
superb site where, until 1809, Alexander
Pope's house stood. When he moved to
Twickenham it was regarded not as an
adjunct of London, and certainly not as
the home of rugby, since William Webb
Ellis had yet to pick up the ball and run
with it. Instead it was thought of as a
rural Elysium a mere two hours' ride
from the capital. Pope wrote of his new
home that there were 'no scenes of
paradise, no happy bowers, equal to
those on the banks of the Thames'.
This was, of course, before the arrival
of Woolworth's and Blockbuster.

Cross the sluice that connects the
Young Mariners' base to the river and
keep on as far as Teddington Lock.
This is actually three locks, including
a massive one, 650 feet long, which can
accommodate a tug and six barges. In
spite of its size, the whole construction
has the feel of a Victorian country railway
halt. The small redbrick office building
dates from 1857, and you expect to see
a twinkle-eyed station master played by
Bernard Cribbins to emerge. In fact, it's
manned by a twinkle-eyed man in a navy
sweater and a nautical cap. There's a
patch of grassland with a bench where
you can sit and watch the boats go by.

A short walk further upstream brings
you to Teddington footbridge, where you
cross over to the Middlesex side. The
expensive houses and their frontages do
not, for the most part, allow you to walk

Eel Pie Island, a village in midstream.

by the river – a riverside path is marked but it turns out to be disappointingly short. So you may as well head up the busy Twickenham Road, going north. If you want to avoid some of the traffic noise, turn left at Waldegrave Park, and almost immediately right down an unnamed narrow alleyway. This crosses Clive Road, and continues as far as the small roundabout at the end of Waldegrave Road. You can stroll into the pleasant Radnor Gardens, a small park facing the river, then rejoin the main A310 at Cross Deep.

At the main traffic lights – facing Sandys, one of the finest fishmonger's in the whole London area – turn right down King Street, and almost immediately right again down Wharf Lane. Reunited with the river, you'll see the footbridge to Fel Pie Island. This is now reopened to the public, and there's nothing to stop you from having a wander round this strange little waterborne village, which varies wildly from chocolate-box prettiness, to executive-style developments, to messy, clanging boatyards. Some of the houses are barely visible through the foliage. One has a substantial collection of Barbie dolls planted in its front garden, as if in hopes that they will reproduce. There are flower-festooned cottages and little houses offering to sell you various works of art. Naturally there is no traffic on the island, so the inhabitants are sometimes able to look to the shore and see their cars bobbing along on the high tide. For years there was a hotel, a popular weekend destination for East Enders, who took boat trips here and ate the eponymous eel pies. In the 1960s it was a blues venue, and the Rolling Stones and The Who played here often, which is one reason why so many of them still live in this part of town. The hotel burned down, and now the island is once again, well, insular.

Marble Hill House

Back on mainland, you'll see a pub called the Barmy Arms, which is especially popular in summer. It's worth going up the next little alleyway, back towards Twickenham, because it takes you into Church Street, a largely pedestrianised thoroughfare filled with restaurants, cafés, knick-knack and toy shops, a bookstore, a coffee and chocolate shop, the usual bookmaker, and an excellent pub, the Eel Pie. At the end of the street is St Mary the Virgin church, one of the more striking in the area, since the building is actually of a handsome Georgian design, but is attached to the original stone 14th-century tower.

Return to the river via Church Lane and admire Dial House, now St Mary's vicarage, and look in at the open-air sculpture garden. From here a small gate leads into York House gardens. (Sometimes the gate is closed, in which case you'll need to do part of the walk

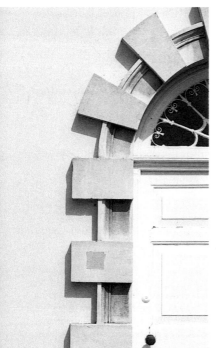

backwards if you want to see this startling confection – *see map*.)

York House has been lived in by many people (now it's the borough council offices). One owner was the Indian magnate Sir Ratan Tata, who installed the extraordinary statues of seven vast and cheerful-looking nymphs. This is a water feature that might even make the *Ground Force* team blench. Cross the extravagant bridge over the road (now known as Riverside), continue past the Japanese garden and the great sunken lawn, probably occupied by boys playing football, and head out towards the tennis courts. To the right you'll see a gate that leads on to Sion Road. Turn right, and head back towards the river.

Here are some of the prettiest Georgian cottages in the whole of west London. The lanes are narrow, cars are few, and it's easy to imagine yourselves as gentlefolk ambling here more than 200 years ago. And to make a fine setting almost perfect, you return to the river at the White Swan pub, one of the most popular along this stretch of river. The pub has its own sitting area between the roadway and the water, and serves outdoor meals on summer weekends. At high tide, however, you might need to take your shoes and socks off to get out.

By this time the river is drawing you east, back towards Richmond. After a while the road, still Riverside, leads to a wide open grassy area. Either veer right and throw bread to the ducks, coots, swans, moorhens, herons and Canada geese, or else turn left through a small gateway leading to Orleans House.

This was actually built by a politician, James Johnston, but is named after Louis Philippe, the Duc d'Orléans, who rented the house for two years from 1815 following his exile from France. He later returned to his homeland as king. (By a curious coincidence the house is a few hundred yards away from what's thought to be the only 'Napoleon Road' in England.) The fine Octagon, a garden

Montpelier Row – 'one of the finest Georgian streets in Greater London'.

pavilion, is worth looking into, and there are interesting art exhibitions in what remains of the main house.

Turn right at the Octagon. A short and woody path takes you to another door in the wall. Cross Orleans Road, a quiet stretch of tarmac mainly serving people who are visiting Marble Hill Park, now straight ahead. This is dominated by Marble Hill House, the Palladian mansion you probably spotted from the Surrey bank. It was built between 1724 and 1729 for Henrietta Howard, who was Countess of Suffolk, and mistress of George II. (The position seems to have been rather a lonely one. By all accounts, the king had a closer relationship with his wife than with Henrietta, but like most powerful men of the day, felt that the possession of a mistress was an important status symbol.)

On leaving the house, return across the park towards Orleans Road, and there turn right. This takes you past more pretty cottages. When you reach a converted chapel on your left, turn right down the narrow lane. This brings you to Montpelier Row, one of the finest Georgian streets in Greater London. At the far end, on your right, is the superb South End House, which for 16 years

was the home of the poet Walter de la Mare. No.15 immediately on your left, at the end of a row of houses built in 1720, is the largest dwelling in the Georgian part of the street. It was once, as a plaque informs us, the home of another poet, Alfred Lord Tennyson. More recently it belonged to Pete Townshend of The Who, a fact that tells you something about how British society has changed over the years. All the houses in the northern part of the street (the southern half is Victorian, though still pretty enough) are magnificent and will provoke stirrings of baleful envy towards their occupants.

At the northern end of Montpelier Row you have a choice. You can go back to the river, by turning right into the park and heading south-east. This will take you on a pleasant walk with woods and parkland on your left and the water on your right. At Richmond Bridge, cross the river, turn left at the Odeon cinema, right at Dickins & Jones, and so on to Richmond station.

If, however, you're beginning to flag, you could cross by the zebra at the end of Montpelier Row, turn left as if back towards Twickenham, and cross over Crown Road at the mini-roundabout, passing the Crown pub, so-called because before Marble Hill House was built George II used to take his mistress to an upstairs room here. Take a bus from the first stop you come to. All except the 33 go to Richmond station.

Or, as a third option, you could turn right after the zebra crossing, go a few yards down Richmond Road, then left down Sandycombe Road. This takes you past Sandycombe Lodge, a handsome white building on the right just after you've crossed St Stephen's Gardens. This was built by the painter JMW Turner for himself and his father, and at the time included a very substantial garden. The house is still privately occupied, though it's open to the public very occasionally. If you're lucky enough to get in, the present owner will show you a golden guinea he found in the garden, dated from the time Turner lived in the house, and almost certainly part payment for a commission.

At the end of Sandycombe Road, turn left, and after about four minutes you will come to St Margaret's station. Four trains an hour (two on Sundays) leave for Richmond and Waterloo. Or there's the H37 bus, which leaves frequently from the stop outside the post office, diagonally opposite the station.

Eating & drinking

Barmy Arms
The Embankment, Twickenham, Middx TW1 3DU (8892 0863). **Open** 11am-11pm Mon-Sat; noon-10.30pm Sun. **Food served** noon-9pm Mon-Sat; noon-3pm Sun.

Some of the best fish in London can be found at **Sandys** fishmonger in Twickenham.

Canyon

The Towpath, nr Richmond Bridge, Richmond, Surrey, TW10 6UJ (8948 2944/www.jamies. co.uk). **Brunch served** 11am-3.30pm Sat, Sun. **Lunch served** 11am-3.30pm Mon-Fri. **Dinner served** 6-10.30pm daily. Relaxed modern mood and excellent brunch.

Crown

174 Richmond Road, Twickenham, Middx TW1 2NH (8892 5896). **Open** 11am-11pm Mon-Sat; 11am-10.30pm Sun. **Food served** noon-3pm, 5-10pm Mon-Fri; noon-10pm Sat, Sun. Thai food.

Eel Pie

9-11 Church Street, Twickenham, Middx TW1 3NJ (8891 1717). **Open** 11am-11pm Mon-Sat; noon-10.30pm Sun. **Food served** noon-4.15pm daily.

Slug & Lettuce

Riverside House, Water Lane, Richmond, Surrey TW9 1TJ (8948 7733/www.slugand lettuce.co.uk). **Open** 11am-11pm Mon-Sat; noon-10.30pm Sun. **Food served** noon-10pm Mon-Sat; noon-9pm Sun.

White Cross

Riverside, Richmond, Surrey TW9 1TJ (8940 6844). **Open** 11am-11pm Mon-Sat; noon-10.30pm Sun. **Food served** noon-3.30pm Mon-Sat; noon-4pm Sun.

White Swan

Riverside, Twickenham, Middx TW1 3DN (8892 2166). **Open/food served** noon-2.30pm, 6-9.30pm Mon-Fri; noon-2.30pm Sat, Sun.

Houses & gardens

Ham House

Ham Street, Ham, Richmond, Surrey TW10 7RS (8940 1950/www.nationaltrust.org.uk). **Open** *House* mid Mar-Oct 1-5pm Mon-Wed, Sat, Sun. *Garden* 11am-6pm Mon-Wed, Sat, Sun. **Admission** £7.50; £3.75 5-15s; free under-5s; £18.75 family. *Garden only* £3.50; £1.75 5-15s; free under-5s; £8.75 family.

Marble Hill House

Richmond Road, Twickenham, Middx TW1 2NL (8892 5115/www.english-heritage.org.uk). **Open** *late Mar-Nov* 10am-2pm Sat; 10am-5pm Sun. **Admission** £4; £3 concessions; £2 5-15s; free under-5s.

Orleans House

Riverside, Twickenham, Middx TW1 3DJ (8831 6000/www.richmond.gov.uk). **Open** *Apr-Sept* 1-5.30pm Tue-Sat; 2-5.30pm Sun. *Oct-Mar* 1-4.30pm Tue-Sat; 2-4.30pm Sun. *Gardens* 9am-dusk daily. **Admission** free.

Radnor Gardens

Cross Deep, Twickenham, Middx (no phone).

York House Gardens

Richmond Road, Twickenham, Middx TW1 3AA (8891 1411/www.richmond.gov.uk). **Open** 7.30am-dusk Mon-Sat; 9.30am-dusk Sun. The gate in the sculpture garden is open: *Termtime* 10am-3pm Mon-Fri, dawn-dusk Sat, Sun. *Holidays* dawn-dusk daily.

Others

Dickins & Jones

80 George Street, Richmond, Surrey TW9 1HA (8940 7761). **Open** 9.30am-6pm Mon, Wed-Fri; 10am-6pm Tue; 9am-6pm Sat; 11am-5pm Sun.

Hammerton's Ferry

see map for location (8892 9620). **Open** 10am-6pm, or dusk if earlier Mon-Fri; 10am-6.30pm, or dusk if earlier Sat, Sun. **Tickets** 60p; 30p under-16s; 40p pushchair; 30p-50p bike.

Merrie Thames Ferry

(07710 229026). Ferries do non-stop trips to Teddington Lock and back. Boats leave at quarter past the hour from 11.15am, the last starting at 4.15pm on weekdays, 5.15pm at weekends and bank holiday Mon. **Tickets** £4.50; £3 under-16s, OAPs.

Odeon

72 Hill Street, Richmond, Surrey TW9 1TW (information & tickets 0871 224 4007/ www.odeon.co.uk).

St Mary the Virgin

Church Street, Twickenham, Middx TW1 3NJ (8744 2693). **Open** call for details. *Services* 8am, 9.30am, 11.30am, 6pm Sun.

Sandys

56 King Street, Twickenham, Middx TW1 3SH (8892 5788). **Open** 7.30am-6pm Mon-Sat.

Westminster Passenger Service Association

Westminster Pier, Victoria Embankment, SW1A 2JH (7930 2062/www.wpsa.co.uk). Boats for Kew, Richmond and Hampton Court leave 10.30am, 11.15am, noon daily (subject to tidal conditions); phone first. **Tickets** *to Richmond* £12; £8 concessions; £6 6-16s; free under-5s.

The garden at **York House** contains seven vast and cheerful-looking nymphs.

Hospital corners

Rabbi Julia Neuberger

An out-patient's tour of south London's hospitals past and present.

Start: Oval tube
Finish: London Bridge tube/rail
Time: 3-4 hours
Distance: 5 miles/9km
Getting there: Northern line
to Oval
Getting back: Jubilee or Northern
lines or rail from London Bridge
Note: there is some overlap
with Steven Appleby's walk.

It has always seemed strange to me that there are parts of London full of hospitals and other healthcare institutions, while others have few to rely on. The plethora of hospitals in inner south London has more to do with population patterns and the nature of Southwark, one of London's oldest areas, than with over-provision, but one can see why study after study of London's hospitals and health system have shown a strange distribution of these institutions, which does not mirror where the people of London now live.

However, to go for a walk and see what remains of the earlier buildings is fascinating in itself. The King's Fund, where I work, was established in 1897 for the hospitals of London, many of which had serious financial problems. It was the then Prince of Wales, later Edward VII, who set up the fund to commemorate his mother's diamond jubilee; so successful was he at raising the funds that until the foundation of the National Health Service in 1948, many of London's voluntary hospitals relied heavily on major contributions from the King's Fund to enable them to serve the poor of London.

So, to set off on our tour, take the tube to Oval, turn right along Kennington Park Road and walk for about 100 yards to opposite the former Belgrave Hospital for Children. You can just pick out its name in the brickwork high up on the south-facing walls, and you can still admire the gold mosaic of the underside of the porch cupola. Otherwise, unless you have a practised eye, you would not necessarily realise it was a former hospital. Yet, in fact, it was very modern for its time. Begun in 1899, it was built by forward-thinking architects Henry Percy Adams and Charles Holden, in a quasi-cruciform design. This allowed a considerable amount of light to percolate through the wards, with open wells, but the most significant feature was that any wing could be isolated at any time if there were an outbreak of infectious disease. And, of course, infectious diseases were still the major threat to small children, and infant mortality, especially among the poor who were most likely to use the hospital, was still distressingly high in 1900. Though you cannot see them, the walls were decorated with nursery rhyme pictures on ceramic tiles, designed by Gertrude Bradley, not dissimilar to others hidden in St Thomas' Hospital (which we pass later).

Walk back up Kennington Park Road for a few yards and turn right into Prima Road alongside the hospital. Glance across at the handsome outside of St Mark's Church Kennington, one of the so-called Waterloo Churches built in 1822, then turn left and cross first Brixton Road, then Camberwell New Road, into Kennington Park. Make your way diagonally across the park to the north-east corner.

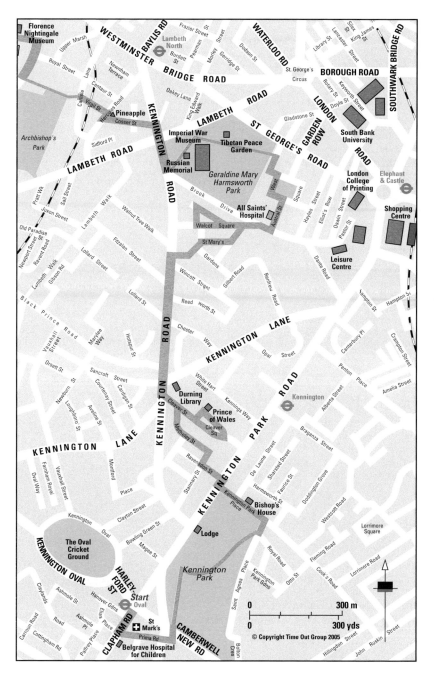

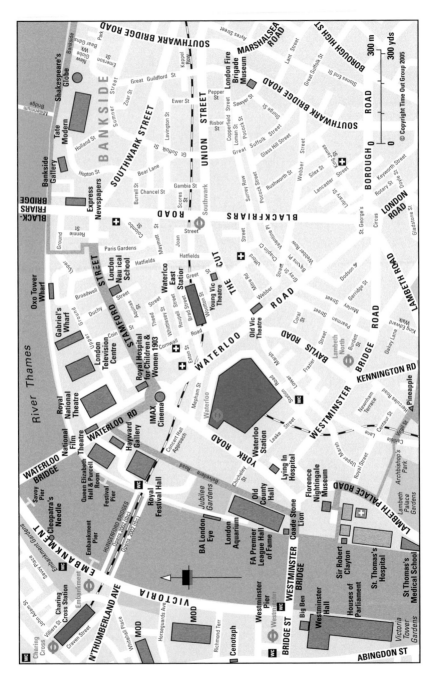

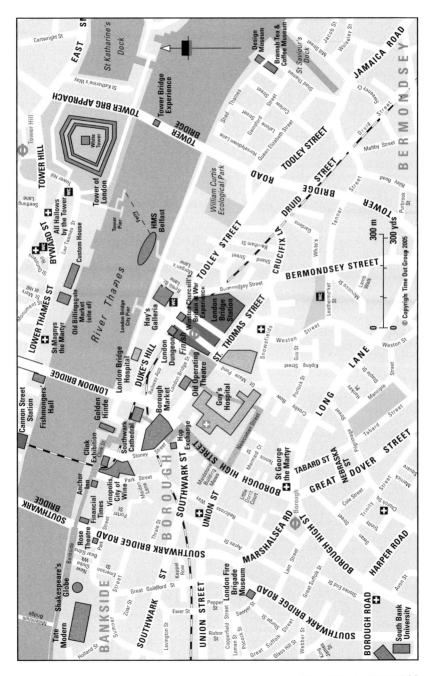

It seems like any other London park at first, with children, dogs and young footballers in roughly equal numbers. But don't miss the lodge, which consists of two mock Elizabethan cottages put up at the Great Exhibition of 1851 by special request of Prince Albert, who wanted to demonstrate what good working-class housing should look like. They were altered, combined and re-erected in the park by their original designer, H Roberts, who also designed the first cheap working-class flats in Streatham Street, Holborn. Emerge from the park at the north-east corner, into St Agnes' Place, with its elegant Georgian houses, and turn immediately left into Kennington Park Place. Take a look at the vast house to your right: Bishop's House, designed in 1895 by Norman Shaw and until recently home to the Bishop of Southwark.

Cross Kennington Park Road into Ravensdon Street, past the rather engaging 'Temperance Works' to an area of definite gentrification. Turn right into Radcot Street, and left into Methley Street, where on the left at the end there is a blue plaque to Charlie Chaplin, who lived there in his poverty-stricken childhood, when the area was more or less a slum. Turn into Bowden Street and then Cleaver Street, just by Lambeth County Court, and make a quick detour into Lambeth's prime address of Cleaver Square, home to politicians and film stars (but not improved by Lambeth Council's having replaced the grass in the middle with gravel). There's a good pub, the Prince of Wales, in the corner if you are getting tired by this stage. There's still quite a good way to go.

Return to Cleaver Street, cross Kennington Lane just by Spanish restaurant the Finca, looking back at the amazing and monstrous, yet attractive, Durning Library on Kennington Lane on the right. Walk up Kennington Road; it's a main road but has some beautiful

houses. Charlie Chaplin appears again on a plaque at No.287, and the traffic rumbles past. So it's a relief to turn right after a few hundred yards up Bishop's Terrace, past more elegant warehouses, and weave past the small pretty houses that surround picturesque greens in St Mary's Gardens and Walcot Square. The whole Walcot Estate is a conservation area, and one is well aware of it with all the front doors painted black. Walcot Square itself dates from 1837 to 1839, but the houses on Kennington Road behind it are mostly earlier, dating from the 1770s to the early 19th century, and considerably more distinguished in their design.

Turn left down Sullivan Road and cross Brook Drive into Austral Street, past the old All Saints' Hospital, which is now an annexe to the Imperial War Museum, but must have been splendid as a public hospital for the poor. Enter elegant West Square with its sprawling trees, and go left around the side to Geraldine Street. You can get a good view of the former 'Bedlam', the old Bethlem Hospital, now the Imperial War Museum, from the door in the wall. Go through the door into the Geraldine Mary Harmsworth Park, an area of amazing contrasts. Not only does it have a Tibetan Peace Garden, well worth a look, but also the Soviet War Memorial to all the Russians who died in World War II – and all this in front of the Imperial War Museum. There's a certain amount of irony in the siting.

The Bethlem Hospital dates back to 1246, but the present building, much of which has been demolished to make way for the enlargement of the park, dates from 1812 to 1815, with the huge portico and dome added even later, in 1838-40. By 1400 it specialised in the care of the insane, hence the term 'Bedlam'. It moved from Bishopsgate to Moorfields after the Great Fire of London, and out to Southwark in 1812, at a time, presumably, when it was thought beneficial for people with mental illness to be in larger buildings in safe, semi-rural surroundings – though this was well before the great expansion of the asylums for the mentally ill sited all round the outskirts of London.

Leave the park on Kennington Road and turn right, crossing Lambeth Road. Go up Kennington Road for a few yards and turn left into Cosser Street. Right into Hercules Road, past the wonderful Pineapple Bar, before turning left into Virgil Street, under the railway lines, and across Carlisle Street, with a view of St Thomas' Hospital ahead. Go through Archbishop's Park, part of the old Archbishop's Palace gardens, with its tennis courts on your left, and cross Lambeth Palace Road to outside St Thomas' Hospital.

St Thomas' was founded in the 12th century on the site of the priory of St Mary Overie, by the present Southwark Cathedral. It was re-dedicated to St Thomas the Martyr after the canonisation of Thomas à Becket in 1173. Between 1207 and 1212 the priory was destroyed in a fire, but it was rebuilt to the east of Borough High Street. When Henry VIII dissolved the monasteries in 1540, the hospital closed, but Edward VI, his son, reopened it in 1552, and granted it to the lord mayor and City of London. Until the formation of the NHS in 1948, the lord mayor retained control (there is still an annual lecture in his honour) and raised funds to keep it going. Between 1693 and 1709 a huge rebuilding programme took place, funded largely by Sir Robert Clayton, a former Lord Mayor of London. But it was still too small, and Thomas Guy, who had made a fortune out of the South Sea Bubble, among other things, and who had become a governor of St Thomas' in 1704, decided a new hospital was needed to reduce the overcrowding. So he, with Richard Mead, physician to Queen Anne, set about getting a lease of land from St Thomas' and establishing a hospital for incurables opposite the big, newly extended St Thomas'. It was

opened in 1725, shortly after Guy's death, and named after him. In 1859, the hospital moved first to Vauxhall Gardens (the old pleasure gardens site, of which the Archbishop's Park is a small reminder), and then to its present site by the Thames in 1871. All this makes some sense of why the main road by Guy's Hospital is called St Thomas' Street, and why Guy Street, south of Guy's, is really quite an insignificant road. The two were long linked, and it seems obvious that now, finally, after hundreds of years, the two should finally form one NHS Trust, and the charitable trusts of the two be merged.

Keeping St Thomas' on your left, walk along Lambeth Palace Road until you come to the car park entrance. By the second roadway (where traffic emerges from the hospital) opposite the Ernst & Young building you'll see the Florence Nightingale Museum. Florence Nightingale's contribution to nursing is legendary and the museum contains many of her belongings as well as giving a comprehensive picture of the way nursing developed during and beyond the Crimean War. Leaving the museum, return to the main road, and climb the ramp a few yards further on into the site of St Thomas' proper. Head towards the riverbank, past, to your left, the impressive Rick Kirby sculpture, *Cross the Divide*, commissioned to mark the millennium. As you look across the river to the Palace of Westminster, with, in summer, the green (House of Commons) or red (House of Lords) awnings on the terrace, note the statue set back to the left, presiding over a strip of grass. It is of Sir Robert Clayton, Lord Mayor of London in 1679 and President of St Thomas' from 1692 to 1707. The statue is one of only four known marble works by Grinling Gibbons.

Return to Westminster Bridge Road, turn left and follow round towards the bridge. Opposite is the so-called South Bank Lion. This is acutally the Coade Stone Lion, the emblem of the former

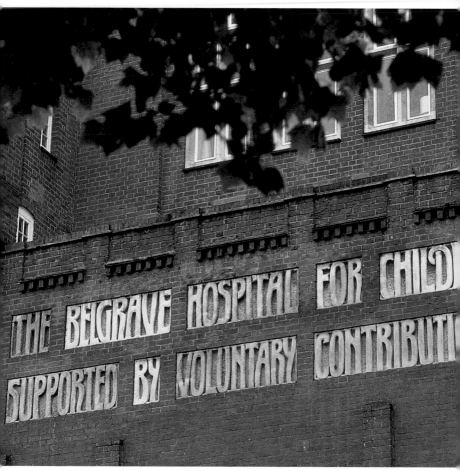

red Lion Brewery which used to be on the site of the Festival Hall. It was red originally, but was painted white in 1951 at the suggestion of King George VI. The original Coade artificial stoneworks were founded here in 1769 on the site of the present County Hall, so this lion is a local.

Cross the road and walk back past the Marriott Hotel, part of County Hall (home to the Saatchi Gallery and a building that leaves me cold apart from an admiration for its vastness), and left down Belvedere Road. As the buildings on your right (with several excellent eating places on the ground floor) make way for the piazza, you can get a great view of the old Lying-In Hospital on York Road to the south. It was built in 1828 by Henry Harrison, its façade boasting four Ionic columns. There are very few examples left of what the old small hospitals looked like, but this is a fine one. Beautifully designed, it was nevertheless a fever trap, for only poor women went to the lying-in hospitals. Anyone wealthier had their babies at home, where the risks of infection were much lower. Even though the risks were not fully understood, it was clear that infant mortality – and maternal mortality – was far higher among poor women than the rich. Puerperal fever was a terrible killer, rife in the lying-in hospitals, even though their founders and those who supported them with charitable contributions believed they were alleviating the troubles of the poor.

Continue down Belvedere Road as far as Waterloo Bridge, passing the London Eye to your left. I loathe the Eye, but it is wonderful to ride in, and the views from it are spectacular. Pass the Royal Festival Hall and the Hayward Gallery. At Waterloo Bridge, turn right up the ramp on to the IMAX roundabout to admire, on the left corner, the Royal Hospital for Children and Women, built in 1903 and now home to the Schiller University.

Cross the road and follow left on to Stamford Street, admiring the splendid terraces on the right, especially the London Nautical School near the far end, followed by the wonderful portico entrance to the Unitarian Chapel with the playground behind it. Shortly after this point, turn left down covered Milroy Walk and on through Marigold Alley towards the river. On your left is the Oxo Tower. I love the view from here – an incredible vista both ways along the Thames from a rooftop viewing gallery.

But we veer right, along the well-trodden Bankside walk, under Blackfriars Bridge and on to the incredibly successful Tate Modern. It has become one of London's greatest attractions, and though you could stop and visit it now – it is a good place for a coffee – it is emptier and easier to get around on a Saturday evening when it opens late and everyone else has gone out on the town. Here, also, is London's 'blade of light' footbridge, a wonderful route between Tate Modern and St Paul's.

Just after the Tate Modern, you come to Shakespeare's Globe, a reconstruction of Shakespeare's theatre, where superb productions of his plays are put on in the open air in the summer months, and with the added bonus of a great restaurant. Then on, under Southwark Bridge; follow the path round to the right when you get to the railway bridge. Don't miss the great view from the viewing terrace of the Anchor Pub, looking towards Tower Bridge and Canary Wharf. A left down Clink Street takes us past the ghoulish Clink Prison Museum, the impressive Vinopolis wine museum and shops, and the ruins of Winchester Palace, the home of the bishops of Winchester, to your right. Then straight on to Pickford's Wharf and the *Golden Hinde*, a reconstruction of the famous ship that Sir Francis Drake sailed in the 16th century.

Don't go on until you have also admired the tablet just by the ship in memory of St Mary Overie. The story is remarkable. Her father was a mean merchant who feigned death in order to get his servants to fast in mourning and therefore save a day's rations. He got it profoundly wrong. So delighted were they by his demise that they started feasting. In a rage, the old man got up. One of his horrified servants threw a pot at him and killed him. At this point his daughter's lover appeared on the scene, but, presumably in joy at getting his rich heiress at last, he fell off his horse and broke his neck. Mary, the daughter, thereafter devoted her life to religion and good causes, and was named a saint for her efforts. St Mary Overie is, in fact, St Mary over Rie, or river, and her church eventually became St Saviour and St Mary Overie, and is the collegiate church for Southwark Cathedral.

Having turned right, away from the river, enter the cathedral. Once inside, turn left and go into the north transept, where you will find a fine monument to Lionel Lockyer, a so-called quack doctor famous for his pills. The excruciating verse dating from 1741 includes the lines 'His virtues and his pills are soe well known/That envy can't confine them under stone'. If you leave the cathedral through the opposite door from the one you entered by, you will be facing the wonderful Borough Market.

If you are doing the walk on a Friday or Saturday, you're in luck: the market is a foodies' haven, with cheese stalls, vegetables, organic meats and other delights. There are lots of places to get a sandwich as well, but my favourite are the snacks on offer outside Brindisa, the Spanish stall, washed down with a wonderful fresh juice, squeezed while you wait.

Exit the market into Stoney Street, turn right briefly into Southwark Street to admire the glorious Hop Exchange at No.24, before crossing and heading down Borough High Street opposite. On the right are the beautifully restored Maidstone Buildings Mews, worth a quick glance, before crossing and turning left into Newcomen Street, and left again into Guy's Hospital, opposite Bowling Green Place. If you go past the modern buildings, you come to the two glorious inner courtyards, with, in Pevsner's words, its 'two far projecting wings forming a *cour d'honneur*'. It is truly beautiful, and you can see yet again the idea of the wings being available for isolation if necessary, because originally there were open arcades on the ground floor. Presumably isolation was a serious issue, as was the fear of overcrowding throughout, so the open spaces were to allow air to circulate.

Before you walk into St Thomas Street through the original gates, it is worth a visit to the tiny chapel in the centre of the left wall of the courtyard. It is by Richard Jupp and dates to about 1780. It has a wonderful, if somewhat sentimental, memorial to Thomas Guy by John Bacon, and among the luminaries commemorated here is William Ewart Gladstone, a hospital governor for 63 years. And, just in case you should miss them, there are glorious Victorian cylindrical radiators, still heating the chapel adequately some 140 years after they were made.

Cross the road and turn left along St Thomas Street into the Old Operating Theatre, Museum and Herb Garret, in what appears to be a church. Indeed, it is a church. The roof garret has Britain's oldest operating theatre (1821) as well as the herb garret once used by the hospital apothecary. This is the oldest part of St Thomas' Hospital. The theatre saw the beginnings of anaesthesia in 1846 and was closed only three years before the first experiments in antisepsis in surgery. It was only rediscovered in 1956 – after the move of the main hospital in 1862, it went into disuse. Do admire it. The surgeons did not wear special clothes; bloodstained grocers' aprons seem to have been the norm. The operating table itself, which came from University College Hospital, is seriously bloodstained, and the sight is disturbing to say the least. But the museum is wonderfully scented with herbs, and time spent catching up on the history of the medicines, as well as handling the equipment for making pills – you can have a go yourself – is time well spent. The various instruments make one glad that surgery has moved on apace and that antisepsis and micro-surgery are well advanced.

It is also worth admiring the building as a whole, for the impressive church was probably designed by one of Sir Christopher Wren's team (he was a governor of the hospital). The operating theatre had to have a good deal of natural light, which explains the presence of the skylight, an eccentric addition to a Wren-style church.

After that visit, you might want to seek the comforts of home via London Bridge station, unless you spotted an interesting place to stop for a meal or a cup of tea or jar of something stronger along the riverfront. Having seen all these past and present hospitals, you should be feeling strong and healthy – and certainly determined to avoid being ill for as long as possible, beautiful though some of them are.

Guy's Hospital

Old Operating Theatre

Eating & drinking

Anchor Bankside

34 Park Street, SE1 9EF (7407 1577). **Open**
11am-11pm Mon-Sat; noon-10.30pm Sun. **Food
served** noon-10pm Mon-Sat; noon-9pm Sun.

The Finca

*185 Kennington Road, SE11 4EZ (7735 1061/
www.thefinca.co.uk).* **Open** noon-3pm, 6-11pm
Mon-Sat; 1-11pm Sun.

Pineapple Bar

53 Hercules Road, SE1 7DZ (7401 2860).
Open/food served 11am-11pm Mon-Sat;
noon-10.30pm Sun.

Prince of Wales

*48 Cleaver Square, SE11 4EA (7735 9916/
www.shepherdneame.co.uk).* **Open** noon-11pm
Mon-Sat; noon-10.30pm Sun. **Food served**

noon-2.30pm, 6-9pm Mon-Thur; noon-2.30pm
Fri, Sat; noon-3pm Sun.

Real Greek Souvlaki & Bar

*Units 1 & 2, Riverside House, 2A Southwark
Bridge Road, SE1 9HA (7620 0162/www.the
realgreek.co.uk).* **Open** noon-11pm daily.

Shakespeare's Globe Restaurant

*New Globe Walk, SE1 9DR (7928 9444/www.
shakespeares-globe.org).* **Open** *May-Oct* noon-
2.30pm, 5.30-10.15pm Mon-Sat; 11.30am-2.30pm,
5-10.15pm Sun. *Nov-Apr* noon-2.30pm Mon, Sun;
noon-2.30pm, 6-9.30pm Tue-Sat.

Churches

St Mark's

*Kennington Park Road, The Oval, SE11 5SW
(7735 4609).* **Open** by appointment. Contact
Rev de Berry for details.

Southwark Cathedral
Montague Close, SE1 9DA (7367 6700/tours 7367 6734/www.dswark.org/cathedral). **Open** 8am-6pm daily (varies). *Audio guide £2.50.*

Museums & galleries

Clink Prison Museum
1 Clink Street, SE1 9DG (7403 6515/ www.clink.co.uk). **Open** *June-Sept* 10am-9pm daily. *Oct-May* 10am-6pm daily. **Admission** £5; £3.50 concessions, 5-15s; free under-5s; £12 family.

Florence Nightingale Museum
St Thomas' Hospital, 2 Lambeth Palace Road, SE1 7EW (7620 0374/www.florence-nightingale.co.uk). **Open** 10am-5pm Mon-Fri (last entry 4pm); 11.30am-4.30pm Sat, Sun (last admission 3.30pm). **Admission** £5.80; £4.20 concessions, 5-18s; £13 family; free under-5s.

Golden Hinde
St Mary Overie Dock, Cathedral Street, SE1 9DE (0870 011 8700/www.goldenhinde.co.uk). **Open** daily, times vary; phone for details. **Admission** £3.50; £3 concessions; £2.50 4-13s; free under-4s; £10 family.

Guy's Hospital
St Thomas' Street, SE1 9RT (7188 7188/ www.guysandstthomas.nhs.uk). **Open** *Hospital Chapel* 8am-9pm daily. The Gordon Museum is not open to the public.

Imperial War Museum
Lambeth Road, SE1 6HZ (7416 5000/ www.iwm.org.uk). **Open** 10am-6pm daily. **Admission** free; donations sppreciated. *Exhibitions* prices vary.

Old Operating Theatre, Museum & Herb Garret
9A St Thomas' Street, SE1 9RY (7955 4791/ www.thegarret.org.uk). **Open** 10.30am-5pm daily (last admission 4.45pm). **Admission** £4.75; £3.75 concessions; £2.75 6-15s; free under-6s; £12 family.

Saatchi Gallery
County Hall, Riverside Building, Westminster Bridge Road, SE1 7PB (7823 2363/www.saatchi-gallery. co.uk). **Open** 10am-8pm Mon-Thur, Sun; 10am-10pm Fri, Sat. **Admission** £9; £6.75 concessions; £26 family.

Shakespeare's Globe
21 New Globe Walk, SE1 9DT (7902 1500/ www.shakespeares-globe.org). **Open** *Tours & Exhibitions* May-Sept 9am-noon daily; Oct-Apr 10am-5pm daily. **Admission** £8.50; £7 concessions; £6 5-15s.

Tate Modern
Bankside, SE1 9TG (7887 8000/www.tate.org.uk). **Open** 10am-6pm Mon-Thur, Sun; 10am-10pm Fri, Sat. *Tours* 11am, noon, 2pm, 3pm daily. **Admission** free. *Temporary exhibitions* prices vary.

Vinopolis
1 Bank End, SE1 9BU (0870 241 4040/www. vinopolis.co.uk). **Open** 10am-9pm Mon, Fri, Sat; 10am-5.30pm Tue-Thur, Sun (last entry 2hrs before closing). **Admission** £12.50; £11.50 concessions; free under-16s.

Parks & gardens

Geraldine Mary Harmsworth Park
Geraldine Street, SE1 (7735 3704). **Open** dawn-dusk daily.

Kennington Park
Kennington Park Road, SE11. **Open** dawn-dusk daily.

Others

Borough Market
Borough Market, between Borough High Street, Bedale Street, Winchester Walk & Stoney Street, SE10. **Open** noon-6pm Fri; 9am-4pm Sat.

British Airways London Eye
Riverside Building, next to County Hall, Westminster Bridge Road, SE1 7PB (0870 500 0600/www.ba-londoneye.com). **Open** Oct-Apr 9.30am-8pm daily. May, June, Sept 9.30am-9pm daily. July, Aug 9.30am-10pm daily. **Admission** £12.50; £10 concessions (not applicable weekends or Jul, Aug); £6.50 5-15s; free under-5s.

Durning Library
167 Kennington Lane, SE11 4HF (7926 8682/ www.lambeth.gov.uk). **Open** 1-6pm Mon; 10am-1pm Tue; 10am-8pm Wed; 10am-6pm Fri; 9am-5pm Sat.

The King's Fund
11-13 Cavendish Square, W1G 0AN (7307 2400/ www.kingsfund.org.uk).

London Marriott
County Hall, Westminster Bridge Road, SE1 7PB (7928 5200/www.marriott.com/lonch).

Oxo Tower Wharf
Bargehouse Street, SE1 (7401 2255). **Open** 11am-6pm daily.

St Thomas's Hospital
Lambeth Palace Road, SE1 7EH (7188 7188).

The number of the Beast

Mark Pilkington

Witness, as if by magic, the London of Aleister Crowley and the Golden Dawn.

> **Start:** Euston tube/rail
> **Finish:** Victoria Palace Theatre
> **Time:** 4-5 hours
> **Distance:** 6 miles/10km
> **Getting there:** Northern or Victoria lines or rail to Euston
> **Getting back:** District, Circle or Victoria lines or rail from Victoria
> **Author's note:** this route is best walked wearing a large top hat and cape. Crowley was sometimes seen perfectly to mimic the stride of a walker in front of him. Once in perfect rhythm, he would then trip lightly, causing the person in front to stumble and fall. This may help to clear your route through busier areas.

'And it is utterly true that he who cannot find wonder, mystery, awe, the sense of a new world and an undiscovered realm in the places of Gray's Inn Road, will never find the secret elsewhere, not in the heart of Africa, not in the fabled hidden cities of Tibet.' Arthur Machen, *Things Near and Far* (1923).

As the sun set on the mechanical marvels of the 19th century, so a new dawn was rising, a Golden Dawn. Formed by coroner Dr William Wynn Westcott, of 396 Camden Road, and historian Samuel Liddell 'MacGregor' Mathers, in 1888, the Hermetic Order of the Golden Dawn grew to be one of the most influential secret magical societies of the 20th century – despite fragmenting into several parts in 1900. As they ascended through its quasi-Masonic degree system, Golden Dawn members were introduced to series of increasingly dense secret teachings that borrowed from both Western and Eastern mystical traditions. The initiates' ultimate spiritual goal was the Knowledge and Conversation of their Holy Guardian Angel, their higher selves, but along the way they would experiment with esoteric practices that are now staples of bookshops' Mind, Body, Spirit shelves, including meditation, visualisation, astrology, tarot, astral projection, Kabbala and ESP.

Over the years Golden Dawn members included the poet WB Yeats, the popular actress Florence Farr, heiress Annie Horniman, esoteric writer AE Waite, supernatural authors Arthur Machen and Algernon Blackwood and, most infamously of all, the Great Beast 666, Aleister Crowley – occultist, painter, poet, mountain climber and novelist, also known as Count Vladimir Svareff, Prince Chioa Khan, Mahatma Guru Si Paramahansa Shivaji and Alastor, Wanderer of the Wastes. This last moniker best suits the peripatetic Crowley, who professed a disdain for London, and spent much of his time travelling. He usually only returned when things weren't working out, living at numerous rented addresses, sometimes several in a year.

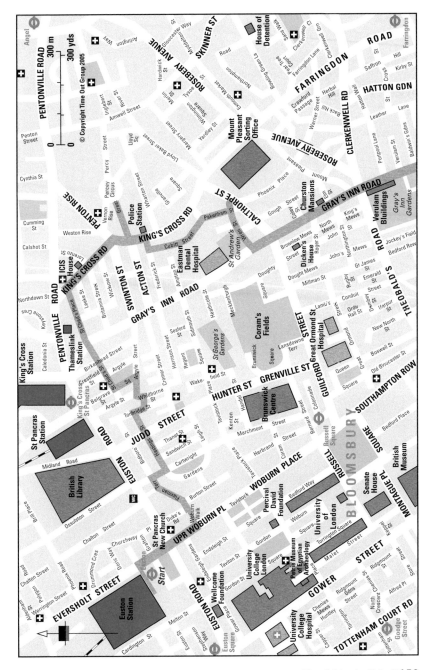

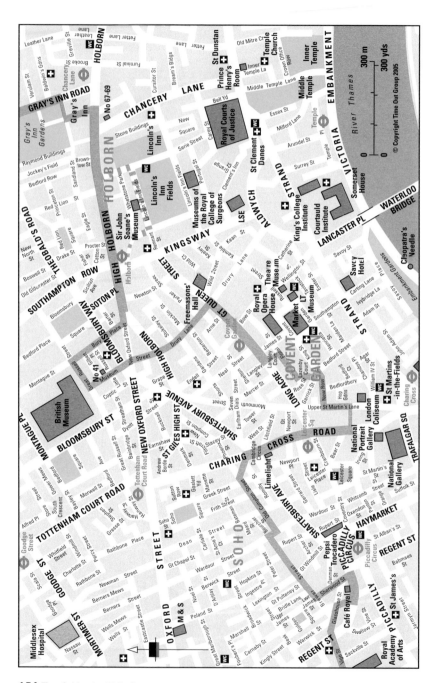

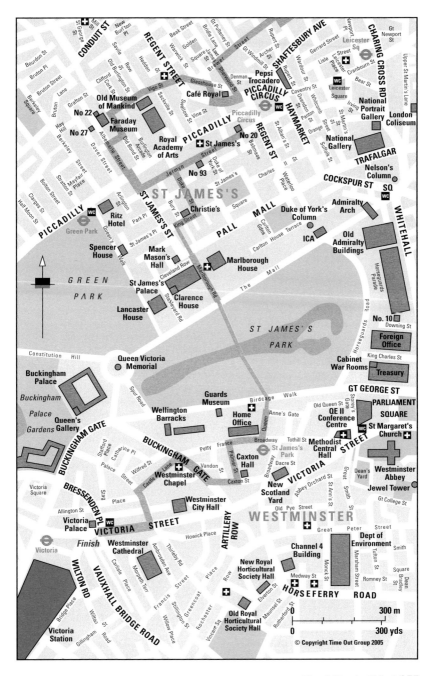

The **Princess Louise**, where pagans and occultists still gather.

Crowley was an extremely complex man, whose rich life and immense influence as a character have birthed at least ten biographies, commanding awe and ridicule in equal measures. Meanwhile, the legacy of his magic and his 'Do What Thou Wilt' philosophy of disciplined libertinism have inspired countless artists, filmmakers, authors and musicians. As a uniquely dedicated, trailblazing magician, Crowley remains unsurpassed in the 20th century. As a man, however, he often had little respect for others, and left in his wake a trail of death, madness and disillusionment. It is perhaps this romantic conflict between cruelty and enlightenment that made him such a powerful figure of his cruel, enlightened century.

Many occultists believe that the influence of every thought, word and deed remains in the aether long after they have been carried out. This is especially true of magical operations. Bear this in mind as you follow our path through sites of ancient power, magical action and other locations of esoteric interest.

Exit Euston station and cross Euston Road towards St Pancras New Church, then turn on to Upper Woburn Place. Take your first left on to Woburn Walk. Above Wot the Dickens! (Charles Dickens lived further down Upper Woburn Place) on the left is a plaque marking the home of William Butler Yeats, who lived here between 1895 and 1919, when it was known as the Woburn Buildings. Yeats – magical motto Demon Est Deus Inversus – was one of the Golden Dawn's most committed members, and deeply resented the 'unspeakable' Crowley's disruptive presence in the Order.

For his own part, Crowley craved the respect that Yeats commanded as a poet. 'What hurt him was the knowledge of his own incomparable inferiority,' he wrote of Yeats, clearly projecting his own bitterness on to the lauded poet. The Golden Dawn split in 1900 after a confrontation between Yeats and Crowley at the Second Order Vault of the Golden Dawn Adepts (at 36 Blythe Road,

Hammersmith), though Yeats would remain magically involved with its members until the 1920s.

Here, too, is the Aquarium bookshop, specialist in Beat writings, with a drugs section that would do the author of *Diary of a Drug Fiend* proud. While scouting the route I noticed a copy of Pel Torro's *Galaxy 666* for sale. Bear left and continue down Flaxman Terrace, turn right at Mabledon Place and cross over on to Hastings Street, taking a moment to note the peculiar redbrick, tomb-like shed in Cartwright Gardens. Crowley would retire to the town of Hastings in his old age and die there in 1947. At the end of Hastings Street, turn right on Tonbridge Street, then slip down Argyle Walk on your left. Follow this until it crosses Whidborne Street and bear left, where you'll see a remarkable free standing house, three rooms high and one wide – which gives some idea of what these streets must have been like before redevelopment.

Turn right into Argyle Street, cut left on to Argyle Square, then head diagonally across to St Chad's Street. St Chad's Well, one of many holy wells in the area, sat at the crossing of Gray's Inn Road and St Chad's Street on the banks of the once-mighty River Fleet. According to legend the well sprang up at the feet of the future King Canute after he killed Edmund Ironside in 1016.

Cross Gray's Inn Road, where Hermes, protector of travellers, tradesmen and thieves, and messenger of divine wisdom, keeps watch above. Continue down St Chad's Place, which leads via a narrow alley to King's Cross Road. Follow King's Cross Road round to the right, past ICIS House and Weston Rise – Weston Super Mare had a Golden Dawn lodge – up to Great Percy Street on the left. Here lived 'MacGregor' Mathers, curator of the Horniman Museum in Forest Hill between 1890 and 1892. Great Percy Street climbs to Percy Circus where Lenin stayed at No.16 in 1905. Before being developed

as suburbs in the late 18th century, this area was a popular heath, containing a grotto known as Merlin's Cave, presumably situated where Merlin Street is now, off Amwell Street.

Turn back on to King's Cross Road and cross over to Frederick Street, opposite what is surely one of London's grandest police stations. Walk a short way down and turn left on to Cubitt Street, passing Wells and Fleet squares whose names are a reminder of the area's past. Cubitt becomes Pakenham Street, from which turn right on to Wren Street, passing the crumbling tombs of St Andrew's Gardens, used as a mass grave for cholera victims in 1832. Approach Gray's Inn Road and turn left, past Irish Books at No.244 and, further up on the other side, the Blue Lion. Look out for the fantastically expressive gargoyle faces carved into the old wooden doors of 1-12 Churston Mansions.

Gray's Inn Road meets Clerkenwell Road, where you can drop into the Yorkshire Grey Brewery for traditional ales brewed on the spot. Once refreshed, continue down Gray's Inn Road. Immediately on the right are the Verulam Buildings, where the writer, actor and, for a year, Golden Dawn member Arthur Machen (magical motto Avallaunius) lived at No.4 from 1895 to 1901.

In many of his supernatural tales, Machen transformed London's familiar streets into eerie landscapes haunted by half-seen, inhuman forms, as in this passage from *The Hill of Dreams* (1907): 'All London was one grey temple of an awful rite, ring within ring of wizard stones circled about some central place. It was awful to think that all his goings were surrounded, that in the darkness he was watched and surveyed, that every step but led him deeper and deeper into the labyrinth.'

Making sure to stay out of the shadows, continue down Gray's Inn Road, cut right into the legal enclave of Gray's Inn Square, then walk across and through an arch to Gray's Inn Gardens. The entrance is graced by twin griffins guarding the entrance to the City. Take a left to return to busy High Holborn. Virtually opposite is Chancery Lane. On this corner stood the first domed church of the Knights Templar, built in 1128. A few feet down Chancery Lane, at Nos.67-9, under the name Count Vladimir Svareff, Crowley lived from 1898 to 1900. From 1899 he shared the large flat with fellow Golden Dawn member Allan Bennett, a chemist who helped to popularise Buddhism in the West. The large flat contained two temples, one white, the other – more of a cupboard – black. The White Temple contained six large (six feet by eight feet) mirrors; while in the Black a statue of a 'coolie' stood on his hands, carrying a table on his feet. Also in the Black Temple was a skeleton, which Crowley 'fed from time to time with blood, small birds and the like. The idea was to give it life, but I never got further than causing the bones to be covered with a viscous slime.'

The two men performed a great deal of ceremonial magic here, summoning a grimoire's worth of spirits and demons. Crowley described shadowy figures seen on the stairwell and said that he once found furniture and magic symbols scattered around, although the flat had been empty. 'It was almost a regular experience,' he writes, 'to hear of casual callers fainting or being seized with dizziness, cramp or apoplexy on the staircase. It was a long time before these rooms were let.' From the doorway, look above No.76 almost opposite, where snarling gargoyles sneer in your direction.

Return to High Holborn and continue left towards the West End. If you fancy a quick detour into Lincoln's Inn Fields and the delights of the Sir John Soane and Hunterian museums, slide down Great Turnstile. Otherwise continue along High Holborn, past the tube and over Southampton Row. It was at this point on my own tour that half a pigeon fell from the sky and landed messily at my feet – an offering from a large crow

glimpsed passing overhead. A little further along High Holborn is the Princess Louise, an atmospheric pub with its 1891 decor intact. Note the horned Pan-like head carved on the wall to the left of the entrance. Meeting upstairs on two Wednesdays a month are the Secret Chiefs, a friendly and open gathering of London pagans and occultists, who hold talks and exchange ideas among much bawdiness and laughter.

As High Holborn splits, take the right-hand path and then another right on to Bury Place, leading to Great Russell Street, and left to the wonders of the British Museum. Golden Dawn members would often be found poring over ancient magical tomes in the old Reading Room, and this was where Yeats first met Mathers. Room 46 of the east wing contains some of the magical apparatus of John Dee, Queen Elizabeth I's astrologer and spy, code name 007. Look for Dee's obsidian scrying mirror, wax tablets bearing magical diagrams, and a gold disc engraved with the four castles seen in a vision by Dee's assistant Edward Kelly. It was using Dee and Kelly's Enochian magical system that Crowley and the poet Victor Neuburg summoned the demon Choronzon in Algeria in 1909, a terrifying encounter that would haunt them both for ever.

Returning to Great Russell Street, turn right and have a quick peek at the amazingly bizarre books in the window of Jarndyce, then head down Museum Street. On your right is the Plough, a popular bohemian hangout and a favourite of Crowley's, known as the Baby's Bottom due to its (still) pink exterior. At No.41 was Mandrake Press, which published Crowley's *Confessions*, as well as some short stories and his novel *Moonchild*, before going bust in 1930 after not even two years in the business. At No.49A is the Atlantis Bookshop, one of London's oldest and best esoteric bookshops, and another favourite haunt of the Beast.

Museum Street crosses Bloomsbury Way, New Oxford Street, then High Holborn, taking you down Drury Lane (past the White Hart, London's oldest licensed pub, though you wouldn't know it) and eventually Great Queen Street, where stands the mighty edifice of Freemasons' Hall. Completed in 1933, this is the third Masonic Hall on the site, the first being completed in 1776, and the second in 1869. It was in the Mark Mason's Hall, roughly where the New Connaught Rooms begin today, that the Golden Dawn held their important ceremonies, including Crowley's initiation on 18 November 1898. The Golden Dawn's founders were all Masons and borrowed heavily from the Craft for their own ceremonies and symbolism. However, Crowley had little time for Freemasonry: 'Many degrees contain statements (usually inaccurate) of matters well known to modern schoolboys.' The Hall, open to the public (see listings), contains an excellent museum of Masonry, as well as a library, which holds a complete run of Crowley's magical journal, *The Equinox*.

At 19-21 and 23 Great Queen Street are two Masonic suppliers, Toye, Kenning & Spencer, and Central Regalia, where you can buy anything from Masonic key rings and golf balls, to the hat, robes and sword of a Templar Knight. Above No.30 is carved 'Masonic Trust for Girls and Boys' – wishful thinking these days, one suspects.

Continue down Long Acre and, resisting the lure of the Pan Pipes, which beckon from Covent Garden, continue past the Tube and turn left into Langley Court, right on to Floral Street, then left on to tiny Lazenby Court (site of the historic Lamb & Flag pub), crossing Garrick Street to reach New Row, where you turn right. Cross St Martin's Lane, into Cecil Court, past the elegant Salisbury pub, unchanged since 1892. Prominent among the cornucopia of antiquarian book and print sellers is Watkins, at No.19, founded by John Watkins in 1897. Sometime in the early 1930s, Watkins is said to have asked Crowley for a demonstration of his magic. Happy to oblige, Crowley told him to shut his

Crowley's fellow Golden Dawn member WB Yeats lived in **Woburn Walk.**

eyes. On opening them, the bookseller was astonished to find all his shelves bare. The books returned with another blink.

Those who dare to cross the ley lines running along the Strand from St Martin's to St Paul's can make the extra journey down to Cleopatra's Needle. Two such obelisks once stood at the entrance to Heliopolis in 1475 BC – the other is now in New York – and six men died to get this one to us. A phantom leaper is sometimes seen here, accompanied by cackling laughter from the water's depths. Beneath the obelisk are several items including a razor, a box of pins, four Bibles in different languages and photographs of the 12 most beautiful Englishwomen of the day. How appropriate, then, that on 23 December 1937, Crowley summoned members of 'all the world's races' here to receive the word of the New Aeon via a new edition of his *Book of the Law*.

Assuming you have remained in Cecil Court, head right up Charing Cross Road past the booksellers to Cambridge Circus and the Palace Theatre. Cross on to Moor Street and head left down Old Compton Street to Comptons, between Dean and Wardour streets. In the heady days of bohemian London, this was the Swiss, a favoured meeting place for artists and writers. According to legend, it was here that Crowley encountered the poet Dylan Thomas, who was composing verse in a notebook. Crowley sat in the shadows on the other side of the room, and also began scribbling. A crumpled piece of paper landed in Thomas's lap as the hulking, dome-headed Beast left the building. Written on the torn scrap were the very lines that Thomas himself had conjured up moments earlier. Thomas was discovered in the early 1930s by Victor Neuburg, Crowley's one-time lover and disciple.

Cross Wardour Street on to Brewer Street, walk some way, then turn left on Sherwood Street, opening on to Piccadilly Circus. Briefly pay your respects to Eros, then turn right on to Regent Street and the Café Royal, a bohemian oasis until the 1920s. Crowley was a regular here, and would often practise the art of drawing attention to himself, at which he excelled. In November 1911, he entered wearing full evening dress and a brass butterfly over his crotch. This he had prised from Jacob Epstein's statue of Oscar Wilde in Paris's Père Lachaise cemetery – the prudish authorities had placed it over an exposed male member. Epstein himself was in the Café Royal for this performance protest, and apparently approved. On another occasion, Crowley strode mightily through the dining hall from Regent Street to Glasshouse Street wearing a conical hat and black cape decorated with mystical symbols. Nobody said a word, convincing him that his cape of invisibility worked.

Vanish right through Air Street and turn left at Glasshouse Street. Cross Regent Street and down Vigo Street on the other side, passing the late lamented Museum of Mankind and next to it the Royal Institution with its stone pantheon of free-thinkers, so many of them also keen esotericists. Left on Old Bond Street, right on to Stafford Street to find two pubs, the Shelley and the Goat Tavern, which we can assume Crowley would have patronised when he lived at 27 Albermarle Street in 1932. In the late 19th century, No.22 housed the meeting rooms of the Hermetic Society, a Theosophical offshoot founded in 1884, of which both Mathers and Westcott were members.

Turn back down Albermarle Street, and right on to the other side of Stafford Street, where, at No.8, was Lowe's, a chemist's managed by one EP Whineray. Here London gents, including Crowley, would acquire exotic – and legal – substances such as opium, hashish and cocaine, as well as perfumes and oils. Whineray supplied Crowley with his Perfume of Immortality – ambergris, musk and civet – which attracted the attentions of women and, according to Crowley, horses, who would whinny

as he passed. What looks like a sign holder in the shape of an exotic jar still hangs over the entrance.

Follow Albermarle Street down to Piccadilly, and across on to St James's Street, home of the gentlemen's club, none of which would have had Crowley as a member. Turn left on to Jermyn Street and head down to No.93, Paxton & Whitfield, a cheese shop since 1797; 93 was the kabbalistic number of Crowley's magical current, Thelema, and this was his last London home before retiring to Hastings in 1945. Further down at No.20 is George Trumper, Gentleman's Perfumier, established 1875. Crowley lived above here in 1939. Some years before, Crowley and the equally eccentric historian Montague Summers had planned to market a unisex perfume called 'It'.

Backtrack down Jermyn Street, past St James's Church, where New Age lectures are held, to Duke Street St James on the left. Head down to Kings Street, past Christie's, and turn right. Have a look at the entirely cosmic glass etchings at No.23, then take a left down the narrow and windy Crown Passage, past the Red Lion, London's second oldest licence, another 23. On Pall Mall, head right for a peek at the current Mark Mason's Hall, 86 St James's Street – the administrative centre of world Freemasonry – and then left down gated Marlborough Road, past the unsettling sculpture of Queen Alexandra. St James's Palace, on the right, was a hospital for leper women until the 16th century.

Pass straight through St James's, London's oldest park. Cross the bridge with its fairy-tale view of Whitehall, and follow the path to the road on the other side; cross over. A passage leads into Queen Anne's Gate, whose beautiful brown-brick houses date back to the early 18th century and housed numerous dignitaries. Carry on to St James's Park tube, and the amazing golem-like statue to the left of its entrance. Right down Petty France, where Milton wrote much of *Paradise Lost*, and left on Palmer Street, to Caxton Street. On your left is Caxton Hall, where on seven Wednesdays in 1910, Crowley, Neuburg and others performed the magical Rites of Eleusis. While the performances disappointed journalists and policemen expecting a drug-crazed devil orgy, their mix of ritual, music and dance was otherwise surprisingly well received.

Turn right on Caxton Street, past the Blewcoat School Building, dated 1709 and now a National Trust outlet. Turn left down Palace Street, and when you get to Victoria Street, turn right and walk on. To your right, looming dark over the shops before Victoria Palace Theatre, is No.24. Crowley's flat here served as the HQ of his own magical order, the Astrum Argenteum (the AA), whose members included Neuburg and the artist Austin Osman Spare, and the offices of his magical journal, *The Equinox*.

And here your journey ends, but Crowley's troubled, magical life would continue for almost another 40 years. The vision of *fin de siècle* London traced out by our walk is sadly fading fast, but the legend of Aleister Crowley, a man who could never have existed at any other time, lives on.

My thanks to Fraters PB, GJM and TC, and Sorore FMM for signs and clues along the way.

Eating & drinking

06 St Chad's Place
6 St Chad's Place, WC1X 9HH (7278 3355/ www.6stchadsplace.com). **Open** 8am-11pm Mon-Fri. **Food served** 8-10am, noon-2.30pm, 6-9.30pm Mon-Fri.

Blue Lion
133 Gray's Inn Road, WC1X 8TU (7405 4422). **Open** noon-1am Mon, Tue, Thur, Fri; noon-11pm Wed. **Food served** noon-midnight Mon, Tue, Thur, Fri; noon-10pm Wed.

Café Royal
68 Regent Street, W1B 5EL (0870 400 8686). **Open** 10am-11pm Mon-Sat. Drinks and snacks.

Comptons of Soho
51-53 Old Compton Street, W1D 6HJ (7479 7961/www.comptons-of-soho.co.uk). **Open** noon-11pm Mon-Sat; noon-10.30pm Sun. **Happy hour** 7-11pm Mon.

Goat Tavern
3 Stafford Street, W1S 4RP (7629 0966). **Open** noon-11pm Mon-Sat. **Food served** noon-8pm Mon-Sat.

Lamb & Flag
33 Rose Street, WC2E 9EB (7497 9504). **Open** 11am-11pm Mon-Sat; noon-10.30pm Sun. **Food served** noon-3pm Mon-Fri; noon-5pm Sat; noon-3pm Sun.

Plough
27 Museum Street, WC1A 1LH (7636 7964). **Open** 11am-11pm Mon-Sat; noon-10.30pm Sun. **Food served** noon-4pm Mon-Sat; noon-4.30pm Sun.

Princess Louise
208 High Holborn, WC1V 7EP (7405 8816). **Open** 11am-11pm Mon-Fri; noon-11pm Sat; noon-10.30pm Sun. **Food served** noon-2.30pm, 6-8.30pm Mon-Fri; noon-8.30pm Sat, Sun.

Red Lion
23 Crown Passage, off Pall Mall, SW1Y 6PP (7930 4141). **Open/food served** 11am-11pm Mon-Sat.

Salisbury
90 St Martin's Lane, WC2N 4AP (7836 5863). **Open** 11am-11pm Mon-Fri; noon-11pm Sat; noon-10.30pm Sun. **Food served** noon-9pm daily.

Shelley's
10 Stafford Street, W1S 4RX (7493 0337). **Open** 11am-11pm Mon-Sat; noon-10.30pm Sun. **Food served** noon-9pm Mon-Fri; noon-5pm Sat, Sun.

White Hart
191 Drury Lane, WC2B 5QD (7242 2317). **Open** 11am-midnight Mon-Thur; 11am-1am Fri; noon-1am Sat; noon-8pm Sun. **Food served** noon-8pm Mon-Sat; noon-7pm Sun.

Wot the Dickens!
3/5 Woburn Walk, WC1H 0JJ (7383 4813). **Open/food served** 6am-6pm Mon-Fri.

Yorkshire Grey Brewery
2 Theobald's Road, WC1X 8HR (7405 2519). **Open** 11am-11pm Mon-Fri; noon-11pm Sat. **Food served** noon-9pm Mon-Sat.

Bookshops

Aquarium
10 Woburn Walk, WC1H 0JL (7837 8417/ www.aquariumgallery.co.uk). **Open** 11am-6pm Mon-Sat.

Atlantis Bookshop
49A Museum Street, WC1A 1LY (7405 2120/ www.theatlantisbookshop.com). **Open** 10.30am-6pm Mon-Sat.

Four Provinces Bookshop
244 Gray's Inn Road, WC1X 8JR (7833 3022/ www.irishdemocrat.co.uk). **Open** 11am-5.30pm Wed-Sat.

Jarndyce Books
46 Great Russell Street, WC1B 3PA (7631 4220/ www.jarndyce.co.uk). **Open** 10.30am-5.30pm Mon-Fri.

Watkins Books
19 Cecil Court, WC2N 4NH (7836 2182/www. watkinsbooks.com). **Open** 11am-7pm Mon-Sat.

Churches

St Pancras New Church
Euston Road, NW1 2BA (7388 1461/ www.stpancraschurch.org). **Open** call for details. *Services* 1.15pm Mon, Wed; 8am, 10am, 6pm Sun.

St James's Church
197 Piccadilly, W1J 9LL (7734 4511/www.st-james-piccadilly.org). **Open** 8am-6.30pm daily. Evening event times vary. **Admission** free; donations appreciated.

Westminster Chapel
Buckingham Gate, SW1E 6BS (7834 1731/ www.westminsterchapel.org.uk). **Services** 11am, 6pm Sun.

Shopping

Central Regalia
23 Great Queen Street, WC2B 5BB (7405 0004/ www.centralregalia.com). **Open** 9.30am-5pm Mon-Fri; 9.30am-2.30pm Sat.

Christie's
8 King Street, SW1Y 6QT (7839 9060/ www.christies.com). **Open** 9am-4.30pm Mon-Fri.

Paxton & Whitfield
93 Jermyn Street, SW1Y 6JE (7930 0259/ www.paxtonandwhitfield.co.uk). **Open** 9.30am-6pm Mon-Sat.

Toye, Kenning & Spencer
19-21 Great Queen Street, WC2B 5BE (7242 0471/www.toye.com). **Open** 9am-5.20pm Mon-Fri; 9am-2.30pm Sat.

George F Trumper
20 Jermyn Street, SW1Y 6HP (7734 1370/ www.trumpers.com). **Open** 9am-5.30pm Mon-Fri; 9am-5pm Sat.

Others

British Museum
Great Russell Street, WC1B 3DG (7636 1555/ www.thebritishmuseum.ac.uk). **Open** *Galleries* 10am-5.30pm Mon-Wed, Sat, Sun; 10am-8.30pm Thur, Fri. *Great Court* 9am-6pm Mon-Wed, Sun; 9am-11pm Thur-Sat. *Highlights tours* (90mins) 10.30am, 1pm, 3pm daily. **Admission** free; donations appreciated. *Temporary exhibitions* prices vary. *Highlights tours* £8; £5 concessions.

Caxton Hall
Caxton Street, SW1 (no phone).

Freemasons' Hall
60 Great Queen Street, WC2B 5AZ (7831 9811/ www.grandlodge-england.org). **Open** 10am-5pm Mon-Fri; 10.30-11.30am Sat.

Gray's Inn Fields
Tours 7458 7800.

New Connaught Rooms
61-65 Great Queen Street, WC2B 5DA (7405 7811/www.newconnaughtrooms.co.uk).

Palace Theatre
Cambridge Circus, Shaftesbury Avenue, W1D 5AY (0870 895 5579). **Box Office** *in person* 10am-8pm Mon-Sat.

Victoria Palace Theatre
Victoria Street, SW1E 5EA (0870 895 5577). **Box Office** 10am-6pm Mon-Sat.

Literature

Book of the Law Aleister Crowley (1904)
The Confessions of Aleister Crowley: An Autohagiography Aleister Crowley (1970)
The Diary of a Drug Fiend Aleister Crowley (1922)
Do What Thy Wilt: A Life of Aleister Crowley Lawrence Sutin (2000)
The Hill of Dreams Arthur Machen (1907)
Moonchild Aleister Crowley (1929)
Things Near and Far Arthur Machen (1923)

Middle East end

Andrew Humphreys

Draw on a sheesha and sip on mint tea for an Arabian night on the town.

Start: Edgware Road tube (Circle, District or Hammersmith & City lines exit)
Finish: Notting Hill Gate tube
Time: 2-3 hours
Distance: 3 miles/5km
Getting there: Circle, District or Hammersmith & City lines to Edgware Road
Getting back: ten-minute walk to Notting Hill Gate (Central, Circle or District lines)
Note: given that part of this walk is through Hyde Park, setting off during daylight hours is probably a good idea. If you do it on a Sunday, you'll catch the open-air art fair along Hyde Park railings between Lancaster Gate and Queensway. However, Edgware Road and Queensway are at their liveliest and most vibrant in the evening.

G ranted, if you look in your A-Z, the Edgware Road and near neighbour Queensway may appear to be in London, but the reality is that they are, in fact, two far-flung suburbs of Beirut and Cairo. If you want to pick up your copy of the Arab world daily *Al Hayat*, cash a cheque at the Bank of Kuwait or catch Egyptian league football on TV in a boisterous sweetly scented, smoke-filled café, then this west central corner, squeezed between Marble Arch and Notting Hill, Hyde Park and Paddington, is where you come.

It's an insular world and one little visited by most Londoners. Falafel, houmous and kebabs we're all familiar with, and sitting cross-legged on rug-covered benches around mosaicked tables with Aladdin's cave lighting – and the rest of the oriental shtick – is very much flavour of the month (see Portobello Road's chic watering hole Bed, Clapham's SO.UK, the recent 'old Araby' makeover of the Duke of York in St John's Wood and, of course, the continued success of Momo). But this is all window dressing and about as true to the modern Middle East as Dick Van Dyke's accent was to London. The East-West dialogue goes much deeper than that. Our fine city is, in fact, the intellectual capital of the Arab world. It's home base for several major international Arabic-language newspapers, Arabic satellite TV stations and the BBC Arabic service, broadcasting out of Bush House and respected across the Middle East for its impartiality. It's a centre for Arab exiles and opposition groups, who enjoy the freedom of speech in Britain that they could never exploit at home, organising revolution by phone, fax and email. Viewed from Riyadh, Damascus and Baghdad, London is also a place of economic opportunity, a provider of quality education for the kids and a shoppers' paradise.

It's the last of those factors, shopping, according to one Lebanese friend of mine, that kicked off the whole Arab London scene. It began in the early 1970s with the quadrupling of world oil prices, from which the Gulf Arabs were the major beneficiaries. Their money brought them to England, a country they were familiar with via our imperial habit of meddling in other people's affairs. It was, after all, the British who drew the map of the modern Middle East; TE Lawrence, better known as Lawrence of Arabia, would boast that he was one of a small group who had pencilled in the borders over dinner. Given the troubled history of the region since, it must have been a very short dinner. Travel writer Jonathan Raban in his *Arabia Through the Looking Glass* (1979) records the sudden arrival (he dates it to summer '73) of white-robed men and their black-clad wives who walked exactly four paces behind on the streets of Earl's Court. The new arrivals also favoured the Edgware Road and surrounding streets, largely because of the plentiful availability of summer-let accommodation, but also because of the proximity to the department stores of Oxford Street, in particular, the Marble Arch branch of Marks & Spencer.

Prior to this, Cairo and Beirut had been the traditional summer heat retreats for the Gulf Arabs, so when they switched to London, along came a whole host of Egyptians and Lebanese – not to mention Iraqis, Morrocans and Yemenis – in their wake to start up the restaurants, cafés, clubs and cinemas to make their moneyed brethren feel at home in the UK. Thirty years on, Marks & Spencer has lost whatever cachet it once had, and in a surprising turnaround, the world now flies to hip and happening Dubai to shop in style. Nevertheless, the Gulf Arabs and assorted Middle Easterners seem attached to London, and the Edgware Road remains their base.

Unfortunately the northern end of the road, where our walk begins at the Hammersmith and City line tube station, is London at its grimmest. As you exit the station, turning right along Chapel Street, the ground vibrates to the tune of the cars and lorries thundering over the Marylebone flyover. Ahead is the Hilton Metropole, currently stuck with one of the most unappealing locations of any London five-star but hoping for payday when the Paddington Basin development behind reaches completion. Few people seem to have had anything good to say about the Edgware Road, and it features rarely in London lore. Graham Greene wrote a haunted cinema tale, 'A Little Place Off the Edgware Road', and in a noirish short story, 'Perfect Casting', contemporary London writer Christopher

Green Valley

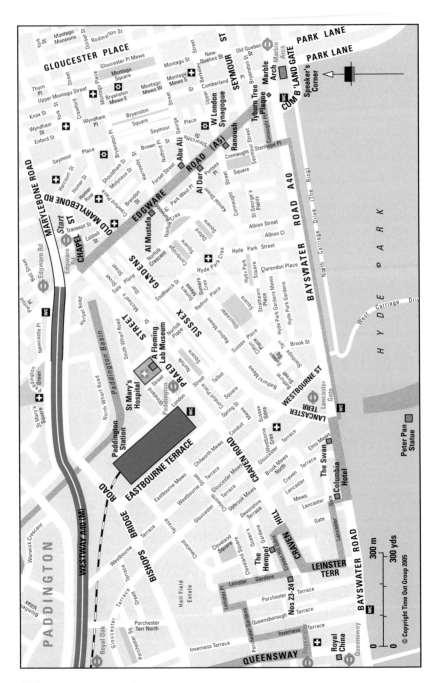

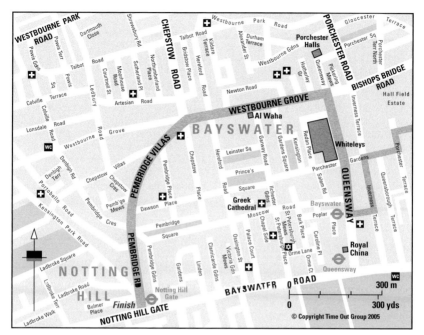

Fowler has a jobbing actor turn up for a fateful audition on the Edgware Road 'skirting filthy puddles to locate a small turning between the kebab shops and falafel bars'. Much more to my liking is the Edgware Road in the opening scenes of *Room to Rent*, a British film directed by Khaled El Hagar, himself an Egyptian immigrant, and starring Juliette Lewis, Rupert Everett and Said Taghmaoui. Shot at night from the perspective of a speeding scooter, it's a pulsating montage of lollipop neon, ethnic faces and Arabic-language signs. It could almost be Beirut, then suddenly a red double-decker cuts through and you realise that this is London. So let's go explore.

Heading south from Chapel Street, the Arabisation begins cautiously with a smattering of bilingual announcements for the likes of Mecca Estate Agents and Halal Meat. It quickly picks up pace and by the time you cross Old Marylebone Road there's been a complete calligraphic revolution. Some shopfronts dispense

with English altogether; their signboards are lettered wholly in elegant wafts of ripples, curves and dots. Names end in 'oush' (Fattoush, Tarboush) and Lebanese becomes the adjective of choice – as in Lebanese restaurant, Lebanese supermarket – used to imply class and sophistication, for the Lebanese are the French of the Middle East. Across the road from Woolworths, Al Mustafa is the first of the Edgware Road's *ba'als*, or grocer's. They are the traditional corner shops that we bemoan the loss of in Britain. Shop here for mangoes, figs and dates, beans and pulses, trays of briny olives and sharp pickled veg, white cheese, rosewater and great big sacks of rice. I especially love these places for the smell of the herbs and spices, so densely pungent that, walking through, you almost expect to leave tracks in the air.

Continuing south, the junction with George Street heralds the real Middle East End heartland. Off to the left is the Abu Ali Café; to the right are Café du Liban,

Al-Dar and Al Shishaw. Somewhere in Syria, Lebanon, Jordan or Egypt on some sun-hammered city centre street must be a series of gaping empty lots where these four establishments were torn out whole, air-lifted, then dropped into place here in London. They are as authentically and unexpectedly Middle Eastern as it gets, particularly Abu Ali. While inside a TV blares the latest Nile-pop hits, outside (English weather permitting) there's usually a pavement line-up of Arab men sucking on sheeshas, the glass-bottom waterpipes, billowing out enough grey smoke to worry world emission regulators.

For a slightly more upmarket smoking experience, try puce and kitschy Al-Dar over the road. One sheesha costs more than a whole packet of fags, but it does take half an hour to smoke. The tobacco used is soaked in apple juice giving it a sweet aftertaste. It's a little sickly (back in Cairo, world capital of sheesha smoking, apple tobacco is for the tourists; real men smoke molasses) but fine if countered with mint tea, the real stuff, with twigs and leaves stuffed in the teapot.

Get lucky and instead of the terrible tinny, clappy pap that passes for Arabic music these days, your café of choice might be playing some of the old stuff, with sensuous swirling strings and the gravelly voice of Umm Kolthum. Bigger than Elvis, bigger than the Beatles, Umm Kolthum was a legend across the Arab world, and when she died in 1975 her funeral drew three million people out on to the streets of Cairo. Elvis Costello's a fan: he included her anthology in his '500 albums you need' listed in *Vanity Fair* in 2000. If you want to hear what impresses him, nip over the road to Falcon, a great Arabic music shop hidden behind a bureau de change frontage. It has a fine selection of Umm Kolthum cassettes, as well as plenty of less essential artists.

A quick detour round the corner on to Upper Berkeley Street brings a reminder that before the Arabs this part of west London was settled by other immigrants – the biblical-looking West London Synagogue was founded in 1841 and still serves a thriving local community, hosting Shabbat and festival services, and Bar and Bat Mitzvahs. Next door, Green Valley is another Lebanese supermarket, notable for its excellent deli counter and flat disks of unleavened bread baked on the premises and sold hot. It also does great syrupy baklava and konafe, but if you buy from here, then you probably won't want to go to nearby Ranoush, the Edgware Road's landmark snack and juice bar. Drop in here for all the standards (tabbouleh, houmous, labneh, falafel, stuffed vine leaves etc), plus excellent chicken liver sandwiches and garlicky shwarma (lamb or chicken) sandwiches. Busy throughout the day, the place really gets buzzing late in the evening when it becomes a west London alternative to Soho's Bar Italia for a post-pub or club caffeine fix or munchie binge.

A few doors down from Ranoush, and owned by the same Lebanese entrepreneur, the restaurant Maroush is another local institution – its first felafels hit the deep-fryer over 25 years ago. It's now the centre of a mini-empire with Maroushes spreading throughout London, but this, the original, still largely caters to the oil-rich, with belly dancing and music until 2am, and a £48 per head minimum charge.

As you approach the bottom end of Edgware Road the bustle of the Middle East fades away and older, darker, English history kicks in. Over the road is a modern glass-fronted JD Wetherspoon pub called the Tyburn – a name which commemorate London's principal place of public execution, in use from 1388 to 1783, where at one time there was a great triangular gallows on which 21 people could be hanged at once. Condemned prisoners were driven here in a cart from the gaol at Newgate. At Tyburn the executioner stopped the cart under the gibbet, placed a noose over the unfortunate's head and gave the horse a lash with his whip, as graphically described by a 17th-century observer: 'Away goes the cart and there swings my gentleman, kicking in the air. The hangman does not give himself the trouble to put them out of their pain but some of their friends or relatives do it for them. They pull the dying person by the legs and beat his breast to dispatch him as soon as possible.'

The spectacle drew huge crowds – an estimated 200,000 witnessed one death in 1714 – and hanging days became public holidays. Today the approximate site of the gallows is marked by a stone in the traffic island at the junction of Edgware and Bayswater roads.

From the pub cross over the road to stand in front of the blue plaque on the corner of Connaught Place stating that statesman Lord Randolph Churchill (best remembered for fathering Winston) lived here at No.2, and admire the beautiful vision of Georgian London presented by the arcade of cream-coloured porticoes with hanging carriage lamps. No.11 at the far end is home to the FA Premier League. Exiting on to Stanhope Place you're presented with another fine view, here of Hyde Park and beyond it the chimneys of Battersea Power Station appearing as four great free-standing white columns, like the lonely remains of some ancient temple – a Baalbek or Palmyra over by the Thames.

A convenient zebra crossing lets you ford the traffic of Bayswater Road and enter the park. Although Bayswater Road is an ancient thoroughfare, part of the Roman Via Trinobantia, serious development of the area didn't begin until after public executions had ended at Tyburn. Then, in the early 19th century, the Bishop of London embarked on an ambitious high-class building scheme on church estates, resulting in the series of attractive terraces, gardens and squares just to the north, such as Sussex Gardens. But it's nicer to walk through the park,

heading west on the path that meanders through the trees. You pass Albion Gate, a grand name for a break in the railings. At Victoria Gate don't be forced back on to Bayswater Road; bear left back into the park and pick up the path again.

From here there's a very pronounced downhill slope to an attractive arrangement of four fountains, an ornate pump house and a long stretch of water, called, with great inspiration, the Long Water. This dip marks the passage of one of the 'lost rivers' of London, the Westbourne, once an open water course, now covered over and piped in, turned into a storm sewer to carry water from roadside gutters. The buried river begins as several streamlets flowing down the hill to the west of Hampstead and flows under Kilburn High Road, Maida Vale and Paddington and into the park. It doesn't empty into the Long Water (which becomes the Serpentine), but is carried in a Victorian conduit constructed beneath the lake's left bank. It eventually empties into the Thames at Chelsea.

Leave the park here by Marlborough Gate, opposite Lancaster Gate tube station. Over the road is one of the area's oldest buildings, the Swan, originally an 18th-century coaching tavern that stood beside a bridge over the (now-buried) Westbourne. Unfortunately the interior has been charmlessly modernised, but the forecourt, looking on to the park, is pleasant enough for a pint. (Real beer fans might want to veer to the right of the Royal Lancaster Hotel and nip down Bathurst Street to the Archery Tavern, purveyor of excellent Badger Best, Tanglefoot and Sussex.)

West a short distance is the Lancaster Gate for which the tube station is named. It's a gorgeous mid 19th-century scheme of townhouse terraces around three sides of a central grassy square. Until 1978 it was arguably one of London's most attractive bits of urban landscaping. Sadly in that year Christ Church, the centrepiece of the square, was pulled down because of structural damage and to the surviving spire was appended a truly foul bit of modern housing development. Most of the surrounding buildings are now hotels, including at Nos.95-99, the Columbia Hotel, whose management banned Oasis after the group's rock 'n' roll room-trashing activities. The episode inspired the song 'Columbia' on *Definitely Maybe*.

We're now well into Bayswater. According to the *London Encyclopedia* the name is probably a corruption of Bayard's Watering, which was once chief of the district's springs and a drinking place for horses. Strange to think, looking at the solid architecture with its air of history and permanence, but all you see is only around 150 years old. At the time they were built the interconnected crescents and squares, like Lancaster Gate, were meant to rival Belgravia, and the area succeeded in drawing wealthy merchants and fashionable Victorian society.

If you walk west to the corner with Leinster Terrace, No.100 is where playwright Sir James Barrie lived from 1902 to 1909 and where he wrote *Peter Pan*. But there was a dip in fortune in the early 20th century and the classic Victorian stucco townhouses, built for large families and their larger numbers of servants, were divided up to provide cheap lodgings. For decades following, the area became synonymous with prostitution, poverty and neglect. It's only in recent times that some measure of prosperity has returned and those cheap lodgings have been upgraded to mid-range chain hotels catering for an international array of visitors. Want to strike up a conversation with Wilma from Montana or Phil and Jo from Auckland? Drop in the Leinster Arms, where you'll hear every accent but English.

The surfeit of tourists has so far meant that Bayswater hasn't gone the way of neighbouring Notting Hill, filled with hip and haughty hangouts,

but the area does boast the Hempel, the most Zen of hotels, discreetly hidden at 31 Craven Hill Gardens, just off Leinster Gardens. Its white-on-white lobby is breathtaking, and one of the starkly minimalist bedrooms even has a bed that hangs from the ceiling. The sort of guests who pay anything from £285 to £1,525 a night for a room tend to like their privacy, and walk-in sightseeing is not encouraged.

Back in the mortal world, notice anything odd about the house at 23-24 Leinster Gardens? Like windows that aren't windows but are painted grey squares. That's because there is no house at Nos.23-24. It's just an elaborate bit of set decoration, a painted wall built to hide an opening to the Underground line below through which early engines would let off steam.

Carry on up the street, take a left at Leinster Place, cross Porchester and Queensborough Terraces and then take the second left into Inverness Terrace. When I said that the area had risen in tone in recent times, there are exceptions and this street is one of them. This is pure, unreconstructed 1970s Bayswater, a street of divey, low rent joints with plastic chairs on the balconies, towels drying over railings, garbage piling up on forecourts and an ever-present whiff of spliff in the air. Appropriately enough Nos.41-49 was where Jimi Hendrix stayed for the first few nights on his arrival in London in September 1966. It must be his lingering spirit that keeps gentrification at bay.

The strains of Arabic begin to surface once again here as you cut right part way down Inverness Terrace, passing by the Lorraine Electronics Spy Shop, stockists of bullet-proof waistcoats, fountain pen microphones, night-vision torches and other Bondian paraphernalia; a sign says 'No browsing'. Spoilsports. This cut-through brings you out on to Queensway, the brash and trashy heart of Bayswater. I love this street. When I

Maroush

was a small kid my parents used to take me every summer to Blackpool, and here in west London the shops full of tourist tat, the pavements crammed with promenading out-of-towners, and the way Hyde Park creates a horizon at the bottom end of the street, all remind me of those holidays. And then there's Whiteley's, lit up at night like the Blackpool Tower building – but minus the tower. What Blackpool never had, though, was Queensway's vibrantly cosmopolitan ambience, a mix of Asian (the Royal China restaurant is London's best for dim sum, with queues at weekend lunchtimes to prove it), South American (to some, the area goes by the alternative name of 'Brazilwater'), Mediterranean and Middle Eastern. Not as overt as on Edgware Road, but the Arab presence is heavy.

Check out the newsstands: the Arabic-language press fills the racks out front with the English papers relegated to the shelves inside. Mobile phones ring with the catchy riff of Khaled's 'Abdel Khader', which in its ubiquity is the Arab-world equivalent of the lambada (but while one's a dance, the other's an ode to an Islamic saint). And of course, there are the eateries: Taza, down the bottom end, is a takeaway joint that does excellent shwarma to rival that at Ranoush; Fakhreldine Express at No.92 does merely average Lebanese fast food but is worth popping in for a look at the Warhol-inspired silkscreen prints on the walls by local Lebanese artist Rana Salam.

Continuing north, Queensway's pre-eminent landmark, Whiteley's, has the dubious distinction of being admired by Adolf Hitler. It's said that he ordered the Luftwaffe not to bomb it during the Blitz because he wanted the place as his headquarters when he conquered Britain. The story behind the great store is the archetypal rags-to-riches tale, with a suitably soap opera-ish ending. William Whiteley was a 20-year-old Yorkshireman when in 1851 he made his first visit to London to see the Great Exhibition. Inspired by the displays of manufactured goods, he made it his aim to create an emporium as grand as the Exhibition's Crystal Palace. Beginnings were humble: premises on Westbourne Grove retailing 'fancy goods' with a staff of two serving girls and an errand boy. But within ten years the business had expanded all along the street and Whiteley advertised himself as 'the Universal Provider', claiming to supply everything 'from a pin to an elephant at short notice'. If this made him popular with shoppers, it was less welcomed by other local tradesmen and they burned Whiteley's effigy on Guy Fawkes' Night in 1876.

No foul play was reported, but it was Whiteley's store that burned in 1897, blazing for seven days in a fire that could be seen from Highgate Hill. The indefatigable Yorkshireman rebuilt, establishing a new store staffed by 6,000. It became a household name, the Harrods of its day; Queen Victoria shopped there (not in person) and in *Pygmalion* Eliza Doolittle is sent to Whiteley's 'to be attired'.

Whiteley's dramatic end came on 24 January 1907 when he was shot dead in his office by a man who claimed to be his bastard son. The store survived and, in fact, flourished, moving in 1911 into the present purpose-built premises on Queensway. After a long, slow, post-war decline, during which time Bayswater became too shabby and under-moneyed to support such an immense retail outlet, Whiteley's finally closed for business in 1981. Happily it reopened at the end of the decade, albeit as a mall. It may not offer the most exciting shopping (it's full of the usual mall contents: Tie Racks, Sock Shops, chain cafés and the like) but it is, nevertheless, an unquestioned success and is largely credited with turning round the fortunes of the area. Café Rapallo on the ground floor of the shopping centre by the escalators is Queensway's most popular Lebanese hangout.

Just beyond the northern end of Whiteley's is the junction with Westbourne Grove. Directly ahead, over the road, is one of London's few remaining Victorian underground public toilets, while just up the hill is Porchester Hall, the pride and joy of Westminster City Council. It's a curious old place (built in 1925) that's all things to everybody. Under one roof it combines a chlorine-scented leisure centre, Turkish baths and a grand hall for hire, used for Christian, Jewish and Muslim weddings, regular tea dances for local OAPs, school exams, an annual tango festival, and miscellaneous PR events (Destiny's Child launched their last album here). It was the venue for Elton John's 50th birthday party, and back in the mid 1980s I remember seeing Mick Jones's then-new band, Big Audio Dynamite, play their debut gig at the Porchester. However, unless you're up for a swim or a steam cleaning, there's little to see at the hall, so head west along Westbourne Grove.

A country lane flanked by tall trees and fields prior to the 1850s, then a shopping centre to rival Oxford Street through until the 1930s, Westbourne Grove is again in the process of transformation. At present it's a fairly low rent sort of place, distinguished by some interesting small businesses and a handful of good restaurants.

At No.26 is my favourite London bookshop, Saqi Books, Middle Eastern specialists – so it helps to have more than a passing interest in early Fatimid architecture or Sufi poetry. Set up 21 years ago by Lebanese fleeing the civil war in Beirut, the shop (and neighbouring Kufa Gallery) occupies the old Westbourne Hall, a Victorian music hall – walk through to the back and you can see the old auditorium beyond a windowed partition wall. Down the street, on the left-hand side is Al Waha, which gets my vote as London's finest Lebanese restaurant; it's smart and intimate with good professional service, and the food is first rate. Further on, Dar Al Dawa is a truly quirky little Islamic emporium, purveyor of mosque alarm clocks, prayer mats and jalabeyyas, the one-piece robes traditionally associated with Middle Eastern men. Just beyond the junction with Chepstow Road, Rico's

is a famed Brazilian haunt for coffee, just-like-home cooking, Portuguese conversation and somewhere to pick up the two free Brazilian magazines published in London. But all this could be due to change. The influence (not to say affluence) of comfortably white Notting Hill is closing in. Recent years have seen the addition of the Elbow Room, the highly fashionable pool hall-cum-bar, and the Reel Poster Gallery, a Cork Street-like space devoted to the sale of original film posters.

To see where the trend is leading, you could carry on along the Grove into W11 proper with its ultra-chic fashion outlets, boutiques and Piers Gough-designed public toilets. You're only half a mile from Dar Al Dawa and still on the same street, but here 'Arab' is no more than an adjective intended to justify serious over-pricing on some antique rug or artefact in a designer ethnic furnishings store. Curmudgeon that I am, I tend to quit my wanderings long before I reach this point and either swing left down Pembridge Villas for the tube station at Notting Hill Gate, or, better still, backtrack and get myself some more baklava and mint tea.

My thanks to Mai Ghossoub, Rana Salam and Khaled El Hagar.

Eating & drinking

Abu Ali Café
136-138 George Street, W1H 5LD (7724 6338). **Open** 9am-11pm daily. Lebanese food.

Al-Dar
61-63 Edgware Road, W2 2HZ (7402 2541/ www.aldar.co.uk). **Meals served** 8am-1am daily. Sheeshas, fruit juices, grills, meze and cakes.

Al Shishaw
51-53 Edgware Road, W2 2HZ (7262 6212). **Open** 5am-1am Mon-Thur; 24hrs Fri, Sat; 5am-midnight Sun. Middle Eastern food and sheeshas.

Al Waha
75 Westbourne Grove, W2 4UL (7229 0806/ www.waha-uk.com). **Meals served** noon-midnight daily. Traditional Lebanese cooking – one of the best.

Queensway's pride – **Whiteley's** shopping mall has boosted the area's fortunes.

Archery Tavern
4 Bathurst Street, W2 2SD (7402 4916).
Open 11am-11pm Mon-Sat; noon-10.30pm
Sun. **Food served** noon-3pm, 6-9.30pm
Mon-Fri; noon-9.30pm Sat; noon-9pm Sun.

Bed
310 Portobello Road, W10 5TA (8969
4500/www.styleinthecity.co.uk). **Open/food**
served 5-11pm Mon-Thur; noon-11pm
Fri, Sat; noon-10.30pm Sun. Moroccan-
themed bar.

Café du Liban
71 Edgware Road, W2 2HZ (7706 1534).
Open 9am-midnight daily. Juices, cakes and
full Lebanese menu, and, of course, sheeshas.

Café Rapallo
Unit 25-26, Ground Floor, Whiteley's,
Queensway, W2 4YQ (7221 3258). **Open**
9am-11pm Mon-Sat; 10am-10.30pm Sun.
Coffees and snacks.

Duke of York
7 Roger Street, WC1N 2PB (7242 7230).
Open noon-11pm Mon-Fri; noon-11pm
Sat; noon-10.30pm Sun. **Food served**
noon-10pm Mon-Sat; noon-9.30pm Sun.

Elbow Room
103 Westbourne Grove, W2 4UW (7221 5211/
www.elbow-room.co.uk). **Open/food served**
noon-11pm Mon-Sat; 1-10.30pm Sun.

Fakhreldine Express
92 Queensway, W2 3RR (7493 3424).
Open noon-midnight Mon-Sat; noon-11pm
Sun. Cold meze, salads and fruit juices.

Leinster Arms
17 Leinster Terrace, W2 3EU (7402 4670).
Open noon-11pm Mon-Sat; noon-10.30pm Sun.
Food served noon-9pm daily.

Maroush
21 Edgware Road, W2 2JE (7723 0773/
www.maroush.com). **Meals served** noon-
midnight daily. Excellent Lebanese fare.

Momo
14 Queen's Place, W5 3HU (8997 0206).
Open noon-2.30pm, 6-10pm Mon-Sat.
Portuguese-influenced Japanese cuisine.

Ranoush Juice Bar
43 Edgware Road, W2 2JR (7723 5929/
www.maroush.com). **Meals served** 8am-3am
daily. Fruit juice extravaganzas.

Rodizio Rico
111 Westbourne Grove, W2 4UW (7792 4035).
Meals served 6-11.30pm Mon-Fri; noon-4.30pm,
6-11.30pm, 12.30-10.30pm Sun. Brazilian BBQ.

Royal China
*13 Queensway, W2 4QJ (7221 2535/www.royal
chinagroup.co.uk).* **Meals served** noon-11pm
Mon-Thur; noon-11.30pm Fri, Sat; 11am-10pm
Sun. **Dim sum** noon-5pm Mon-Sat; 11am-5pm
Sun. The best dim sum in London.

SO.UK
*165 Clapham High Street, SW4 7SS (7622
4004/www.soukclapham.co.uk).* **Open** 5pm-
midnight Mon, Sun; 5pm-2am Tue-Sat. **Food
served** 6-10pm daily. A global mix of food.

Swan
66 Bayswater Road, W2 3PH (7262 5204).
Open 10am-11pm Mon-Sat; 10am-10.30pm Sun.

Taza
35A Queensway, W2 4QJ (7727 7420). **Open**
9.30am-midnight daily. Middle Eastern style café.

Tyburn
*18-20 Edgware Road, W2 2EN (7723 4731/
www.jdwetherspoon.co.uk).* **Open** 10am-11pm
daily. **Food served** 10am-10pm Mon-Sat; 10am-
9.30pm Sun.

Film & literature

Arabia Through the Looking Glass
Jonathan Raban (1979)

A Little Place Off the Edgware Road (from
Twenty-One Stories, Graham Greene, 1954)

The London Encyclopedia ed Ben Weinreb &
Christopher Hibbert (1983)

Perfect Casting Christopher Fowler (from
London Noir, ed Maxim Jakubowski, 1994)

Peter Pan JM Barrie (1904)

Pygmalion George Bernard Shaw (1916)

Room to Rent (Khaled El Hagar, 2000, UK)

Hotels

Columbia Hotel
*95-99 Lancaster Gate, W2 3NS (7402 0021/
www.columbiahotel.co.uk).*

Hempel
*31-5 Craven Hill Gardens, W2 3EA (7298 9000/
www.the-hempel.co.uk).*

Hilton London Metropole
*225 Edgware Road, W2 1JU (7402 4141/
www.hiltonlondonmet.com).*

Shopping

Al Mustafa
133-135 Edgware Road, W2 3HR (7402 7707).
Open 8am-midnight daily.

Dar Al Dawa
97 Westbourne Grove, W2 4UW (7221 6256).
Open 9am-10pm daily.

Falcon
82 Edgware Road, W2 2EA (7723 5121).
Open 10am-10pm Mon-Fri; noon-10pm
Sat, Sun.

Green Valley
*37 Upper Berkeley Street, W1H 5QE (7723
2545).* **Open** 8am-midnight daily.

Lorraine Electronics Spy Shop
*59 South Audley Street, W1K 2QS (7493 4007/
www.lorraine.co.uk).* **Open** 9am-6pm Mon-Fri;
10am-5pm Sat.

Marks & Spencer
*458 Oxford Street, W1C 1AP (7935 7954/
www.marksandspencer.com).* **Open** 9am-9pm
Mon-Fri; 9am-8pm Sat; noon-6pm Sun.

Reel Poster Gallery
*72 Westbourne Grove, W2 5SH (7727 4488/
www.reelposter.com).* **Open** 11am-7pm Mon-Fri;
noon-6pm Sat.

Saqi Bookshop
*26 Westbourne Grove, W2 5RH (7221 9347/
www.saqibooks.com).* **Open** 10am-6pm Mon-Sat.

Whiteley's Shopping Centre
*Queensway, W2 4YN (7229 8844/
www.whiteleys.com).* **Open** 10am-8pm
Mon-Sat; noon-6pm Sun.

Others

FA Premier League
*11 Connaught Place, W2 2ET (7298 1600/
www.premierleague.com).*

Marble Arch Odeon
*10 Edgware Road, W2 2EN (0871 224 4007/
www.odeon.co.uk).*

Porchester Hall
Queensway, W2 5HS (7792 2823).

West London Synagogue
*33 Seymour Place, W1H 5AU (7723 4404/
www.wls.org.uk).*

Whittington's cat and Winchester Geese

Joy Wotton

Explore the sites of the bishop's brothels on Bankside and walk the medieval streets trod by London's most famous mayor.

Start: Monument tube
Finish: Monument tube
Time: 3-4 hours
Distance: 3.5 miles/5.5km
Getting there: Circle or District lines to Monument
Getting back: Circle or District lines from Monument
Note: City churches and pubs are usually closed at weekends, and the Guildhall is closed to the public from time to time for civic functions. It is also worth consulting Rick Jones's walk and Liza Picard's walk as there is some overlap.

The modern City of London appears an unpromising starting point for a walk that explores the sleazier side of medieval London. Can any trace of the bawdy women known as the Bishop of Winchester's Geese or the many 'houses of easement' or public conveniences set up by legendary mayor Dick Whittington be found beneath today's erections of concrete and steel? Closer examination of the street map reveals many old-sounding names from Love Lane to Bread Street. The Great Fire of London and the air raids of the Blitz may have destroyed almost all of medieval London, but following each event the City was rebuilt in such haste that the medieval street layout survived almost untouched. This walk makes use of modern bridges and of Queen Street, one of the two new roads created after the Great Fire, but apart from that it sticks to the streets and alleyways (not to mention the brothels and prisons) medieval Londoners knew.

At Monument station follow the exit sign to Fish Street Hill and the Monument. Walk down towards the Monument and consider the destruction of the medieval City of London in 1666 by the Great Fire, as devastating in its way as the Blitz. The fire raged for five days from Pudding Lane up to Pye Corner in Smithfield. 44 livery halls, 13,200 houses and 87 churches were burned down. Shopkeepers set up booths in the still smouldering ruins in a desperate endeavour to keep London going as the economic capital. Sir Christopher Wren's vision of a modern road layout with his cathedral at its hub never really stood a chance. Trade had to be restored before the economic centre moved elsewhere, and it would have taken as many years then as it would now to buy up the hundreds of property owners in the City. In the end, a modern scheme of rebuilding was imposed on the medieval street structure, making it possible to walk today the streets that Dick Whittington (and perhaps his cat) knew, and explore the stewes (brothels) and prisons of Old London Town.

Follow Fish Street Hill down to the Thames. This was the major approach to Old London Bridge, which stood about 30 feet east of the current version. Cross over Lower Thames Street to St Magnus the Martyr. In 1420, Sir Robert Wattes, chaplain to the Fishmongers' Guild, 'was taken in adultery with Alice Sourby in

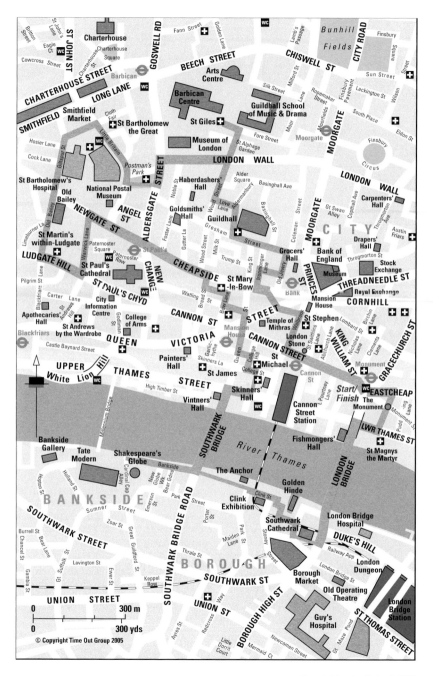

The Monument

the stewes neare St Magnus' church at the Bridge entrance'. The open tower allowed a public footpath to lead through it and up on to Old London Bridge. The tower clock hung out over the bridge. In the churchyard is some petrified Roman piling, perhaps from a Roman bridge downstream, and broken stones from the 1830 bridge. So many fragments of this bridge are still in London that it's a wonder they managed to re-erect it at Lake Havasu City, Arizona.

Inside St Magnus church is a model of the 1400 bridge, made in 1987 by David T Aggett. The bridge was 21 feet wide, and so crowded with houses and shops that in places the road was only five feet wide. Over 1,000 figures on the model bridge are busy – fishing, selling, throwing out slops – and at the first gap on the west end, the artist has installed himself as a modern policeman. The medieval parish of St Magnus stretched across the bridge and into Southwark, a sure indication of how important control of this route was.

Come out of the churchyard and turn left. Follow a sign on the left to London Bridge and Southwark Cathedral. Walk up the subway stairs and across London Bridge. In the centre of Old London Bridge was a chapel to Thomas Becket, who signed the Ordinance of 1161 that licensed the Bankside stewes or brothels, the year before he unwillingly became archbishop. A large public lavatory on London Bridge is known to history only because in 1306 William de Prestone was chased by debtors through the streets of London until he reached London Bridge and 'went unto the privie there… and then he left the prevye by an other entrance' and escaped. In 1305, the head of 'Braveheart' William Wallace was stuck up above the gatehouse, the first of what was to become a gruesome display.

The bridge was closed during the Peasants' Revolt of 1381 by William Walworth, a fishmonger and London's mayor. However, the rebel leader Wat

Tyler took it without a fight when he threatened to burn it down. Having burned down the Clink Prison, he led his rebels over the bridge to destroy the Fleet and Newgate prisons. Later, Mayor Walworth stabbed Tyler at Smithfield, pulling him from his horse to the ground, where he was finished off. Henry V rode across the gaily bedecked bridge after his victory at Agincourt.

Take the steps on the right down to Green Dragon Court and Southwark Cathedral, previously the Priory Church of St Mary Overie or 'over the river' or 'ferry'. It was founded in 1106 and is one of the largest medieval buildings in London. Richard II's poet laureate, John Gower, has a gaudy tomb on the left in the north aisle. The background to the Shakespeare monument in the south nave is a low relief of Bankside and Old London Bridge. Mentally excise those Tudor theatres and add a large number of white-painted, detached houses standing in their own grounds, with the sign for each brothel painted flat on each house front. Stewes could be distinguished from inns, because inns would hang their signs at right angles to the street.

Leave the cathedral and follow Cathedral Street round to the right towards the reconstruction of Drake's ship the *Golden Hinde* in St Mary Overie's Dock. This is a free landing place where St Saviour's parishioners are entitled to load goods free of toll. (At the Reformation St Mary Overie became St Saviour's.) The original *Golden Hinde* was the world's first floating maritime museum after Elizabeth I ordered the ship's preservation, following Drake's epic voyage around the world.

From the *Golden Hinde*, walk on via Pickfords Wharf to the remains of the 12th-century Winchester Palace, the town home of the bishops of Winchester from the 1140s until 1626. The bishop owned most of the land occupied by the Bankside brothels along the Thames's south bank. He first licensed the brothels in 1161, and the bawds became known as Winchester Geese.

Following the Peasants' Revolt, the Great Hall of Winchester Palace was extended by Henry of Yeovil. The women's prison remained in the courtyard, but the men's prison was transferred to the vaults under the Great Hall. Gratings at street level served as begging points for starving prisoners, and the area could be flooded at high tide. The constant clinking and clanking of manacles and fetters, chains and bolts may have given the prison its ominous name – the Clink.

Pickfords Wharf runs into Clink Street, where a man in irons welcomes you to the Clink Prison Museum. Turbulent Southwark, with its tavern fights, bull- and bear-baiting, bawds and strumpets, boasted five prisons – the Compter, the King's Bench, the Marshalsea, the White Lyon and the Clink. The Clink began as a small, obscure prison, owned by the Bishop of Winchester and used to maintain order in his licensed brothels along Bankside. The Tudor historian John Stow, who wrote the first detailed history of London in 1598, speaks of it as having been a prison 'for such as should brabble, frey or breake the Peace on the banke, or in the Brothell houses'. The term 'in the clink' has become a synonym for imprisonment anywhere.

Walk under the railway bridge to find the Anchor pub. Samuel Pepys watched the Great Fire from here: 'All over the Thames, with one's face in the wind, you were almost burned with a shower of fire-drops. When we could endure no more, we went to a little ale-house on the Bankside, over against the Three Cranes, and there staid till it was almost dark, and saw the fire grow… in a most horrid, malicious, bloody flame, not like the flame of an ordinary fire… it made me weep to see it, the churches, houses all on fire, and a horrid noise the flames made, and the crackling of the houses at their ruin.'

Six bridges can be seen from the Anchor pub terrace: westwards Southwark, the Millennium and

Blackfriars bridges, and eastwards Cannon Street, London and Tower bridges. The first of the bishop's licensed brothels on Bankside, Le Castell upon the Hoop, stood where the Anchor now is. All the brothels now lie under the area running from the Anchor, through the reconstruction of Shakespeare's Globe, to 49 Bankside (named Cardinal's Wharf). In 1547, from east to west they were: Le Castell upon the Hoop, the Gonne, Le Antylopp, the Swanne, Le Bulhede, the Crane, Le Herte, Le Olyphaunt, Horseshoe Inn, the Leonem, the Hartyshorne, the Beere, the Little Rose, Le Rose, the Barge, the Bell, the Cock, Le Unycorne, Le Flower de Lyce, Le Boreshed, Le Crosse Keyes and the Cardinals Hatte. The Rose was owned by William Walworth.

Walk westward along the riverside, passing murals of the 1564 Frost Fair under Southwark Bridge. The stewes end at 49 Bankside (Cardinal's Wharf). Here, or so popular legend would have it, Catherine of Aragon sheltered from a storm and Christopher Wren took lodgings while building St Paul's Cathedral. Unfortunately there is no hard evidence to support this, and the stories about Catherine and Wren may have been made up in around 1950 when Malcolm Munthe, son of the author of *The Story of San Michele*, lived here.

Cardinal Cap Alley dates back to 1360. It was not named after Cardinal Wolsey, Bishop of Winchester from 1529 to 1530, but may commemorate Thomas Boyce, the first Englishman to be created a cardinal in 1310, or Cardinal Ottoboni who visited England in 1266. Further on, Bankside Power Station, now the Tate Modern, was built on the site of the 14th-century Great Pike House whose fishponds supplied local clergy with fish.

The view across Millennium Bridge to the uphill approach to St Paul's Cathedral gives an impression of how vast and lofty old St Paul's was – the longest cathedral in Christendom according to Cynthia Harnett's *Ring Out Bow Bells!*, a novel

featuring Dick Whittington. But we return to cross Southwark Bridge and descend into Queen Street Place.

This was once the parish of St Martin Vintry, where the wine-trading vintners worked, set so close to St Michael Paternoster that it seems incredible a second church could have been required. Here Whittington built a huge public lavatory, a 128-seater (64 for men and 64 for women) known as the Longhouse, which was purged by the Thames twice a day at high tide. Today the City Corporation offers less generous facilities.

Cross over Upper Thames Street. Dick Whittington's parish church, St Michael Paternoster Royal, lies ahead on the right. 'Royal' refers not to the patronage of kings, but to the wine merchants from La Reole in Gascony who traded here. Walk through Whittington Gardens, enjoying the fountain. The small garden beyond the hedge contains a long concrete bar marking the boundary of the medieval church Whittington knew. In his day the church was ruinous. He decided to rebuild it and bought some land in 1411 so that it could become a collegiate church.

Inside the church, the Whittington window by John Hayward is the westernmost one on the south side. If the church is closed, the outline of the black cat can be seen in the window to the right of the entrance. It shows young Whittington – with spotted bag and faithful cat – and the streets of London, apparently paved in gold.

The real Richard Whittington was born in 1358 or so, the youngest and possibly illegitimate son of Sir William de Whityngdon, lord of the manor of Pauntley, Gloucester. Urban society was then fluid, with good chances of advancement for a keen young man, so he walked to London, trained as a mercer, and married Alice Fitzwarren. Legend says she was his master's daughter, but her father was Sir Ivo Fitzwaryn, a wealthy landowner.

Golden Hinde

The Clink Prison Museum
THIEF-CATCHER
USED BY " CHARLIES " BETWEEN
1700 UNTIL THE EARLY 1800'S.

Clink Prison Museum

Whittington prospered. It was a good time to be a mercer – the rich spent lavishly on clothes and many flush London mercers became bankers as well. By the age of 35 he was an alderman and sheriff. He became an imaginative benefactor, building public conveniences and drinking fountains and in many parts of the City. He left money for the rebuilding of Newgate Prison (a more charitable action than this at first appears) and built a wing to St Thomas' Hospital for unmarried mothers. He lent huge sums of money to Richard II, Henry IV and Henry V. At a feast in the Guildhall, he once threw bonds worth some £60,000 into a fire to free Henry V from debts incurred by the French campaign. Whittington was made Mayor of London in 1396, 1397, 1406 and 1419. He was a London MP in 1416. He died in March 1423 and, childless, left his wealth to the City. And all anyone remembers these days is that he had a cat!

A stone to the south of the altar at St Michael Paternoster marks the site of Whittington's grave. He was first buried here beside his wife Alice, who had died in 1414. In the reign of Edward VI, wrote Stow, 'the parson of the church, thinking some great riches to be buried with him, caused his monument to be broken, his body to be spoiled of his leaden sheet'. In the reign of Mary Tudor, he was reburied a third time, and then left in peace until the Great Fire destroyed all trace of his tomb. *Brewer's Dictionary of Phrase & Fable* claims the following cheery epitaph was destroyed then, too. It contains all the facts that everyone knows, and these facts are wrong.

The cat does not appear in the legend until a ballad of 1605 ('now this scullion had a cat'), Whittington was 'four times Mayor' rather than 'three times Lord Mayor' and he was never knighted.

Beneath this stone lies Whittington,
Sir Richard rightly named,

Who three times Lord Mayor served in London
In which he ne'er was blamed.
He rose from indigence to wealth
By industry and that,
For lo! he scorned to gain by stealth
What he got by a cat.

During excavations in 1949, the mummified corpse of a 14th-century cat was found. This was, of course, thought to be the cat, and the body was exhibited in a glass case at the Guildhall. Subsequent vicars were pestered not by requests for spiritual guidance, but by urgent demands to see the cat. A later vicar destroyed the cat, but today you may be invited, as I was, to 'come into the vestry and see a photograph of a 14th-century mummified cat', surely one of the most original chat-up lines ever devised.

Whittington's cat and *Puss-in-Boots* both helped their owners to fortunes. The cat was first pictured in a 17th-century engraving by Robert Elstracke, when public demand led him to turn a skull he had painted beneath the mayor's hand into a cat. Legend says that while Dick was Mr Fitzwarren's apprentice, he sent his cat abroad as part of one of his master's trading ventures. The king of Barbary, whose land was plagued by rats and mice, purchased the cat for an enormous sum. The real cat may have been a corruption of the French word 'achat' (purchase). More probably, Whittington traded using a ship known as a cat, with a narrow stern, projecting quarters and deep waist, bringing coals from Newcastle to London in his cat. The blackened faces of the coal-heavers, and their incomprehensible accents, led to the tale that he was trading with the Moors.

During recent rebuilding at St Michael Paternoster, the main entrance was moved to its present position. To find the original entrance to the church, turn right as you leave the church and walk up College Hill. The second set of heavy doors, next to a plaque about Richard Whittington, marks the old church entrance and the new entrance to the Whittington Hall. His home once stood further up at 19-20 College Hill, and next door, a plaque to the second Turners' Hall marks the site of Whittington's College in honour of the Holy Ghost and St Mary. Whittington left money to found a College of Priests to pray for his family and benefactors. William Brooke, rector of St Michael's, was made its first master with a salary of ten marks besides the oblations of the church. It maintained a high reputation, for its last master, appointed in 1537, was Richard Smith, the first Regius Professor of Divinity at Oxford. Close by was Whittington's Hospital, founded in 1424, an almshouse whose 13 inmates each had 'a celle or a litell house with a chymne and a pryvey and other necessaries'.

Go past College Hill Chambers and turn left into Cloak Lane, along which the River Walbrook once flowed. Turn right into Queen Street, one of the two new roads laid out after the Great Fire, and continue over Cannon Street and Queen Victoria Street. Then turn left into Watling Street, probably an offshoot of the Roman road between Dover and St Albans. On the left is Ye Old Watling, a tavern newly built, with incredible bad luck, just before the Great Fire broke out on 2 September 1666.

Turn right up Bow Lane and left into Bow churchyard. To be born within the sound of Bow Bells makes a child a cockney, and the church of St Mary-le-Bow housed 'the Great Bell of Bow' of the nursery rhyme 'Oranges and Lemons'. Legend says that Whittington was so badly treated by the cook that he ran away (with his cat), but rested on Highgate Hill. He heard Bow Bells ringing out – 'Turn again, Whittington, thrice Mayor of London Town' – and returned to Fitzwarren's house and future fortune. The Whittington Stone

lies today at the foot of Highgate Hill, near Salisbury Walk (see Lloyd Bradley's and Richard Holmes's walks). That Dick heard the bells ringing at all is remarkable, for they were often late, much to the apprentices' fury who could not leave work until the bells had rung. John Stow in his 1598 *Survey of London* comments acerbically that 'the young men 'prentices, and other in Cheape, they made and set up a rhyme against the clerk, as followeth:

> *Clarke of the Bow bell with the yellow lockes,*
> *For thy late ringing thy head shall have knocks.'*

Dick Whittington founded the Society of College Youths at St Mary-le-Bow. This very select body of bell-ringers still plays at state funerals and weddings at St Paul's Cathedral and Westminster Abbey.

Leave the churchyard and go into the church of St Mary-le-Bow, which has a lively history. In 1090, 'by tempest of wind', the roof of the church was torn off and some persons were slain. Four rafters, each 26 feet long, were pitched into the ground of the high street with such force that, says John Stow, 'scantly four feet of them remained above ground, which were fain to be cut even with the ground, because they could not be cut out (for the city of London was not then paved, and a marish ground).'

In 1196, William Fitz Osbert, a seditious tailor, 'took the steeple of Bow, and fortified it with munitions and victuals'. He was forced out with fire and dragged by his heels to be hanged at Smithfield. There, says Stow, 'he forsook Mary's son (as he termed Christ our Saviour) and called upon the devil to help and deliver him. Such was the end of this deceiver, a man of an evil life, a secret murderer, a filthy fornicator, a pollutor of concubines, and (amongst other his detestable facts) a false accusor of his elder brother.'

The tale of Laurence Ducket or Dubet is the most brutal and bloody of all. In 1284, Ducket 'grievously wounded' Ralph Crepin in Cheapside and fled into the church to seek sanctuary. At dead of night, certain evil persons, friends of Ralph, entered the church, found Laurence hiding in the steeple, and strung him up in one of the windows so that it looked as if he had killed himself. This fooled the magistrates, and the body was drawn by the feet and buried in a ditch outside the city wall. However, a boy who had witnessed the murder came forward, and after investigation 16 men were hanged and 'Alice, that was chief causer of the said mischief, was burnt' (one can only wonder whose lover she was). The church was interdicted and its doors and windows stopped up with thorns. But the most unlikely part of all is that Laurence's body was found, taken out of the ditch and honestly buried in the churchyard. Given that the ditch outside London Wall was an open flowing sewer, finding the body can have been no easy task.

Leave the church and cross Bow churchyard diagonally, passing the statue of Captain John Smith, founder of Virginia. Turn right, back onto Cheapside. As you continue west towards St Paul's Cathedral, Bread Street is the first street on your left. One of the few whorehouses within the city walls in Norman times stood here, and the Bread Street Compter or prison lay on the opposite side of the road. Fraudulent bakers were punished for selling inferior bread by being drawn on a hurdle from Guildhall 'through the great streets of Chepe' to the pillory, the defective loaf hanging from their necks.

Continue along Cheapside. To your right is Wood Street – at whose crossing with Cheapside lay one of the 12 Eleanor Crosses erected by Edward I at every place where his wife's funeral cortège rested on its way to Westminster Abbey. The Wood Street Compter was divided into three sections: 'the masters' side' for the wealthy, 'the knights' side' for the comfortably off and 'the hole' for the poor.

Follow Cheapside, keeping St Paul's on the left, up to Newgate Street. Here, at the junction with King Edward Street, was Greyfriars, where Dick Whittington laid the foundation stone of a library on 21 October 1421. The manuscript library he founded at the Guildhall was stolen in the time of Edward VI by the Duke of Somerset, who borrowed them in five cart-loads 'with an intent never to be returned', like certain other library users.

Continue along Newgate Street and turn left down Warwick Lane, which leads through to Ludgate Hill. In the days of Henry VI, the Earl of Warwick stationed 600 men in Warwick Lane, 'in whose house there was oftentimes six oxen eaten at a breakfast, and every tavern was full of his meat; for he that

had any acquaintance in that house, might have there so much of sodden and roast meat as he could prick and carry upon a long dagger.'

Walk down Ludgate Hill, looking for the plaque high on the wall of St Martin-within-Ludgate marking the site of the original Lud Gate on London Wall. A row of tolerated brothels at Baynards Castle near Ludgate were known as 'Duke Humphrey's Rents' because they belonged to Humphrey, Duke of Gloucester and 'Protector of the Realm' during Henry VI's childhood.

Carry on downhill and turn right up Old Bailey, whose route leads you just outside London Wall. Walk past the gloomy, grim entrance to the Central Criminal Court built on the site of Newgate Prison. Stones from the prison have been incorporated in the rustic work of the lowest storey. A crackdown on crime in the 1420s led to a clean sweep of 'untrewe lyvers' in the City: 'In harvest tyme weren two bawdes sett upon ye pillorie and three Strumpettes held in New Gate.' Newgate was rebuilt by Dick Whittington. Unsubstantiated tradition says a carved cat existed on Newgate Prison before the Great Fire.

Cross over Newgate Street and carry on up Giltspur Street, passing on the left the church of St Sepulchre, where Captain John Smith of Virginia is buried. Here, Newgate prisoners prayed around their open coffins on the morning of execution. John Rogers, a Bible translator and the first Protestant to be sentenced to death in the reign of Mary Tudor, was vicar here. He was first imprisoned in the Clink and later brought 'over the Bridge on procession to Newgate' and burnt at Smithfield.

Walk up Giltspur Street, passing Cock Lane on the left where Whittington erected a public 'two-holer privy'. As its name suggests, Cock Lane has a saucy history. In 1241, it became the 'assigned place' to which City whores were exiled. Owned by St Paul's Cathedral, it was probably governed in much the same way as the Bankside stewes of the Bishop of Winchester. From 1384, bawds were taken to Aldgate, 'wearing a hood of ray, holding a peeled white Rod… with minstrels pronouncing cause… marched through the Chepe and through Newgate to Cokkeslane there to take up her abode.' On the corner of Cock Lane is the Golden Boy of Pye Corner, marking the furthest reach of the Great Fire.

Follow the road round to the right at West Smithfield, whose story includes public executions in the past and animal butchery today. Walk past St Bartholomew's Hospital, founded in 1123 by one of Henry I's courtiers, Rahere, who made a vow to found a hospital and priory while lying sick in Rome. It was repaired in 1421 by Whittington and is today the oldest charitable institution in London still on its original site. On the right is a memorial to Sir William Wallace, butchered here in 1305, before his head was stuck up on Old London Bridge.

Opposite is the entrance to one of the eight medieval churches in London to survive the Great Fire, the priory church of St Bartholomew the Great. Rahere also obtained licence to hold a fair for three days to provide an income for the hospital and priory, which led to riotous goings-on at Bartholomew Fair from 1102 to 1855. As a ballad from 1641 has it:

Cutpurses and Cheaters, and Bawdy-house Keepers
Punckes, Aye! and Panders and casheered Commanders…
Alchemystes and Pedlars, Whores, Bawds and Beggers
In Bartholomew Fair.

Walk left along Little Britain to the junction with King Edward Street. The entrance to Postman's Park is just beyond. Cross through the park, passing the cloister wall, erected in 1880 at the suggestion of the artist GF Watts, with

its memorial plaques to heroic Londoners, including a dancer burnt as she tried to save her partner from flaring footlights and a little boy who died saving his brother with the poignant words, 'Mother, I saved him. I could not save myself.' Come out on Aldersgate Street. Opposite is a plaque about the Aldersgate of London Wall, which stood here until 1761. An important gate during the medieval period, it gave access to St Bartholomew's Priory and the meat market, fair and execution grounds at Smithfield. In 1380, London Wall enclosed what seems to modern eyes a very small city of some 50,000 people.

Walk north up Aldersgate towards the horrible roundabout where the Museum of London stands. If time allows, explore the museum and find in the medieval section a doctor's urine testing flask, close to a drawing that shows Dick Whittington on his deathbed, watching a doctor who holds a flask. At the roundabout turn right along London Wall. On the right at Noble Street are the remains of part of the medieval city wall and a Roman fort, built circa 120. More of the wall can be seen on the opposite side of the road.

Continue along London Wall to the traffic lights and turn left up Wood Street. Look for St Giles Cripplegate on your left. A water conduit east of the church came from Highbury, and Whittington built a water tap or fountain in the churchyard wall in the shape of a bear's head, which Stow sourly reports was in his day 'turned into an evil pump, and so is clean decayed'. He also built fountains at Bosse Alley, Billingsgate, and Trigge Lane, Queenhithe. North of the city wall, in a large swamp called Moorfields, lay the source of the River Walbrook, one of the lost rivers of London.

Return to Wood Street. A report of 1420 condemns John Sherman, a cooper, 'for kepynge Duckes to the nuisance of his neighbours… and the Wood Street Stewehouse is a nuisance because it is a common house of Harlotry, a great

Southwark Cathedral

resort of theeves and Preestes and their Concubines… likewise the privy is a nuisance because of great corruption.'

At the corner with St Alphage Garden, a plaque marks the site of Cripplegate, another of the City gates. From 1217 to 1277 there was a Grope Street in Cripplegate ward, known today as Grub Street.

Cross London Wall and go down Wood Street, passing the church tower of St Alban's, destroyed during World War II. Turn left down Love Lane to find the ruins of St Mary Aldermanbury and a monument to the editors of Shakespeare's First Folio. Love Lane, like Poultry, was a red-light area from time immemorial, 'so-called of wantons there'.

Turn right into Aldermanbury and go past the Guildhall Library, one of the most splendidly helpful places for any London historian. By the end of the 13th century, the 'City' was established and being administered from the Guildhall. Turn left into Guildhall Yard to see the Great Hall, a magnificent medieval civic building that has survived the years despite all that the Great Fire and the Blitz, George Dance the younger and Sir Giles Gilbert Scott could do to it. The Guildhall was built during Whittington's lifetime by John Croxton, in about 1411-30. The original pavement was provided by Whittington, and the black oval line marks the outline of the Roman arena of the amphitheatre that once stood here.

Opposite is the entrance to the Great Hall, where city magnates have met for 600 years. First glazed by Whittington, the windows now list all the mayors of London, and Whittington appears in the west window several times. Take your binoculars. A modern window, erected by the Worshipful Company of Glaziers, on the right of the main entrance shows important moments in London's history, including you-know-who with his cat. The banners of the 12 great Livery Companies hang overhead. The Mercers' banner is on the left of the Dais.

At the east end of Guildhall Yard is the Guildhall Art Gallery. Facing you are busts of four *Great Londoners* by Tim Crawley (1999). They look too large, the lines too deeply graven, for their setting. Much more successful, at the left-hand end, is a charming statue of *Richard Whittington and Cat* (1997) by Lawrence Tindal. Dick is rather a pudding-faced youth, but he stands triumphantly on one of the rats slain by a very cute cat indeed. The art gallery has a splendid interactive system allowing one to access over 31,000 Guildhall images – including an 1807 ballad about Dick Whittington's ghost's search for his cat at Mansion House, which was not even built in Dick's day.

Leave Guildhall by the paved way at the east end of St Lawrence Jewry and turn left along Gresham Street. Take the second turning on the right along Old Jewry. This was the heart of the Jewish Quarter, and the Old Synagogue stood here until 1272. Some 15,000 Jews were expelled from England in 1290, their houses confiscated and their mortgages going to the Crown. All around here was a red-light district. Gropecuntlane stood to the east of Old Jewry and belonged to the wealthy Henri de Edelmonton in 1276. The Bordhawe dates from 1125, and by 1405 it was known as Burdellane (Brothel Lane). Here in 1423 'One Margaret procured a younge girl, Isobel Lane… for a certayne Lombard, and other unknowne men, who deflowered her agaynste her wille. She then sent Isobel over to the Stewes for immoral purposes.' The tone of condemnation in this account suggests a real desire to clean up the City.

Turn right down St Olave's Court, past a dinky Wren church that is now a lawyers' office. Turn left along Ironmongers Lane, passing Prudent Passage on your right. On the left is Mercers' Hall and a grim-looking chapel with the Mercers' sign above the doorway. High on the wall at the corner with Cheapside is a plaque commemorating the fact that Thomas Becket was born here in 1120, the son of Gilbert Becket, another mercer.

Walk left up Cheapside and Poultry, cross the road and walk down through Bucklersbury Passage, the lowest point of the River Walbrook, towards a church. This is St Stephen Walbrook, built on the foundations of a Roman Mithras temple. Walk right down Walbrook – the actual course of the river is about 25 yards to the west and it emerges into the Thames by Cannon Street Bridge.

Turn left along Cannon Street. The London Stone is set in the wall of a bank at the corner of Cannon Street and St Swithin's Lane. To be honest, no one is very sure what this piece of limestone signifies. Roman remains at the Governor's Palace beneath Cannon Street station mean it may be a Roman milestone marking the centre of Londinium. Or not. The first mention occurs in 1188, when there is a reference to Henry, son of Eylwin de Londenstane, subsequently Mayor of London.

Continue along Cannon Street towards Monument station and the walk's end, considering the remnants of the medieval city we have seen. Walking through massive modern Bucklersbury and down Walbrook, we were conscious of the River Walbrook, covered and bricked up over the centuries. Stink ponds and cess ways though such lost rivers as the Walbrook, the Fleet and the Tyburn often were, the presence of water running through the City is one of the sights that most divides medieval London from us. From time to time, plans are laid to restore the Fleet, but the immense ecological changes this would cause (not to mention the cost) must mean this is never likely to happen. Trying to establish the route of London Wall from Ludgate to Newgate and discovering where Dick Whittington erected his 128-seater are satisfying experiences. But nothing rivals standing in St Magnus Churchyard at the very point where people went up on to Old London Bridge for establishing a link with medieval London.

Eating & drinking

Anchor Bankside
34 Park Street, SE1 9EF (7407 1577). **Open** 11am-11pm Mon-Sat; noon-10.30pm Sun. **Food served** noon-10pm Mon-Sat; noon-9pm Sun.

Ye Olde Watling
29 Watling Street, EC4M 9BR (7653 9971). **Open** 11am-11pm Mon-Fri. **Food served** noon-9pm Mon-Fri.

Shakespeare's Globe Restaurant
New Globe Walk, SE1 9DR (7928 9444). **Open** *May-mid Oct* noon-2.30pm, 5.30-10.30pm daily. *Mid-Oct-Apr* noon-2.30pm Mon, Sun; noon-2.30pm, 6-9.30pm Tue-Sat.

Buildings & museums

Clink Prison Museum
1 Clink Street, SE1 9DG (7403 6515/www.clink. co.uk). **Open** *June-Sept* 10am-9pm daily. *Oct-May* 10am-6pm daily. **Admission** £5; £3.50 5-15s.

Golden Hinde
St Mary Overie Dock, Cathedral Street, SE1 9DE (0870 011 8700/www.goldenhinde.co.uk). **Open** daily, times vary; phone for details. **Admission** £3.50; £3 concessions; £2.50 4-13s; free under-4s; £10 family.

Guildhall
Gresham Street, EC2P 2EJ (7606 3030/ www. corpoflondon.gov.uk). **Open** *May-Sept* 9.30am-5pm daily. *Oct-Apr* 9.30am-5pm Mon-Sat. Closes for functions so phone ahead. *Tours* groups of 10+ only (by arrangement). **Admission** free.

Guildhall Art Gallery
Guildhall Yard, off Gresham Street, EC2P 2EJ (7332 3700/www.guildhall-art-gallery.org.uk). **Open** 10am-5pm Mon-Sat; noon-4pm Sun. **Admission** £2.50; £1 concessions; free under-16s. Free to all after 3.30pm daily, all day Fri.

Guildhall Library
5 Aldermanbury, EC2V 2HH (7332 1868/ www.cityoflondon.gov.uk). **Open** 9.30am-5pm Mon-Sat (some restrictions on Sat). **Admission** free; donations appreciated.

Mercers' Hall
Ironmonger Lane, EC2V 8HE (7726 4991/ www.mercers.co.uk). **Open** by appointment only.

The Monument
Monument Street, EC3R 8AH (7626 2717/
www.towerbridge.org.uk). **Open** 9.30am-5.30pm
daily. **Admission** £2; £1 5-15s; free under-5s.

Museum of London
150 London Wall, EC2Y 5HN (0870 444 3852/
www.museumoflondon.org.uk). **Open** 10am-
5.50pm Mon-Sat; noon-5.50pm Sun. **Admission**
free. *Exhibitions* £5; £3 concessions.

Old Bailey
corner of Newgate Street & Old Bailey, EC4M 7EH
(7248 3277/www.oldbaileyonline.org). **Open** 10am-
1pm, 2-4.30pm Mon-Fri. **Admission** free (no under-
14s admitted, 14-16s accompanied by adults only).
No cameras, mobile phones, large bags or radios
allowed into the court; no storage facilities. Stairs
may pose problems for some visitors.

Postman's Park
between King Edward Street & Aldersgate Street,
EC2 (7332 1456). **Open** 8am-dusk daily.

St Bartholomew's Hospital Museum
West Smithfield, EC1A 7BE (7601 8152/guided
tours on Fridays 7837 0546). **Open** 10am-4pm
Tue-Fri. **Admission** free.

Shakespeare's Globe
21 New Globe Walk, SE1 9DT (7902 1500/www.
shakespeares-globe.org). **Open** *Tours & Exhibitions*
May-Sept 9am-noon daily; Oct-Apr 10am-5pm daily.
Admission £8.50; £7 concessions; £6 5-15s.

Tate Modern
Bankside, SE1 9TG (7887 8000/www.tate.org.uk).
Open 10am-6pm Mon-Thur, Sun; 10am-10pm Fri, Sat.
Tours 11am, noon, 2pm, 3pm daily. **Admission** free.

Churches & cathedrals

St Bartholomew the Great
West Smithfield, EC1A 7JQ (7606 5171/
www.greatstbarts.com). **Open** *Mid Feb-mid Nov*
8.30am-5pm Tue-Fri; 10.30am-1.30pm Sat; 8am-
1pm, 2.30-8pm Sun. *Mid Nov-mid Feb* 8.30am-
4pm Tue-Fri; 10.30am-1.30pm Sat; 8.30am-1pm,
2.30-8pm Sun.

St Giles Cripplegate
Fore Street, Barbican, EC2Y 8DA (7638 1997/
www.stgilescripplegate.com). **Open** 11am-4pm
Mon-Fri. *Services* 8am, 10am, 4pm Sun.

St Lawrence Jewry
next to Guildhall, Gresham Street, EC2V 5AA
(7600 9478). **Open** 8am-2pm Mon, Tue, Fri;
8am-1pm Wed, Thur. **Admission** free.

St Magnus the Martyr
Lower Thames Street, EC3R 6DN (7626 4481/
www.stmagnusmartyr.org.uk). **Open** 10am-4pm
Tue-Fri; 10am-1pm Sun. *Services* 12.30pm Tue,
Thur; 1.15pm Fri; 11am Sun.

St Martin within Ludgate
40 Ludgate Hill, EC4M 7DE (7248 6054).
Open 10am-4pm Mon-Fri. *Service* 1.15pm Thur.

St Mary-le-Bow
Cheapside, EC2V 6AU (7248 5139/
www.stmarylebow.co.uk). **Open** 6.30am-6pm
Mon-Thur; 6.30am-4pm Fri.

St Michael Paternoster Royal
College Hill, EC4R 2RL (7248 5202/www.
missiontoseafarers.org). **Open** 9am-5pm Mon-Fri.

St Paul's Cathedral
Ludgate Hill, EC4M 8AD (7246 4128/
www.stpauls.co.uk). **Open** 8.30am-4pm Mon-
Sat. *Galleries, crypt & ambulatory* 9.30am-4pm
Mon-Sat. Special events may cause closure; check
before visiting. *Tours* 11am, 11.30am, 1.30pm,
2pm Mon-Sat. **Admission** *Cathedral, crypt &*
gallery £8; £3.50 6-16s; £7 concs; free under-6s;
£19.50 family. **Audio guide** £3.50; £3 concs.

St Sepulchre-without-Newgate
10 Giltspur Street, EC1A 9DE (7248 3826/
www.st-sepulchre.org.uk). **Open** noon-2pm
Tue, Thur; 11am-3pm Wed. *Concerts* 1pm Wed.
Service 1pm Thur.

St Stephen Walbrook
39 Walbrook, EC4 (7626 8242). **Open** 10am-
4pm Mon-Thur; 10am-3pm Fri.

Southwark Cathedral
Montague Close, SE1 9DA (7367 6700/tours
7367 6734/www.dswark.org/cathedral). **Open**
8am-6pm daily (varies). *Audio guide* £2.50.

Literature

Ring Out Bow Bells! Cynthia Harnett (1953)
A Survey of London John Stow (1598)
The Diary of Samuel Pepys (1660)

Others

City Information Centre
St Paul's Churchyard, EC4M 8BX (7332 1456).
Open *Easter-Sept* 9.30am-5pm daily; *Oct-Easter*
9.30am-5pm Mon-Fri; 9.30am-12.30pm Sat.

City Parks & Gardens Office
7374 4127/www.cityoflondon.gov.uk.

Night lights
Steven Appleby

Riverside reflections.

Start: Bush House, Aldwych
Finish: Millennium Bridge
Time: 1 hour
Distance: 1 mile/2km
Getting there: Central or
Piccadilly lines to Holborn
Getting back: Circle or District
lines or rail from Blackfriars
Note: try to start at dusk or later.

Eating & drinking

The Admiralty
*Somerset House, Strand, WC2R 1LA (7845
4646).* **Open** *noon-2.30pm, 6-10.30pm Mon-Sat;
noon-2.30pm Sun.*

Film Café
*National Film Theatre, South Bank, SE1 8XT
(7928 3535). Bar* **Open** 11am-11pm Mon-Sat;
noon-10.30pm Sun.

India Club
*Strand Continental Hotel, 143 Strand, WC2R 1JA
(7836 0650).* **Open** *noon-2.30pm, 6-10.50pm daily.*

Mezzanine
*Level 1, Royal National Theatre, South Bank,
SE1 (7452 3600/www.nationaltheatre.org.uk/
food).* **Open** *5.30-11pm Mon-Sat.*

Oxo Tower Bar, Brasserie &
Restaurant
*8th floor, Oxo Tower Wharf, Barge House Street,
SE1 9PH (7803 3888/www.harveynichols.com).
Bar* **Open** 11am-11pm Mon-Sat; noon-10.30pm
Sun. *Restaurant* **Lunch** *noon-2.30pm Mon-Sat;
noon-3pm Sun.* **Dinner** *6-11pm Mon-Sat; 6.30-
10pm Sun. Brasserie similar times to restaurant.*

Galleries & arts centres

Hayward Gallery
*South Bank Centre, Belvedere Road, SE1 8XX
(9870 169 1000/www.hayward.org.uk).*

Open *During exhibitions* 10am-6pm Mon, Thur,
Sat, Sun; 10am-8pm Tue, Wed; 10am-9pm Fri.
Admission £9; £4 concessions; £3 12-16s;
free under-12s.

Royal National Theatre
*South Bank, SE1 9PX (box office 7452 3000/
www.nationaltheatre.org.uk).* **Open** *Box Office*
10am-8pm Mon-Sat. *Foyers, exhibitions &
bookshop* 10am-10.45pm Mon-Sat.

Somerset House
*Strand, WC2R 1LA (7845 4600/www.somerset-
house.org.uk).* **Open** 10am-6pm daily; extended
hours for courtyard & terrace. **Admission**
Courtyard & terrace free. *Exhibitions* £5; £4 concs.

South Bank Centre
*Belvedere Road, South Bank, SE1 8XX (7921
0600/www.rfh.org.uk).* **Open** *Box office* 9am-9pm
Mon-Sat; 9.30am-9pm Sun. Royal Festival Hall
closed for renovation until 2007.

Tate Modern
*Bankside, SE1 9TG (7887 8000/www.tate.
org.uk).* **Open** 10am-6pm Mon-Thur, Sun;
10am-10pm Fri, Sat. *Tours* 11am, noon, 2pm,
3pm daily. **Admission** free.

Others

BBC World Service Shop
*Bush House, Strand, WC2B 4PH (7557 2576/
www.bbcshop.com).* **Open** 10am-6pm Mon-Fri;
10am-5.30pm Sun. noon-5pm Sun.

British Airways London Eye
*Riverside Building, next to County Hall,
Westminster Bridge Road, SE1 7PB (0870 500
0600/www.londoneye.com).* **Open** *Oct-Apr*
9.30am-8pm daily. *May, June, Sept* 9.30am-9pm
daily. *July, Aug* 9.30am-10pm daily. **Admission**
£12.50; £10 concessions (not at weekends or Jul,
Aug); £6.50 5-15s; free under-5s.

Oxo Tower Wharf &
Gabriel's Wharf
*Bargehouse Street, SE1 (7401 2255/www.
oxotower.co.uk).* **Open** 11am-6pm daily.

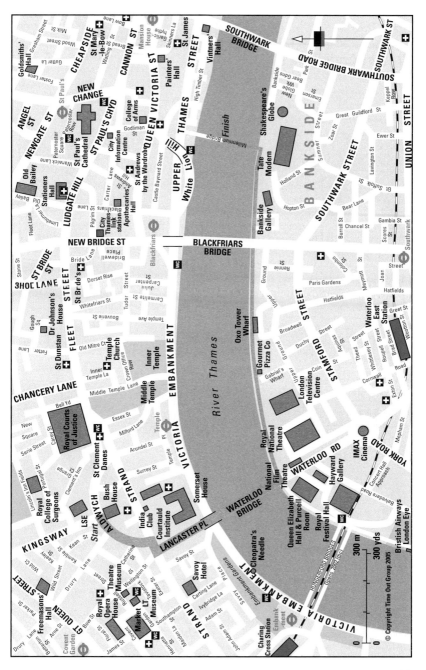

NIGHT LIGHTS

Steven Appleby

I love London at night, particularly the riverside. It is beautiful and still makes me feel as thrilled to be in London as I first was when I arrived 20 years ago.

While waiting for it to get dark you could eat in one of the capital's oldest Indian restaurants, the canteen-like India Club Restaurant.

Let's start at Bush House, home of the BBC World Service, which often keeps me company through the night when I'm working on drawings or can't sleep. Don't miss the two half-undressed men holding hands in the portico. What they have to do with radio I have absolutely no idea.

Pause for a moment as you walk down past the side of Somerset House. The Inland Revenue have offices in this wing and if you look down over the balustrade you can imagine the naked prisoners – clothing and all other possessions sold to pay their overdue taxes – lying on stone cots behind the barred windows.

Just past Somerset House, stand on Waterloo Bridge and look left. The night is lit by car headlights and tail lights moving along the Victoria Embankment. Corporate flagships shine in the distance from the City and Docklands. St Paul's glows with white light and the Thames sparkles as it reflects the strings of bulbs in the trees, the party boats and streetlights.

Walk across Waterloo Bridge. On your right are the lights of the flickering neon sculpture on top of the Hayward Gallery, the soft lilac glow of the Festival Hall, the dark silhouette of the London Eye (unlit but for the flashes of cameras) and, finally, the Houses of Parliament and Big Ben's clock tower.

From the bridge take left-hand steps down to the South Bank

Walk towards the Oxo Tower.

Overhead, the winking lights of aeroplanes criss-cross the sky constantly.

OXO TOWER

LONDON TELEVISION CENTRE

NATIONAL THEATRE

I like the National Theatre, with its unceasingly burbling electronic information sign, best at night. Its bulk is lightened, its planes and corners emphasised by by the shadows light creates. Inside are bars, cafés, gallery spaces and a bookshop, all wonderful for people-watching. Walking further, you'll come first to Gabriel's Wharf, then the Oxo Tower; both brimming with restaurants, designer shops and craft work spaces.

The darker it gets, the more beautiful the river becomes.

The silhouettes of unlit things, like this barge, are just as atmospheric as the lights.

Walk out along the pier next to the Oxo Tower and listen to the sound of boat engines across the water. It makes a change from cars and buses.

I look for the lights of space-craft but, as I've never seen one, I can't recommend that you should look too.

I also look down into the dark water hoping to see the dim lights of water babies, once London chimney sweeps, as they swim past.

Just past Blackfriars Bridge are the surreal remains of the London, Chatham & Dover Railway Bridge. Great, red pillars stand gloomily in the water like a giant, flooded radio set.

After the rail bridge you come to Bankside and the Tate Modern, black against the sky, pierced deep into its interior by shafts of glass and light.

NORTH→

SOUTH←

Finally, walk across the new Millennium footbridge (assuming it's reopened) towards St Paul's. One thing you WON'T see in the sky are stars. There's far too much artificial light for their faint natural light to be visible.

The **Royal Festival Hall** and **St Paul's**.

Sewage and celebrity

David Aaronovitch

A waterworld of canals and creeks, dotted with media hideaways.

Start: junction of Regent's
Canal and Kingsland Road
Finish: junction of Regent's
Canal and Kingsland Road
Time: 4-5 hours
Distance: 10 miles/16km
Getting there: Northern line or rail to
Old Street, then 243 bus; or Central,
Circle, Metropolitan or Hammersmith
& City lines or rail to Liverpool
Street, then 149 or 242 bus
Getting back: 243 bus to Old Street
(Northern line or rail); or 149 or 242
bus to Liverpool Street (Central,
Circle, Metropolitan or Hammersmith
& City lines or rail)
Note: this is a long walk beside
water, but has virtually no contact
with traffic.

Forget escape to Arcadia, or a tour round village London. In fact, I'll give anyone a pound who can answer the question at the end of this ramble, and prove that they've travelled deep into the cockney hinterland. For me this walk was not an attempt to discover rusticity in an urban setting, but an adventure to a part of the capital that, as a Londoner, I hardly knew.

Its uniting theme was water. Following water is almost always rewarding – rivers were the earliest highways, and the canals were built as industrial arteries centuries before there were containers or white vans. They go to places that roads don't, and in ways that roads can't. And London is full of unexpected waterways, many hardly known even to people who live within a coot's call, let alone visitors from far away.

On a Bank Holiday Monday, early, I parked the car on the verges of the infamous Stonebridge Estate in Hackney, near where two poles, one on either side of the Kingsland Road, announce the existence ten feet below (and out of sight) of the Regent's Canal. There a set of steps took me down to the towpath, and my first sight of the water. I headed east, towards Limehouse.

I wasn't quite alone. Even at eight a few early risers were around. Separated from the flats and roads by a low bank and railings, the dog-walkers were exercising their pooches, one or two cyclists were slowly making their way God knows where, and men who looked like boxers were jogging purposefully, blowing out their cheeks.

This section of the canal was built to link the Grand Union at Paddington with the Thames at Limehouse. Once large amounts of coal and steel travelled this way by barge, the horses straining along the towpath, resting only at the locks while the gates were opened and closed. The street names around here – Eagle Wharf Road, Wharf Place, Seacole Road – are a reminder of the trade that breasted this now placid strip of blue-grey-green.

A more recent force had worked hard to turn the path into public space. For the first 100 yards an enterprising council committee or housing association had commissioned mosaics to be set in the brickwork, culminating in a magnificent eight-foot laburnum on Haggerston Road Bridge. As if in response to this consideration, the towpath was free of the old fridges, smashed glass and exploded rubbish bags visible through the railings.

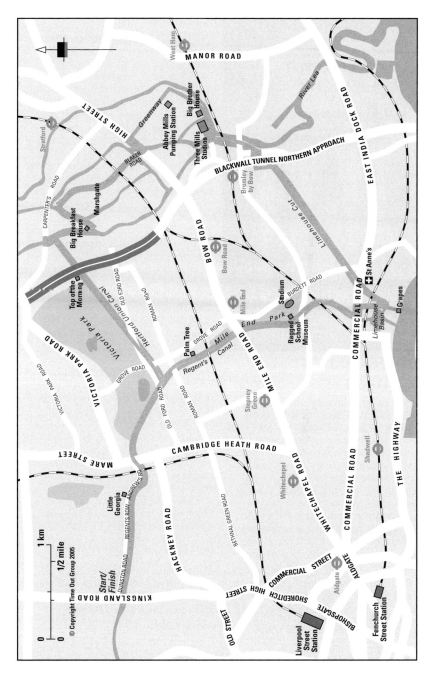

Victoria Park

Peg Sliderskew. A heron stood, lithe and still, by the Mare Street bridge, peering into the depths, only flapping slowly away when I was within three feet or so. Old factories appeared between the canalside housing, buddleia trees growing from their walls and disused wharves.

Past a few gardens, some bijou with statuettes, some overgrown, one with a canoe moored at the end, and I found, on my side of the water, that I was travelling beside green. This had become a landscape of rose-beds and railings, ponds and racing Dobermanns. The VR motif on the neat bridge suggested 19th-century philanthropy, and my passage beside Victoria Park. In 1839, the Annual Report of the Registrar General of Births, Marriages and Deaths drew the attention of the authorities to the high mortality suffered by the people of east London. The solution, he concluded, was a park. The following year a petition signed by 30,000 Londoners was sent to Her Majesty. The result was Victoria Park with its ornamental gateways, lakes and lawns. In 2005 it still looked superb.

Past the sad remnants of the Royal Cricketers – once a favourite narrow-boaters' pub – and for the moment my path took me away from the railings and flowers, taking the right fork of the canal, the one marked for the Thames and Limehouse. Soon I was at Mile End Park, with, rising beyond it, the famous Green Bridge, a bridge of sod and trees that spans the A11. Here, along the towpath at 9.30am, sat friendly anglers with bright red maggots in flat tins, framed by a perfect, isolated early Victorian terrace, and – should they need a jar later – the Palm Tree public house. On the night of 12-13 June 1944, as commemorated by a plaque on the parallel Grove Road, the first doodlebug had cut its engine and fallen free and deadly near here. For years this would have been a bombsite.

Now I was marching towards the far Canary Wharf Tower, the blinking light at its phallic tip, while a pair of Canada

Every type, condition and colour of municipal housing sat on either side of the water: renovated '50s blocks in London brick with new blue balconies, Orwell Court in off-red brick and white wood, trees in the yard, a dismal long grey warehouse of a block, its car park punctuated with carburettors and wrecks. On my side of the railings two interloping Canada geese landed noisily on the territory of a third who, akk-akking angrily, drove them off. In front of two gasometers a yellow wagtail skitted across the water.

A sign offered an escape to Broadway Market and London Fields, and I could see a clean brick building proclaiming itself to be the 'Sir Walter Scott. Rebuilt 1909'. But it was now Little Georgia, the time still only 8.25, and the birds had won me over. On the other side of the water a dusty road led to a sequestered enclave worthy of Dickens, where Empress Coaches sat alongside a fire-damaged Victorian house, fit for Arthur Gride and geese paraded the other way, six yellowish goslings gaggling behind. Unmanned locks announced the descent towards the Thames: Mile End Lock, Johnson's Lock, near the gleam of the Mile End stadium and the old brick of the Ragged School Museum, a patch of bluebells, a great continuous curve of new, low-rise housing and then Salmon Lane Lock, ugly boxed iron bridges and finally Commercial Road lock.

The path was fractured here, stopped dead, and I went left up some steps on to the four lanes of Limehouse Road. I turned right, heading for the octagonal tower of St Anne's, Limehouse, one of Hawksmoor's three great docklands churches, begun in 1714. A right into Island Row, past the '20s red of the Catholic Church of Our Lady Immaculate, with its weird statue of Jesus high above, brought me to the northern edge of Limehouse Basin. To gain the Thames, I had to pass by some modern houses on my left, cross a footbridge, and take my pick from signs offering either the Basin and the Thames or the Limehouse Cut. Right now I chose the river.

Limehouse Basin was once the Regent's Canal Dock, transit place for tons of dark, heavy goods, but today it was clearly a beloved province of Bellway Houses – proud builders of speculative housing – which had helped surround the yachted water with new buildings, some with yellow slopes atop them like Day-Glo sou'westers. On the deck of the *Calypso*, out of Southampton, a woman with sunglasses was bringing croissants and coffee to her blue-sweatered menfolk; the kids from the scruffier *Joja* spat toothpaste into the dock. Underneath us, unheard, traffic was speeding to and from Canary Wharf in the tunnel of the Limehouse Link.

Twenty more yards brought me past the old Limehouse Lock, and on to the bridge at Narrow Street. I could, if I wanted and had it not been so early still, now drink at Booty's just to my right, or

St Anne's, Limehouse

walk a few yards to the Grapes, supposed prototype of the Six Jolly Fellowship Porters in *Our Mutual Friend*. Instead I took in the sight of the Thames at this point, with – right and left – its banks covered by buildings under 30 years old.

I retraced my steps back to the signposts, where a woman with thick glasses and a small dog was picking a bouquet of daffodils from the carefully tended beds. 'Those Pakistanis,' she complained guiltily, 'they've bin pullin' the flowers up. I saw 'em. I'm takin' these to the 'ospital.' I wished her joy of them, and went on down to the canal again, to the Limehouse Cut. 'Escape platform,' a sign said disconcertingly. 'Wait here at high tides.' But it was obviously low tide, and no need to stay.

The cut was narrower and more industrial, dating back to a 1760s desire to link the Thames with the River Lee. Under the bridges there were still the cobbles and raised brick courses that would prevent the horses' hooves from slipping. Courses for horses, you could say. A warehouse conversion offered balcony views of a part-submerged rusting barge, a grim estate gave on to a vista of high-tech workshops.

Then this, too, came to a bad end. Up a concrete ramp and I surveyed the brutal ribbon of the A102 Northern Approach to the Blackwall Tunnel, and thought my good times were finished. On my left was a subway. I took it, crossed and doubled back, and now the signs promised the unlikely pleasures of the 'Lee Valley Walk'.

I found myself on a path by some water again, and so, unsuspecting, entered a new world, the world of the Lee, Bow Creek and the Bow Back rivers. A gatekeeper in the shape of an amiable drunk stamped my passport. ''S good here,' he told me, reeling. 'Good people. Nice place. Jus' carry on an' you can't go wrong.' I told him that I hoped he'd have a good day. 'I've already 'ad a good day,' he said.

I could smell the sea. I was on a long narrow island between two wide and fast-moving tidal rivers, both part of Bow Creek, the lowest part of the River Lee. Bridges occasionally spanned island and waters, carrying trains and cars between Bromley-by-Bow and West Ham, but leaving me to the weeping willows, the flowers, the birds and the upturned car, improbably transported to the middle of the flow. Ahead of me were the oast-house-shaped roofs of the Three Mills, remnants of the tidal mills that, for centuries, ground the wheat for the bakers of Stratford. House Mill, dated 1776, may have been the largest tidal mill in Britain.

Behind them was the Three Mills Film Studio, just the place to start a business cheaply, and go on to make a mint. In these studios in 2001 the prefabricated media band *Hear'say* – the first band to go to Number One with both their debut single and album – recorded their first tracks. The security man on the gate wouldn't answer any questions about the studios, but did suggest that if I followed the path to my right between the mills, I might find something to interest me. High above the water I skirted a wall of graffiti, and found myself at a narrow bridge, with a sign nearby to Abbey Mill. Just over the bridge was a pathway leading to a gate, a gate blocked by a security guard in shades. Posters warned of man-eating dogs. Here, in 2000, and every year since, several young people have been sequestered for weeks, their every movement filmed and debated, and then evicted on the votes of TV viewers. The show is called *Big Brother*.

Standing sentinel on the empty *Big Brother* house was the silhouette of a very different building. Constructed in a bizarre Byzantine-Gothic style (Romanesque with excrescences) and topped off with a magenta cupola, this was the Abbey Mill pumping station. Abbey Mill was built in 1868 as one of the first sewage stations commissioned in the wake of the Great Stink of London. The engineer, Sir Joseph Bazalgette (whose bust is on the Embankment), devised a sewage system that would collect the outpourings of London, treat them and then dump them beyond Dagenham, and Abbey Mill was his baby. In a nice piece of serendipity it was his relative, Peter Bazalgette, who founded Bazal Productions and – from the place where his ancestor pumped crud to Essex – transmitted his entertaining nonsense to Britain.

Passing over the small bridge and around the invisible house, on a path flanked by silver birches and cowslip, I saw another heron on the mudbanks of the Prescott Channel, and at a much more substantial bridge – with the pumping station close by on my left – turned left down the Greenway, towards the A11, beyond which I hoped to find water again.

I crossed at the lights, passed into Blaker Road and found the unpromising beginning of a waterway. The path seemed to end at a bridge, but ducking through a wet tunnel and under the broad

Canary Wharf viewed from Limehouse.

Abbey Mill pumping station.

Three Mills Studios

brick span of another bridge, I came out into a Secret Garden and lost contact with the world of roads and cars. I was on the City Mills river, one of the seven Bow Back rivers that make this area a St Petersburg yet to be discovered.

These courses fell into disrepair in the 1900s, were dredged in the '20s as part of the limited British New Deal, fell into disrepair again after the war, and are now re-emerging once more. Behind, hidden, was a vast area of sidings. Old factories lined the opposite bank, one with hundreds of tyres spilling out across the water. The wind was catching in the

broken corrugated iron roof of another. But all around me, on my high path, butterflies rose from the flowers and trees.

This Eden past, a turquoise bridge took me left, towards the Old River Lea Towpath, skirting Marshgate. A quarter of a mile further, having passed under two colossal black pipes straddling the river, I rejoined the Lee Navigation, last seen at Three Mills, joining a party of ramblers down from Enfield (rambling capital of the Home Counties) as they headed right and north by Old Ford Lock. And here, standing beside an astroturf lawn, in the shade of a gigantic garden gnome, was a maroon lock cottage, a speed-taker's idea of a second home. On the wall I could see a blue plaque (now gone) telling passers-by that a minor celeb named Denise Van Outen had lived here between 1996 and 1999. The house was once used as the set for a TV programme called *The Big Breakfast.*

Not far north a canal broke off from the river to the left. This was the Hertford Union, which would take me back to Victoria Park and the Kingsland Road. Here, once again, the mood changed, back to urban, public space. It was warm now, mid-morning, and there were crowds by the Top of the Morning pub, walking beside River Lock Cottage or buying lollies from the ice-cream vans parked on the bridges. Bright narrow boats were on the cut, the first of the day. The main expanse of Victoria Park appeared on the right, full of strollers and cyclists.

More cyclists zoomed along the towpath, coming from behind at a lick. Whatever happened, I wondered, to bicycle bells? A badly misplaced motor-bike parted the walkers on the towpath. The herons and Canada geese had fled, giving way to the people. At Acton locks, in the lee of the great estates, boats passed through in holiday style, watched by men with Eastern European accents who drank beer.

And so I came to the end. Just two more things to say. Remember the Bow Back rivers: you read it here first. Finally your question for a pound is this: repro what? David.Aaronovitch@btinternet.com gets the prize.

Eating & drinking

Booty's Riverside Bar
92A Narrow Street, E14 8BP (7987 8343). **Open** 11am-11pm Mon-Thur; 11am-midnight Fri, Sat; noon-10.30pm Sun. **Food served** 11am-9.30pm Mon-Fri; noon-6.30pm Sat; noon-9.30pm Sun.

Grapes
76 Narrow Street, E14 8BP (7987 4396). **Open** noon-3pm, 5.30-11pm Mon-Fri; noon-11pm Sat; noon-10.30pm Sun. **Food served** noon-2pm, 7-9pm Mon-Sat; noon-3.30pm Sun.

Little Georgia
2 Broadway Market, E8 4QJ (7249 9070). Café **Open** 9am-6pm Mon; 9am-7pm Tue-Sat; 10am-7pm Sun. *Restaurant* **Dinner served** 7-10pm Tue-Thur, Sun; 7-10.30pm Fri, Sat. Sublime Georgian food in a delightful local restaurant.

Top of the Morning
129 Cadogan Terrace, E9 5HP (8985 9917). **Open** 11am-11pm Mon-Sat; noon-10.30pm Sun. No food served.

Churches

Catholic Church of Our Lady Immaculate
636 Commercial Road, E14 7HS (7987 3563). **Open** *Services* 9.30am Mon, Thur, Fri; 6pm Sat; 11.15am Sun.

St Anne's
Commercial Road, Limehouse, E14 7HP (7987 1502). **Open** *Services* 10.30am, 6pm Sun.

Parks & waterways

British Waterways
1 Sheldon Square, Paddington Central, W2 6TT (7286 6101/www.britishwaterways.co.uk). **Open** 9am-6pm Mon-Fri.

Lee Valley Walk
01992 702200/www.leevalleypark.com. Phone for information.

Mile End Park
E1 (7264 4660/www.towerhamlets.gov.uk).

Victoria Park
E14/E9 (8985 1957/www.towerhamlets.gov.uk). **Open** 6.30pm-dusk daily.

Others

Mile End Stadium
Rhodeswell Road, E14 7TW (8980 1885). **Open** 9am-10.30pm Mon-Fri (last ticket sold 9pm); 9am-6pm Sat, Sun (last ticket sold 5pm). Sports facilities.

Ragged School Museum & Towpath Café
46-50 Copperfield Road, E3 4RR (8980 6405/www.raggedschoolmuseum.org.uk). **Open** 10am-5pm Wed, Thur; 2-5pm 1st Sun of mth.

Three Mills Studios
Three Mills Lane, E3 3DU (7363 3336/www.3mills.com).

Under and over the Archway

Lloyd Bradley

An up-and-down trail of highways and woodland.

> **Start:** Archway roundabout
> **Finish:** Archway roundabout
> **Time:** 3-4 hours
> **Distance:** 4.5 miles/7.5km
> **Getting there:** Northern line to Archway
> **Getting back:** Northern line from Archway
> **Note:** this is a very hilly walk, but with two wooded parks it has proved a success with children.

To say I've only ever lived in London flatters me. Compared with the geographical truth of my 40-plus years it makes me sound like some sort of urban Ernest Shackleton. The ludicrously narrow reality is that I've spent practically all my life on two adjoining pages of the (old) A-Z, pages 29 and 45. There was a period back when the 1960s became the 1970s, when Mum was inconsiderate enough to move us to Chalk Farm and my life briefly crept across into the gully of page 44, but we tend not to talk about those dark days. I scurried back to NW5 and the magic number 45 as soon as financially possible.

Five decades in an area contained by the bottom end of Kentish Town, Alexandra Palace, Hornsey Road and Highgate might seem dull to the extreme, but that's pretty much the point. Social slothfulness lends itself to this deeply unfashionable, usually unmentionable part of London because it's got everything anybody could possibly want. Mostly within mooching distance, too. And to a large degree it's an area left to its own devices, as, lacking the obvious heritage of Highgate village or the wannabe ambience of Crouch End, nobody who didn't live there cared that much about it. Taking Fortess, Junction and Archway Roads as its spine, this was a Bermuda Triangle of upward mobility. Aspiration went AWOL and, as a result, the area hasn't so much evolved as simply hung about. In fact, all I can say to describe it from a sociological standpoint is that, like my essentially aimless self, it's still there.

But to travel the northern half (we wouldn't want to overdo anything by attempting the whole manor) is to happen across some of the most apparently inappropriate, scandalously underappreciated, never less than enjoyable aspects of London life. Once again, happily within mooching distance.

To begin to appreciate pages 29 and 45, you have to start just about where they join, at the Archway roundabout, where Junction Road, Archway Road, Holloway Road and Highgate West Hill converge. No, sorry, not *at* the Archway roundabout, but *on* it.

Cross the highways on to this oversized traffic island in the middle of one of the capital's most hostile road junctions and you're at the heart of Lloyd Bradley's London, both geographically and culturally. Thus the ideal place to begin our mooch. Sorry, our walk.

What's happened on the Archway roundabout in the last couple of years pretty well sums up the surrounding area:

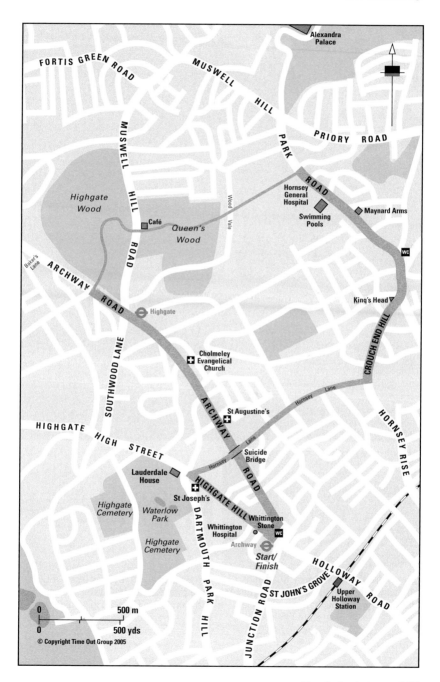

Alexandra Palace

FORTIS GREEN ROAD

MUSWELL HILL

PARK

PRIORY ROAD

MUSWELL HILL ROAD

Highgate Wood

Café

Queen's Wood

Wood Vale

Hornsey General Hospital

Swimming Pools

Maynard Arms

WC

Baker's Lane

ARCHWAY ROAD

King's Head

CROUCH END HILL

Highgate

SOUTHWOOD LANE

Cholmeley Evangelical Church

St Augustine's

Hornsey Lane

HORNSEY RISE

HIGHGATE HIGH STREET

ARCHWAY ROAD

Hornsey Lane

Suicide Bridge

Lauderdale House

HIGHGATE HILL

Highgate Cemetery

Waterlow Park

St Joseph's

DARTMOUTH PARK HILL

Whittington Hospital

Whittington Stone

WC

Highgate Cemetery

Archway

Start/ Finish

HOLLOWAY ROAD

JUNCTION ROAD

ST JOHN'S GROVE

Upper Holloway Station

0   500 m

0   500 yds

© Copyright Time Out Group 2005

The actual **Archway**.

here different traditions and approaches to life that, anywhere else, would seem to collide, coexist with such naturalness you feel there's hope for the rest of the planet. Take the Archway Methodist Church,

whose building dominates the site. In the foyer are aerial views of the area from the 1930s, and, surprisingly, it's virtually impossible to tell which road is which. Now, in thoroughly modern fashion, the church is the weekday home to Kentish Town Montessori School. The Toll Gate Café, with its original curved windows and fancy pastel colours, is very much the hip-menued upmarket bistro, yet directly opposite is the Archway Tavern, one of London's most celebrated Irish pubs. There's been an inn on that site since the 18th century and some of the guys at the bar look as if they've been there since then waiting for it to open. Indeed, so solid is the Archway Tavern that even the recent revamp hasn't altered its essence or clientele. It doesn't actually appear that too much has changed around the TV screen that is usually showing racing, and, most importantly, whoever runs the cellar still knows how to keep Guinness. But in the true spirit of apathy, there's quite a crossflow of traffic between the two, as an ideal Sunday involves papers and a superb lunch at the Toll Gate followed by beer and the Sky game at the Tavern. Why cross the road?

But we've got to. The Archway roundabout is the ideal place to appreciate the Archway itself, which dominates the area as it carries Hornsey Lane across Archway Road. The cast-iron single span might be the area's best-known landmark – for obvious reasons locals know it as Suicide Bridge – but it's only been there 100 years, since the original John Nash (he did Marble Arch and the Nash Terraces in Regent's Park) brick arch was demolished. It would be nice to think that Archway-ites wanted the old one down in case it brought attention to the area, but the truth is the spans were too narrow. However, perhaps appropriately considering its architectural pedigree, the first structure was somewhat extravagantly known as the Bridge of Sighs. Apparently people used to jump off that one, too.

Of course, suicides could have been avoided if the original tunnel that, in 1812, was dug under the hill that Hornsey Lane ran across hadn't collapsed 120 yards into the hill. But then Archway

would've had to be called something else. Lower Highgate? Thankfully not. To set off up the Archway Road on the left-hand side means you go up above the road beneath the bridge and can almost touch its underside – it's difficult not to worry about how this could possibly hold up the weight of traffic passing overhead. Momentarily the Bridge of Sighs becomes the Bridge of Shudders.

Carry on up the Archway Road towards Highgate. On the other side of the road is a bizarre juxtaposition: at 164 Archway Road, Amano is a shop that sells knitwear. Next door is a gun shop. But then Archway Road was never the most self-evident shopping street, and after a combination of rising rents and road widening schemes forced many 'proper' shops out, its retail opportunities speak volumes about the area in general. Bordering on the chichi likes of Highgate, Crouch End and Muswell Hill, it's like the poor relation, hence the merchandise of choice in the shops at the top of Archway Road is both top quality and none too rigorously used – hand-me-downs from the more fortunate neighbours. Ironically a proportion of this bric-a-brac is the sturdy stuff left behind by the professional classes that used to occupy the Archway Road's big Victorian piles – some with the original porch tiles still intact – and is now being re-bought by the professional classes drifting back into the flats those houses have now become.

Don't be put off by the rather depressing sight of the Alternative Life Centre, which looks like nobody's lived there for years (in fact, they've moved to Leytonstone), or the two most hideous churches in London – St Augustine's and Cholmeley Evangelical Church, the former obviously never having cared about looking vile, while the latter has so many ill-conceived pillars and split levels it looks like Las Vegas on a budget. Amble on up Archway Road, because from around the Jackson's Lane junction to the police station by Church Road, the browsing among the second-hand emporiums is as interesting as it can be rewarding. Bones is great for high-class, reasonably priced tat. Particular favourites, though, are Wild Guitars – I can't play a note, I just like looking at this fabulous collection of vintage twang – and Ripping Yarns, a bookshop that repays endless rummaging. Unfortunately the marvellous second-hand furniture shop, Home to Home, which used to be adjacent, has closed down. This is a great shame as sometimes you'd buy so many bargain books in the first shop it was extremely useful to be able to get your hands on an attractively priced bookcase next door.

Just on from these shops was Rose's Ale House (now closed), which looked like somebody's front room and had its own song painted on a board outside:

Bring us a barrel and set it up right
Bring us a barrel to last us the night
Bring us a barrel no matter how high
We'll drink it up lads, we'll drink it dry.

Although this end of Archway Road can get away with that sort of behaviour, now you know why this will never be confused with Highgate – not even with 'Highgate Peripheries' – in spite of there only being about 200 yards separating this very spot from the heart of the village.

Rod Stewart grew up on this end of the Archway Road, just before it becomes the Great North Road. He lived over his dad's newsagent's on the corner of Baker's Lane (where the petrol station is now – it's not the most beautiful of spots), his brother had the builder's yard that used to be just around the back, and Rod played football for the local amateur side, Highgate Redwing. His dad used to manage them and my dad used to take me and my brother to watch them on a Saturday afternoon at their home games in Highgate Wood. Which is where we're about to turn into (taking the left forking path) after we've crossed Archway Road outside the police station.

Highgate Wood is one of London's most underestimated parks; in other words another embodiment of how this part of town keeps itself to itself. Mostly dense forest criss-crossed with paths, it's won awards for conservation and generally being brilliant and is every bit as fascinating as Hampstead Heath. Trees have grown here since the ice age, and you'll find Highgate Wood mentioned in the Domesday Book as the Ancient Forest of Middlesex. Since then it's been known as Brewhouse Wood and Gravel Pit Wood and, during the 16th and 17th centuries, grew oak for Royal Navy shipbuilders. There's a good chance that what were once Highgate Wood trees did battle against the Spanish Armada in 1588. This 70-acre space is a wildlife paradise, thanks to careful management and thoughtful conservation programmes. Rare birds include sparrowhawks, owls, golden orioles and woodpeckers; several species of bat live here; squirrels and foxes frolic; there are butterflies and moths unique to the wood; female stag beetles have been recorded; and more than 50 species of trees and shrubs flourish, as does a variety of very rare fungi.

It's unlikely you'll see them all in the same visit, but your best chance is to go creeping about through there as soon after daylight as possible in high summer. Or, in the middle of the wood, by the playing field where Rod Stewart once ruled, is a walk-through information centre that is so detailed about what else lives in Highgate Wood it'll show you the correct usage of a Bat Box, and has a working worm farm. There are also details of the wood's activity programme, which involves seasonal guided walks, bat watches, beetle safaris and, for the kiddies, the Storytelling Tree. Highgate Wood also has one of the most exciting-looking children's playgrounds, tucked away by the Archway Gate, where we came in.

It would be easy to explore here until, at dusk, the resident parkies tour the wood ringing the bell before they lock the gates,

Highgate Wood

but we've got to head east and out of New Gate, across Muswell Hill Road -— via the Queen's Wood Café if it's a weekend and we're peckish – into Queen's Wood.

Queen's Wood never closes. It makes Highgate Wood's dense foliage look like a Capability Brown garden and has all the Brothers Grimm qualities of a genuinely dangerous wood. Even in summer, as you descend to its centre, it remains

pretty scary as the trees are so thick it's practically dark at midday and although you're only yards away from several main roads you can hardly hear a thing. It was somewhere our mums warned us never to go – with or without a grown-up – and the story they used to put about was that a few feet under the surface was a massive burial pit for victims of the Great Plague. We did, of course, and most weekends there was a good chance that anybody passing any of the entrances would have been knocked down by gangs of formerly fearless nine-year-olds sprinting out of the woods after a bush had rustled behind them.

The burial pit story was always 'proved' by saying this was why it had never been properly cultivated, let alone developed, but it never rationalised the berserk, totally unexplained and perfectly pointless paddling pool that lies in the very centre of Queen's Wood, which, as far as I can remember, has never had water in it. If to walk down from the road in such an uncompromisingly natural setting is a slightly surreal experience, to arrive at this silent, waterless pool is pure David Lynch. (As for the local legend about Queen's Wood being a plague pit, although I've looked in a dozen or so history books and not found mention of it, I think I'll stick with it. It's probably far

Crouch End **Clock Tower**.

more interesting than the truth, and I'd be the last man to call all those well-meaning mothers liars.)

Take the larger path that goes left away from the pool and brings you out in Wood Vale, and go straight across to the path that runs down the side of the cricket ground to Park Road in Hornsey, where we'll turn right and head on to Crouch End Broadway. The culture shock is almost immediate.

Past the hospital and the swimming pool, which used to be open air and the redevelopment of which is proof that little kids are getting softer – my school used to have an annual long-distance swimming race there, in the depths of winter, and you were expected to enter. But I guess such lowering of standards is all part of what Crouch End imagines it's become, an astonishing misguidedness that manifests itself in the private members' bar on the other side of the road just before you turn to the clock tower. If the notion of a Groucho-style private members' establishment in Crouch End isn't daft enough, this being Crouch End it has set up in a shopfront so the privileged few with membership can be seen by us poor unfortunates who are desperate to get in. Otherwise what would be the point of paying the fees? Hurry on and turn into the Broadway. The Sunday second-hand bookstall outside the supermarket and the King's Head pub on the corner of Crouch End Hill are worth wasting an hour or two between them. The King's Head is a fine example of the positive power of progress: 25 years ago my old Sunday football team, the JBs (we were soul boys and nearly called ourselves Wood Green Express), would go there after training at Crouch End Junior School. Blues, jazz, comedy and a Salsa Cellar every Monday are a vast improvement on surly bar staff and long periods of boredom interrupted by the occasional knifing.

Now we continue up the hill towards Hornsey Lane, thankfully leaving Crouch End behind. Don't get me wrong, there are

some interesting shops and restaurants down there – the Fairwinds Trading Co. (easternish antiquey things) and Banners (Caribbean/Mediterranean cooking) in Park Road and the Sable d'Or Patisserie (fancy cakes) in the Broadway – but it all seems to be trying too hard. The only relaxed place is the Maynard Arms way back in Park Road, which is what, in spite of its pretensions, Crouch End is all about – if the place had a bit more class, or a bigger salad bar, you could almost imagine it was a Harvester.

At the top, Crouch End Hill turns into Hornsey Lane and to say there's not much left of the original would be a vast understatement. Although Hornsey Lane appears in local records as far back as the 16th century, these days only Nos.2 and 4 have survived from the 1700s. But then this was the thoroughfare that was cut in half to make way for the Archway Road, and we're about to come out on top of Suicide Bridge looking down at it. The view is simply fabulous, across east and south-east London – unfortunately there are too many tall buildings close by to see straight down south – and it seems much further down than it did looking up at the bridge a few hours ago. It's this that makes Archway what it is and why it has to be appreciated from both perspectives. When I was a kid looking down from the top on a clear day, I used to feel like all of London belonged to me. I just didn't want to go to any of it, other than this special patch.

Then, on the left, in spectacular contrast, is St Aloysius School, a dreary prefab-looking affair that replaced the original 18th-century St Aloysius College some time around the 1960s. The boys that go there have changed as much as the building itself. Whereas it used to be knickerbockered young gentlemen pupils who would gaze out from the terraces across the woods and fields to views as distant as the East End, no doubt contemplating the classics, in the late 1960s my old school uniform (from

Stationers school in Crouch End, which is now a park) was like a red rag to the 'Alley Wash-House' kids. If the Stationers lads who lived in the Jewish flats on the other side of Hornsey Lane mistimed their journey home, they'd end up running a gauntlet of Aloysius's most thuggish. Naturally a crew from my school would have to seek retribution the next afternoon, so more of them would come down to ours the following day, and so it would escalate, usually dodging traffic in Crouch End Broadway, until the police would put a stop to it. More than 30 years later, I still quicken my step past that school, braced for the inevitable ambush.

And there's no need to hang about now. Although, when you get to Highgate Hill (now we're back on to page 45), before you turn left grab a minute to take in St Joseph's Church – or St Joseph's Retreat – right opposite you. This enormous, glorious, Gothic pile has nearly enough statuary alcoved within its walls to fill a museum and is topped off with two magnificent domes. St Joe's sheer scale and splendour are testament to the growth of Catholicism in the area. When the original chapel was erected in 1858 it was because there were two dozen registered Catholics in the area and they had nowhere to worship. The expanding congregation warranted the present building a mere 30 years later, and it has remained open when so many around there haven't. The Presbyterian Church opposite (at the end of Hornsey Lane) has been 'luxury loft-style apartments' since the 1970s. Of course, that St Joseph's fabulousness now resides under 113 years of Archway grime is testament to a parallel growth of apathy in the area.

Let's get down the hill. Halfway down, on the right, is the Whittington Stone, a small monument commemorating Dick Whittington who 'turned again' on that very spot 600 years ago. Remarkably it looks like a tombstone topped off with a cement cat, and while the wrought-iron work surrounding it is doubtlessly there to prevent vandalism it looks like a cage

to keep the cat from running away, which seems somehow spookily appropriate for this original Archway celebrity. However, just a few yards more and we're back at the roundabout and the Archway Tavern, and we can honour him properly with one of those immaculate pints of Guinness.

Eating & drinking

Archway Tavern
1 Archway Close, N19 3TX (7272 2840). **Open** 11am-11pm Mon-Wed; 11am-2am Thur-Sun. **Food served** noon-3pm Mon-Fri; noon-5pm Sun.

Banners
21 Park Road, N8 8TE (8348 2930). **Open/food served** 9am-11.30pm Mon-Thur; 9am-midnight Fri; 10am-4pm, 5pm-midnight Sat; 10am-4pm, 5pm-11pm Sun. Child-friendly brasserie serving anything from huge breakfasts and comfort food to jerk snapper and cocktails.

King's Head
2 Crouch End Hill, N8 8AA (8340 1028). **Open** noon-11pm Mon-Sat; noon-10.30pm Sun. **Food served** noon-10pm daily.

Maynard Arms
70 Park Road, N8 8SX (8341 6283). **Open** noon-11pm Mon-Sat; noon-10.30pm Sun. **Food served** noon-6pm daily.

Queen's Wood Weekend Café
42 Muswell Hill Road, N10 3JP (8444 2604). **Open** 10am-5pm Sat, Sun. A quaint vegetarian café serving hot and cold snacks.

Sable d'Or Patisserie
43 Broadway, N8 8DT (8341 7789). **Open** 8am-6.30pm Mon-Sat; 8am-6pm Sun. Café, pâtisserie and boulangerie.

Toll Gate Café
6 Archway Close, N19 3TB (7687 2066). **Open** 8.30am-4pm Mon-Fri; 10am-4pm Sat, Sun. Serving fine breakfasts and lunches.

Churches

Archway Methodist Church
Archway Close, N19 3TD (7272 2241). Phone for service times.

Cholmeley Evangelical Church
272 Archway Road, N6 5AU (8347 9658/ www.cholmeley-church.org.uk). **Open** by appointment. *Service* 11am Sun.

Church of St Joseph

*St Joseph's Retreat, Highgate Hill, N19 5NE
(7272 2320).* **Open** 7.30-9.30am, 6.30-7pm daily.
Services 7pm Sat; 8.10am, noon, 7pm Sun.

St Augustine's

*Archway Road, N6 5BH (8374 6985/www.saint
augustine.org.uk).* **Open** *Services* 9am, 6pm Mon-
Fri; 6pm Sat; 9.15am Sun. *Mass* 10am Weds, Sun.

Shopping

Amano

164 Archway Road, N6 5BB (8347 4333).
Open 9am-6pm Mon-Fri; 11am-6pm Sat.

Bones

263-267 Archway Road, N6 5BS (8348 4496).
Open 10.30am-5.30pm Mon-Sat.

Fairwind Trading Co

*47 Park Road, N8 8TE (8374 6254/
www.fairwindtrading.com).* **Open** 11am-6pm
Mon-Fri; 10am-6pm Sat; noon-5pm Sun.

Ripping Yarns

*355 Archway Road, N6 4EJ (8341 6111/
www.rippingyarns.co.uk).* **Open** 11am-5pm
Tue-Fri; 10am-5pm Sat; 11am-4pm Sun.

Wild Guitars

*393 Archway Road, N6 4ER (8340 7766/
www.wildguitars.com).* **Open** 10am-7pm Mon,
Wed-Sat.

Woods

Highgate Wood

*Muswell Hill Road, N6 (information hut 8444
6129/www.cityoflondon.gov.uk/openspaces).*
Open 7.30am-dusk daily. For information,
contact Haringey Conservation (*see below*).

Queen's Wood

Queen's Wood Road, N6. For information,
contact Haringey Conservation (*see below*).

Others

Jackson's Lane Community Centre

*269A Archway Road, N6 5AA (8341 4421/
www.jacksonslane.org.uk).* **Open** 10am-10pm
daily. Hosts a variety of activities for adults and
children, with a good vegetarian café and bar.

Kentish Town Montessori School

*Archway Methodist Church, 8 Flowers Mews,
N19 3TD (7485 1056).* **Open** 9am-3pm Mon-Fri.

Park Road Pool

*Park Road, N8 8JN (8341 3567/www.haringey.
gov.uk).* **Open** 7am-7.30pm Mon; 7am-9.30pm
Tue-Thur; 7am-7pm Fri; 7.15am-7.30pm Sat;
7.15am-5pm Sun. **Admission** £3.20; £1.50
4-16s; free under-3s.

Wildlife Events in Haringey

Contact David Bevan or Jan Wilson at Railway
Fields Local Nature Reserve (8348 6005), or write
to Conservation Unit, Contract House, Park View
Road, N17 9AY.

Queen's Wood

Off-centre
Gareth Evans

The secret, the hidden and the unusual.

Start: Holborn tube
Finish: Westminster Bridge
Time: 4-5 hours
Distance: 5.5 miles/9km
Getting there: Central or Piccadilly lines to Holborn
Getting back: Circle, District or Jubilee lines from Westminster
Note: for reasons of space, not all the places mentioned in the text are included in the listings. There is some overlap with the walks of Mark Pilkington, Liza Picard, Robert Elms and Nicholas Royle.

As I climb the long escalator up from the Central line at Holborn station, I look once more at a page photocopied from the Collins Dictionary. The word in question is secret. No, I'm not keeping it from you. It's 'secret'. Sourced from the Old French and Latin words meaning 'concealed' and 'to sift', it prompts a number of interesting definitions: 1. kept hidden or separate from the knowledge of others. 2. known only to initiates. 3. hidden from general view or use. 4. operating without the knowledge of outsiders. 5. an underlying explanation that is not apparent. This handy spread seems to cover all the bases, as that's what this walk around and through the city's teeming heart is about. The secret, the covert, the hidden, the privately known, the publicly overlooked (London is, after all, the topographical equivalent of Churchill's quote about the Russians – 'a riddle, wrapped in a mystery, inside an enigma'). It's about a few different

ways of viewing that seemingly most explicit part of the capital, about some well-established yet mysteriously undervisited sites there, and also about some of the less obvious communities that inhabit its crowded streets.

Inevitably it's a partial and partisan account. After all, one person's secret is another's screaming tabloid headline. They say a little knowledge is dangerous, and really a lot of the stuff is tedious, so this offers itself as the ramblings – in every sense – of a curious amateur, fired up by changing architecture, strange juxtapositions and new contexts, the cubist nature of multiple coexistent histories and timeframes.

I keep in mind as inspired guides the writings and actions of the Paris Surrealists and the later Situationists with their respective strategies of urban knowing, as *flâneurs* and participants in the *dérive*, wandering through the modern city and participating in its ceaseless spectacle. Friends once navigated Cambridge using a map of Eastbourne in true Situationist fashion, heeding Ezra Pound's call to 'make it new'. But closer to home, the mission manifesto must come from the primary observations of Iain Sinclair, maverick Hackney-based prose-magus and latest in a distinguished line of pacing London visionaries. Appearing in his essential collection of capital meditations *Lights Out For the Territory*, the following really says it all: 'Walking is the best way to explore and exploit the city… Drifting purposefully is the recommended mode, trampling asphalted earth in alert reverie… noticing everything.'

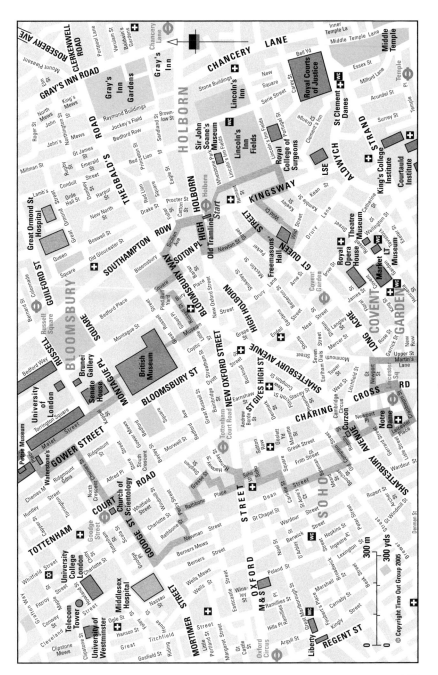

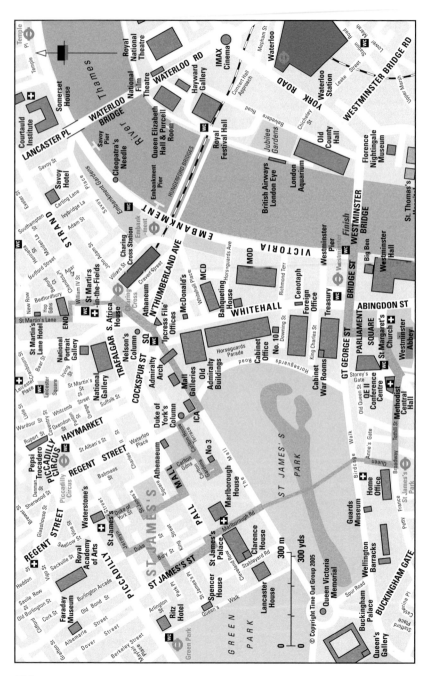

Alignments of telephone kiosks, maps made from moss… torn and defaced promotional bills… the crystalline patterns of glass shards…'.

From books, then, we can now say yes to life, and start out, through TS Eliot's 'unreal city'.

Given that Holborn's road system is about as noisy and public a space as you can find, it seems a good place to start digging into the unseen. The name itself comes from the long-buried brook, the Holebourne, marking our first encounter with London's hidden river system. Sitting in a river valley, London is laced with numerous tributaries, streams and brooks, most of which are covered over or incorporated into the sewer network, leaving only their names to impact on the overground environment, in street monikers and the like.

Despite being located on the outer edge of the financial City, one of the few areas of the metropolis to follow some sort of old-style weekend shutdown, Holborn does not appear to offer any prospect of relaxation. However, the pleasures of leisure have never been far from the district's heart. Until a century ago, when Kingsway was carved through its centre to ease traffic congestion, most of the area was a squalid spill of slums knocking on the door of the legal Inns of Court. But it was also a party place to be. Novelist and biographer Peter Ackroyd, with Sinclair one of the most committed chroniclers of the city's secret side, reveals in his recently published 'biography' of the capital – a huge tome too heavy to bring with us – that the area had been a major haunt of the gay community, among others. The only reference to Holborn's current sexual life comes from the prostitute phonecards to be found, here as everywhere in London, stuck up in the phone booths nearby or trampled underfoot in the commuter rush.

But, just as almost everywhere else in the city, once you drop off the main drag, a sense of calm can fall like soft rain, and

the subtle diversities of architecture and activity start to reveal themselves. We begin by turning almost immediately left and therefore south down Kingsway just a few metres before ducking left again into the unappealing alley-like Gate Street. At the end on the corner you find the Ship Tavern. Stop here and check the history board. It will reveal that the pub was built in 1549 and rebuilt in 1923. In the heyday of anti-Catholicism it served as a vital shelter for the faith's clergy, with priest's holes and covert masses. However, once that all died down, the tavern hedged its bets by backing the Masons and becoming a lodge, number 234 in fact, consecrated by Grand Master the Earl of Antrim in 1786. This is not too surprising, given that soon we will be pulling in at Freemason central across the road. More on that later, but what the panel doesn't reveal is that they also serve superb beer-battered fish and chips. We can't stop this soon, so on it is.

Turning our backs on the pub, we veer right towards Lincoln's Inn Fields, green centre of the legal profession, dossers' once notorious bed-down and home to two unique museums. On the north side of the square sits the Blitz-surviving Sir John

13 Portsmouth Street: disputed site of Dickens's **Old Curiosity Shop**.

Soane's Museum, the immaculate house and collection of the cultural magpie and architect of the Bank of England. Whether it's Hogarth's panelled *Rake's Progress* or a basement Egyptian sarcophagus you're after, Soane's your man. However, if it's anatomical excess that bakes your biscuit, try a pre-meal visit across the grass to the cabinet of curiosities that is the Royal College of Surgeons' Hunterian Museum.

We stick to the right now, heading south past the well-appointed Georgian houses. At the corner, it's right into Sardinia Street, noticing that if we went straight on we would find at 13 Portsmouth Street, dating from c1567, the much disputed location of Dickens's Old Curiosity Shop.

Moving very swiftly on, we head down Sardinia to Kingsway, where we can gaze down to the arching sweep of Aldwych, home to the London School of Economics – headed by New Labour and Third Way guru Anthony Giddens. The now closed

Aldwych tube station lies off to the right on the Strand, one of many in the Underground system to be shut. It's occasionally used for events; in 1999 the great writer and critic John Berger teamed up with Théâtre de Complicité director Simon McBurney to present *Vertical Line*, a mind-expanding descent back 30,000 years to the time of the first cave paintings. It ended in the absolute dark of the derelict tunnel, with Berger's voice describing deep time and its implications, and was an unforgettable experience.

Now cross over and on into Wild Court, and at the end turn right into Wild Street, admiring the fine housing block ahead, a potent reminder that the most secret side of the city is the private, residential one… Out in the suburbs the balance of private and public is reversed, but here we need constantly to remember that for some – on all rungs of the wealth ladder –

the heart of the operation is also home, and not just a rat run or booze hall.

We continue, past blanked windows, then turn into Great Queen Street and there it is, the reason for the excessive 'net curtain' activity. The 20th-century art deco frontage of the massive Freemasons' Hall looms over us. Opened on 19 July 1933, this is Masonic HQ, the clock below its tower commemorating the 250th anniversary of the original Grand Lodge (24 June 1717). It holds a beautiful Grand Temple along with nearly 20 other smaller spaces and is a favourite stop in the annual London Open House weekend each September, when huge numbers of doors are thrown wide to all comers. Hundreds of buildings take part but many of the most interesting interiors, like this one, are free to enter all year round.

My grandfather was a Mason and would regularly feed my curiosity – but tell me nothing – about what he did every Tuesday. I used sneakily to wear his Masonic cufflinks on special occasions and think they might save my life, like Sean Connery's necklace did, in *The Man Who Would Be King*. Despite sterling efforts towards more transparency in recent years, it's hard not to feel the Masons still have something disconcerting going on. They help each other out of tricky situations and get the best seats at games. A bit like good friends, but with much more power and amusing trouser habits. They're probably watching now. This, after all, is the heart of Lodgetown. If we turn left and face towards Covent Garden, we can see several pubs with Masonic associations. Look past Drury Lane along Long Acre to see the Sun Tavern on the left – the solar orb being a key Masonic symbol – and on the right we have the self-explanatory Freemason's Arms.

But the Masonic high road is Great Queen Street, described in the 1800s as the first regular street in London. Moving east towards Kingsway (interesting, all this royalty, in such proximity to

the Hall), it's Masons all the way. At Nos.31 (William Blake was apprenticed to an engraver here from 1771 to 1778) and 26 the plaques are most certainly clear – Masonic Trust for Girls and Boys, Masonic Housing Association, Royal Masonic Benevolent Association, Compass Housing Association. Further associations are served from Nos.19-21 further on. It's a parallel welfare state. I resolve immediately to use all my inherited familial influence to secure an invitation to join. Then I can pick up some cufflinks legitimately from one of the three shops next up. Central Regalia has all the paraphernalia, plus the acclaimed volumes *Jokes For Toasts* by Jack Bright, *Beyond the Craft* and *The Square*, a Masons' monthly. Most resonantly, it's at No.23. This number is a deeply significant one, full of occult import – check the Net for serious amounts of conspiracy speculation. Did Central choose this? Has the whole street, nay the entire city, been constructed around this street-number necessity? I reel with the implication and almost miss the riches – the engraved golf balls, the toy cars and dividers, the silk teddy bear ties in the window of Masonic supplier Toye, Kenning & Spencer, established 1685. That's 32 years before the Grand Lodge opened. What were they doing then, the early Masons, were they hanging out on street corners like spotty teens without a youth club?

Buzzing with wild theories, I lurch left under the arch of offices into Newton (also a Mason) Street. There is a madness in this method. As I veer, I ponder with a growing awareness the intricate networks of sign and detail we are encountering, patterns as fine as a spider's web in the morning light that might reveal that the secret life of the city possesses a constantly shifting but underlying order.

A hundred yards later, we hit High Holborn, turn right and move with haste back towards Holborn tube. If we're out on the asphalt in the late afternoon, we can observe colossal numbers of workers waiting to enter the station, looking a lot like tired punters at the back of a field at Glastonbury. We do not join them but head instead left up Southampton Row 50 yards to the tiny nook that is Coffee Matters, probably London's only Fair Trade organic coffee stop. The quality of the caffeine here is very high.

Refreshed and reasonably rational, we proceed up the road almost to the Cochrane Theatre and cross back over Southampton Row, noticing the gaping maw of Hell, or rather the abandoned tram tunnel – its rails sloping down to locked gates – that is central London's most visible introit to the concealed, 'official' world beneath our feet. Once planned to serve as the mainstay of the UK's post-nuclear war government, it's empty now.

The 'pleasures' of the tube are perhaps overly familiar but its sealed, almost lost stations exert a huge fascination. They are just the most haunting aspect of an interior, underground system – of mail railways, sewers and streams, vast fuel and water pipes, government passages and bunkers, catacombs, bullion reserves and storage areas – that give partial rise to the idea of the city as a body, with its requisite veins, arteries and muscles beneath the skin.

Carry on across the road, then turn left and almost immediately right into the pedestrianised and colonnaded Sicilian Avenue. Exit at the other end and turn left into Bloomsbury Way, noting across the road the shady plane trees of Bloomsbury Square. The double helix formation of the 450-space car park beneath the green is designed precisely so as not to disturb their roots. For a long time I thought that this was the car park featured in the film of Len Deighton's stylish 1960s thriller *The Ipcress File*. I told a large number of people. I almost charged admission. Now I find that it's actually under Hyde Park, at Marble Arch. Nevertheless, *The Ipcress File*

provides a useful filmic parallel for our visits to certain establishments later on.

Continue west along Bloomsbury Way, passing soon the offices of the Swedenborg Society at No.20. Honouring Stockholm-born Emanuel Swedenborg (1688-1772), a Christian mystic of international standing, the house stocks his numerous texts, many written or published in London, including his best-known tract, *Heaven and Hell*. In fact, he died in the capital and exerted a huge influence on London's own visionary par excellence, poet William Blake.

Now we cross the road and wind along the left flank of the square, turning sharp left just over halfway into the gated entrance of Pied Bull Yard, a covert entrance to Bloomsbury and particularly its renowned knowledge quarter – with books almost the local currency. The yard is an oasis of calm, with cafés, a camera shop that sells photography monographs, and the elegant manuscript and first-edition dealer Gekoski.

We turn left now into the adjoining Galen Place. Pass out through the wrought-iron gates, over Bury Place and into Little Russell Street. As we stroll past a crop of shining office plaques to our left, it seems right to recall the keen observation by Milan Kundera in his novel *Slowness* that we slow down to remember and speed up to forget. How true this is. At this point I am moving so slowly I am probably a liability. The series of linked squares that characterise this district actively encourage an afternoon's reading. It's a fine spring day and this street is a slice of the old town that seems preserved in amber. People are out in corners of sun, having a break from work, a smoke, and the undressed backs of buildings stand easy in the light. To our left is the rear of Hawksmoor's St George's church. The architect and his surviving churches have now become key players in the psychogeographical mapping of the city through their roles in Iain Sinclair's

Freemasons' Hall

Lud Heat and the bestselling novel *Hawksmoor* by Peter Ackroyd.

Retracing our steps, we stride out towards the imposing edifice of the British Museum, the gravitational core of the area. Everything locally exists in relation to this colossal collection. As we go, we pass more bookshops, notably first-edition dealer Ulysses. These old places are cultural repositories, daily more valuable as time slides into the future. Especially for the bindings they display. In a few decades will there be a culture gap as today's publications collapse from poor packaging?

The British Museum is certainly looking at the big picture. Alongside Washington's Smithsonian, it's the greatest single manifestation of human abilities there is. Once you're inside, the effect really kicks in. Sir Norman Foster's dazzling new ceiling for the Great Court – with 3,312 panes of glass – makes this the largest covered square in Europe.

At its heart is the legendary rotunda of the 1857 Reading Room, with a dome the size of St Paul's and open to us all now that the library proper has shifted to Euston Road. They've all been through here, an A-Z of names hangs on either side of the door, with Karl Marx just one of the most significant (interestingly, after the 1905 uprisings, Lenin found himself in London and plotted the 1917 Soviet revolution from the basement of a pub on Tottenham Court Road). Climb the flights of stairs outside for a great view of the desks from the gallery and then circle round either side and out through the museum's back exit into Montague Place. Turning right before the lights into Malet Street, we enter studentland. To our right is the University of London and then the radical lifelong-learning of Birkbeck College; on the left it's the School of Hygiene and Tropical Medicine. Note the high tower of Senate House, which doubled

MI6 building.

for the Ministry in Michael Radford's 1984 adaptation of George Orwell's *Nineteen Eighty-Four*.

Off the road and within the learning complex several interesting sites beckon. The Brunei Gallery of Middle Eastern and Oriental Art hosts temporary exhibitions, while the Petrie Museum of Egyptian Archaeology is a dazzling personal assembly, including the world's oldest dress (2800 BC).

A little further north we pass RADA (Royal Academy of Dramatic Arts) with its Gielgud, Shaw and Vanbrugh Theatres. Opposite there's the University of London Union, which hosts an excellent second-hand book market every Thursday and Friday. Its operation is a touch like David to the Goliath we encounter as we turn left into Torrington Place. Currently a huge Waterstone's bookshop, it was for decades the flagship store of Dillons booksellers and is still often referred to as such. It also houses a wide-ranging second-hand section as well as floors of new and remaindered titles and a coffee shop in the basement.

Having browsed, we move off and left, down the long, straight Gower Street. This resolutely uncommercial avenue presents a modest façade, mostly houses-cum-offices and hotels/hostels, but at its Euston Road end, on the right, there stood until recently one of the key sites of the British secret service, the security service HQ, now a building site. This is perhaps the 'secret' that first comes to mind when thinking of the city. The watching and listening game conducted across the centre from anonymous outposts, office blocks, unsigned houses, behind banal frontages. There is an endemic fascination with this parallel world, and we shall come across several more examples as we drift.

For now, we continue south, right into Chenies Street. On the low roof of No.20 to the left I once saw a guy sitting with a perfectly still, hooded falcon. I watched them for ages but they didn't move. Falcons are sometimes

hired to clear office ledges of pigeons, but knowing this in no way reduced the poised mystery of the sight.

There is little subtle about Tottenham Court Road, which we reach after passing the Drill Hall and North Crescent, with its ugly, cake-like Eisenhower Centre marking one of two entrances to a deep-level shelter that stretches from here to the west side of Tottenham Court Road. In 1942, the shelter was adapted as UK headquarters for General Eisenhower.

Little more than a century ago, Tottenham Court Road was a semi-rural road of cowsheds and storage barns. Now it's the city's prime electronics marketplace and a grimly busy mini-canyon, signing off with an erection at each end: to the south it's the Grade II-listed 1960s Centre Point, while up north Euston Tower raises its 36 floors. The 17th floor allegedly houses the highly guarded MI5 'Watcher' service – disguised agents who follow people – with the rooftop aerials (that don't officially exist) broadcasting information directly to their concealed earpieces.

Along with Bloomsbury, this district has seen numerous famous residents down the centuries. James Boswell, for example, boozed and whored his way around it during the six years it took to write his biography of Samuel Johnson. But it's also home to a much less familiar population. Many immigrant communities live in council housing off or behind the elegant streets and squares.

Humming Marianne Faithfull's superior take on Donovan's *Sunny Goodge Street*, we pick up speed. From here on south it's post-production all the way, as we enter the shiny chrome domain of edit suites, digital design houses, big glass and more latte lounges than you can swing a cockney in.

While we down a swift pint in the reasonably unaltered Cambridge pub, we think about the few traces of oppositional filmmaking that have flourished here, for example the work of Chris Petit.

Former editor of *Time Out*'s film pages and maker of prescient road movie *Radio On* (1979) as well as a number of collaborative digital works with Iain Sinclair, Petit is also a novelist and his dark, Ballardian work *Robinson* (reissued by Granta in September 2001) is a fecund exploration of a mind warping in these very streets. A Petit short story, *Newman Passage*, delves into the locational atmospheric ancestry of the book and its mysterious heart. We turn left into Newman Street towards a rendezvous with this strange alley-yard that featured heavily in Michael Powell's controversial camera-killer flick *Peeping Tom* (1960).

Once in the passage, do not turn into the terminal yard, utterly ungentrified, but continue straight on, under the sign for the 'upstairs pie room' belonging to the 'famous' Newman Arms – in a zone where you're only as good as your last sting for that chocolate bar that tastes 'like an orgasm', it's refreshing to find some down-home cooking still filling the belly – and right into Rathbone Street. Despite the dubious appeal of Percy Passage across the road, we continue on into a blizzard of eateries.

On into Percy Street and Rathbone Place – critic William Hazlitt (1778-1830) lived in both – and the air continues to thicken with filmic rumour and gossip. Traditional Italian joint Marino's (No.31) is a fine venture but no escape from the intrigue. The same goes for Jerusalem, a Belgian beer and dining joint in the cellars a few paces further on. We go on past Percy Mews (a road to nowhere) and nudge left into Gresse Street, then continue past Stephen Mews, colonised by the British Film Institute. Now, with few options left, we duck right into what seems to be a private car park but is actually the east end of Evelyn Yard. Across the tarmac and out in the far corner past the Black Horse and we find ourselves back on Rathbone Place just yards from Oxford Street. It's in small

enclosures like this where you can hear the hidden industry of the area: voices, phones, printers – the hum of offices, facilities houses and the like, unseen but utilising every spare inch of this charged patch. Of course, the most concealed places here are rooftops, a neat conceit utilised by long-time Soho aficionado Christopher Fowler in his novel *Roofworld*.

Oxford Street itself drowns out all sonic finery. Even on foot there's talk that soon you might have to choose a pavement lane, dependent on the speed of your shopping. A consumption coliseum, where the weak of credit fall by the wayside, left with the language students handing out flyers, the breadbasket perfume pushers and the tanktop charity doorstoppers. It's a choked fume gutter, and its junction with Tottenham Court Road a few yards east is one of the least pleasant corners in the entire city. Velocity is essential here to escape its sordid gravity, but we will just step briefly into a gem of an alley, Hanway Street, a few feet to our left.

What seems at first like a urine-soaked short cut is on one level exactly that, but it's also a secreted arc, a characterful compendium of small businesses, including record shops, restaurants, a flamenco café and Bradley's famous Spanish Bar (don't forget there's a downstairs). 18th-century anarchist writer William Godwin used to run a bookshop at No.9.

The fact that some maps show Hanway Street to be joined to Evelyn Yard at the Bradley's end – where no rupture in the wall of building appears ever to have existed – only adds to the mood. It's also the setting for a pivotal scene in characterful London writer Nicholas 'connoisseur of dereliction' Royle's recent novel *The Director's Cut* (2000), a page-turning thriller of obsessions both cinematic and sexual that mines the celluloid memory of the capital for a richly textured homage to both place and the past.

We retrace and cross over into Soho Street, pass the Hare Krishna HQ with its veggie café and hit Soho Square, surrounded by distributors, publishers and studio offices. A trace of green is particularly welcome here, and I'm not alone in thinking so. On any decent day the place is packed, with suits, bikers, tourists and lunchers.

We swing to the right and into the first turning, Carlisle Street where, at No.18, we would have found the offices of Peter Whitehead's pioneering publishing house Lorrimer, responsible for a highly collectable series of screenplays (the first of which was Jean-Luc Godard's dystopian urban sci-fi *Alphaville*). Whitehead was the director of a crop of seminal 1960s counter-cultural documentaries about swinging London, then falconer to the Saudi royal family and now a writer of sexually charged Internet conspiracy fiction. He was also the subject of *The Falconer*, a controversially received docu-fiction by Chris Petit and Iain Sinclair for Channel 4.

Turning left into Dean Street, we are faced now with the children of such media initiatives. It's image generation overload all around as we become nostalgic for what feels now like a more democratic spread north of Oxford Street. Of course, it's never that simple and like any other seemingly singular part of the city there are always other countervailing forces at work. Soho, after all, has been at the centre of things for a long time.

In the 1800s it had a very large and wealthy population, until a cholera outbreak in 1854 scared the rich away and it became an entertainment zone, radical haunt and immigrant nexus. In *The Forsyte Saga*, his novel of the 19th century, John Galsworthy describes it as '... untidy, full of Greeks, Ishmaelites, cats, Italians, tomatoes, restaurants, organs, coloured stuffs, queer names, people looking out of upper windows... it dwells remote from the British Body Politic'. By 1981 fewer than 3,000 people lived in the district. While most of the numerous visitors – after whatever activity – slope home on the night buses for the suburbs, the centre does, however, still retain an active residential core, the majority of whom are East Asian. Indeed, the first hint of the approaching Chinatown is across the street at No.81, the Wen Tai Sun Chinese newsagency with its vibrant window display.

We've passed the equally energised home of new drama, the new Soho Theatre building (No.21), and now come across another first for this route, a strip joint, a 40-year-old sex club with 'continuous full nudity'. This full-frontage display, however, is increasingly rare. It wasn't so long ago that Soho was entirely unreconstructed, its currency skin and kin, its rents low, but major clean-ups in the 1980s and '90s mean that most carnal business is more covertly pursued. There's just enough left to let people feel they're still somewhere edgy. Now the main focus of the central London sex industry is scored to a ringing tone, with a call made to one of the innumerable cards mentioned earlier.

One of the major freedoms any city affords is, of course, sexual liberation and the chance to experiment. Thus these adverts for services rendered appear across the capital, but their character changes slightly dependent on district. And where once the ads were hand-drawn illustrations of relative coyness, the now forthright visual promotion of 'she-males', pre-ops, bizarre, submission and the like suggests that things have got altogether harder.

There are estimated to be dozens of domination dungeons in central London, but a more disturbing statistic is that up to 70 per cent of women working in the sex industry are from Eastern Europe and beyond, lured here under false pretences or literally bought as sex slaves in hometown markets. This population of the missing – echoing the wider community of the absent or disappeared publicised every week in the *Big Issue* – has very little chance of escape. What might seem harmless with nostalgic hindsight (but read Ackroyd's *London* for the real horror of historical whoredom) gains a much tougher edge when it's contemporary. This business might be a continuation of the area's established character, but knowing the current socio-economic forces in operation, you can't help but feel desperately sad and concerned for the women involved.

Continuing on down Dean Street, we spot some fine surviving townhouses (No.68, from 1732, is fully panelled, with upstairs and downstairs cesspits, plus secret attic rooms). Then at No.67 it's the first of our private members' clubs, Blacks, conveniently coloured as such on its ground floor – entry is via the basement. Opposite at No.41 there's the green door of the upstairs Colony Room, legendary artists' drinking hole and front room to some of the biggest names and egos in the business, from Francis Bacon to Tracey Emin. A couple of steps further on and we hit newish kid on the block, the Groucho Club, with its media crowd excess and a major waiting list. More on these (not so) discreet establishments when we reach their main concentration in St James's.

Were we to cross Old Compton Street – the axis of gay Soho – at this point, we would come to the French House (so-called because de Gaulle used to grab a bite here when the Free French forces were in London).

Old Compton Street is a fine and relaxed operation. Almost every property has a host of tales, including some top-grade coffee shops and their attendant enticing window displays, whether cafés like Pâtisserie Valerie (No.44), established in 1926, or stores such as the Algerian Coffee Company (No.52), next door to the Admiral Duncan pub, target of a tragically fatal nailbomb attack in 1999.

We turn left now and quickly right into Frith Street, home of Ronnie Scott's famous jazz club (No.47) and the Frith Gallery (No.60), a fine contemporary art space housed in an original residence. Cross the road and head south, noting celeb barber's Cuts at No.39, scissors to the stars (Goldie, Bowie, Guy Ritchie and Alexander McQueen). Pioneer of styles such as the Fin, Short Buddha and Super Hair Row, its presence prompts a brief plea for the return of singeing and friction. These lost arts of barbering were explained to me by my regular tonsorial specialist, a Greek Cypriot in Spitalfields. He remembers that until 20 years ago they were regularly requested.

Newly coiffured we duck left into Romilly Street, pass the grand frontage of Kettner's restaurant (founded 1867) and there it is – the legendary Coach & Horses drinking establishment. Note first the ultra-cheap shorts and then pause to remember possibly its most loyal patron, the late Jeffrey Bernard. Writer and Drinker, JB (suitably spirited initials) defined a certain Soho attitude. A friend once interviewed him after alcohol had claimed both his legs, in his flat in the Berwick Street tower. He found a terribly sad man who could no longer venture out even the few necessary yards.

We turn right now, immediately across the high street of Theatreland, Shaftesbury Avenue – throwing a glance right as we do so to log the art house renaissance cinema that is the Curzon Soho, with its attendant cafés and bars – and into Gerrard Place, the heart of Chinatown, with phone info and street names in Mandarin, restaurants everywhere (are there huge subterranean noodle pits as featured in the equivalent New York set-ups seen in the movie *Year of the Dragon*?) and a great sense of having moved thousands of miles and not just a couple of yards. Pagodas and triumphal gates shape the streetscape and there's no question who runs things on this patch.

We shuffle on through the crowds and into Little Newport Street, past the Tokyo Diner – a growing number of Japanese outfits suggests a slight realignment might be imminent – and a herbal medicine centre. It's along here we also glimpse our first doorway cards for walk-up busty models and the like.

We turn back now and along Lisle Street before nudging left into Leicester Place, past cheap second-run cinema the Prince Charles, home to regular sing-along screenings of such films as *The Sound of Music* and *The Rocky Horror Picture Show*. Next to it is the altogether different interior of the French Catholic church of Notre Dame. It's hard to imagine any tranquillity within walking distance, but the church is a circular, high-domed and elegant wonder of contemplation, unfussy, welcoming and, while still a working building, is not averse to you coming in for a quiet few minutes' breather. One of four Catholic churches in the West End, it was built in 1865 but suffered major hits in the Blitz and was subsequently rebuilt. In 1959, Jean Cocteau designed several striking murals for the altar alcoves, and they appeared in *Love is the Devil*, the recent biopic of artist Francis Bacon. Discerning musicians occasionally perform here and yet it remains underknown.

Interiors like this can obviously serve as escape routes from the noise, crowds, traffic – and rain – of the metropolis. Such spaces become havens of ambitious, but workable, scale: smaller is beautiful and the human reach predominates. They often completely confound the expectations of their streetside appearance. Narrow frontages can open into vaulted excess behind shopfronts, while classical façades might deliver exotic quarters of decorated delight. At such moments, the secret nature of the capital – its capacity endlessly to surprise – truly comes into its own.

British Museum

Out in the open again we break through the massed ranks into Leicester Square itself, either plughole of the civilised world or a democratic centre of the visiting international community. Its grassy focus, the original common land of Leicester Fields, is perhaps not so far removed from its cattle pasture origins. After all, it's a place to partake in the public voyeurism of city street life – but mind the pickpockets on hand to fleece the unwary – and so there's little here of a secret hue.

Turning left into Cranbourn Street, we meet Charing Cross Road, once residence of the late, great Derek Jarman and another home of London's book trade, especially the second-hand wing (disturbingly this historic pursuit is currently threatened by rent hikes that could atomise the local atmosphere here; books are as crucial to this road as snogging is to a school disco). Looking across the street from the corner, we can see the blue and silver chrome signage of the excellent Middle Eastern deli Gaby's, several doors down from the Wyndham Theatre.

We cross now, turning left then quickly right into Great Newport Street. Hidden away frontage-wise, but still hugely popular, are the two galleries, shop and café of the hip and happening Photographers' Gallery. Next door is the modestly dimensioned but equally significant Arts Theatre, where Peter Hall's seminal production of Beckett's *Waiting for Godot* opened on 3 August 1955. Things there might not be so ground-breaking now, but the venue's position is secure when the ancestry's that influential.

Turn right now and over the road to St Martin's Lane, and continue on down past one of the few remaining examples of late Victorian tavern design, in the form of the Salisbury's hand-cut glass and carved mahogany. Opposite, notice the slim frontage of the Quakers' Friends Meeting House and gallery. Then we pass Cecil Court and its bookdealing pedestrian

calm. Many antiquarian dealers still lodge here, while well-stocked newer arrivals include the Italian Bookshop. Esoterica pioneer Watkins Books holds a vast array of unusual titles.

Whether the Manhattan minimalism of the St Martin's Lane Hotel will be quite so enduring is another matter. This Starck/Schrager-designed playground is undeniably elegant and of the moment, but it will always be tainted for me by the fact that it sits on the site of what was perhaps London's finest art cinema. The Lumière was a sensational underground auditorium, a single-screener of generous dimensions and immense comfort forced to close by rising rents. As a bumpkin teenager making solo cultural sorties into the capital, I was drawn to it as a place in which one could be changed. It premièred some essential works. Most memorable for me was Wenders's *Paris, Texas*. It is hard to walk past the still present cinema entrance awning without stopping to recall the opening scenes of that poetic desert epic.

But we succeed, the walk drawing us ever on. Tucked in next to the English National Opera is a tiny alleyway, one of the narrowest named thoroughfares in London – Brydges Place. A piss-stained rut, it's therefore a perfect location for the designer grimness of the imaginatively named private club 2 Brydges Place. Just before it, an archway takes us south into William IV Street, over into Adelaide Street and down to the Strand and Charing Cross station, the Geographical centre of London, from which all distance calculations are made. On the way we pass St Martin-in-the-Fields to our right, with its market stalls and two basement cafés.

Cross over the Strand. It was originally a riverside bridlepath, but is now set back from the river, and carries endless traffic. Turn right in front of the station, and come to Trafalgar Square. This most public of London piazzas, with its New Year revels and countless pigeons, has been the culmination of many political marches and demonstrations, with speeches given from the foot of Nelson's Column. Epicentre of the infamous 1990 Poll Tax riots, it was also home to the long-running anti-apartheid protests (South Africa House looms over the eastern side of the square). Its fourth plinth in the north-west corner, empty for years, is now the capital's most prominent site for contemporary sculpture, with each work given a 12- to 18-month slot. Watch this space, and where better to do so (if only it were possible) than from the third-floor window of the building whose prow separates Northumberland Avenue from Whitehall. Look up above the shops to find the viewing position spymaster Dalby would have enjoyed from his *Ipcress File* office.

Moving just a few yards forward, before crossing it we turn to look down Whitehall – into the very gut of state authority – and can't quite glimpse the familiar logo of the McDonald's (just beyond the Old Shades pub) that was trashed in the 2000 May Day anti-capitalist protests. Carry on over the road and then down the Mall beneath the Admiralty Arch. Off to the left is another *Ipcress File* location, the lane where Michael Caine's Harry Palmer is beaten up a tad.

To avoid this bit of rough we cross over and head down the Mall towards Buck House, past first a bastion of conservative art, the Mall Gallery, and then 50 yards further on, in the same colonnade, the cultural Molotov cocktail that is the Institute of Contemporary Arts (ICA). It is impossible to imagine what the cultural vanguard might be like without the seminal exhibitions, films, events, performances and talks the ICA has organised since 1948. Its galleries, cinemas, theatre, bookshop and bar are hopelessly crammed, but it is an essential venue, introducing key international practitioners and encouraging experimental British artists

across all media. There was talk a few years ago that the venue might utilise the unoccupied stacks near Tate Modern, but there is something very suitable, however impractical, about the operation's incendiary position in the heart of the establishment.

And the area we're about to enter is unquestionably that. Out of the ICA and right up the wide steps to the Duke of York Memorial brings us to Carlton House Terrace. Rising over the east side of Waterloo Place is an unattractive 1960s block perfectly suited, in the time-honoured way, to watching people from. This gets us in the mood, as the culture of *The Ipcress File* meets surveillance reality. The dispersed and anonymous nature of much covert-purpose architecture means it's naturally hard to find and not obviously placed. But certain tasks need to be kept in the neighbourhood and retain an element of seduction. One such business is the recruitment of Oxbridge whizz-kids for the spygame. A left leads into the L-shaped Carlton Gardens where, rumour has it, this still goes on. Pass first No.4, once home of Lord Palmerston and also base for de Gaulle and the Free French forces when they weren't scoffing in Soho. A left turn into the close and you can almost smell the secrecy. No.3 is our goal. No sign at all except for the small request to 'please hand deliver any mail'. So why keep the letter box? It's all a test, I'm certain. Across the grass, No.1, with its domed unblinking eye of a security camera in the gatepost, looks equally ambiguous. Loop past it and the de Gaulle statue and then left into the rest of the street until we meet Pall Mall.

If that was where they win the kids, then St James's is where they dine them. We are in the throbbing tuxedo of clubland now, and not a DJ in sight. These ventures are of the old-school persuasion, where the real business, of business and government, is still most likely done, especially as the two have always been intimate. Women are a rare

St George's Bloomsbury

species here, tolerated now in most clubs but only grudgingly. To our right are clubs, the Reform (No.104), the Travellers (No.106), and further away, but probably the grandest, the Athenaeum. To our left, the RAC and then the Oxford & Cambridge. No name plaques here. Either you know where you're going or it's not for you. A glimpse of halls and foyers is all we're going to get. Indeed, St James's is where you often see people without coats. These are people who walk under the permanent awning of affluence.

We walk left past these restricted areas and then cross over and into St James's Square. Of course, the central grass is local and locked – what else? – but we can still circle it. In the top left corner, at No.14, we find the London Library, which is, in perfect keeping, 'open to

members'. Swinging round to the right past Chatham House (1737 and home to three PMs), now the Royal Institute of International Affairs, we turn left into Duke of York Street and up the slope towards St James's Piccadilly, the Wren-designed church, hosting recitals, a Tuesday antique market and the new spirituality of its 'Alternatives' programme. Visionary Russian film director Andrei Tarkovsky spoke here in 1984.

We're standing now on Jermyn Street. A minor aristo could walk naked into this street and be fully equipped in no time from the myriad specialist outfitters. All the labels, particularly the long-standing ones, are on show here. Hawes & Curtis, George Trumper, Herbie Frogg and Bates the Hatter (the window display says it all – Burlington,

Trilby, Hilton, Peach Bloom, Weekender, Newbury, Soft Casual and Forester are a mantra of high-class headgear).

Turn right and on the left there's the back entrance to one shop that's a little more of the moment. Waterstone's has its flagship branch here. This largest bookshop in Europe is in the former Simpsons department store. Cafés, bars, restaurants, Internet access and more sofas than a student crashpad make this a great place to break the journey. You can, if you want, buy the Russian edition of *GQ* in the basement.

Revived, we turn back past the church, and the immaculate windows of Fortnum and Mason, noting that the sex sale cards in the phonebooths are now offering more hotel visits. Money still talks but walks less here, it seems. Pass Princes' Arcade on the right and then we turn left into Duke Street and down it, past a number of fine art dealers. This is not the modern art of Cork Street, north of Piccadilly, let alone the cutting edge conceptualism of Shoreditch. Very traditional they all are, as are the bookshops that accompany them. But there was, until recently, one anomaly. At No.44 stood White Cube, the tiny but influential exhibition space run by old Etonian Jay Jopling, dealer for Damien Hirst and the Young British Artists, bridge between the old money and the new art, playing both fields. It has since moved to more spacious premises on Hoxton Square.

Turning right into Ryder Street now, we can catch a few local voices. These aren't just plummy accents. It sounds like this lot have whole orchards in their mouths. We pass auctioneer Christie's wine department without breaking our stride – it's just too painful – and turn left into St James's Street, with the seminal 1960s *Economist* building at No.25 to our right.

St James's Street is the second local concentration of clubs, including Brooks's across the road at No.60, while at No.37 the oldest (founded 1693) is ultra-aristo White's. Notice the turning for Blue Ball

Yard, which is really where the seriously conservative Carlton Club should be. That's a little further down at No.69, recognisable by its paranoid camera overload. Even Mrs Thatcher had to be made an honorary man to earn full membership.

Continue on down and we rejoin Pall Mall at its western end, making an L that doesn't stand for left wing. These are the border streets of a small, threatened kingdom that some people probably rarely leave. We are off, however, across the road and through the black gates of Marlborough Road, heading for our first decent open space of the whole walk, the ordered St James's Park. Horse droppings in the road as we pass the walls of St James's Palace (built in 1532 on the site of a leprosy hospital) suggest there might be some royalty nearby, which is, of course, the case.

Joining the Mall again briefly, we cross into the park and head down towards the footbridge crossing the lake. To the east the graceful curve of the London Eye lifts above the treeline. This park is exactly the sort of place where spies should meet, to stand in twos by the water and say things like 'the geese are flying south for the winter' or 'the man knows aunty is knitting'. And so they do, Dalby and Ross anyway, in *The Ipcress File*.

Having crossed the inappropriately named Birdcage Walk into Queen Anne's Gate, we are faced with the unsecret state, in the form of the Stalinist monstrosity that is the Home Office. Of staggering scale and ugliness, this is a criminal construction. Notice the hanging curtains designed to deflect glass incoming from a streetside bomb blast. We proceed to turn left at the end – with St James's tube station facing us – into Broadway and on into Tothill Street. Had we continued on Broadway we would shortly have come to New Scotland Yard, police HQ, with its provocative crime museum.

On the right now we notice the Sanctuary pub, our first trace of this unique area near Westminster Abbey. The church's historical role as protector of the oppressed and persecuted continued until 1697, but perhaps its clergy could consider reviving the practice to provide succour for those refugees and the poor hounded by the many recent social and welfare 'reforms' enacted just 200 yards away in Parliament. Escape of another kind also beckons, in the form of the little-known and amazingly secluded 900-year-old College Garden, reached via the Abbey's Great Cloisters.

With Methodist Central Hall on our left (it has a decent café downstairs) we pass along Broad Sanctuary towards Parliament Square. In front of us what looks like a nuclear bunker is actually a toilet complex, which has won the 'City of Westminster Loo of the Year Award'. On the left is the huge QEII Conference Centre, underneath which is probably London's largest bugging centre (an outreach project of the Cheltenham-based GCHQ) situated in a nuclear bomb-proof bunker.

The square itself was taken over by protesters taking part in the May Day 2000 protests. Called 'guerilla gardening', the event was conceived as a symbolic greening of the city. The police had soaked the lawn prior to the event, hoping this would dissuade the assembly from hanging around. But the dowsing served to loosen the turf, making it easy to remove and place on the asphalt in front of the House of Commons. A potent visual statement and some kind of small victory that generally went unreported due to the later violence from a tiny minority of participants.

Walking clockwise around the square, we pass Abraham Lincoln and his massive sculpted chair and we ruminate on the uses and abuses of power, on the relationship between the individual and the political system, and on the increasing irrelevance of Parliament in the face of growing superstate and corporate authority.

Perhaps visitors will soon be coming to Westminster as part of a democratic heritage tour.

By now we are at the top of Parliament Street, leading into Whitehall, just across the road from the once notoriously grass-mohicaned Winston Churchill statue. Were we to walk down a few yards to the first turning on the left, King Charles Street, site of the Foreign Office, we might well come across Turkish Cypriots demanding recognition of their territory. Peaceful protest seems essential to democracy, not, as some portray it, a threat. If the chain of opposition is broken, then there is no defence against authoritarianism.

Political broadcasting over, we can now cross the road and take a quick look inside the spacious, forward-looking Westminster tube station, part of the extended Jubilee line that goes on to Greenwich. But we're not leaving quite yet. Cross over Bridge Street to its right side and then stroll out on to Westminster Bridge.

It seems entirely suitable to finish above the river, an open ending without closure. We can see that it alone has been responsible for the city's presence, and therefore for all the versions and visions of London we have encountered. The city never fully yields all its secrets. It is at once intensely private and brazenly public. Here, in transit, surrounded by innumerable languages and nationalities, by the personal headlands of every citizen, we can appreciate that London is both a profoundly English and reticent metropolis, but also now a fecund and vibrant city of the world. A seemingly ceaseless national and international magnet, attracting people prepared to engage with its heightened dynamic and perverted energy, it shows a constantly changing face.

On this crossing, on 3 September 1802, William Wordsworth wrote that 'earth has not anything to show more fair'. But the same river prompted William

The **ICA**.

Blake to describe it as 'chartered', and he also noted the 'marks of weakness… and woe in each face'. In this last century, TS Eliot would observe a similar despair. Watching the crowd on London Bridge, he wrote, 'I had not thought death had undone so many'. This sort of sensibility may be an inevitable by-product of living in such a large settlement. The anonymity that some crave is the undoing of others.

But as we stand, above the river, almost above time itself and history, we can look upriver to the west and know that London will eventually cease. Despite Victorian novelist Richard Jefferies's apocalyptic titular assertion that *After London* there is nothing except a putrid swamp, an escape route is provided if needed. That is, if the building that doesn't exist will let you pass. Far down on the South Bank, looking through Lambeth Bridge's second stack from the right, we can just make out the green and pale stone ziggurat that is the Babylonian HQ of MI6. Designed by Terry Farrell and costing £240 million, it is an official denial, a public secret. Fortunately you can't fool all the people all the time, but its existence is a rare example of the authorities adopting a Zen practice. Employing opposites, they have made the most secret, unaccountable institution the most visible.

And so, as we turn to disappear back into the great democratic throng, we can muse on the thought that, in theory at least, London is a city of infinite visions. You can make and remake your own as it suits you. This has been just one trawl through its beating heart. To borrow from novelist Geoff Ryman – author of among other things *253*, the tube train novel without rival that celebrates the diversity of the capital's population – London really is a city where, 'silent as settling snow, experience falls on prepared ground'.

Eating & drinking

Admiral Duncan
54 Old Compton Street, W1D 4UD (7437 5300). **Open** noon-11pm Mon-Sat; noon-10.30pm Sun.

Bierodrome
67 Kingsway, WC2B 6TD (7242 7469/www. belgo-restaurants.com). **Open** noon-11pm Mon-Sat. **Food served** noon-3pm, 6-11pm Mon-Fri; noon-11pm Sat.

Black Horse
6 Rathbone Place, W1T 1HL (7307 9911). **Open** 11am-11pm Mon-Fri; noon-11pm Sat. **Food served** noon-5pm Mon-Fri; noon-4pm Sat.

Bradley's Spanish Bar
42-44 Hanway Street, W1T 1UT (7636 0359). **Open** noon-11pm Mon-Sat; 3-10.30pm Sun.

Cambridge
48 Newman Street, W1T 1QQ (7636 1332). **Open** 11am-11pm Mon-Fri; noon-11pm Sat; noon-10.30pm Sun. **Food served** noon-3pm, 6-8pm daily.

Coach & Horses
29 Greek Street, W1V 5LL (7437 5920). **Open** 11am-11pm Mon-Sat; noon-10.30pm Sun.

Coffee Matters
4 Southampton Row, WC1B 4AA (7242 9090). **Open** 7am-6pm Mon-Fri; 9am-3pm Sat.

Freemason's Arms
81-82 Long Acre, WC2E 9NG (7836 3115). **Open** 11am-11pm Mon-Sat; noon-9pm Sun. **Food served** noon-3pm, 5-9pm Mon-Fri; noon-9pm Sat; noon-4pm Sun.

French House
49 Dean Street, W1D 5BG (7437 2799). **Open** noon-11pm Mon-Sat; noon-10.30pm Sun. **Food served** *Bar* noon-3pm Mon-Sat. *Restaurant* noon-3pm, 6pm-midnight Mon-Sat. Soho fixture with downstairs bar and first-floor dining room serving Modern European fare.

Gaby's
30 Charing Cross Road, WC2H 0DB (7836 4233). **Food served** noon-midnight Mon-Sat; noon-10pm Sun. Felafel and houmous.

Govinda's
9 Soho Street, W1 (7437 4928/www.iskcon-london.org). **Open** noon-8pm Mon-Sat. Cheap Indian vegetarian cooking.

Jerusalem
33-34 Rathbone Place, W1T 1JN (7255 1120/ www.thebreakfastgroup.co.uk). **Open** noon-11pm Mon; noon-midnight Tue, Wed; noon-1am Thur, Fri; 7pm-1am Sat. **Food served** noon-3pm, 6-10.30pm Mon-Fri; 7-10.30pm Sat.

Kettner's
29 Romilly Street, W1D 5HP (7734 6112/www.
kettners.com). Bar **Open** 11am-1am Mon-Sat;
11am-10.30pm Sun. *Restaurant* **Meals served**
noon-1am Mon-Sat; noon-midnight Sun.

Marino's
31 Rathbone Place, W1T 1JH (7636 8965).
Open 7am-7pm Mon-Fri; 9am-5pm Sat.

Pâtisserie Valerie
44 Old Compton Street, W1D 4TY (7437 3466/
www.patisserie-valerie.co.uk). **Open/food**
served 7.30am-8.30pm Mon, Tue; 7.30am-9pm
Wed-Fri; 8.30am-9pm Sat; 9.30am-7pm Sun.

Salisbury
90 St Martin's Lane, WC2N 4AP (7836 5863).
Open 11am-11pm Mon-Fri; noon-11pm Sat; noon-
10.30pm Sun. **Food served** noon-9pm daily.

Sanctuary House
33 Tothill Street, SW1H 9LA (7799 4044).
Open 11am-11pm Mon-Sat; noon-10.30pm Sun.
Food served 11.30am-9pm Mon-Sat; noon-9pm
Sun.

Ship Tavern
12 Gate Street, WC2A 3HP (7405 1992). **Open**
11am-11pm Mon-Sat. **Food served** 11am-3pm
Mon-Fri.

Sun Tavern
66 Long Acre, WC2E 9JD (7836 4520). **Open**
11am-11pm Mon-Sat; noon-10.30pm Sun. **Food**
served noon-4pm Mon-Fri; noon-5pm Sat, Sun.

Tokyo Diner
2 Newport Place, WC2H 7JP (7287 8777/ www.
tokyodiner.com). **Meals** noon-midnight daily. .

Buildings & parks

Foreign Office
King Charles Street, SW1A 2AH (7270 1500/
www.fco.gov.uk).

Methodist Central Hall
Storey's Gate, SW1H 9NH (7222 8010/www.c-h-
w.com). **Open** 9am-6pm daily. *Services* 11am,
6.30pm Sun.

QEII Conference Centre
Broad Sanctuary, Westminster, SW1P 3EE (7222
5000/www.qeiicc.co.uk). **Open** 8am-6pm Mon-Fri.

RADA
62-64 Gower Street, WC1E 6ED (7636 7076/
www.rada.org).

St James's Palace
Cleveland Row, SW1 (7930 4832/
www.royal.gov.uk).

St James's Park
The Mall, SW1 (7930 1793/www.royalparks.
gov.uk). **Open** dawn-dusk daily.

St Martin's Lane Hotel
45 St Martin's Lane, WC2N 4HX (7300 5500/
www.stmartinslanehotel.com).

School of Hygiene & Tropical Medicine
Keppel Street, WC1E 7HT (7636 8636/
www.lshtm.ac.uk).

Cinemas & theatres

Cochrane Theatre
Southampton Row, WC1B 4AP (7269 1600/
www.cochranetheatre.co.uk). **Open** *Box office*
10am-6pm Mon-Fri. **Tickets** £3-£15.

Hall
16 Chenies Street, WC1E 7EX (7307 5060/
www.drillhall.co.uk). **Open** *Box office* 10am-7pm
Mon-Sat; 10am-6pm Sun.

English National Opera
St Martin's Lane, WC2N 4ES (7632 8300/
www.eno.org). **Open** *Box office* 10am-8pm Mon-
Sat. **Tickets** £5-£65.

Prince Charles Cinema
Leicester Place, WC2H 7BP (today's films 7734
9127/www.princecharlescinema.com).

Soho Theatre
21 Dean Street, W1D 3NE (7478 0100/
www.sohotheatre.com). **Open** *Box office* 10am-
7.30pm Mon-Sat.

Wyndhams Theatre
Charing Cross Road, WC2H 0DA (0870 060
6633/www.theambassadors.com/wyndhams).
Open *Box office* 24hrs daily.

Film & literature

After London Richard Jefferies (1885)
The Director's Cut Nicholas Royle (2000)
Hawksmoor Peter Ackroyd (1985)
Heaven and Hell Emanuel Swedenborg (1758)
The Ipcress File Len Deighton (1962)
The Ipcress File (Sidney J Furie, 1965, GB)
Lights Out For the Territory Iain Sinclair
(1997)

London: A Biography Peter Ackroyd (2000)
Lud Heat Iain Sinclair (1975)
Newman Passage Christopher Petit (from *The Time Out Book of London Short Stories*, ed Maria Lexton, 1993)
Nineteen Eighty-Four George Orwell (1949)
Nineteen Eighty-Four (Michael Radford, 1984, GB)
Peeping Tom (Michael Powell, 1960, GB)
Radio On (Christopher Petit, 1979, GB/WGer)
Robinson Christopher Petit (1993)
Roofworld Christopher Fowler (1988)
The Life of Samuel Johnson James Boswell (1791)
Tunnel Visions Christopher Ross (2001)
253 Geoff Ryman (1998)
www.nohzone.com Peter Whitehead (2001)

Museums & galleries

British Museum
Great Russell Street, WC1B 3DG (7636 1555/ www.thebritishmuseum.ac.uk). **Open** *Galleries* 10am-5.30pm Mon-Wed, Sat, Sun; 10am-8.30pm Thur, Fri. *Great Court* 9am-6pm Mon-Wed, Sun; 9am-11pm Thur-Sat. *Highlights tours* (90mins) 10.30am, 1pm, 3pm daily. **Admission** free; donations appreciated. *Temporary exhibitions* prices vary. *Highlights tours* £8; £5 concessions.

Brunei Gallery
SOAS, 10 Thornhaugh Street, Russell Square, WC1H 0XG (7898 4915/www.soas.ac.uk). **Open** 10.30am-5pm Mon-Fri.

Freemasons' Hall
60 Great Queen Street, WC2B 5AZ (7831 9811/ www.grandlodge-england.org). **Open** 10am-5pm Mon-Fri; 10.15-11.45am Sat (booking necessary for Sat; £10 charge).

ICA Gallery
The Mall, SW1Y 5AH (7930 3647/www.ica.org.uk). **Open** *Exhibitions* noon-7.30pm daily. **Admission** £1.50, £1 concessions Mon-Fri; £2.50, £1.50 concessions Sat, Sun.

Hunterian Museum
Royal College of Surgeons, 35-43 Lincoln's Inn Fields, WC2A 3PE (7869 6560/www.rcseng.ac.uk/ services/museums). **Open** 10am-5pm Tue-Sat. **Admission** free.

Petrie Museum of Egyptian Archaeology
University College London, Malet Place, WC1E 6BT (7679 2884/www.petrie.ac.uk). **Open** 1-5pm Tue-Fri; 10am-1pm Sat. **Admission** free.

Sir John Soane's Museum
13 Lincoln's Inn Fields, WC2A 3BP (7405 2107/ www.soane.org). **Open** 10am-5pm Tue-Sat; 6-9pm first Tue of every mth. **Tours** 2.30pm Sat. **Admission** free; donations appreciated. **Tours** £3; free concessions.

Private members' clubs

Athenaeum Club
107 Pall Mall, SW1Y 5ER (7930 4843).

2 Brydges Place
2 Brydges Place, St Martin's Lane, WC2N 4HP (7240 7659).

Blacks
67 Dean Street, W1D 4OH (7287 3381).

Brooks's Club
St James's Street, SW1A 1LN (7493 4411).

Carlton Club
69 St James's Street, SW1A 1PJ (7493 1164/ www.carltonclub.co.uk).

Colony Room Club
41 Dean Street, W1D 4PY (7437 9179/ www.colonyroom.com).

Groucho Club
45 Dean Street, W1D 4QB (7439 4685/ www.thegrouchoclub.com).

Royal Automobile Club
89 Pall Mall, SW1 (7930 2345/ www.royalautomobileclub.co.uk).

Reform Club
104 Pall Mall, SW1Y 5HS (7930 9374).

Travellers Club
106 Pall Mall, SW1Y 5EP (7930 8688/ www.thetravellersclub.org.uk).

United Oxford & Cambridge University Club
71-77 Pall Mall, SW1Y 5HD (7930 5151).

White's Club
37 St James's Street, SW1A 1JG (7493 6671).

Religion

Notre Dame de France Church
5 Leicester Place, WC2H 7BX (7437 9363/ www.notredamechurch.co.uk). **Services** 12.15pm, 6pm Mon, Wed-Fri; 12.15pm, 6pm, 7.30pm Tue; 12.15pm, 6pm, 7.15pm Sat; 10am, 11.30am Sun.

St George's Bloomsbury
7 Little Russell Street, WC1A 2HR (7405 3044/ www.stgeorgesbloomsbury.org.uk). **Open** 9.30am-5.30pm Mon-Fri; 10.30am-12.30pm Sun.

St James's Piccadilly
197 Piccadilly, W1J 9LL (7734 4511/www.st-james-piccadilly.org). **Open** 8am-6.30pm daily. Evening event times vary. **Admission** free; donations appreciated.

Shopping

Algerian Coffee House
52 Old Compton Street, W1D 4PB (7437 2480/ www.algcoffee.co.uk). **Open** 9am-7pm Mon-Sat.

Atlantis Bookshop
49A Museum Street, WC1A 1LY (7405 2120/ www.theatlantisbookshop.com). **Open** 10.30am-6pm Mon-Sat.

Bates the Hatter
21A Jermyn Street, SW1Y 6HP (7734 2722/ www.bates-hats.co.uk). **Open** 9am-5.15pm Mon-Fri; 9.30am-4pm Sat.

Central Regalia
23 Great Queen Street, WC2B 5BB (7405 0004/ www.centralregalia.com). **Open** 9.30am-5.30pm Mon-Fri; 10am-3pm Sat.

Cuts
39 Frith Street, W1D 5LL (7734 2171). **Open** 11am-6.30pm Mon-Fri; 10am-6pm Sat.

George F Trumper
9 Curzon Street, W1J 5HQ (7499 1850/ www.trumpers.com). **Open** 9am-5.30pm Mon-Fri; 9am-1pm Sat.

Harvie & Hudson
77 Jermyn Street, SW1Y 6NP (7839 3578/ www.harvieandhudson.com). **Open** 9am-5.30pm Mon-Sat.

Herbie Frogg
18-19 Jermyn Street, SW1Y 6HP (7437 6069/ www.herbie-frogg.co.uk). **Open** 9.30am-6pm Mon-Sat.

Italian Bookshop
7 Cecil Court, WC2N 4EZ (7240 1634/ www.italianbookshop.co.uk). **Open** 10.30am-6.30pm Mon-Sat.

Paradiso Bodyworks
60 Dean Street, W1D 6AH (7287 6913). **Open** 11am-7.30pm Mon-Sat.

RA Gekoski
Pied Bull Yard, 15A Bloomsbury Square, WC1A 2LP (7404 6676). **Open** 10am-5.30pm Mon-Fri.

Toye, Kenning & Spencer
19-21 Great Queen Street, WC2B 5BE (7242 0471/www.toye.com). **Open** 9am-5.20pm Mon-Fri; 9am-3pm Sat.

Ulysses
40 Museum Street, WC1A 1LU (7831 1600). **Open** 11am-6pm Mon-Sat; by appointment Sun.

Waterstone's
203-206 Piccadilly, SW1Y 6WW (7851 2400/ www.waterstones.co.uk). **Open** 10am-10pm Mon-Sat; noon-6pm Sun.

Watkins Books
19-21 Cecil Court, WC2N 4EZ (7836 2182/ www.watkinsbooks.com). **Open** 11am-7pm Mon-Sat.

Wen Tai Sun Chinese News Agency/Art & Craft Co
80 Dean Street, W1D 3SL (7437 5188). **Open** 10.30am-7pm Mon-Fri; 11am-4pm Sat; 11am-6pm Sun.

Others

Birkbeck College
(University of London), Malet Street, WC1E 7HX (7631 6000/www.bbk.ac.uk).

Compass Housing Association
31 Great Queen Street, WC2B 5AG (7831 5879). **Open** 9.30am-5pm Mon-Fri.

London Library
14 St James's Square, SW1Y 4LG (7930 7705/ www.londonlibrary.co.uk). **Open** 9.30am-5.30pm Mon, Fri, Sat; 9.30am-7.30pm Tue-Thur.

London Open House
www.londonopenhouse.org.

Masonic Housing Association
31 Great Queen Street, WC2B 5AG (7831 5879). **Open** 9am-5pm Mon-Fri.

Swedenborg Society
20 Bloomsbury Way, WC1A 2TH (7405 7986/ www.swedenborg.org.uk). **Open** 9.30am-5pm Mon-Fri.

University of London
Senate House, Malet Street, WC1E 7HU (7679 2000/www.lon.ac.uk).

A tale of two tribes
Courttia Newland

The busy activity of Ladbroke Grove and Portobello Market contrasts sharply with the wealthy serenity of Notting Hill.

Start: Ladbroke Grove tube
Finish: Ladbroke Grove tube
Time: 2-3 hours
Distance: 4 miles/6km
Getting there: Hammersmith & City line to Ladbroke Grove
Getting back: Hammersmith & City line from Ladbroke Grove
Note: Portobello antiques market operates only on Saturdays.

One constant source of amazement when walking through the Portobello Road area is the diversity of its people and buildings. The road and market effect a subtle yet unmistakable transformation from poor to rich, or vice versa, depending on the direction in which you're walking. The area has seen three distinct phases: from acres of farmland sprang the rat-infested slums of the 1950s, which finally turned into the coffee shop and wine bar haven of today. There's nothing to say that change won't keep on coming, which contributes to the feel of a district on the cutting edge, where everything happens.

From Ladbroke Grove tube station, visitors are deposited on to a main street of the same name, though this is not where your walk really begins. The true diversity of 'the Grove' is only revealed by walking northwards until you meet the fire station, then taking the left-hand road opposite, which leads to St Charles Square. In 1599 it was here, or more exactly at the bottom of Chesterton Road where the Lancaster West Estate now stands, that you would have found the Notting Barns, one of two farms previously occupying the area.

Walk as far as you can and you'll be faced with St Pius X Church, formerly the most ambitious Catholic venture in 19th-century Notting Hill. Take a right, then your first left and you'll come across a Carmelite Monastery beside St Charles' Hospital, which along with the square took its name from St Charles of Borromeo. The hospital opened in 1889, but in those times it was known as St Marylebone Infirmary, accommodating 760 patients. It was also the only hospital in the immediate vicinity.

As you pass along Exmoor Street and head on towards Barlby Road, try not to be too spooked by the Funeral Home of John Nodes, in business since 1854. A right turn at the end of the road will take you to a roundabout. Walk straight across and into the Wornington Green housing estate past West Indian takeaway Yum Yum. Then straight all the way, passing more council blocks, Kensington & Chelsea adult college, and a sunken football pitch showcasing the best in spray-can graffiti art, until you come to a small zebra crossing and a smattering of varied shops.

You have just met Golborne Road, where the collection of fish 'n' chip bars, Moroccan restaurants and Portuguese coffee shops fully reflects the area's worldwide flavour. Stop and take in the many languages and dialects, a far cry from the quiet meadows and pastures that existed here over a century ago. Nothing is what it was, even as recently as 15 years back. Turn right and walk until you come

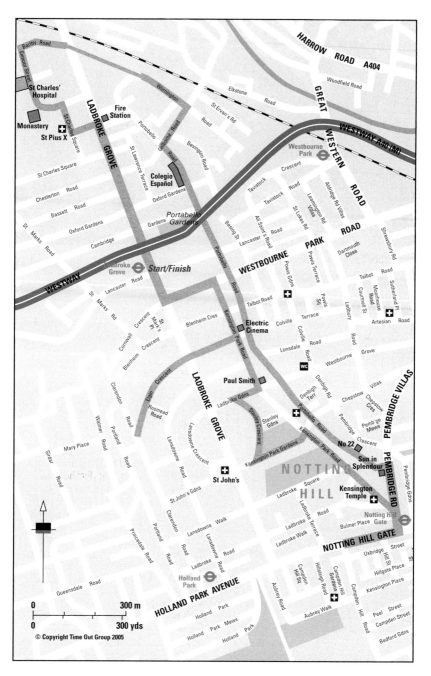

The moneyed splendour of **Notting Hill**.

to another zebra crossing, just in front of the Bed bar. You've joined Portobello Road very near its humble beginnings.

In 1599 the entire area had been known as the North Kensington Farms, though in later years it became the Portobello Estate. This was due to the proximity of the second local farm, the Portobello, which took its name from Admiral Vernon's capture of Puerto Bello in the Gulf of Mexico, around 1739. The lane, as it was called back then, was just that – a fairly rural affair until 1864. In a booklet published in 1882, an anonymous inhabitant wrote that until the last century a walk down this lane was one of the most pleasant in the whole of London. By 1919, according to records, there was only a smattering of stalls and shops. The market opened only on weekdays, but by 1927 an official order was passed London-wide: Portobello and other similar roads opened six days a week, with licensed stalls and market inspectors to ensure compliance with strict trading rules and regulations.

From then until now, Saturdays find this road filled with stalls and people, though on weekdays and Sundays the pace is sedate, more serene. To the right is the Colegio Español, the local Spanish school, formerly a convent incorporating the St Elizabeth Home for Children. To the left is a council estate, the actual site of Portobello Farm; where once there were pigs, produce and fields, now comes the tinny sound of community radio. Further ahead is the first of many eateries, including Uncle's, one of my personal favourites. There's a scattering of one-off clothes shops and a haven for jazz record collectors, Honest Jon's, all in the space of one square block. Ahead and above you, cars whizz by on the Westway, the motorway overpass opened in 1970 to provide a straight route into the city. Local protestors campaigned for its closure at the time, and were answered by the building of the housing estates that dot the area. The mix between village and city is a thin line here; even thinner is the fade between tourism and the varied local communities.

Stand on this block in late August, when the Notting Hill Carnival takes place, and you'll find yourself astounded by the sheer numbers of people. The celebration originates from a Trinidadian tradition, when slaves were forbidden to play musical instruments and wear costumes, except for when the imported European Carnival took place. Slaves were also banned from the streets at night unless accompanied by their masters.

When the laws were repealed in 1833, slaves took to the streets. They mimicked their former masters by using powder to make their faces paler, and wore elaborate costumes that mocked the way they dressed. It became a regular tradition and soon spread all over the West Indies in many different variations; for example, in Barbados the carnival is used to celebrate 'Crop Over', a time when all of the farmyard crops have been harvested.

When native Trinidadians eventually came to England, they brought with them a deep love and remembrance of their annual celebration. A civil rights activist, Claudia Jones, founded her own festival sometime in the late 1950s. It was known as the Caribbean Carnival and was held indoors near Euston; as its popularity grew, it gained the attention of people outside the black community. The first official carnival was moved to the streets of Notting Hill in 1965, owing a great deal to the efforts of Rhaune Laslett. Ms Laslett was a social worker who strove for racial tolerance among the area's inhabitants by including steel pan music in a local festival that previously excluded West Indian residents.

Laslett's actions were partly a response to the race riots that blazed through the area on 1 September 1958, when the black immigrant population finally fought back against the mounting racial persecution doled out by the Ladbroke Grove Teddy Boys. Since the arrival of West Indian and African immigrants in their largest numbers to date, the white population of England had shown their displeasure in many ways. All over the country so-called 'minorities', who in global terms were the majority, were forced to undergo violent attacks, racial abuse and segregation in both the workplace and rented accommodation. In Ladbroke Grove the attacks became commonplace. White gangs often drove around looking for victims. Hate groups such as the Aryan Knights sent threatening letters to the offices of black publications. White women who were known to have married or had relations with blacks had their homes petrol-bombed and were driven out on the streets. All of this came to a head on that powder keg of a summer night, when, according to one participant, 'the entire community was up against us'. The resulting riot centred mostly on the streets around Blenheim Crescent. The fighting lasted three days. It was the worst race riot Britain had seen, if not the last, and a turning point for the community as a whole.

Since then, Carnival has grown in strength year on year, though in recent times the safety element has become a subject of debate, as crowds of revellers that once numbered in the thousands have recently topped the million mark. Instead of steel pans and floats – traditionally Trinidadian components – the Jamaican sound systems have taken over, mainly due to the musical tastes of a generation born in this country more than any allegiance to a particular island. There is talk of moving the carnival to nearby Kensington Gardens, which some say will destroy the mood and feel of something that was always a West Indian affair. The future of this massive event hangs in the balance, another token of the area's fight for survival.

On a Sunday the only people you'll find are music enthusiasts and second-hand bargain hunters, along with the odd local. If the weather's good, you can purchase some food and sit in Portobello Green, a small square of park that's a quiet haven

from serious shopping. Here you'll find yourself surrounded by second-hand books and clothes. Somewhere under a huge canopy there's a stall offering affordable Thai food, light on the pocket but heavy on taste.

Walk beneath the Westway and pass more stalls, as well as an arcade that boasts among other things, children's clothes shops and jewellers specialising in silver. Emerge into a square at the end of Tavistock Road, located on your left, where in the early 1990s you could catch travelling performers, including African drummers, mime artists, fire eaters and acrobats. Here vegetarian food can be enjoyed. Wander further and come across bars, hairdressers and underground barbers favoured by locals and tourists alike. Every other step is like an unspoken fight between commerce and necessity; women's clothes shops nestle on the same block as Tesco; Starbucks sits directly opposite a small butcher's. The Warwick Castle, in the middle of what was formerly

Dressed to impress on **Portobello Road**.

Cornwall Road (now Westbourne Park Road), has gone by the same name since the days when it was nothing more than a simple inn. As you move on, you'll see more of the same. Big business going toe to toe with smaller, long-established stores – and, on this block at least, winning the fight.

Keep walking and you'll come across the Electric Cinema, the country's oldest purpose-built movie house. It first opened in 1911 as the Imperial Playhouse, and film enthusiasts have battled for years to keep it alive. Its reopening in 2001 struck a vital blow for lovers of art house films nationwide, as well as Portobello Road purists. The Electric Brasserie has since opened next door, thus further bridging the gap between art and commerce. John Reginald Christie, the serial killer, was a relief projectionist at the Electric during World War II. Christie preyed mainly on transient young women and prostitutes who frequented the area. He and his wife lived in a ground-floor flat at 10 Rillington Place; the cul-de-sac, bounded by St Mark's Road to the east, was demolished.

In the next block you'll find high-quality antique stores and art galleries, such as Apart, home to some of the finest craftspeople the area has to offer. Continue on an upward rise to find yet more antique stores on the right, in sharp contrast to the clusters of council flats on the left. Here, the antique stalls and shops are in abundance.

The more observant walker will notice the subtle change in atmosphere a couple of blocks on. It's less about what you can buy, and more about what sights there are to be seen. At 22 Portobello Road stands the former house of novelist, essayist and literary critic George Orwell, author of such classics as *Nineteen Eighty-Four* and *Animal Farm*. If you feel you deserve a rest after all this, then a local-style pub at the very top of Portobello, the Sun in Splendour, is the perfect watering hole.

You will have reached Notting Hill Gate, where many places of interest are located. Maps dating between 1675 and 1769 detail the toll houses and gates that gave the area its name. A Turnpike Trust was conceived to pay for maintenance to the nearby Bayswater Road and to prevent any robberies or murders. This move proved unpopular at the time, as none of these obligations was properly met, and the toll, which stood at three pennies, was deemed too expensive. By 1864 these toll houses, sometimes squat wooden huts large enough for only a few bodies, were removed, much to the joy of local residents.

In 1863 the first underground in the world, the Metropolitan railway line, was opened. It was extended from Paddington to South Kensington via Notting Hill in 1868. A year later, the *Kensington News* reports that four houses in Westbourne Park Passage fell in, due to tunnels dug under premises that were newly built at the time. No one was hurt. Complaints were aired about the decline of shrubs and foliage that residents blamed on smoke from the trains. The Metropolitan line station was eventually demolished, but by 1900 a Central line station had taken its place. The return fare for a journey on what was then a 30-minute steam train ride was priced six pence. Very little remains of the buildings that once stood on that spot, besides an old post office. The area was redeveloped as recently as the late 1950s, when the main road was widened to accommodate a more 'high street' feel.

A high street this certainly is. There are coffee shops, second-hand books and clothes shops, the Gate Theatre, a cinema of the same name that's strong on international film, and also the Coronet, which shows films of a more commercial nature. The Coronet, originally a theatre, was forced to make the switch to moving pictures 20 years later, and though it has had to fight long and hard against going dark, the cinema still enjoys a healthy and prosperous existence. It was also one of the last cinemas in England that permitted

Electric Cinema

smoking, though burning tobacco was finally banned a few years ago.

Further along the high street are more clothes shops and a great Italian restaurant, the perfect place for an after-movie munch. Many of the pubs to be found here existed in the form of taverns doing business way back in the 1800s. Sitting inside one, you can believe it. The pubs are steeped in tradition.

From the very top of Notting Hill turn back on yourself, passing shops and the Gate Theatre until you meet Kensington Park Road. You'll see Kensington Temple on your left, and Southbank International School on your right. Here is an institution that takes pride in the diversity of its students, with over 45 nationalities represented within its walls, a fitting philosophy after the area's more colourful history. You'll pass a collection of high-class flats that are linked by underground tunnels. I know this because I used to deliver papers to these buildings as a teenager.

Walk further to encounter private gardens that resemble those Hugh Grant and Julia Roberts broke into in *Notting Hill*. Houses priced at millions can be found in the streets around this end of Notting Hill, the luxury cars that line them a vivid testimony to the wealth of its community.

Turn left on to Kensington Park Gardens, with St John's Church at the end, and you'll find an area rich in artistic and academic history. Take your first right and follow the map past the sweep of elegant stuccoed houses in Stanley Gardens and back to the lights.

Opposite you'll see the spot where designer Paul Smith has located his west London base. This was formerly a prestigious restaurant and hotel, mostly remembered for the friendly nature of a beautiful parrot that greeted its many guests at the entrance. Continue down to your left, perhaps diverting left to pass the pastel-coloured houses that line Elgin Crescent. Many well-known names have lived on this road, including novelist Katherine Mansfield who lived at No.95, and architect Sir Hugh Casson, who helped transform the derelict Holland House, which stands in the centre of Holland Park, into the youth hostel that still exists today.

Return to Kensington Park Road to find yourself in Westbourne Grove. The final irony is that this is where the 1958 riots took place – hard to believe when you look at this block today in all its glory. Over 300 West Indians apparently holed up in a house here waiting for white rioters to try to burn them out. The fighting turned the tide of violence back on to the racists and led to many arrests. Nowadays, these events are only vague memories.

If you can afford to, stop and try the food, which is delicious. If not, continue walking and you'll find an assortment of cafés and wine bars more suited to the modest pocket. When you can walk no further, take a left on to Westbourne Park Road, then head down to the traffic lights and take the first right back on to Ladbroke Grove. From here, the tube station is just a matter of yards away; but you could always stop for a last drink in the Ion Bar, situated right by Ladbroke Grove tube station, before leaving for home.

Eating & drinking

Bed
310 Portobello Road, W10 5TA (8969 4500).
Open/food served 5-11pm Mon-Thur; noon-11pm Fri, Sat; noon-10.30pm Sun.

Electric Brasserie
191 Portobello Road, W11 2ED (7908 9696/ www.electricbrasserie.com). **Open/food served** 8am-midnight Mon-Sat; 8am-11pm Sun.

Ion Bar
161-165 Ladbroke Grove, W10 8GJ (8960 1702/ www.meanfiddler.com). **Open** 5pm-midnight Mon-Fri, Sun; 11am-midnight Sat.

Luna
192 Kensington Park Road, W11 (7229 0482). **Open** 12.30-11.30pm Mon-Sat; 12.30-11pm Sun.

Prince Albert
11 Pembridge Road, W11 3HQ (7727 7362). **Open** noon-11pm Mon-Sat; noon-10.30pm Sun. **Food served** noon-9.30pm daily.

Sun in Splendour
7 Portobello Road, W11 3DA (7313 9331). **Open** noon-11pm Mon-Fri; 11am-11pm Sat; noon-10.30pm. **Food served** noon-4pm, 6-10pm Mon-Fri; noon-8pm Sat, Sun.

Uncle's
305 Portobello Road, W10 5TD (8962 0090). **Open** 9am-5pm Mon-Fri; 9am-6pm Sat, Sun.

Warwick Castle
6 Warwick Place, W9 2PX (7432 1331). **Open** noon-11pm Mon-Sat; noon-10.30pm Sun. **Food served** noon-3pm, 6-9pm daily.

Yum Yum
312 Ladbroke Grove, W10 5NQ (8968 1477). **Open** 10am-10pm Mon-Thur; 10am-11pm Fri, Sat. West Indian takeaway.

Cinema & theatre

Coronet
103-105 Notting Hill Gate, W11 3LB (7727 6705/www.coronet.org).

Electric Cinema
191 Portobello Road, W11 2ED (7908 9696/ bookings 7229 8688/www.the-electric.co.uk).

Gate Cinema
87 Notting Hill Gate, W11 3JZ (0870 755 0063/ www.picturehouses.co.uk).

Gate Theatre
11 Pembridge Road, W11 3HQ (7229 0706/ www.gatetheatre.co.uk).

Religion

Kensington Temple
Kensington Park Road, W11 3BY (7727 4877/ www.kt.org). **Open** 9am-7pm daily.

St John's
Lansdowne Crescent, W11 2NN (7727 4262). **Open** Services 10.30am, 6pm Sun.

St Pius X
79 St Charles Square, W10 6EB (8969 6844). **Open** 7am-4pm Mon-Fri; 7am-7pm Sat, Sun. *Services* 8.20am Mon-Fri; 6pm Sat; 8am, 10am, noon Sun.

Shopping

Apart
138 Portobello Road, W11 2DZ (7229 6146). **Open** 10.30am-5.30pm Tue-Fri; 11am-5pm Sat; noon-4.30pm Sun.

Les Couilles du Chien
65 Golborne Road, W10 5NP (8968 0099/ www.lescouillesduchien.co.uk). **Open** 9.30am-5.30pm Mon-Thur; 8am-5.30pm Fri; 9am-5.30pm Sat.

Golborne Fisheries
75-77 Golborne Road, W10 5NP (8960 3100). **Open** 8am-6pm Mon-Sat.

Honest Jon's
278 Portobello Road, W10 5TE (8969 9822). **Open** 10am-6pm Mon-Sat; 11am-5pm Sun.

Paul Smith
Westbourne House, 122 Kensington Park Road, W11 2EP (7727 3553/bespoke 7727 3820/ www.paulsmith.co.uk). **Open** 10.30am-6.30pm Mon-Thur; 10am-6.30pm Fri, Sat.

Others

Colegio Español
317 Portobello Road, W10 5SZ (8969 2664).

Parkside Health
St Charles' Hospital, Exmoor Street, W10 6DZ (8969 2488).

Southbank International School
36-38 Kensington Park Road, W11 3BU (7229 8230/www.southbank.org).

Exiles, rebels and iconoclasts

Bonnie Greer

The revolutionary poet Rimbaud, who escaped Paris for London, was one of many exiles to find a safe haven in the streets of Soho.

Start: Goodge Street tube
Finish: St Anne's churchyard, Soho
Time: 2-3 hours
Distance: 3 miles/5km
Getting there: Northern line to Goodge Street
Getting back: short walk to Piccadilly Circus (Bakerloo or Piccadilly lines)
Note: although there is a route mapped through Soho, it is probably best to find a homely café and read the text before finding your own path through its streets.

'I am the pedestrian on the main road…'
Les Illuminations, Arthur Rimbaud

Whenever I tell people that I moved to London from New York's East Village, they usually check my temperature and ask if I'm all right. Granted, these are usually media or literary types who think that NYC is some kind of mecca – maybe it is, but it also betrays the secret British belief that America is best.

The US is a great place if you like uniformity and there is no town more uniform at the end of the day than the Big Apple. Often, while seated at a café in St Marks Place, filled with 'Loisaida' art-types aiming to be on the cover of *Time*, I longed to be over here. London

looked mad, bad and dangerous to know, and anyway, the great French poet, Arthur Rimbaud, one of my favourite writers, said that it was 'healthy', filled with the kind of atmosphere that an artist needed, one where there were very few poseurs.

Jean Nicolas Arthur Rimbaud, schoolboy poet and country bumpkin, had, quite simply, before leaving his teens, revolutionised French poetry. He smashed the outmoded use of the Alexandrine and introduced free verse, in which nothing needed to rhyme or have rhythm. This may seem like old hat now, but remember, we are living in post-Rimbaud times. He was the Eminem of his day, and his theory of the derangement of the senses – 'just do it' – has inspired writers from Karl Marx to Nick Cave. His words were the battle-cry of the 1968 student revolts. He is the godfather of punk, the apostle of youth as destroyer of history – a firm believer in drink, dirt, depravity, but not the Deity.

By the age of 17, Rimbaud had fled his conventional background to become a part of the Paris Commune in 1871. The Commune was the revolutionary government set up by Paris after France's defeat at the hands of the Prussians. The Commune proclaimed itself a nation of free-thinkers and free-lovers.

France eventually declared war against Paris and smashed the Commune in a week of bloody reprisals. Rimbaud and his lover, the other great poet of 1870s France, Paul Verlaine, escaped Paris for the free air of London.

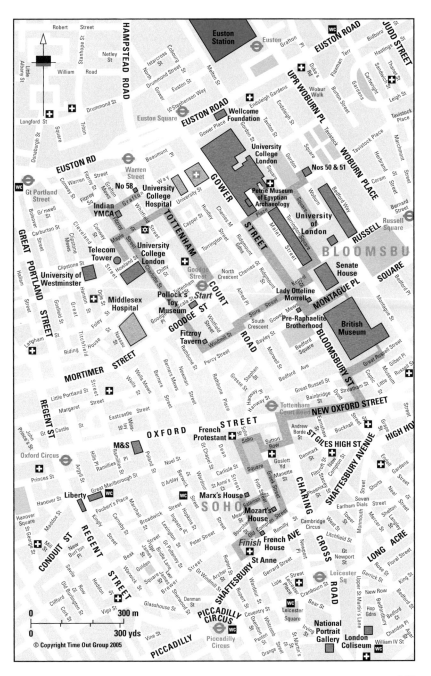

BT Tower

Even today, Rimbaud's poems are terrifyingly beautiful in what they confront and the icons they smash. The intensity of his affair with Verlaine makes *Natural Born Killers* look like an episode of *Teletubbies*.

Rimbaud effectively stopped writing before he was 20 and became a trader in Africa. He died in his late 30s, not knowing that he had changed the face of poetry for ever. His motto was that art should be absolutely modern in the most complete sense and that the natural state of humans is to be on the move.

Since Rimbaud is always right, and being a self-proclaimed exile from Reagan America, I came to live in the poet's favourite city. It was the right choice. London has always been home to exiles, both from outside and from within British culture itself.

The teenage Rimbaud, along with Verlaine, caught the ferry from Ostend to Dover on the night of 7 September 1872, arriving in London two days later.

They went straight away to Langham Street, to the room of the Communard poet Vermersch, a boyhood idol of Rimbaud's. He told them that he had a room in nearby Howland Street and offered it to them. The house at 34 Howland Street is no more, torn down in 1938 to make way for a telephone exchange. That fits, because communication was, and still is, one of the main activities of the area. Those who had escaped France after the destruction of the revolutionary city government in Paris were reduced, in London, to writing business letters for francophile Americans and giving French lessons to the English middle class. But at least they were still alive.

Rimbaud, enemy of all things conventional, was happy enough, when he had to, to advertise himself as a French teacher and travelling companion. Once, he even brought his mother over to front for him on job interviews. After all, you can't eat a poem.

To start, turn left when you come out of Goodge Street station on the Northern line, walk for a couple of minutes along Tottenham Court Road, then turn left into Maple Street. A few streets along on the left, at the foot of the BT Tower, is all that is left of Cleveland Mews. This is where Rimbaud once held his French classes.

Vermersch's grubby room has been swallowed up into what is now the BT Tower. If you stand at the base of it, somewhere in the corner opposite there is usually an accumulation of cigarette butts cast aside by the tobacco-exiles from the assorted glass and concrete edifices nearby.

Rimbaud himself smoked quite a lot, so I consider the butts a kind of monument to him. The literary colossus would have considered this litter the unabashed freedom of expression that his life and art demanded. He loved the fact that London doesn't give a monkey's.

The narrow mews passage can still give you a sense of what the area must have looked like when Rimbaud and Verlaine arrived fresh off the boat-train from Charing Cross station in the dense, yellow fog.

At the other end of the mews is Howland Street. The buildings there, including a campus of the University of Westminster, have a soulless and alien air, yet their brisk utilitarian essence is what Rimbaud admired in this 'nation of shopkeepers'.

I like to think that it was probably around here, in a pub somewhere, that he completed his monumental *Une Saison en Enfer*, the work that was an encyclopedia of European art, thought and religion. It was in London, too, that Rimbaud worked on his subsequent collection, *Les Illuminations*, whose title he was fond of saying with an English pronunciation.

While the 'Immortals' of the language watchdog the Académie Française choke on the above, smoke a fag to the god-of-no-bullshit, and then set off for Fitzroy Square. Across from the Indian YMCA, there is, at 39-45 Grafton Way, a very fine statue of another exile, Francisco de Miranda. De Miranda was a Venezuelan patriot and independence leader, who lived in London from 1802 to 1810 and later died in Spain. His house is still standing, round the corner in Grafton Way at No.58. The house bears a blue plaque in honour of de Miranda and, beneath it, another for Andres Bello, the 'Poet, Jurist, Philologist and Venezuelan Patriot' who also lived there in 1810.

Backtrack down Fitzroy Street to Charlotte Street. Look behind you and catch the looming presence of the BT Tower, a phallic symbol that Rimbaud would have found appropriate. Window

Rimbaud captured by Henri Fantin-Latour.

British Museum

after window in this area advertises movies, television, travel, things that help us to leave the places of our births, and to place ourselves in the unfamiliar, away from the tried and the true. Charlotte Street rewards the pedestrian with its melange of styles from three architectural eras and its odd air of gentility.

Turn left just before the end of Charlotte Street into Windmill Street. On the corner is the Fitzroy Tavern. This is the heart of Fitzrovia, a country unto itself in the 1930s and '40s. The louche and the disreputable, and those aiming to be, gathered here to write and drink and talk about writing and drink. And drink.

Dylan Thomas, that exile from 'starless and Bible-black' Wales, got legless here before he moved on to deeper exile in New York, notoriety at the White Horse Tavern in Greenwich Village and eventual death in the Chelsea Hotel. In London he was one of the internal exiles, those who had escaped their class to become part of another class called 'bohemian'. The spirit of Rimbaud is here, too. He wrote that this part of London, and the streets around Regent Street, were full of black people. He compared our presence here in the early 1870s to… a snowfall.

Well, he was a poet after all, but I am sure that among that 'avalanche' were poets and artists who had come to claim the Mother Country as their own, and some who had come to overthrow it, too.

Cross Tottenham Court Road into Store Street. You will pass the very pretty South Crescent; parts of its gently sloping colonnades are a bluish colour in the right light, a relief from the dull grey of the buildings around it, as is the tiny, periwinkle-blue Service Station, like something on a side lane in the Land of Oz.

At the bottom of Store Street is the looming Portland stone edifice that is , part of the University of London, created in the same neo-classical '30s style of the BBC's Broadcasting House in Langham Place.

You are now at the junction with Gower Street. Turn left, walk up a little way and turn right, past the enormous branch of Waterstone's on the corner, into Torrington Place. This will take you into Gordon Square, one of the 'sanctum sanctorums' of the Bloomsbury Group. Nos.50 and 51 were the London homes of Lytton Strachey, Vanessa and Clive Bell, Duncan Grant and Virginia and Leonard Woolf.

Virginia Woolf is, of course, an icon of women's writing, and her husband Leonard helped to found the League of Nations, the forerunner of the United Nations; Duncan Grant and Vanessa Bell were part of Omega, which brought an English stamp to Italianate arts and crafts; while Lytton Strachey reinvented biography with his *Eminent Victorians*.

Whether you love or loathe this group of Edwardian trustafarians, along with their art, their political stance and their forthright sexual activities, these upper-class rebels turned the system on its head.

Weave through the university campus to 10 Gower Street, towards the lower end of the street. Lady Ottoline Morrell, the aristocrat who helped finance many of the endeavours of the Bloomsbury Group, had a house across from Bedford Square. Today some would call her a mere groupie, but she was a serious patron of the arts. DH Lawrence, who attended her soirées in Gower Street, returned her hospitality and enthusiasm by satirising her in *Women in Love*.

Lawrence had a lot of nerve. He was an escapee, too, as she was, from the class into which he had been born. Maybe Lady Ottoline, with her desperate desire to be in with the in-crowd, struck too close to home for Lawrence. Opposite is the house where the Pre-Raphaelite Brotherhood was founded in 1848, some of whose members we shall be visiting later.

Gower Street becomes Bloomsbury Street as we follow Rimbaud's route to the place that he loved best of all: the British Museum. One of Rimbaud's most prized London possessions was his Reader's Ticket, which admitted him to the library here. This was his spiritual home, the symbol of the freedom that London had to offer. There were also all the free pens and ink a boy genius could want, and it was warm.

According to Graham Robb's excellent biography of Rimbaud, the Reading Room had French-speaking librarians, who did not judge the way Rimbaud dressed or smelled. It even had a good, moderately priced, restaurant that sustained him during the ten hours of reading he sometimes did a day. He would have sat in the same room that Karl Marx used when he worked on the book that had revolutionised the world, inspiring Rimbaud and his compatriots in Paris: *Das Kapital*.

Being Rimbaud, he had no compunction about lying about his age to the powers-that-be in order to get one of the precious reading tickets. A ticket enabled him to read Communard literature, still suppressed in France, but not the works of the Marquis de Sade, which were safely locked away by the Keeper of Printed Books.

The Anglo-Italian Rossetti family once had a home not far away. Christina the poet, Dante Gabriel the painter and their brother William had played in the shadow of the museum. Not only did Dante Gabriel help found the Pre-Raphaelites some 30 years earlier, challenging the conventions of English painting, but he had also had his late wife's body disinterred because he had left a poem inside the coffin. Rimbaud would have got on well with Dante Gabriel.

Sometimes, walking through the museum, I wonder if Rimbaud would have taken a break from storming the bastions of French poetry, and looked at the exhibits, especially those from Egypt and the rest of Africa. Could it have been here that he decided to leave Europe and poetry behind some day and venture further into the heart of darkness?

French Protestant Church in Soho Square.

Come out of the museum into Great Russell Street, and follow the map down to Charing Cross Road where you turn into the little passageway off Charing Cross Road called Sutton Row.

Take your time if you like the smell of frying onions and leaflets thrust in your face inviting you upstairs somewhere to study your native tongue. Otherwise, carry straight on into Soho, the little bit of land deep in the heart of London that is not for ever England. Rimbaud would have known that parts of Soho were called 'petty France' by the natives. A Frenchman could get along just fine here without ever having to speak a word of English. There were pâtisseries, boulangeries, hatmakers, and, of course, wine shops galore.

Seventy years later, the French House in Dean Street, known locally as 'the French', became the favoured watering hole of Charles de Gaulle and the French Resistance. In the days when France had surrendered not only to the Germans but to the enticements of their greying daddy-figure, Pétain, hero of World War I, de Gaulle knew that Soho would provide a welcome haven for those who marched to a different drum.

On a path in the fenced-off part of Soho Square, as you enter it from Sutton Row, is a statue of King Charles II, Royal Bad Boy Number One. Charles had dozens of children, but unfortunately for England, Scotland and Ireland, none of them was legitimate. He placed the theatre under his protection so that he could have his pick of the actresses, some of whom did a little whoring on the side. Last but not least, he went to his death a Roman Catholic in violation of the agreement that had restored him to the throne in the first place. The 'Merry Monarch' definitely did his own thing, and if a king could be an iconoclast, Charles fitted the bill.

The Huguenots, the French Protestants who escaped persecution in the 16th century, have left their legacy, too, not only in the names of Laurence Olivier and General Sir Peter de la Billière of Gulf War fame, but in the only French Protestant church left in London, located on the west end of the square.

Walk down Greek Street, named for the Greek church that stood nearby, further evidence of the area's cosmopolitan past. Rimbaud attended lectures of the 'Cercle d'Etudes Sociales' at the Hibernia Store pub that sat at this end of Old Compton Street. Socialists, anarchists and fellow travellers could meet to argue the issues of the day. Rimbaud took a grave risk in attending these meetings. Boys younger than he were still being deported to Devil's Island in Guyana for their part in the Paris uprising. The long arm of General MacMahon and his avenging Federal Army could reach even into a smoky den in Old Compton Street.

Karl Marx's daughter, Eleanor, was there, too. She could walk over from the family home above the present-day Quo Vadis restaurant in Dean Street, which we can walk to via Frith Street. According to Graham Robb, a certain Monsieur Barjau, a newsagent in Frith Street, while pretending to help the exiled Communards, was passing along

The **French House**, de Gaulle's local.

their details to the French police. Like Scotland Yard, they, too, took a lively interest in the area.

Lurking on the edge of this scene was Oliver Madox Brown, son of Ford Madox Brown, brother-in-law of William Rossetti. He could be considered the English Rimbaud, playing with his rat collection in Fitzroy Square and writing weird poetry.

Other foreign iconoclasts and exiles who found Soho to their liking were Mozart, that breaker of musical rules, who lived for a time at 20 Frith Street, and the man who revolutionised popular music in the 20th century, Louis Armstrong.

'Satchmo', who had been given his nickname by an English journalist, was in exile from racism, gangsters, debt and women when he came to Soho in 1933. He hung out in the long-extinct

restaurant the Bag of Nails in Wardour Street, where he managed to find some authentic down-home red beans and rice, escorted by his British doppelganger, Nat Gonella.

Louis always bragged that the Chinese restaurants in Greek Street were better than the ones in New York. Also, no one harassed him if he lit a joint and enjoyed his beloved marijuana. He loved weed so much that he had a special name for it: 'muggles'. He made a famous record called 'Muggles', which was one of Soho's anthems in the 1930s, and called his band the Vipers, another name for people who smoke marijuana.

Most people only think of Louis as the smiling old buffer who sings 'What a Wonderful World'. Only the truly hip know what Louis was really about. He was into his muggles and flying, without

Venezuelan patriot
Francisco de Miranda.

the aid of a broomstick, long before Harry Potter came along. Why do you think the man smiled so much?

But the ultimate Soho exile has to be poor old King Theodore of Corsica. He even put up Corsica itself to pay for his medical treatment after he fled his native land, but ended up dying penniless here on 10 December 1756. His memorial slab is in the churchyard of St Anne at the southern end of Wardour Street.

When Rimbaud returned to Paris, he urged his fellow 'Vivants', those who opposed the Old Guard of French poetry, to go to London. Long after he had left behind his youth and his work, he was seen in the Place Bastille dressed as an English merchant seaman.

Rimbaud represents all of us who, over the centuries, have chosen London as what the poet called our *'ville inconnue'*, so what better place to toast him and all the other rebels, exiles and iconoclasts, than back in Dean Street at the French House.

Maybe we won't indulge ourselves with absinthe as he and Verlaine would do during their 'green hour', but the French is just about the best place I know to raise a glass and read *Les Illuminations* – a French masterpiece inspired by London.

Eating & drinking

L'Escargot Marco Pierre White

48 Greek Street, W1D 4EF (7437 2679/ www.whitestarline.org.uk). Ground-floor restaurant **Lunch served** noon-2.15pm Mon-Fri. **Dinner served** 6-11.30pm Mon-Fri; 5.30-11.30pm Sat. *Picasso Room* **Lunch served** 12.15-2pm Tue-Fri. **Dinner served** 7-11pm Tue-Sat. A long-established French restaurant.

Elena's L'Etoile

30 Charlotte Street, W1T 2NG (7636 7189). **Open/food served** noon-2.30pm, 6-10.30pm Mon-Fri; 6-10.30pm Sat.

Fitzroy Tavern

16 Charlotte Street, W1T 2LY (7580 3714). **Open** 11am-11pm Mon-Sat; noon-10.30pm Sun. **Food served** noon-2.30pm, 6.30-9.30pm Mon-Thur, Sat, Sun; noon-2.30pm Fri.

French House

49 Dean Street, W1D 5BG (7437 2799). **Open** noon-11pm Mon-Sat; noon-10.30pm Sun. **Food served** *Bar* noon-3pm Mon-Sat. *Restaurant* noon-3pm, 6pm-midnight Mon-Sat. This Soho fixture serves drinks downstairs and Modern European food in the first-floor dining room.

Pâtisserie Valerie

44 Old Compton Street, W1D 4TY (7437 3466/ www.patisserie-valerie.co.uk). **Open** 7.30am-8.30pm Mon, Tue; 7.30am-9pm Wed-Fri; 8.30am-9pm Sat; 9.30am-7pm Sun. Breakfasts, brioches, soup and sandwiches, but above all, cakes.

Quo Vadis

26-29 Dean Street, W1T 6LL (7437 9585/www. whitestarline.org.uk). **Lunch served** noon-2.30pm Mon-Fri. **Dinner served** 5.30-11pm Mon-Sat. Fine French cuisine in art deco setting.

Literature & music

Eminent Victorians Lytton Strachey (1918)
Les Illuminations Arthur Rimbaud (1884)
Das Kapital Karl Marx (1867)
Muggles Louis Armstrong (included on *The Complete Hot Five and Hot Seven Recordings*)
Rimbaud Graham Robb (2000)
Une Saison en enfer Arthur Rimbaud (1873)
What a Wonderful World Louis Armstrong (included on *The Very Best of Louis Armstrong*)
Women in Love DH Lawrence (1921)

Others

British Museum

Great Russell Street, WC1B 3DG (7636 1555/ www.thebritishmuseum.ac.uk). **Open** *Galleries* 10am-5.30pm Mon-Wed, Sat, Sun; 10am-8.30pm Thur, Fri. *Great Court* 9am-6pm Mon-Wed, Sun; 9am-11pm Thur-Sat. *Highlights tours* (90mins) 10.30am, 1pm, 3pm daily. **Admission** free; donations appreciated. *Temporary exhibitions* prices vary. *Highlights tours* £8; £5 concessions.

University of London

Gower Street, WC1E 6BT (7679 2000/ www.lon.ac.uk).

Waterstone's

82 Gower Street, WC1E 6EQ (7636 1577/ www.waterstones.co.uk). **Open** 9.30am-8pm Mon, Thur-Sat; 10am-8pm Tue, Wed; noon-6pm Sun.

YMCA Indian Student Hostel

41 Fitzroy Square, W1T 6AQ (7387 0411/ www.indianymca.org).

The return of the king

Liza Picard

Following the Civil War and the Great Fire of 1666, London witnessed the restoration of the monarchy and the rebuilding of the city's streets.

Start: Museum of London, London Wall
Finish: Banqueting House, Whitehall
Time: 3-4 hours
Distance: 6 miles/9.5km
Getting there: Central line to St Paul's, or Circle, Metropolitan or Hammersmith & City lines to Barbican. Both followed by a short walk
Getting back: short walk to either Embankment (Bakerloo, Circle, District or Northern lines) or to Westminster (Circle, District or Jubilee lines)
Note: the first part of this walk is through the City, where most places are closed at the weekend (though not the Museum of London). The two Inns of Court cannot be walked through at the weekend, although they can be visited. There is also some overlap with Joy Wotton's walk.

Charles II came to the throne in May 1660, after the most turbulent period in British history. His father, Charles I, had believed that he could reign without Parliament, because he had been appointed by God. Parliament did not share this view, and civil war broke out in 1642. Charles I's army was consistently beaten by the Parliamentarians, especially when they were commanded by Oliver Cromwell. In 1647, the parliamentarians seized Charles, and after a formal trial, he was executed in 1649. Meanwhile his eldest son had escaped to the Continent. After an unsuccessful attempt to regain his throne by invasion, he could only wait about in European courts, with little money and uncertain prospects. The English tried various alternative systems of government, even offering the crown to Protector Cromwell. After some wavering, he declined the offer. The gap created by his death in 1658 highlighted Charles II's potential role as ruler. In 1660, he was invited to resume his father's throne, almost as if nothing had happened. Little remains of the London that welcomed back its citizens' king, on his 30th birthday, with wild acclamation. But this walk will give some feel for the city during the period now known as the Restoration.

The best place to start is the Museum of London, built in 1975 on a large traffic island and apparently as inaccessible as a medieval castle. Don't be put off. Take the tube to the Barbican or St Paul's, look around for some rather reticent signs, trail up some malodorous stairs and you should get there, on first-floor level.

The museum is reorganising itself at present, so as to display better its magnificent collection on the history of London, but the whole process won't be finished for some years. Meanwhile the 17th-century gallery is well worth a visit as a starting point, to get your eye in. If you know of anything specific that you want to see, and that isn't on display when you visit, call and make an appointment. Staff are very helpful. One unforgettable object that you

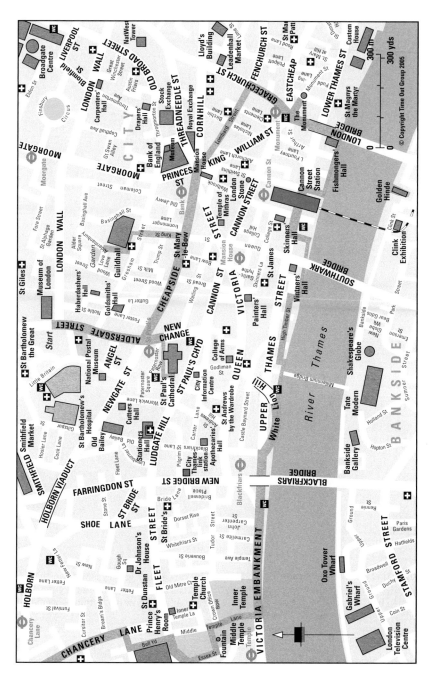

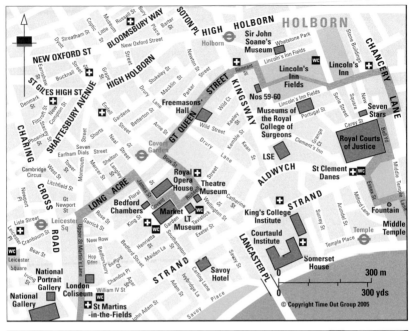

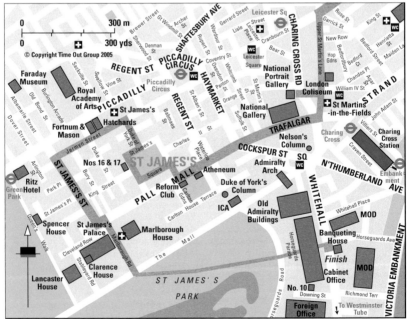

should see is the Lord Mayor's coach, a magnificent vehicle made in the 18th century, reputed to produce acute travel sickness in its occupants. (There's also a pleasant branch of El Vino in the first-floor passageway leading to the museum entrance, should you need a glass of wine to fortify yourself for the journey ahead.)

When you emerge from the museum, head for St Paul's Cathedral, nearby and unmissable. It is the fourth cathedral to be built on the site, which, according to legend, was used by the Romans for a temple to Diana. The church that stood there until the Great Fire of 1666 used to have the tallest spire in the known world, until it was hit by lightning in 1561, causing alarm and despondency. Was this the judgement of God? – in which case it was obviously up to the Church to pay for rebuilding it. Or was it only a natural disaster, to be made good by the City? This promising theological argument rumbled on for a century, during which accusations of sleaze and corruption flew back and forth and any funds that were collected for the rebuilding somehow never got there. It must have been a relief to some when the whole thing went up in smoke.

St Paul's exemplified a problem that faced the rebuilders all over the city. The fire left walls sticking up like rotten teeth, which had to be levelled before rebuilding could begin. The wooden internal beams of St Paul's burned with furnace heat between the stone walls, melting the lead on the roof. The molten lead flowed into the crypt and destroyed the stock of the Stationers' Company, which had been stored there for safety. On the way it welded together the stones that remained standing when the flames died down, making the task of demolition exceedingly difficult and dangerous. As manpower, alone, gradually turned the ruins into rubble, carts lumbered up Fleet Street to clear the site. Charles II had the forethought to order that the hardcore from old St Paul's should be used to

make a foundation for Fleet Street, to withstand the HGV traffic. He was a very practical man, when he wasn't chasing Lady Castlemaine and others.

St Paul's is magnificent. The ground floor is cluttered with tombs and monuments, some of which are interesting in their own right, but if you have a good head for heights go up as far as you can. On a fine day you get a good view of London from the gallery at the base of the dome – but the London Eye is much better. It's not for the exterior view that I recommend those narrow stairs, but for looking down, and across, and appreciating the grandeur of Wren's design – try the Whispering Gallery, 100 feet from the floor.

Because other buildings were more urgently needed, Wren didn't begin work on St Paul's until 1675, after the kind of bickering that's all too familiar whenever any groundbreaking design is proposed. The version that eventually went up was his third modification. The foundation stone was laid with Masonic rites – Wren was a Freemason – in June 1675, and the whole superb edifice was finished in 35 years. Astonishing, when you remember that the only sources of power were men and horses.

From the south side of St Paul's, look towards the river and you should be able to see the Millennium Bridge, which promised so much but turned out to look like the backbone of a fish that the cat's been at. The first version was closed soon after opening so engineers could modify the design and control its worrying oscillations, but all is stable now.

Walk round the east end of the cathedral towards St Paul's tube station and take a right along Cheapside. It's a bit dreary now, but in its heyday it was *the* place to shop. Its name doesn't mean that goods were sold for very little – it comes from the Old English word for market. It was at the core of London life for centuries. In the 14th century tournaments used to be held on the

The **Monument**.

City of London's administration, where the lord mayor throws an annual dinner attended by most of the cabinet, movers, shakers, and so on. The prime minister usually makes a state-of-the-nation speech. You may well have seen the inside of the Guildhall on television on those occasions – all rather Victorian. But the exterior walls of the original medieval building survived the fire, despite being, as an eyewitness described it, 'for several hours together after the fire had taken it, without flames (I suppose because the timber was such solid oake), in a bright shining coale as if it had been a palace of gold or a great building of burnished brass'. Some of the beams were reused by Wren in his rebuilding. He managed to get it finished by 1671, in time for the lord mayor's banquet that year. It was again set alight in December 1940, and again some of the medieval beams were reused in the reconstruction. Lady Jane Grey and Archbishop Cranmer were both tried here, in 1553; so was one of the conspirators in the Gunpowder Plot to blow up James I and his Parliament in 1605.

If you should ever have time to spend in researching the history of London, the Guildhall Library, at the west side of the Guildhall, is incomparable in the richness of its collection and the helpfulness of its staff. It also has a good bookshop, if you want to take something of London away with you. There's a charming little garden made around the ruins of St Mary Aldermanbury just to the north-west of the library entrance, where you can eat your sandwiches – there are plenty of good sandwich shops in Gresham Street and thereabouts, but I suggest stocking up before the rush of City types – and enjoy the scent of lavender and the memorial to John Heminge, without whom Shakespeare's plays might not have survived in print.

Opposite the Guildhall is St Lawrence Jewry, a Wren church of great charm and tranquillity. It was damaged in the last war, but mercifully was restored without

open ground to the north of it, 'the stone pavement being covered with sand, [so] that the horses might not slide when they strongly set their feet to the ground'. There was a Great Conduit or public water fountain that spouted wine on special occasions, and one of the crosses that Edward I put up in 1290 to mark the resting places of his wife's coffin as it wended its way from Nottinghamshire to Westminster Abbey. (The one at Charing Cross is a Victorian pastiche, not even on the right spot.)

On your left is King Street, the only new street made after the fire. All the rest were reinstated more or less where they had been – often since the Romans first laid out the city – because it would have taken too long to do a thorough root-and-branch replanning of the capital. Trade could not wait that long.

Look up King Street to the medieval Guildhall, still the headquarters of the changing its character. At its western end is a tiny triangular space used to make one of the most successful gardens in this city of unexpected little gardens. There's nothing there but water and greenery, but it's just right.

Cheapside suddenly becomes Poultry, where those who sold chickens once lived. At the Mansion House (the lord mayor's residence), cross over to Lombard Street. It was named for the bankers from the north of Italy who transacted London's banking business from the 12th century until we began to get the hang of it in the 17th. This is the only place I know that gives a faint idea of the street signs that creaked and swayed above the heads of pedestrians in pre-fire London. They were forbidden by the building regulations that tidied up London after the fire. Retailers' identifications had to be confined to boards fixed flat on to the wall, the original shopfronts.

At the end of Lombard Street turn right into Gracechurch Street and you will see the Monument, a whopping great pillar (to be more exact a column of Portland stone 202 feet high – the tallest isolated stone column in the world), with a flaming golden urn on top. It marks the spot 202 feet eastward in Pudding Lane where the Great Fire broke out. (Why they couldn't have put it on the actual spot I don't know. Perhaps it was an early case of 'Not In My Back Yard'.) It cost, in 1671-77, £13,450 11s 9d. You can still go up it today, but note that it's quite a climb – James Boswell tried back in the 18th century and regretted it halfway up.

The inscriptions on the base are interesting. '[The Fire] consumed… 13,200 dwelling houses… the ruins of the city were 436 acres… to the estates and fortunes of the citizens it was merciless, but to their lives very favourable…' In fact, of course, everyone had been too busy to count the houses, and I strongly suspect that many people died, especially the poor, who likewise were uncounted. In 1681, the inscription was amplified:

Lombard Street

'Papistical malice, which perpetrated such mischiefs, is not yet restrained.' On the west side, the fire was blamed on 'the treachery and malice of the popish faction' and 'their horrid plot of extirpating the protestant religion'. By the time James II, a Roman Catholic, succeeded his brother Charles II in 1685, these sentiments were no longer politically correct and they were expunged.

It's a shame that buildings have crowded round the Monument. It deserves a better setting.

From the Monument, King William Street leads to London Bridge, from which you can see the Tower of London. If you want to visit it, try to avoid the middle of the day. It's magical in the early evening mist, and there's a splendid view of that miracle of Victorian engineering, Tower Bridge. In the 17th century it was on every tourist's itinerary, because of the menagerie there and the crown jewels.

Gateway to **Lincoln's Inn**.

The other obligatory tourist visit was Westminster Abbey, to see the royal tombs. The two were abbreviated even then to 'doing the tombs and lions'.

From here it is a lengthy stroll along the riverfront to beyond Blackfriars Bridge. The Thames Path (west) – keeping to the north of the river – is what you should follow, and although at times you need to jink inland up and down a couple of streets, or up and over a bridge, most of the stretch can be walked beside the river. Descend the steps on the west side of London Bridge, and think about Old London Bridge.

The bridge that was sold and re-erected in Lake Havasu City, Arizona, was a 19th-century version. The one you should be thinking about dates from about 1176. For almost 600 years, until 1750, it was London's only bridge across the Thames. Charles II and his supporters, all splendidly dressed, rode across it in May 1660, at the end of their journey from Holland. (He was in debt to his tailor for years.) It had 19 arches, on stone piers protected by 'starlings', which produced a dangerous millrace between them unless you got the tide exactly right. Samuel Pepys managed to misjudge it, and 'the tide being against us when we were almost through, we were carried back again with much danger'. Among the other amenities of the bridge were houses, some of them seven storeys high, on each side; arches over the roadway, providing a handy place on which to display traitors' heads; a chapel originally dedicated to St Thomas à Becket, until his memory fell out of favour with the monarch and the chapel was tactfully rededicated to St Thomas the Apostle; a drawbridge; and Peter Moritz's waterwheels.

Moritz was a Dutch hydraulic engineer who worked out how to move water from the river up to the heart of the city. The city authorities ill-advisedly gave him a lease of one of the arches, at ten shillings a year – for 500 years. His business expanded and by the time his lease expired his descendants had made millions. Water supply was big business then, even if it tasted foul, having arrived via elm or lead pipes. People mostly drank a weak kind of beer, and they didn't need much for washing, because they didn't often wash. If you didn't want to swell the profits of Moritz's company, or of the other companies that operated in competition (and that were constantly digging the roads up to repair their leaky wooden mains), you could usually get water from one of the many public fountains, or pay a waterman to deliver some from the fountains or straight from the river. Thames water wasn't too bad if you let it settle for a while – it was pure enough for a sturgeon caught there in 1667.

You should now be emerging from under Blackfriars Bridge. By the Blackfriars Millennium Pier you are directed up some steps and on to the roadside, with the Sea Containers' House towering on the other side of the river. Cross the road at the first lights, and continue west along Victoria Embankment as the buildings give way to a green vista, the Temple. Lawyers have worked in the Temple since the 14th century. The name comes from the original owners, the order of Knights Templar, pledged to redeem Jerusalem from the infidel. Walk up Middle Temple Lane and wander about.

The Temple just escaped the fire, but was badly damaged in the Blitz. It has been mostly sympathetically restored, except for the 12th-century Templars' Church, where well-meaning refurbishment has killed any atmosphere. Look out for Fountain Court, where a small charming fountain makes the only noise in a quiet haven. There are some very good pubs round here (lawyers knowing how to enjoy life), not least the Devereux, which you pass as you exit Temple through the Essex Street gateway, just north of the fountain. The Devereux used to be a gay meeting place – several centuries ago.

You'll emerge into the Strand opposite the Royal Courts of Justice, a Victorian confection exemplifying the idiosyncrasy of English law. Bell Yard runs up the right side of the courts to Carey Street. There's a pleasant old pub called the Seven Stars in Carey Street if you're thirsty, but if you're seriously hungry by now there are plenty of trendy wine bars in Chancery Lane – turn right along Carey Street and you're there. A little way up Chancery Lane on the left is the redbrick gateway to Lincoln's Inn, another lawyers' precinct. If you're traffic-weary, enjoy the peace and quiet, but keep going through the Inn, and you get to Lincoln's Inn Fields.

Although most executions took place at Tyburn, near the present Marble Arch, the authorities sometimes decided to execute malefactors at the scene of their crime. All very well in theory, but not so pleasant if it went on outside your house, unless you made a virtue of necessity and sold places at your windows (executions being very popular spectacles). When 14 conspirators in the Babington plot to murder Queen Elizabeth I were sentenced to be hanged, drawn and quartered in Lincoln's Inn Fields in 1586, Sir Antony Babington was still conscious when he was eviscerated. Queen Elizabeth bent the rules for the others, and ordered that their bowels should not be removed until they were well and truly dead. The bits of bodies – the quarters – were nailed up here and there, some of them over the arch in Bishopsgate. You never knew when you might come upon one, although no doubt your nose gave you good warning. Lord Russell was beheaded here in 1683 (where the bandstand now is) for his part in another anti-monarchist plot.

The square was London's first garden square. In the 17th century it was a very good address, and most of its houses were built in the Palladian style, an example of which can be seen on the far (west) side, where there's what looks like a pair of houses, Nos.59-60. They were built as one, Lindsay House, in 1640.

The earliest square of all was Covent Garden Piazza. As the crow flies, it's due west from here with a bit of south. The easiest way there is to go to the north-west corner of the Fields, where another 17th-century house projects over the pavement making an evocative arcade. Go along under the arches, cross Kingsway, and take Queen Street immediately facing you. After a bit it's renamed Long Acre, and you'll notice signs of a trendy district, such as foreign food shops, chairs on the pavement and fashion boutiques. You're now in Covent Garden. Turn left down Bow Street (from where the first policemen, the 'Bow Street Runners', operated in the early 18th century), and you can't miss the icing-sugar splendour of the Opera House and its tall glass extension. But for 17th-century purposes leave it on your right and enter the market area. On a good day there are all kinds of street entertainments going on, in the open space by the church and all around.

The story behind the name is this. In 1534, Henry VIII declared himself head of the Church in England so that he could divorce his first wife Catherine of Aragon and marry his beloved – and pregnant – Anne Boleyn before the baby arrived (the baby in due course became Queen Elizabeth I). This split with the Church in Rome also conveniently enabled Henry to appropriate the wealth and land of the monasteries, and to give or sell the ex-monastic properties to deserving courtiers. The Earl of Bedford was in the right place at the right time, and acquired the lands that had belonged to the Abbey (or Convent) of Westminster Abbey.

By 1627 the fourth earl decided that the area was ripe for development, and commissioned the startlingly innovative Inigo Jones, fresh back from Italy, to build him a square of substantial houses 'fit for the habitations of Gentlemen and men of ability'. To begin with they sold like hot cakes. English landed gentry, who on their native heaths were monarchs of all they surveyed, moved in to live cheek by jowl with men of ability. There were pleasant gardens at the back of the houses, and provision for servants and carriages, but somehow it didn't feel quite like home, and when another development of even grander houses came on the market, there was a general move west, and Covent Garden became notorious for coffee houses, brothels and other shady places of entertainment. None of the original houses are left, but the arcaded buildings along the north side, Bedford Chambers, give you a rough idea of how the square must have looked.

The new development that the wealthy moved to is our next port of call: the area round St James's Palace. To get there, find Long Acre again. In the 17th century Long Acre was where you went to buy the ultimate status symbol, a carriage. Samuel Pepys bought a second-hand one here, for £53, a lot of money in those days. He was so proud of it. Walk westward, towards Leicester Square tube station, until you meet St Martin's Lane on your left. Go down it towards Trafalgar Square, but stop if at all possible at the National Portrait Gallery, on the other side of the road, behind the National Gallery. The National Portrait Gallery has a restaurant with a stunning view over London. The food's good, too. And the pictures, arranged chronologically century by century, are fascinating.

The National Gallery has a hedge of fig trees trained on its walls, in case anyone should feel that the nudes inside are rude and need figleaves. As you pass, note the statue of James II, or Jacobus Secundus, in neatly fitting Roman armour outside. Before the

The **Tower of London** can be seen from London Bridge.

Battle of Trafalgar was fought in 1805, the space covered by the square was the royal mews, where the royal hawks were kept.

Leave the National Gallery behind you and walk along Pall Mall (pronounced 'pell mell' by the pernickety; it was a game played with a mallet and a ball, faintly like croquet). There are some solemn gentlemen's clubs on your left, such as the Athenaeum, which has a frieze picked out in blue and gold above the main windows, based on the frieze round the Parthenon in ancient Athens, and the Reform Club where Phileas Fogg began his trip in *Round the World in Eighty Days*. Further along at Nos.80-82 is Schomberg House, built in 1698, a bit late for the purist looking for Restoration buildings but still an indication of the favoured architecture of the times. On the other

side of the road, there are two streets leading into St James's Square, which is where you want to be.

I can't promise you any original 17th-century houses. They've all been recycled many times. But the square still has an air of peace and prosperity. In its time, the square was ground-breaking: literally, since it was built on a green-field site practically next door to the royal palace of St James's, and legally, since Henry Jermyn, Earl of St Albans and one of Charles II's closest cronies, persuaded the King to give him the freehold of the land. This was very unusual. The Crown preferred to keep the ultimate title to land in its own hands, and grant only a lease for a definite period. If you don't at once grasp the intricacies of English land law, don't worry, you won't be the first to have problems. Just take it from me that Harry Jermyn was lucky. The redbrick three-

St Paul's
Cathedral

storey houses that were snapped up so eagerly were not obviously palatial, yet by 1720 they housed six dukes, seven earls and miscellaneous other grandees, especially courtiers. Jermyn's business associates included Sir Thomas Clarges (hence Clarges Street, not to be confused with Claridge's Hotel) and the post-fire property speculator Nicholas Barbon (originally named by his Anabaptist father 'If-Christ-Had-Not-Died-For-Thee-Thou-Hadst-Been-Damned' Barbon), credited with the invention of fire insurance. Two stirring scenes that took place in the square are worth noting. In 1815, the Prince Regent was at a party in No.16 when Major Percy, dramatically blood-stained, panted in carrying the French army's eagles and the news of the victory at Waterloo. The Prince's hostess complained that her party was ruined, but the Prince gracefully thanked *Colonel* Percy. On the other hand, the Prince's blowsy wife, who lived in No.17, used to enlist public support during her trial for adultery (it wasn't proved) by appearing on the balcony every morning to wild acclaim. Londoners do love adultery in high places.

Leave the square behind you and take Duke of York Street to Jermyn Street. Opposite is the church of St James. It's well worth ignoring the stalls in the courtyard selling tat for good causes, and going in to experience the elegant peaceful interior. Wren, commissioned by Jermyn, finished it in 1684, and he was particularly pleased with it; for instance, a congregation of 2,000 could hear every word. Not for Wren 'the murmur of the mass'. Nowadays the 2,000 are more likely to be the audience at some admirable concerts.

If you go through the courtyard into Piccadilly and turn left, you will come across that wonderful emporium Fortnum and Mason, and also Hatchards, the most obliging booksellers I know. But for 17th-century London, stay in Jermyn Street and go left until it meets St James's Street.

Look to your left, down the hill, and you see the best picture of the Tudor palace where Charles II lived, and where the present monarch welcomes foreign ambassadors: St James's Palace.

London never has had a purpose-built royal palace. Henry VIII took over Cardinal Wolsey's mansion at Whitehall because it was more comfortable than his own rambling medieval palace next door at Westminster. By the time he had added bits here and there it was more like a small village, traversed by a main road, than a coherent royal dwelling. Meanwhile he built himself a small redbrick country house in the fields, on the site of a leper hospital dedicated to St James. It was handy for hunting, which Henry adored, and only a short commute from his official residence. To make sure of good hunting he enclosed, or in the technical term of the day 'emparked', a stretch of land round it. The Palace of Whitehall burned down in 1698, but by then the monarchs, including Queen Elizabeth I, who also loved hunting, and Charles II, had grown to prefer St James's anyway. The gatehouse at the bottom of St James's Street, and the courtyard inside it, are the only parts of the original palace left. The rest of the palace suffered the usual fate of old timber-framed buildings. It burned down in 1809, although it was fairly convincingly restored.

Charles II enlarged Henry VIII's deer park and opened it to the public. Go down the side of the palace, by Marlborough Road, and into St James's Park. (By the way, don't go there alone when it's dark. For some reason the park has had a shady, even dangerous, reputation once the lights are dim, ever since the 17th century.) The blend of water and greenery has altered since Charles's day, when the park was laid out with a long straight stretch of water (then called a 'canal') and straight avenues of trees, all designed in the French taste of Charles's mother, Queen Henrietta Maria. There were gondolas – a gift from the Doge of Venice

– on the canal, and in the winter it froze and Pepys saw people 'sliding on skeates' made of animal bone there. There were cassowaries and other exotic birds in gilded cages along Birdcage Walk, and on the canal. Charles often walked in the park with his brother James, and fed the ducks. It was a happy place.

St James's Park also witnessed the last journey of Charles I, as he walked one January morning to his place of execution, the Banqueting Hall in Whitehall. To get there, turn your back on Buckingham Palace (yet another unsuccessful makeover of a private house as a royal residence) and cross Horse Guards Parade, through the archway where the sentries sit on their horses like equestrian statues. (It is very unfair to drop pennies into their boots.) Inigo Jones's Banqueting Hall confronts you across the road. It's magnificent, inside and out. You should go in and enjoy it. It was on a scaffold built outside one of the first-floor windows that Charles I was executed on 30 January 1649. When the executioner displayed the severed head to the crowd, there was silence, followed by, as one witness records, 'such a groan by the thousands then present, as I never heard before and I desire I may never hear again'.

So, 21 years later, Charles II must have been profoundly pleased to keep the members of the House of Commons waiting there, until he condescended to take their oaths of loyalty, on his birthday, 1 May 1660. The Restoration was now complete.

Eating & drinking

Devereux
20 Devereux Court, off Essex Street, Strand, WC2R 3JJ (7583 4562). **Open/food served** 11am-11pm Mon-Fri.

Fortnum & Mason
181 Piccadilly, St James's, W1A 1ER (7734 8040/www.fortnumandmason.com). **Open** 10am-6.30pm Mon-Sat; noon-6pm Sun.

Seven Stars
53-54 Carey Street, WC2A 2JB (7242 8521). **Open** 11am-11pm Mon-Fri; noon-11pm Sat. **Food served** noon-9pm Mon-Sat.

El Vino
3 Bastion High Walk, 125 London Wall, EC2Y 5AP (7600 6377). **Open/food served** 8.30am-9pm Mon; 8.30am-10pm Tue-Fri.

Buildings

Banqueting House
Whitehall, SW1A 2ER (7930 4179/ www.hrp.org.uk). **Open** 10am-5pm Mon-Sat (sometimes shut at short notice; phone to check). **Admission** £4; £3 concessions; £2.60 5-15s; free under-5s.

Buckingham Palace & Royal Mews
SW1A 1AA (7766 7300/Royal Mews 7766 7302/www.royal.gov.uk). **Open** *State Rooms* Aug, Sept 9.30am-6pm daily (last entry 4.15pm). *Royal Mews* Oct-July 11am-4pm daily; Aug, Sept 10am-5pm daily. Last entry 45mins before closing. **Admission** *Palace* £13.50; £11.50 concessions; £7 5-16s; free under-5s; £34 family. *Royal Mews* £6; £5 concessions; £3.50 5-16s; £15.50 family.

Guildhall
Gresham Street, EC2P 2EJ (7606 3030/ www.corpoflondon.gov.uk). **Open** *May-Sept* 9.30am-5pm daily. *Oct-Apr* 9.30am-5pm Mon-Sat. Last entry 4.30pm. Closes for functions, phone ahead to check. *Tours* by arrangement; groups of 10 or more only. **Admission** free.

Guildhall Library
5 Aldermanbury, EC2V 2HH (7332 1868/ www.cityoflondon.gov.uk). **Open** 9.30am-5pm Mon-Sat (some restrictions on Sat). **Admission** free; donations appreciated.

Lincoln's Inn
Chancery Lane, WC2A 3TL (7405 1393/ www.lincolnsinn.org.uk). **Open** *Grounds only* 9am-5.30pm Mon-Fri.

Middle Temple
Middle Temple Lane, EC4Y 9AT (7427 4800/ www.middletemple.org.uk). **Open** 10am-11.30am, 3-4pm Mon-Fri. **Admission** free.

The Monument
Monument Street, EC3R 8AH (7626 2717/ www.towerbridge.org.uk). **Open** 9.30am-5.30pm daily. **Admission** £2; £1 5-15s; free under-5s.

Royal Courts of Justice

Strand, WC2A 2LL (7947 6000/www.hmcourts-service.gov.uk). **Open** 9.30am-1pm, 2-4.30pm Mon-Fri. No court cases during Aug & Sept.

Tower of London

Tower Hill, EC3N 4AB (booking 0870 756 7070/recorded info 0870 756 6060/www.hrp.org.uk). **Open** *Mar-Oct* 10am-6pm Mon, Sun; 9am-6pm Tue-Sat (last entry 5pm). *Nov-Feb* 10am-5pm Mon, Sun; 9am-5pm Tue-Sat (last entry 4pm). *Tours* every 30mins, all day. **Admission** £14.50; £11 concs; £9.50 5-15s; free under-5s; £42 family.

Churches

St James's Church

197 Piccadilly, W1J 9LL (7734 4511/www.st-james-piccadilly.org.). **Open** 8am-6.30pm daily. Evening event times vary. **Admission** free; donations appreciated.

St Lawrence Jewry

next to Guildhall, Gresham Street, EC2V 5AA (7600 9478). **Open** 8am-2pm Mon, Tue, Fri; 8am-1pm Wed, Thur. **Admission** free; donations appreciated.

St Paul's Cathedral

Ludgate Hill, EC4M 8AD (7246 4128/www.stpauls.co.uk). **Open** 8.30am-4pm Mon-Sat. *Galleries, crypt & ambulatory* 9.30am-4pm Mon-Sat. Hours may change; special events may cause closure; check before visiting. *Tours* 11am, 11.30am, 1.30pm, 2pm Mon-Sat. **Admission** *Cathedral, crypt & gallery* £8; £7 concessions; £3.50 6-16s; free under-6s; £19.50 family. **Audio guide** £3.50; £3 concessions.

Museums & galleries

Museum of London

150 London Wall, EC2Y 5HN (0870 444 3852/www.museumoflondon.org.uk). **Open** 10am-5.50pm Mon-Sat; noon-5.50pm Sun. **Admission** free. *Exhibitions* £5; £3 concessions.

National Gallery

Trafalgar Square, WC2N 5DN (7747 2885/www.nationalgallery.org.uk). **Open** 10am-6pm Mon, Tue, Thur-Sun; 10am-9pm Wed. *Tours* 11.30am, 2.30pm daily; also 6pm, 6.30pm Wed; 12.30pm, 3.30pm Sat. **Admission** free. *Special exhibitions* prices vary.

National Portrait Gallery

2 St Martin's Place, WC2H 0HE (7306 0055/www.npg.org.uk). **Open** 10am-6pm Mon-Wed, Sat, Sun; 10am-9pm Thur, Fri. **Admission** free.

Banqueting House

Tate Modern

Bankside, SE1 9TG (7887 8000/www.tate.org.uk). **Open** 10am-6pm Mon-Thur, Sun; 10am-10pm Fri, Sat. *Tours* 11am, noon, 2pm, 3pm daily. **Admission** free.

Others

Athenaeum Club

107 Pall Mall, SW1Y 5ER (7930 4843). Private members' club.

British Airways London Eye

Riverside Building, next to County Hall, Westminster Bridge Road, SE1 7PB (0870 500 0600/www.ba-londoneye.com). **Open** *Oct-Apr* 9.30am-8pm daily. *May, June, Sept* 9.30am-9pm daily. *July, Aug* 9.30am-10pm daily. **Admission** £12.50; £10 concessions (not applicable weekends or Jul, Aug); £6.50 5-15s; free under-5s.

City Information Centre

St Paul's Churchyard, EC4M 8BX (7332 1456). **Open** *Easter-Sept* 9.30am-5pm daily. *Oct-Easter* 9.30am-5pm Mon-Fri; 9.30am-12.30pm Sat.

Hatchards

187 Piccadilly, W1J 9LE (7439 9921/www.hatchards.co.uk). **Open** 9.30am-7pm Mon-Sat; noon-6pm Sun.

Reform Club

104 Pall Mall, SW1Y 5EW (7930 9374). Private members' club.

St James's Park

The Mall, SW1 (7930 1793/www.royalparks.gov.uk). **Open** dawn-dusk daily.

Pepys's progress

Claire Tomalin

A riverside walk from Tower Bridge to Greenwich in the footsteps of diarist Samuel Pepys.

Start: Tower Bridge, south side
Finish: Royal Naval College, Greenwich
Time: 3-4 hours
Distance: 5.5 miles/9km
Getting there: District or Circle lines, or DLR to Tower Hill, followed by short walk over Tower Bridge
Getting back: DLR from Cutty Sark.

Pepys inspired me with the idea for this walk. In his diary he describes walking along the south bank of the Thames to and from 'Redriff' (Rotherhithe), Deptford and Greenwich. This was in the 1660s, when he lived and worked on the north bank of the river, close to the Tower. There was no bridge there then – London Bridge to the west was the only one – but there were plenty of boats to ferry you across, and as an official of the Navy Board he could always commandeer one. He often went part of his journey by boat and the rest on foot; the tide was a consideration, and he enjoyed walking. He walked in summer and winter, in rain, sunshine and fog, by day and by night. Pepys walked to Deptford one January evening hoping to visit his mistress, missed her and walked home again. In April he took his wife, her maids, their boy and their dog along the riverside path to gather cowslips and enjoy a picnic of cold meat; another time they visited the Jamaica House, a Jacobean mansion standing in its pleasure gardens: it was still there in 1860. He often stopped

for a drink at a waterside inn, the Halfway House, between Deptford and London. When he was alone he liked to read a book as he walked along the field paths – there were no paved roads. Rotherhithe was a village of a few hundred houses. Deptford had John Evelyn's famous garden, a few streets, the old church of St Nicholas, and the shipyards, where the greatest ship of the age, the *Naseby*, had been launched in 1652, with the figure of Cromwell on its prow and the words 'God with us' inscribed above. In this ship, hastily renamed the *Royal Charles*, Pepys sailed to Holland in 1660 to bring over Charles II.

Imagine the river, unembanked, with a wide beach at low tide and many streams flowing into it through meadows, orchards, gardens and windmills. Looking across to the north bank, there was little to be seen, once you were east of the Tower, but a few church spires. Thinking about how the scene has changed over the centuries, yet with the river always the most powerful element, first made me want to walk in Pepys's footsteps.

From Tower Bridge to Greenwich is about four miles. This is a serious walk, not a stroll, and although it is almost all beside the water, and now fairly well signposted as the Thames Path, there are a few diversions, such as through the Pepys housing estate in Deptford and past decaying industrial buildings and building sites. I recommend stout shoes and a sunny day when the water sparkles and the winds on the river are not too nippy. Best to start in the morning; there is no shortage of places where you can

find food and drink along the route.
You can even give up cravenly halfway,
turning inland just beyond Rotherhithe
and walking along the winding Surrey
Canal to Canada Water tube station on
the Jubilee line – but that would be a pity.

Start on the south bank, beside Tower
Bridge. You get a perfect view of the
Tower here, looking like a toy, dwarfed
by the spectacular 20th-century buildings
behind. Follow under the bridge to come
out into Shad Thames, a canyon of a
street with old industrial gantries or
walkways crossing high above you and
many new shops and cafés. You are in
Bermondsey, close to Horsleydown Lane;
and Horsleydown, so-called because it
was grazing ground for horses, is where
Pepys came as a boy seeking news of
his father who had sailed from here to
Holland during the Civil War and lost
touch with his family.

Samuel Pepys – diarist and stroller.

Turn left as soon as you can on to the
Thames Path, which takes you along the
riverbank, past overpriced restaurants on
your right, a spritsail barge anchored in
the river and the Design Museum – this is
the only busy part of the walk. You reach
St Saviour's Dock, crossed by an elegant
modern wooden footbridge, and after
this you will find hardly anyone about,
even on a fine Sunday. Sometimes you
have to leave the riverfront, here called
Bermondsey Wall, but you are never far
from it. There are smart modern flats all
about you, some made in old warehouses,
some entirely new, almost all worth
looking at. There are still some empty lots
awaiting development, too, and last time
I was here someone had scrawled a notice
in big letters, 'Build your Heliport in your
own back garden, not ours'.

Dickens used this area in *Oliver Twist*,
making Bill Sikes go to ground, after the
murder of Nancy, in a real place called
Jacob's Island, where rotting ancient
houses were surrounded by tidal streams.
It was known as 'the Venice of drains',
and the streams were built over after
the cholera epidemic of 1850. There is
now only Jacob Street, and the Dickens
housing estate, to remember it by.
Walking on, you come to charming
Fountain Square on the riverfront, with
modest, well-built low-rise flats on two
sides. Beyond this, Fountain Stairs, and
if the tide is out you can go down to a
small strip of sand and shingle with a
'No Landing allowed' sign. There are
stairs down to the water all along this
walk, some with names going back to
Pepys's day; they were like so many
stations on an underground or bus route,
places where you could take or leave
a boat to suit yourself.

Still on Bermondsey Wall, you come
to a group of bronze statues, a cat on the
wall, a little girl leaning against it, and
a man sitting on a bench opposite them,
holding out one hand to frame his view of
them. It's a memorial to Dr Alfred Salter,
MP, who devoted his life to the poor of

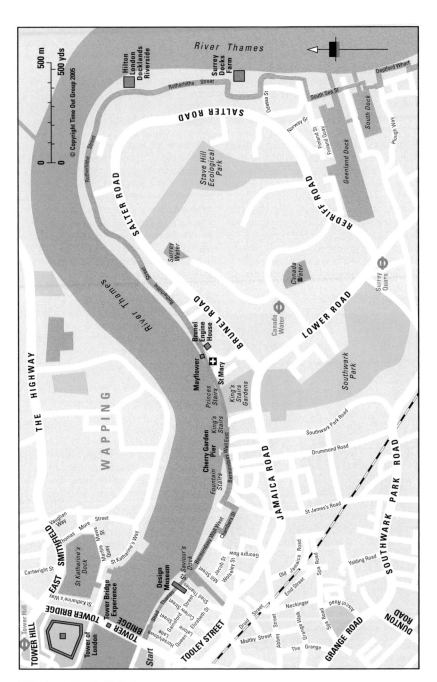

River Thames

500 m
500 yds

© Copyright Time Out Group 2005

Hilton London Docklands Riverside

Surrey Docks Farm

Deptford Wharf

Rotherhithe Street

South Sea St

South Dock

Odessa St

Norway Gr

Finland St

Finland Dock

Finland Quay

Greenland Dock

Plough Way

SALTER ROAD

Stave Hill Ecological Park

REDRIFF ROAD

Rotherhithe Street

SALTER ROAD

Surrey Water

Canada Dock

Canada Water

Surrey Quays

Surrey Quays

Canada Water

BRUNEL ROAD

LOWER ROAD

Brunel Engine House

Mayflower

St Mary

Princes Stairs

King's Stairs Gardens

Southwark Park

River Thames

Cherry Garden Pier

King's Stairs

Bermondsey Wall East

Southwark Park Road

Drummond Road

THE HIGHWAY

WAPPING

Fountain Stairs

JAMAICA ROAD

St James's Road

SOUTHWARK PARK ROAD

Vaughan Way

More Street

Thomas Street

Marble Mews Quay

St Katharine's Way

Bermondsey Wall West

Chambers St

Jacob St

George Row

Mill Street

Wolseley St

Old Jamaica Road

Spa Road

Yalding Road

Cartwright St

St Katharine's Dock

EAST SMITHFIELD

St Katharine's Way

Tower Bridge Experience

TOWER BRIDGE

Design Museum

St Saviour's Dock

Shad Thames

Mill Street

Druid Street

Enid Street

Neckinger

Spa Road

Ascot Road

DUNTON ROAD

Tower Hill

TOWER HILL

Tower of London

TOWER BRIDGE

Start

Shad Thames

Horselydown Lane

Lafone Street

Gainsford Street

Curlew Street

Elizabeth St

TOOLEY STREET

Maltby Street

Abbey Street

The Grange

Grange Walk

GRANGE ROAD

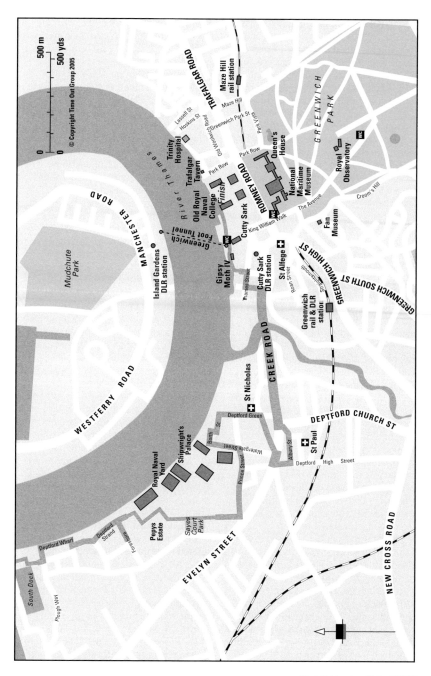

500 m
500 yds

© Copyright Time Out Group 2005

Maze Hill rail station

TRAFALGAR ROAD

Maze Hill

GREENWICH PARK

Lassell St
Hoskins St

Greenwich Park St
Old Woolwich Road

Park Vista

WC

Trinity Hospital

Trafalgar Tavern

Park Row

Park Row

Queen's House

Royal Observatory

ROMNEY ROAD

Old Royal Naval College

River Thames

Finist

Croom's Hill

National Maritime Museum

The Avenue

Cutty Sark

MANCHESTER ROAD

Greenwich Foot Tunnel

King William Walk

WC

Fan Museum

Mudchute Park

Island Gardens DLR station

WC

Gipsy Moth IV

Cutty Sark DLR station

Thames Street

St Alfege

Roan Street

GREENWICH HIGH ST

Stockwell St

Greenwich rail & DLR station

GREENWICH SOUTH ST

WESTFERRY ROAD

CREEK ROAD

St Nicholas

Deptford Green

DEPTFORD CHURCH ST

Royal Naval Yard

Shipwright's Palace

Barth St

Watergate Street

Prince Street

St Paul

Albury St

Deptford High Street

NEW CROSS ROAD

Pepys Estate

Sayes Court Park

EVELYN STREET

Deptford Strand

Footpath

Deptford Wharf

South Dock

Plough Way

Bermondsey. His only child, Joyce, born here in 1902, died of scarlet fever, and the group is called *Dr Salter's Daydream*. Diane Gorvin, the sculptor, has positioned the figures so that if you stand or sit beside him you see his daughter framed by Tower Bridge, and the dome of St Paul's. A moment to pause and reflect on human goodness and sorrow.

Next you arrive at Cherry Garden Pier, where the cheerful red-and-white City Cruise ships are anchored. In Pepys's time there were cherry orchards here from which he bought cherries to take home; and at the south end of Cherry Garden Street was the Jamaica House tavern already mentioned, where he got his maids to run races over the bowling green, and bet on them.

The river is getting wider all the time: you can almost imagine you smell the sea. You are approaching Rotherhithe, traditionally inhabited by sailors, passing the King's stairs where you may meet men fishing for eels; I talked to one who told me there are 140 species of fish in the river today, and added that he went to the Samuel Pepys school nearby and didn't like it. Walking on, you are again between high buildings with walkways above the street, and large 'Danger Keep Out' signs. In the pretty centre of Rotherhithe there are cobbled streets, a fine 18th-century schoolhouse decorated with two figures of children, and a handsome church, St Mary. It was built in 1714 after the earlier church had been flooded so often that it could no longer be restored: Pepys mentions 'Redriffe church… sometimes overflown with water' in 1666.

All the way from Bermondsey to Deptford was marshy land liable to flooding. The houses were built mostly along the river, with pasture and market gardens behind, and farms. There was still a pack of foxhounds kept here in the 18th century, and even in the 19th there was haymaking in summer, and the cuckoo was heard in spring; Rotherhithe remained part of Surrey until 1900.

One of the pleasures of this walk are the many juxtapositions of style and period. Here you find 19th-century mill buildings and warehouses converted into yuppie flats in the 1980s next to the Mayflower, another picturesque pub with cosy panelled rooms for cold days and terraces over the river for warm ones. It's so-named because this is where the *Mayflower* started from before it picked up the pilgrims sailing to America. Then there is Brunel's 1842 Engine House, now a small museum commemorating the building of the first tunnel under the Thames by Marc Brunel, the French engineer who fled from revolutionary France, and his son Isambard. The work, carried out between 1825 and 1843, was dangerous, and after its opening festivities, when Queen Victoria walked through it, it degenerated into little more than a dosshouse until, in 1865, a railway line was run through it. The museum is excellent, with a pumping engine, video show and good displays.

After this, go on for a while and across a red-painted metal bridge, one of several swing bridges, over another Thames inlet, Surrey Water (this is where you can turn off towards Canada Water tube station).

Now you are in Rotherhithe Street, the longest in London (about two miles). Most of the housing is new, not for the locals, not for the poor – at any rate on the waterfront – but gated communities, flats with signs reading 'Warning – City Surveillance in Operation', underground garages and heritage names: 'Hampton Court', 'Windsor Court', 'Balmoral Court', 'Blenheim Court'. There are neo-Georgian terraces with flights of steps up to fan-lighted front doors and, again, garages underneath. A series of squares are named Helena, Sophia, Elizabeth; a dainty modern obelisk and colossal old anchor decorate Pageant Crescent. It's only people who are in short supply, at any rate in the open air. There are buses along Rotherhithe Street, and one or two Indian restaurants and pubs, but you get

Stop on **Shad Thames**, where the industrial port meets modern development.

the impression that the inhabitants of the new buildings leave them only to get into their cars and drive away. Curious, because the architecture is undistinguished, but the riverside walks are for the most part beautifully laid out and paved, with areas of grass and trees, well-designed railings, benches and ramps, even good litter bins. There are still the old steps down to the river at intervals, with sea birds at the water's edge or perched on wooden piles, and the modern flotsam of supermarket trolleys; far away on the other side of the water it looks like Valhalla, huge dreamlike blocks, a brick ziggurat – and straight ahead at this point you see the giant Canary Wharf Tower.

Because Rotherhithe Street takes you right round the loop in the river the views keep slipping and changing as you go. Occasionally you have to turn inland, but mostly you can keep by the water's edge. Presently you arrive among small houses and gardens built for local people. Most of their grandfathers must have worked as dockers, because this is the area of the old Surrey docks. The first was built in the 16th century, and more

in Pepys's lifetime. The Great Wet Dock built in 1699 for whalers became the Greenland Dock (which we'll come to later), where the ships unloaded timber from the Baltic, and the streets are still called Odessa Street, Norway Street, Finland Street and so on.

My husband remembers walking through this area in the 1950s, when the river was walled off from view, and just catching a glimpse of a Russian ship from a bridge, the *Sverdlovsk*, with sailors standing on deck. Then in 1956 he himself sailed on the *Vyacheslav S Molotov* from here to Leningrad, by way of Copenhagen, Stockholm and Helsinki, with the first post-war students to visit Russia.

During World War II the docks suffered the worst fire in London when incendiary bombs hit a timber store. Who could have believed then that the last ship would leave the docks in 1970? By 1974 an ornithologist observed 100 species of birds on the abandoned waters. A few years later most of the docks were filled in for redevelopment. Then different ideas came into fashion and they dug out Lavender Pond again and surrounded it with an Ecology Park, where now you

The soaring towers of **Canary Wharf**, which can be seen from many points on the walk.

Design Museum

can see dragonflies, herons, kingfishers and water birds of all kinds.

There's another surprise in Rotherhithe Street – a Hilton, partly built around an old shipbuilding yard, with terraces over the river. It makes a good place to stop for coffee, sandwiches, loos. Here you are close to Nelson Dock, so named following the Battle of Trafalgar in 1805, where the first steamship was built in 1818. On you slog, reaching more water steps and a well-built 18th-century redbrick wall, behind which is the Surrey Docks Farm: box-edged flower beds, a wind turbine, small animals. Back on the riverside walk, there's another group of bronze figures, all animals this time, pigs, fox and geese, donkey and goats, approaching the farm from the other side.

You've reached the end of Rotherhithe Street at last, arriving at Greenland Dock, and then South Lock, with some handsome modern houses around the wide water inlets across which the path takes you. Soon you pass a boundary stone marking the old Surrey/Kent county border. Of course, this is no longer the divide – you are merely leaving

Southwark for Lewisham – but it marks your entry into Deptford. From here, on Deptford Strand, you have a view of Greenwich almost exactly as Pepys must have seen it, with its green hill, trees and observatory.

Deptford is tragically sad and shabby, like an old woman in squalid rags who was once noble and beautiful; and like an old woman, it has treasures worth discovering, among them two extraordinary churches, some exquisite houses, and a lot of history. Here Pepys's friend John Evelyn made his celebrated garden at Sayes Court. In May 1665, after Pepys had visited Evelyn, he walked home in the dusk with two other guests, both, like him, Fellows of the Royal Society, the scientist and architect Robert Hooke and John Wilkins, inventor of a scheme for a universal language, 'two worthy persons as are in England, I think, or the world'. During the Great Fire of 1666 Pepys stored some of his household goods at Deptford, and he and his colleagues sent for men from the Deptford yard to come and blow up houses in the City to save the Navy office. But Pepys

Not looking too ropy – the **Cutty Sark**.

came to Deptford chiefly to supervise the shipbuilding yards. He also had his bookcases built there by a naval joiner, Simpson: they are the first bookcases known to have been specially made for a private collector in England, and they can still be admired in Magdalene College, Cambridge, although technically they probably belong to the Royal Navy, because Pepys did not pay for them. No doubt he felt he was entitled to them as perks. He had another reason for visiting Deptford. Bagwell, a ship's carpenter, thought he might get promoted if he offered his wife to an official as powerful as Pepys. And Pepys, still a young man, and torn between guilt and pleasure, could not resist the sexual thrill poor Mrs Bagwell gave him, and would arrive at her door like a tom cat on his rounds.

After Evelyn left his house in 1694 he let it to Peter the Great of Russia who was paying an educational visit to England. The Tsar wrecked the gardens with his high-spirited games, which included having himself pushed over Evelyn's thick holly hedges in a wheelbarrow. He also attended Quaker services in the Deptford Meeting House in the High Street; it survived until 1907 and the shop on the site bears a plaque. Evelyn's house became a workhouse and was then demolished, but there is a ghost of a memory of his gardens in the shape of a municipal patch of greenery, Sayes Court Park, with an ancient, twisted mulberry tree, fenced round, and still bearing fruit.

You have to leave the riverfront and go through what were the victualling yards, now the Pepys housing estate, blocks built in the 1960s that look due for demolition. Then, skirting the walls of the shipbuilding yards, along Prince Street to Watergate Street. Turn left and you arrive at water steps with a monster of a building to their right, shutting off the river, and to their left the high wall of the yards and locked black metal gates.

Behind these is a surprise, a family house built in 1708 by a master shipwright, Joseph Allin, replacing the gabled Tudor house that stood there in Pepys's time. It is known as the Shipwright's Palace because Allin overspent his budget, and it has been miraculously preserved: three storeys high, with barley sugar banisters, big empty rooms full of light from sky and river, and nearly an acre of garden, now grass and cherry trees, stretching in front to the river. Even Pevsner does not mention it.

House and garden are currently being restored; the house hosts exhibitions and may be toured by individuals or groups. Telephone (*see listings*) for exhibition details or to request information.

Walk along Borthwick Street, where Christopher Marlowe was murdered, to Deptford Green and you come to the parish church of St Nicholas on Deptford Green. A church has stood here for a thousand years and the tower is partly medieval, but the body of the church was rebuilt in the 1690s and restored after it was bombed in World War II. Marlowe is buried in the churchyard – no one knows the exact spot – and he would have appreciated the big stone-carved skulls and bones set over the gates. The churchyard is full of glorious things: a Jacobean pulpit resting on the shoulders of a tiny, frowning boy carved out of wood, his fingers and toes perfect, his knees showing the strain. A magnificent reredos from Pepys's time has wood carvings of two near-life-size figures, reclining, St John with his eagle opposite an Old Testament prophet. Even better is a carved wooden panel showing Ezekiel in the Valley of the Dry Bones, also 17th century. Skeletons are being brought to life by the four winds, and you can see flesh being laid on the bones and hair growing again. It is a bit like a 17th-century Stanley Spencer resurrection, and I wonder if it alludes to the plague of 1665.

If you have time for a detour in Deptford, cross Creek Road and walk up the High Street to see the other church on your left, St Paul's, built about 1720 by Thomas Archer, who had studied in Rome; and don't miss the terraced houses in Albury Street from the same period. On the north side, almost every door still has its ornamental wooden carving, complete cherubs with dimpled knees, some bearing dividers, geometrical drawing instruments or quill pens; or a pair of cherub heads, and fruit and flowers, apricots, hops, sunflowers. Some have been stolen, and all desperately need to be cherished and preserved, because there is nothing else like them in London. Poor as Deptford is, and beset with problems, it is growing more aware of the value of its treasures; but it needs encouragement and support.

Now return to Creek Road to cross what was once the clear Ravensbourne river and is now Deptford Creek, more mud than water. This is the grimmest stretch of the whole walk and you would hardly guess you are entering Greenwich, famous for its handsome old houses, for the royal and naval buildings of Inigo Jones and Christopher Wren, and for its glorious park, none of which is in sight here. Turn left as soon as you are over the creek (Norway Street), then first right into Thames Street and first left again into Horseferry Place, and you will find yourself on the Greenwich riverfront, approaching the *Gipsy Moth*, the *Cutty Sark* and the pier. You have been walking for something between three and four hours, depending on how many detours and stops you have made, and this can be the end of the walk. So if you are tired, check the time of the next river boat returning to Tower Bridge, Charing Cross or Westminster – they are pretty frequent – buy your ticket, get on board and fall on to a seat. Cups of tea are on sale, and there are loos. As you pull away from the pier, look back and admire the view of Greenwich rising behind you; and as you whizz back to London you can pick out the landmarks past which you have walked.

But if you have any energy left, remember that you are only a few minutes from the great group of buildings that make up the Royal Naval College and National Maritime Museum at Greenwich, and from the park. Pepys made the last official expedition of his life here in 1694, with Christopher Wren, to consider plans for building the hospital for old sailors that later became the college. And, earlier in his life, Pepys enjoyed many walks in Greenwich Park and found it as fresh and agreeable as it remains today, with plenty of grass to lie on to recover from your exertions. There were times when he walked on from Greenwich to Woolwich, and reported hearing nightingales as he went – but we have to draw the line at Greenwich, and say goodbye to him here, and only imagine him as he makes his way further along the river, listening to the nightingales as he goes.

Eating & drinking

Blueprint Café
Design Museum, 28 Shad Thames, Butlers Wharf, SE1 2YD (7378 7031/www.conran.com). **Lunch served** noon-3pm daily. **Dinner served** 6-11pm Mon-Sat. No café, this, but a decent Conran restaurant.

Hilton London Docklands Riverside
265 Rotherhithe Street, SE16 5HW (7231 1001/www.hilton.co.uk/docklands). **Open** *Bar* 2-11.30pm daily. *Restaurant* 7-10pm Mon-Thur, Sun; 6-10.30pm Fri, Sat.

Mayflower
117 Rotherhithe Street, SE16 4NF (7237 4088). **Open** noon-11pm Mon-Sat; noon-10.30pm Sun. **Food served** noon-3pm, 6.30-9pm Mon-Sat; noon-4pm Sun.

Churches

St Mary
St Marychurch Street, SE16 4JE (7231 2465). **Open** 7am-6pm Mon-Thur; 8am-6pm Sat, Sun. **Services** 9.30am Sun.

St Nicholas
Deptford Green, SE8 3DQ (8692 8848) **Open** *by appointment* 9.30am-1.30pm Mon-Fri. **Services** 10am, 6pm Sun.

St Paul's
St Paul's Courtyard, SE8 3DS (8692 0989). **Open** ring for details.

Literature

The Diary of John Evelyn (1818)
The Diary of Samuel Pepys (1660)
Oliver Twist Charles Dickens (1838)

Surrey Docks Farm

Museums

Brunel Engine House
Railway Avenue, SE16 4LF (7231 3840/
www.brunelenginehouse.org.uk). **Open**
1-5pm Thur-Sun. **Admission** £2; £1
concessions, 5-16s; free under-5s; £5 family.

Cutty Sark
King William Walk, SE10 9HT (8858 3445/
www.cuttysark.org.uk). **Open** 10am-5pm daily
(last admission 30min before closing).
Admission £4.50; £3.25 concessions;
£3.20 5-16s; free under-5s; £12 family.

Design Museum
28 Shad Thames, SE1 2YD (7403 6933/
www.designmuseum.org). **Open** 10am-5.45pm
Mon-Thur, Sat, Sun; 10am-9pm Fri. **Admission**
£6; £4 concessions; free under-12s; £16 family.

National Maritime Museum
Romney Road, SE10 9NF (8858 4422/
www.nmm.ac.uk). **Open** *Jul, Aug* 10am-
6pm daily, *Sept-June* 10am-5pm daily.
Admission free.

Old Royal Naval College
King William Walk, SE10 9LW(8269 4747/
www.greenwichfoundation.org.uk). **Open**
10am-4.45pm daily. **Admission** free.

Shipwright's Palace
Watergate, SE8 3JF (8692 5836). **Open** varies;
phone for information. **Admission** free.

Surrey Docks Farm
Rotherhithe Street, SE16 5EY (7231 1010).
Open 10am-1pm, 2-5pm Tue-Thur, Sat, Sun.
Admission free; donations welcome.

Parks & paths

Greenwich Park
Blackheath Gate, Charlton Way, SE10 (8858 2608/
www.royalparks.gov.uk). **Open** 6am-dusk daily.

Sayes Court Park
Sayes Court Street, SE8 (8318 3986/
www.lewisham.gov.uk). **Open** 8am-dusk daily.

Stave Hill Ecology Park
Salter Road, SE16 (7525 1050/www.southwark.
gov.uk). **Open** 10am-4pm Mon-Fri.

Thames Path
Maps available from tourist information centres
in Central London. You can also try the Thames
Barrier Information & Learning Centre (8305
4188/www.environment-agency.gov.uk) or the
Heart of England Tourist Board (01905 763436/
www.visitheartofengland.com).

Others

Greenwich River Boats
Thames River Services (7930 4097/
www.westminsterpier.org). London Transport
Information (7222 1234/ www.tfl.gov.uk).
Both organisations indicate the range of
boat services operating on the Thames.

Rags to riches

Simon Thurley

Mosques, old breweries and almshouses line the route from Mile End through Spitalfields to Liverpool Street.

Start: Mile End Park
Finish: Liverpool Street tube/rail
Time: 3-4 hours
Distance: 3 miles/5km
Getting there: Central, District or Hammersmith & City lines to Mile End
Getting back: Central, Circle, Metropolitan or Hammersmith & City lines or rail from Liverpool Street
Note: there are small museums and two markets on this walk (check opening times in listings).

If you are not familiar with the East End, and perhaps even if you are, you will wonder, as you leave Mile End station, why you are there. So, first, a little history. For 400 years the wealth and success of this part of London were built on shipping. Deep water berths east of London Bridge brought the docks that in turn stimulated a massive concentration of trade and industry. In fact, in its heyday the East End had a manufacturing output greater than Manchester and Liverpool put together. When both the docks and the industry died, only 30 or 40 years ago, they left an urban landscape bruised by ugliness, poverty and neglect. But today all that is changing and the East End is busy reinventing itself. This walk will persuade you, if you needed it, that the East End is one of the most fascinating, dynamic and visually arresting urban areas in the world.

Having said that, the view from the south side of the road is pretty bleak,

the only point of interest being the Green Bridge to your left. That is, in fact, where this walk begins. To get there, turn left out of the tube and just before the bridge turn right up Grove Road, walking up the west side. You pass a bus stand, behind which is Clinton Road, one of the charming 19th-century terraces, most of which were demolished to make the park after the war. Sandwiched between two sections of park, Clinton Road survives as a reminder of the type of housing that covered the entire East End before the Nazis flattened it. Look down this road to some rather pretentious gates at the end that mark the entrance to the park proper.

We head away from all this on to the bridge that leads into the park. Mile End Park as you see it today is the product of a 1996 £12.6m lottery grant matched by money from English Partnerships and Tower Hamlets. It is the most visible symbol of the incredibly rapid change that is affecting the East End. Only ten years ago this area was neglected and flyblown; today it is the pride of residents and the local authority alike.

You will by now be standing on its centrepiece, the Green Bridge that gracefully rises above the fume-filled A11 Mile End Road uniting the various sections of the park for the first time. From here you can see the towers of Canary Wharf and the spire of St Anne's Limehouse amid a panorama littered with bad high-rise housing developments. On your right, more or less at eye level, is the belfry of the church of Guardian Angels, Mile End. The bridge, if you are interested, is designed by Piers

Limehouse Basin

Gough from CZWG architects, a
local resident and leading architect.

Stay on the gravel section of the bridge
– the tarmac path is used by local cyclists
who have little sympathy with walkers
holding guidebooks. As you come off
the crown of the bridge there are three
gravelled paths on your right. Take the
third down into the water gardens. The
stainless steel benches and bins have
indeed proved to be vandalproof, although
the promised park rangers will have
to work harder to keep the omnipresent
local vandals at bay. Behind you are the
green glazed walls of Venus in the Park
restaurant, one of the first earth-sheltered
passive solar heat buildings in the UK.

Follow the ponds and waterfalls around
and back to the path until you see a much
more conventional bridge linking the park
with the enormous Ocean Estate, the
source, perhaps, of the vandals who are
the scourge of this part of the East End.
You will have now arrived at the Regent's
Canal. Begun in 1812 and intended to link
the Grand Junction Canal (at Paddington
Basin) with the East End docks, it is nine

miles long and was largely designed by
the architect John Nash. We turn left and
follow it along the towpath.

The first part of this walk is
dominated by views of Canary Wharf
and the towers on Canada Water. On
your left now there is a series of modern
housing developments for the rich, with
barred and shuttered windows and drive-
in garages for protection, while on the
other side of the canal all is dereliction
and decay.

Soon the modern flats give way to much
older canal-side warehouses. The last of
these is of particular interest, as it was
here that Dr Barnardo set up the second
of his Ragged Schools in 1877. There were
two schools, one for girls and the other for
boys. From this small seed have grown
the 170 or so homes of his organisation
today. Since 1990, the school here has
been a museum with a café. You probably
don't need (or deserve) refreshment yet,
but the museum, containing a history
of East End life, is worth a visit. At this
point we leave the canal. If you are really
enjoying it, you could take a detour of

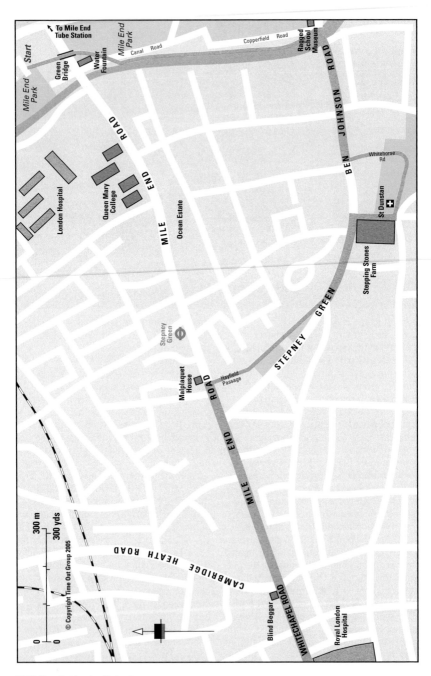

To Mile End
Tube Station

Start

Mile End Park

Mile End Park

Green Bridge

Water Fountain

Canal Road

Copperfield Road

Ragged School Museum

BEN JOHNSON ROAD

ROAD

MILE END

Whitehorse Rd

London Hospital

Queen Mary College

Ocean Estate

St Dunstan

Stepping Stones Farm

STEPNEY GREEN

Stepney Green

STEPNEY

Malplaquet House

Hayfield Passage

ROAD

MILE END

CAMBRIDGE HEATH ROAD

Blind Beggar

WHITECHAPEL ROAD

Royal London Hospital

300 m

300 yds

© Copyright Time Out Group 2005

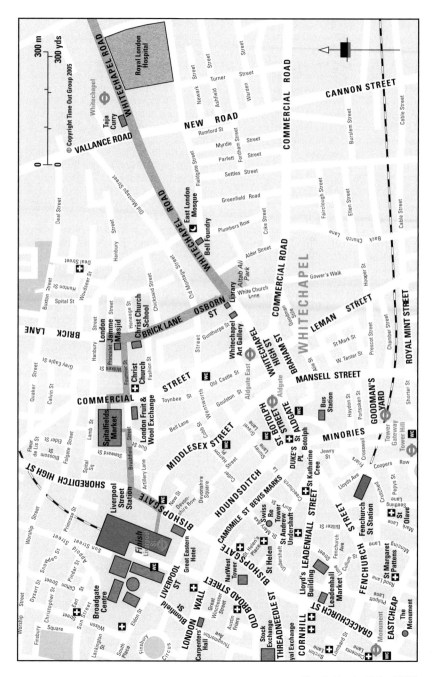

about 25 minutes by continuing beyond the bridge and down to the Limehouse Basin. It's a dead end so you will want to rejoin this walk here at the Rhodeswell Road Bridge. Steps on either side of the bridge lead you up to the road.

Use the bridge to cross the canal. Although the Swiss Re Tower (the 'Gherkin') is clearly visible at the end of the road, you are now entering one of the most deprived areas of London – the Ocean Estate. The estate has been awarded a series of enormous development awards, including £56.6m in 2000. This will gradually help improve the ghastly housing stock.

Signs of regeneration are all about. The side streets on both sides of the road are lined by new blocks of housing swathed in scaffolding. But we walk determinedly on from all this and look for Whitehorse Road on the left. Turn down here and, just before you reach the Little Star pub, pause to look down Durham Row. This is a tiny fragment of old Stepney that escaped both Hitler and the local planners. Nos.5 and 7 are perfectly preserved early 19th-century shops. Very charming.

Rejoin Whitehorse Road and keep going past the playground on your left and turn into the churchyard on the right. Can you believe that you are in the middle of the East End? The rural aspect of St Dunstan and All Saints is extraordinary. The churchyard, now managed by Tower Hamlets Council, is vast and surrounded by beautiful cast-iron railings made by the local Whitechapel firm of Deeley and Clarke in 1844. Most of the gravestones have gone, but a few tombs survive. An example is that of Thomas Ward, a ship owner, whose handsome sarcophagus you will pass railed in by a low iron screen. On the far side of the churchyard you can see a row of almshouses built in 1856 by the Mercers Company, one of the livery companies active in charitable work in the East End.

I'm not going to give a history of the church (which is fascinating) as it is written on a board at the foot of the tower at the west end. If it's open, do go in, if only to see the extraordinary stained glass in the east end depicting bombed Stepney with a homoerotic risen Christ hovering above. The church is flourishing, so it's not always locked. Leave the churchyard by the main entrance opposite the tower and exit on to Stepney High Street. Opposite you on the corner of Stepney Way is the Stepping Stones City Farm. Founded in 1979 and funded by Tower Hamlets Council, it is a very pleasant place to visit, with well-kept happy farm animals. It's worth buying half a dozen eggs (the duck eggs are particularly good).

When you have had your fill of nature, return to Stepney High Street and turn left. When you reach the mini-roundabout, turn left again. You should now be on Stepney Green (you will know you are in the right place if the farm is on your left). The ruined arch is the entrance to a college for Baptist ministers demolished in 1948. Cross the road at the zebra crossing and enter the grassy bit of Stepney Green surrounded by modern high railings. A cobbled way should run alongside on your right, the last blue glazed cobbled lane in London. Apart from a Victorian clock tower and water fountain on the left, everything of interest is on the right – the planners demolished the rows of Georgian houses formerly on the other side of the road in the 1960s.

Before we plunge on into 18th-century Stepney, turn around and get your last glimpse of Canary Wharf. If you are clever, you can make the pyramid of 1 Canada Square look as if it is the top of St Dunstan's.

Stepney Green is the historic heart of Stepney, always previously called Mile End Old Town. Some of its old glories survive. A decent block of late 19th-century flats, Stepney Green Court, is followed by the old Jewish school at No.71, now a suite of artists' studios, home to several famous painters. You may even see a paint-splattered figure

Spitalfields Market

leaving the gates. Beyond are two fine mid 18th-century houses, sad remnants of Stepney's finer days.

The best houses come next. The finest is No.37, the oldest and most handsome in the East End. Built in 1690 for an East India Company sea captain, Dormer Shepherd, it looks like a William and Mary rectory in Somerset. This is because in the 1690s Stepney was the countryside and this was a very fine country house. Note the overthrow (on the gate) with the letters MG, the initials of the house's second owner, Mary Gayer. Next door at No.35 is a slightly later, but also fine house, until recently a clinic, now restored to a family home. A terrace of houses from the 1730s follows, showing what Stepney and the other side of the road once were. It is a miracle that they survived both the Blitz and the post-war planners. No.29 is known as Roland House and was both home to Dr Barnardo and for many years the HQ of the Boy Scouts in the East End.

Now get on to the cobbled lane Hayfield Passage. This disgorges you on to the Mile End Road (over which the living bridge rises further up). Cross over towards Currys and PC World. These new stores occupy the site of the former Charrington Brewery, a fine fragment of which exists on the right-hand corner of the site (dating from 1872).

We will be going left, but turn right and walk up the road for 50 yards. There you will see a very fine pair of houses dating from 1741 recently saved from demolition by the Spitalfields Trust. The right-hand house (Malplaquet House) has stone eagles and a fabulous front garden. Its great arched doorcase is original. Now retrace your steps past the horrid superstores and past another fine terrace dating from 1717 (also saved by the Spitalfields Trust). Houses like these lined this great arterial road during the 18th century, gradually being either converted into shops or replaced by larger shops, pubs and breweries like Charrington's.

An example of one of the larger shops is the extraordinary building now shared

Whitechapel Bell Foundry

by Blockbuster Video and a downmarket DIY centre. This was designed in 1927 to be the Selfridges of the East End. A small shop remains incongruously sandwiched in the midst of the otherwise majestic department store, having turned down lucrative offers to sell. Opposite is another fine original house, No.102, with a grotesque mask on the keystone above the door. You are now in the heart of the Bangladeshi restaurant trade. At least three dozen Indian restaurants lie within five minutes' walk. If you feel so inclined, the Passage to India is by far the best (and the longest established). The choice is thin if you don't like Indian food. You could try the acceptable Chinese, Sinh Le. It's probably best, however, to keep going. Better places are in store.

As you make your way down the north side of the broad tree-lined pavement there is a surprising amount of sculpture. First a bust of Edward VII erected by local Freemasons, and then a life-size statue of William Booth, the founder of the Salvation Army. This was erected in 1979 on the 150th anniversary of his birth. Booth's mission started in the Whitechapel Road in 1865 and is commemorated by another statue 100 yards further on.

On your right are more architectural gems. First the charming Park House (now a solicitor's office) and then the sensational Trinity Almshouses, built in 1695 a few years after 37 Stepney Green by another sea captain, Henry Mudd. As well as the mellow brickwork and the tranquil setting, admire the original iron railings and the four ships perched on the gables. (The originals of these are now in the Museum of London.) The inscriptions and the contorted gargoyle-like keystones are worth a look, too. A little further on at No.27A is a remarkable house, built in 1905 by the engineer of the Albion Brewery, that gives some idea of the money to be made by brewing in the East End.

You will have now reached a massive intersection with the famous Blind Beggar pub on one corner. It's an adequate place to refresh your spirits, if they are wilting. It was here that Ronnie Kray shot George Cornell, a crime that put the Kray twin inside for life. Next door is another brewery building, the spectacular Mann Crossman and Pauline brewery – more evidence, if any was needed, of the brewing wealth of Whitechapel. It looks more like a palace than a factory, but now contains flats and a health centre.

This is where the Mile End market starts – the main reason for doing this walk Monday to Saturday. The market is incredibly cosmopolitan. The people, the smells, the sounds and the sights are Asian and some of the exotic vegetables will certainly find their way into your shopping with the duck eggs from Stepping Stones Farm. Your pace will slow as you soak up the atmosphere. But remain vigilant as there is still plenty of history and architecture to absorb.

You certainly will not miss the London Hospital on the other side of the road, now merged with Guy's and St Thomas' into a mega-trust. It is a vast complex, the best side of which you are looking at. It was founded in 1740, but the fine façade you are admiring was completed in 1890. It fronts an older building that you can see behind it dating from 1757. Dr Barnardo trained here in 1866. It was here also that John Merrick, the Elephant Man, immortalised in the film of the same name with John Hurt, was treated and died. He was discovered living in appalling conditions directly opposite the entrance, at 259 Whitechapel Road (now Ukay Sarees) and was rescued and taken across the road for treatment. The small but interesting museum round the back traces the history of the hospital, and some of its more distinguished characters such as Merrick and nurse Edith Cavell, executed by the Germans in 1915.

The market ends at a black-and-white-striped former public convenience, now the Taja Curry hut, on the corner of Vallance Road. This is the heart of Kray country – their house (now demolished) was just right up the road. Keep on going and on the right you will see the vast 150-bed Salvation Army hostel. The Army still has a major presence in the East End.

Then we come to the East London Mosque on the south side, a rather sad architectural effort compared to the elegant Regent's Park Mosque. The brick looks cheap and the detailing flat. What a shame considering the enormous Islamic impact in the area. Let's move on quickly past the huge number of wholesale clothing shops supplying cheap clothes to the street markets of Britain. We are now looking for one of the highlights of Whitechapel, the bell foundry. It is on the south side of the road and was established here in 1570 having moved from Houndsditch where it was founded in 1420 – surely the oldest business in London. The present beautiful buildings date from 1738

37 Stepney Green

and in them such bells as Big Ben and America's Liberty Bell were made (again, a small museum traces the foundry's history).

The last sight on the Whitechapel Road is the old churchyard of St Botolph, now Altab Ali Park. The church, now gone, was built just outside the city walls and was dedicated to a patron saint of travellers. A fragment of the old building is built into a charming water fountain and a single fine tomb survives, dated 1774. You can see the layout of the church on the grass.

Now you have an option. The walk continues down Osborn Street, effectively Brick Lane, but before you follow it you might like to digress a mere 20 yards to drop into either the Whitechapel Library or the Whitechapel Gallery. The gallery was built between 1897 and 1899 to bring art to the East End. The philanthropist John Passmore Edwards financed it and the library next door. The gallery, housed in a beautiful art nouveau building by Charles Harrison Townsend, still fulfils its original function of bringing the best of contemporary art to this part of London. You might like to wander in – it's free.

Back up Osborn Street, however, and Brick Lane is next. On the outskirts of the city, this narrow lane was a centre of brick and tile manufacture in the 16th century. Today it makes even the Mile End market look positively parochial in its internationalism. On the left is the stonemason A Elfes Ltd, its windows full of Jewish headstones. They remind us that one of the successive waves of immigrants to the East End was the Jews. Today the principal ethnic group is the Bangladeshis, after whom Tower Hamlets Council has embarrassingly tried to name the area (Banglatown). In reality this area is Spitalfields and has been since the Middle Ages despite waves of immigration. The name literally means the field of St Mary Spital, the medieval hospital that lies forgotten under the market. The parish is now that of Christ Church, which we shall see in a moment.

Keep walking down the lane, enjoying the atmosphere and passing the Victorian Christ Church School on the left. It has a nice plaque. You are looking for the London Jamme Masjid. This fine brick-built mosque was at first a chapel for French Protestant refugees or Huguenots built in 1743. The date is on the sundial in Fournier Street. It was then used by the Methodists and Jews before becoming a mosque. No better illustration exists of the dynamism and diversity of the East End. We are going down Fournier Street, one of the best 18th-century streets in London. Originally inhabited by rich weavers, dyers and cloth merchants whose weaving business was located in this area, the street today is full of architects, artists and aesthetes. Many moved in during the 1970s and were responsible for saving this atmospheric quarter from demolition. The artists Gilbert and George own Nos.12 and 10 – note that their doorcase is identical to that of Malplaquet House on the Mile End Road. Also note the old shop front at No.33A, opposite. (You may acquire a taste for these lovely old houses and wish to explore further. It is only a small detour to do this. Take Wilkes Street on the right at the far end and then Princelet Street on the right again. Keep following round to complete a circuit.)

The whole area is dominated by Christ Church, the Portland stone parish church with a vast spike for a spire. It was designed by Nicholas Hawksmoor as one of a group of East End churches built in poor areas to keep the populace on the straight and narrow. It has been recently restored and is well worth a look inside (on Tuesdays and Sundays only). It's not essential to do so, as the glory of the thing is its urban setting, brilliantly conceived by Sir Christopher Wren's young pupil, Hawksmoor.

Right at the end of Fournier Street is the Ten Bells pub now associated with one of the famous Whitechapel murders committed by Jack the Ripper in 1888.

If you are really interested in the gory details of this crime and others, there are plenty of Ripper tours that cover this crime and the five others. Several meet at Aldgate East tube station a quarter of a mile up the road on the left. Take a strong stomach and a big pinch of salt with you.

Now on into Spitalfields Market, once one of the largest vegetable markets in London and now a bric-a-brac, crafts and organic food market. There are always a few stalls here, but the big day is Sunday. The main part is Victorian, built in 1887. A later extension has recently been demolished to build more offices – no great architectural loss as it was undistinguished. Beneath it the Museum of London excavated the old cemetery of St Mary Spital, exhuming over 12,000 skeletons. Beneath that the archaeologists found an important tomb of a Roman noblewoman, now on show at the museum's main site on London

Wall. There are lots of food options here – if you are hungry, just follow your nose.

When you have finished exploring the market, rejoin Brushfield Street and pass the imposing London Fruit and Wool Exchange. Make your way towards the looming mass of the Broadgate Centre on Bishopsgate. Before you get there you will pass more of old Spitalfields. On the left are very good 18th-century shops including Nos.40, 42 and 44. Glimpse down the streets on your left and see more charming shops, pubs and cafés. At the end of the street you suddenly reach the 21st century. You also reach money, and lots of it. Broadgate, the massive 1980s development, now the most valuable possession of the massive British Land Company, is before you. It is vast and strangely impressive. You will probably be too exhausted to explore it now, but, if you haven't before, make a note to return. On your right is the new ABN AMRO bank by the architects EPR partnership. Now feeling a little out of place, we turn left and push our way down the crowded pavements.

Immediately on the left is the Bishopsgate Institute. It should ring a bell. Like the Whitechapel Gallery, it was designed by Charles Harrison Townsend. It contains an excellent local history library. As you move down Bishopsgate you will see your destination, Liverpool Street station, named not after the great Roman and medieval road on which you stand, but after a tiny street off it. You pass Bishopsgate Police Station, which contains the single largest piece of granite ever used in a building, weighing five and a half tons. Nearby, handy for the boys in blue, is the 24-hour Ponti's Café. If everything else is closed, you might need it by now; if not, there are about 60 sandwich shops within five minutes' walk. Or the Great Eastern Hotel has no fewer than five Conran eateries in it, if that is to your taste. Like so many people in the City over the centuries, you have come from rags to riches. What a contrast.

Eating & drinking

Blind Beggar
337 Whitechapel Road, E1 1BU (7247 6195).
Open 11am-1am Mon; 11am-11pm Tue-Sat; noon-10.30pm Sun. **Food served** noon-2.30pm Mon-Sat; noon-3pm Sun.

Great Eastern Hotel
54-56 Great Eastern Street, EC2A 3QR (7613 4545). Ground floor bar **Open** noon-midnight Mon-Fri; 6pm-midnight Sat. *Below 54 bar* **Open** 7.30pm-1am Fri, Sat. *Restaurant* **Food served** 12.30-3pm, 6.30-10.45pm Mon-Fri; 6.30-10.45pm Sat.

Little Star
162 Whitehorse Road, E1 0NW (7790 3319).
Open 11am-11pm Mon-Sat; noon-10.30pm Sun.

Passage to India
49 Mile End Road, E1 4TT (7790 7205).
Open noon-2pm, 6pm-midnight daily. Traditional Indian curries.

Ponti's Café
176 Bishopsgate, EC2M 4ND (7283 4889).
Open 24hrs daily. Sandwiches, all-day breakfasts, cappuccinos and the like.

Sinh Le
41 Mile End Road, E1 4TP (7790 1154).
Open noon-11.45pm Mon-Fri; 5pm-12.30am Sat; 1-5pm, 6-11pm Sun. Spicy and non-spicy Chinese cuisine.

Taja
199A Whitechapel Road, E1 1DE (7247 3866).
Open 11.30am-3pm, 5.30pm-midnight Mon-Thur; 11.30am-3pm, 5.30pm-1am Fri, Sat; 1.30pm-midnight Sun. Vegetarian and non-vegetarian Indian curry house.

Ten Bells
84 Commercial Street, E1 6LY (7366 1721).
Open noon-11pm Mon-Sat; noon-10.30pm Sun.

Venus in the Park
552 Mile End Rd, Mile End Park, E3 4PL (8880 6634). **Open** noon-3pm, 6-11.30pm Mon-Fri; 6-11.30pm Sat; 2-11pm Sun.

Libraries & agencies

Bishopsgate Institute
230 Bishopsgate, EC2M 4QH (7247 6844/ www.bishopsgate.org.uk). **Open** 9.30am-5.30pm Mon-Fri. *Library* 10am-5.30pm Mon, Tue, Thur, Fri; 10am-8.30pm Wed.

Salvation Army (Women's Hostel)
60 Old Montague Street, E1 5LF. Reopening in February 2006.

Spitalfields Historic Buildings Trust
18 Folgate Street, E1 6BX (7247 0971).

Whitechapel Library
77 High Street, E1 7QX (7247 5272/www.tower hamlets.gov.uk). **Open** 9am-8pm Mon, Tue, Thur; 9am-6pm Fri; 9am-5pm Sat.

Museums & galleries

Museum of London
150 London Wall, EC2Y 5HN (0870 444 3852/www.museumoflondon.org.uk). **Open** 10am-5.50pm Mon-Sat; noon-5.50pm Sun. **Admission** free. *Exhibitions* £5; £3 concessions.

Royal London Hospital Archives & Museum
St Philip's Church, Newark Street, E1 2AA (7377 7608/www.bartsandthelondon.org.uk). **Open** 10am-4.30pm Mon-Fri. **Admission** free; donations appreciated.

Ragged School Museum & Towpath Café
46-50 Copperfield Road, E3 4RR (8980 6405/www.raggedschoolmuseum.org.uk). **Open** 10am-5pm Wed, Thur; 2-5pm 1st Sun of mth. **Admission** free; donations appreciated.

Stepping Stones City Farm
Stepney Way, E1 3DG (7790 8204). **Open** 9.30am-5.30pm Tue-Sun. **Admission** free.

Whitechapel Art Gallery
80-82 Whitechapel High Street, E1 7QX (7522 7888/www.whitechapel.org). **Open** 11am-6pm Tue, Wed, Fri-Sun; 11am-9pm Thur. **Admission** free; one paying exhibition per year.

Whitechapel Bell Foundry
32-34 Whitechapel Road, E1 1DY (7247 2599/www.whitechapelbellfoundry.co.uk). **Open** *Museum & shop* 8.30am-4.30pm Mon-Fri. *Tours* (booking essential) 10am, 2pm selected Sat; check website for dates. **Admission** *Tours* £8; under-14s not admitted on tours.

Parks

Altab Ali Park
Whitechapel High Street, E1.

Mile End Park
E1 (7364 4147/www.towerhamlets.gov.uk).

Religion

Christ Church
Commercial Street, E1 6RY (7247 7202/www.christchurchspitalfields.org.uk). **Open** 11am-4pm Tue; 1-4pm Sun. *Services* 10.30am Sun; phone for details of other times.

East London Mosque
82-92 Whitechapel Road, E1 1JQ (7247 1357/www.eastlondonmosque.org.uk). **Open** 10am-5pm daily.

Guardian Angels Roman Catholic Church
377 Mile End Road, E3 4QS (8980 1845). **Services** 8.45am Mon, Tue, Thur, Fri; 9.30am Wed; 5.30pm Sat; 9am, 10.30am, 6pm Sun.

Jamme Masjid Mosque
59 Brick Lane, E1 6QN (7247 6052). **Open** daily, phone for details.

St Dunstan & All Saints
Stepney High Street, E1 4ST (7702 8685/www.stdunstanstepney.org). **Open** *Aug* 1-5pm daily; also by appointment. *Services* 9am, 5pm daily; 7.30pm Wed; 11am Thur.

Shopping

A Elfes
17 Osborn Street/Brick Lane, E1 6TD (7247 0163/www.memorialgroup.co.uk). **Open** 9am-4.30pm Mon-Fri; 10am-1pm Sun.

Spitalfields Market
Commercial Street, Aldgate, E1 (7247 8556). **Open** 10am-5pm Mon-Fri, Sun.

Whitechapel/Mile End Market
Whitechapel Road, E1. **Open** 8.30am-5.30pm Mon-Wed, Fri, Sat; 8.30am-1pm Thur.

Others

ABN AMRO
40 Artillery Lane, E1 7LS (7678 5770/www.abnamro.com).

British Waterways
46 Goodhart Place, Limehouse Basin, E14 8EG (7308 9930/www.britishwaterways.co.uk).

London Fruit & Wool Exchange
Brushfield Street, E1.

A digression with Mr Coleridge

Richard Holmes

Follow in the footsteps of the great British poet, critic and philosopher up Highgate Hill to Hampstead Heath.

Start: Archway tube
Finish: pagoda by Kenwood House, Hampstead Heath
Time: 2 hours
Distance: 2 miles/3.5km
Getting there: Northern line to Archway
Getting back: bus 210 to Archway or Golders Green (both Northern line)
Note: once you've climbed busy Highgate Hill, this is a tranquil walk through Highgate village and across the Heath.

William Hazlitt used to say that the fundamental problem with Coleridge, the opium poet of 'Kubla Khan', was that he could never walk in a straight line. This was not due, unfortunately, to drink, drugs or any other form of chemical interference. (Coleridge took brandy as well as opium, and usually the two combined in a delicious, sweet, fiery, dark red cocktail known as laudanum.) It was because Coleridge lacked – according to Hazlitt – intellectual purpose and moral determination. Coleridge always digressed from the path.

In the walk that follows, I shall try to draw inspiration, and even some philosophy, from this admirable example of Romantic deviance. Indeed, in a book dedicated to walking logically from A to C via B, it might be worth contemplating the Coleridgean alternative method. It raises such metaphysical questions as whether a walk really has an end, as well as a beginning; or whether the middle – if it exists at all – does not reveal itself rather as the walk's particular theme or mood, rather than as a mere geographical halfway point (judged by time? distance? thirst?); and then only in retrospect, well after the event.

Hazlitt was highly observant, and critical, of the Coleridgean digression. Whether striding across a wide field, or sauntering along a broad pavement or picking his way down a narrow muddy footpath (and we shall encounter all these formats on this walk), Coleridge would characteristically deviate and meander from the straight and narrow, drifting unconsciously from side to side, just as he drifted in his talk from subject to subject, seeming in both – in Hazlitt's striking phrase – 'to slide on ice'.

The first time he noticed this, it struck Hazlitt (then an 18-year-old art student who noticed such things) as 'an odd movement' for a seasoned walker like Coleridge. Coleridge had, after all, walked through the Highlands of Scotland, Snowdonia, the Lakeland fells, the Quantocks, the Hartz Mountains in Germany, and the volcanic foothills of Sicily. It was only later (as a 30-year-old radical journalist who had just missed the French Revolution) that Hazlitt connected it with Coleridge's 'instability' of moral purpose and 'involuntary change' of political principle.

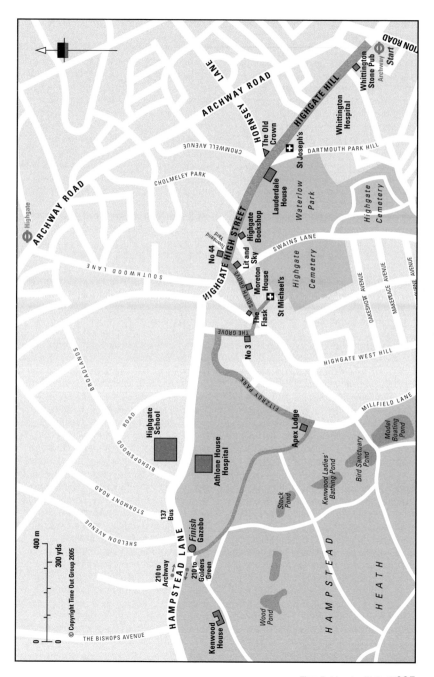

In other words, Coleridge's deviant and digressive approach to walking unconsciously revealed all the faults that Hazlitt (the son of a nonconformist preacher) so bitterly accused him of: political turncoat, plagiarism, drug addiction, platonic adultery, intellectual humbug, mystic fraud and so on.

Hang on to these high matters as you fight your way out of Archway tube. For this is where our walk certainly begins, rising out of the deep Northern line with its grim Piranesi escalators, up through a blizzard of old kebab wrappings (excellent takeaway on the corner with Junction Road), to emerge under a leaden April sky into one of the foulest traffic intersections in the borough of Camden, where the Holloway Road spouts its roaring articulated lorries (surely an oxymoron) up the Archway Road towards Suicide Bridge (an apocalyptic view, but don't try it), the North Circular and the M1.

Do not attempt to cross any road. Avert your gaze, and lift your eyes to the hills, from whence cometh better things. Turn sharp left, and stride off up the steep and bricky incline of Highgate Hill, with its distant idyllic hint of trees, spires and domes. Now we are on our pilgrimage to find Mr Samuel Taylor Coleridge ('poet and gentleman-philosopher in a mist' – his own description) in his final incarnation as the 'Sage of Highgate'.

It was up this very Hill that Coleridge himself climbed in April 1816 (in fact probably ensconced in the mail coach from Covent Garden) to meet the man who would save his life, or at least amazingly prolong it, Dr James Gillman of Highgate. To find Coleridge effectively on this expedition, we must, of course, be more indulgent than Hazlitt, and study, put into practice, and reflect upon Coleridge's own peculiar art of digression. For this is less of a Walk, and more of A Digression with Mr Coleridge, as I have explained. But as the French Michelin Guides still say, 'Cela vaut le détour.'

When Coleridge first came up here, the unpaved road climbed steeply through open fields and parkland as far as Lauderdale House, 500 yards up on the left (or western) side. There were already, however, several infirmaries and numerous inns for sick or thirst-crazed travellers. Many of the latter remain as pubs, growing more frequent as the incline gets steeper. Long, long ago I used to organise an annual winter drinking expedition, or *anabasis*, up or down this Hill, calling at every tavern en route for a modest half-pint. It became known to its participants (a doctor, a painter, an MI6 officer and a man from the Foreign Office who spoke ten languages) as the Highgate Run.

It was highly philosophical in tone, but over more than a decade we never established the exact number of pubs on the Hill. Curiously, the calculation always varied each year between eight pubs (four pints) and thirteen pubs (six and a half).

This was an early lesson in the unreliability of biographical fact, as well as the mysteries of historical topography: there one year, gone the next, like all of us. As Coleridge once said about biography, 'How mean a thing is a Fact, unless illuminated by a Comprehensive Truth.' The comprehensive truth here is not, I think, that we were too drunk to count; but that none of us ever really wanted to find out. So that the Highgate Run achieved a vaguely mythical status, an expedition that always had a start but never a definite end, and so was always worth trying again. As the critics would now say, we permanently evaded closure. This, as I have suggested, is an interesting idea to apply to walks in general.

My favourite pub remains the cavernous and unreformed Old Crown, about halfway up on the right (or eastern) side, which used to serve appalling sand-wiches, no doubt dating from the Regency. However, if you panic earlier, less than three minutes from the start is the modern Whittington Stone Pub, just before the grim redbrick towers and blue gantries

Hampstead Heath, scene of many of Coleridge's favourite digressions.

Kenwood House – then home to Lord Mansfield – near which Keats and Coleridge met.

of the Whittington Hospital, on the site of a 17th-century Plague House. Alternatively there is (on the opposite side of the Hill, for you must start meandering early) the Whittington Antiquarian Bookshop, which this afternoon is selling an almost complete set of the old *London Mystery* magazine, which seems appropriate.

Whittington? The name strikes a light in any Londoner. For this is the fabled site of that earlier salvation story, or rags-to-riches tale, which took place at the time of Chaucer's pilgrims. It was here that the young penniless Dick Whittington, as he left London, seemed to hear the church bells below him calling his name: 'Turn again, Whittington, thrice Mayor of London Town.' So he turned back down Highgate Hill to fame and fortune in the City.

And here, just outside the Stone pub, is an ancient, white milestone that records the incident. It now sits unexpectedly in the middle of the modern pavement, surrounded by a protective black wrought-iron cage about nine feet high, somewhere between a cake-stand and a crown. Inside, crouched on the stone, is a life-size bronze statue of Dick Whittington's faithful cat, looking anxiously over its shoulder. The mayoral dates are inscribed on the stone: 1397, 1406, 1420. But the cat is more recent, 1964, and today carries a jeering blast of gold spray-paint down its back.

So we have that characteristic combination of history, sentimental myth and modern vandalism, which shapes so much of the walker's experience of London today. The philosopher John Stuart Mill (who came to visit the Sage at Highgate) said that while most people would ask of such a story as Dick Whittington's, 'What is the truth of it?', Coleridge himself would always ask a much bigger question, 'What is the meaning of it?' Is it about fairy-tale luck, chance and destiny; or about its very opposite, gritty determination, natural talents, persistence against the odds?

Coleridge once wrote a whole essay on luck and superstition, asking in what sense you could say a great commander (Nelson) or a great scientific discoverer (his friend the research chemist Sir Humphry Davy) could be described as 'lucky' in their achievements. So was Dick Whittington just lucky? Or was he, in fact, a brilliant entrepreneur, a natural money-maker, a City whizz-kid, whose time had come? (Maybe the *gold* spray on his cat is quite subtle.)

Figuring this out will take you beyond the green dome of St Joseph's Roman Catholic church (once an inn called the Black Dog), beyond Lauderdale House (Nell Gwynn slept here with the Merry Monarch, Charles II) and beyond the iron

A digression with Mr Coleridge

gates of Waterlow Park with its spreading cedar tree. If you meander again over to the right-hand side, on to the raised path called the Bank, you will see the first of many stunning views south-eastwards over London. For the first time you begin to get the feel of the place as Highgate village, and why Coleridge thought of this philosophically as his retreat to the rustic high ground.

Cross back, and next to the park gates is one of my favourite shops, Highgate Fruiterers, which always has great buckets of flowers and tubs of exotic plants set out over the pavement. On cold days they keep them warm with umbrella-style gas heaters. Coleridge began to cultivate pot plants in his Highgate years (his favourite was the myrtle), but he also revived a schoolboy prank of sneaking into neighbours' gardens in springtime, and tearing off great branches of apple and cherry blossom. In spring 1823 he was caught red-handed (or flower-fisted) by his Highgate neighbour Mrs Chisolm, who was not unnaturally furious.

Coleridge saved the situation (just) by sending her a hand-written, 60-line humorous poem entitled 'The Reproof and Reply: or, The Flower-Thief's Apology'. It contains the wonderfully bad couplet (from the author of 'Kubla Khan'): 'And if I plucked the flower "that sweetest blows", Who walks in sleep, needs follow must his nose.' There's vandalism, and there's poetic vandalism, maybe.

You can buy a copy of Coleridge's *Complete Poems* at the Highgate Bookshop, which is small but perfectly formed, a few yards further up the Hill on the corner with Bisham Gardens. While you're at it, look out for another unknown Coleridge Highgate poem, *The Delinquent Travellers*, which is by contrast amazingly fast and funny, and could be seen as a sort of Ancient Mariner's hornpipe. I once got Simon Callow to recite it at top speed on Radio 3, and the recording ended in a roar of helpless laughter.

We are getting near to Dr James Gillman's house now. But before we get to Pond Square, which is the centre of Highgate village, digress again across the Hill (to the right-hand side) to the little cobbled opening of Townsend Yard. Here, totally unmarked, is a major Coleridge sacred site. Because this is where Coleridge obtained for many years (unknown to Dr Gillman) his secret supplies of opium. If you walk on up the Hill a few yards to 64 High Street, you will find the present chemist's, Bailey and Saunders. This has always been the official Highgate chemist's, since early Victorian times. But Coleridge patronised an earlier and alternative shop, belonging to TH Dunn, back down at No.44 on the corner with Townsend Yard.

No.44 is now an estate agent's. In Coleridge's time it had an elegant double-bow frontage, with five slim Doric columns, giving directly on to the High Street. But it also had a side door into the 'back shop', with an old gas lamp above it, opening discreetly on to Townsend Yard. This side door and lamp-fitting can still be seen, just a few feet into the yard. Here you can imagine Coleridge coming to collect his secret opium, without any prescription required, purchasing it as laudanum in a flat half-pint bottle, at the (specially reduced) price of five shillings. If this thought is too much, cross swiftly back over to the Angel Inn, on the corner with Pond Square.

We know all these details from the memoirs of Mr Dunn's young chemist-assistant, Seymour Porter, then a teenager, who used to make a point of serving Coleridge in the back shop, because he found him so kindly and so fascinating to talk to. Porter was also sometimes allowed to join Coleridge on his walks round Highgate, when the Sage would 'gratify him with a few minutes' dissertation' on some wildly unexpected subject. Coleridge was always good with the Youth.

On one memorable occasion in 1824, Porter found Coleridge transfixed outside the chemist's shop, watching a long funeral cortège of closed carriages pulled by black-plumed horses, slowly struggling up Highgate Hill. It was the cortège carrying Lord Byron's body. Byron was brought back all the way from Missolonghi, where he had died of malaria during the Greek War of Independence. He was a martyr to the Greek cause, but he was going to be buried in his ancestral ground in Nottinghamshire.

Porter says that Coleridge stood here on the pavement, and delivered a long, public, spontaneous encomium on Byron's life and poetry, saying that the sins of the former would eventually be forgotten, while the glories of the latter would make him immortal. I suppose a cynical biographer might say that the exact opposite has come to pass. Yet Coleridge might reply that this, too, was 'a mean Fact', and not a 'comprehensive Truth'. There have been a thousand loose-living Lords; but only one Childe Harold.

With this cheering reflection, a few strides will bring you finally to Pond Square, where the 271 buses wait next to the Chinese Herbal Medicine shop. Turn to your left, ignoring if you can the successive temptations of the Angel Inn, Strada restaurant, and my own favourite the Café Rouge. This end of the square was always a mecca of refreshment, and in Coleridge's day was occupied by the enormous Lion Brewery. Tops of hills are thirsty places. As you walk on under the trees, you will remark sadly that Pond Square has no pond, but only a large triangle of raised gravel and a public toilet lurking in the bushes. And yet the ghostly influence of the pond (there were two circular ones when Coleridge first arrived) still seems to spread a kind of lake-like tranquillity about this part of the village.

We are in sight of Dr Gillman's house now. But first pause again under the trees in front of the Highgate Literary and Scientific Institution (founded 1839), in a building that was once partly a school and partly a stables. The 'Lit and Sky',

as its fond members now call it, runs a remarkable annual lecture programme and maintains a flourishing lending library. You can peer in politely at its comfortable old-fashioned reading room, with insidious armchairs and welcoming fire, and consider joining for a small fee.

But the institution also contains, hidden away in its whitewashed and air-conditioned basement, a superb archive of Coleridgeana, with wonderful collections of old manuscripts, newspaper articles, critical essays, Victorian illustrations, local maps and biographical documentation. Upstairs it also has a dedicated Coleridge Room, now resplendently decorated in Regency gold-and-dark-green stripes, with the Sage's portrait on the wall. A Coleridge Digression could very well end, or at least come to permanent pause, in this meditative place.

Here you can find one of the best collections of Coleridge's poetry, published notebooks, prose editions, critical works and biographies in the whole of England. There are tables for scholars, and a kindly and attentive librarian. On this chill April afternoon there is also an undergraduate from Cambridge preparing for her Tripos exams, with a slight gleam of perspiration upon her golden brow. We begin to discuss Coleridge's views on ghosts ('Madame, I have seen too many to believe in them'). This seems to cheer her up, but bearing in mind that Coleridge's wife once complained that he had talked for five hours non-stop at his god-daughter's christening, I slip away.

Back in Pond Square continue across the entrance to Swain's Lane, a steep and shadowy little road that leads down to Highgate Cemetery. If you turn off here, you will spend the rest of the afternoon among the celebrity tombs, an eternal digression. Contrary to popular belief, Coleridge was never buried there. In addition, the romantically sounding Swain's – surely a Lover's Lane, one

Spirits tired by the walk up Highgate Hill can be refreshed in **Waterlow Park**.

thinks – is now described by local historians as a corruption of Swine's Lane, referring to the pigs that were once driven down it weekly to Smithfield Market. With modern traffic, it has rather reverted to type, though it is now said – somewhat optimistically, I should have thought – to be haunted.

So press on, still under the trees, as Pond Square becomes South Grove. Here at last, immediately on your left, is the fine brick Georgian frontage of Dr James Gillman's residence, Moreton House. It has been restored, after a fire, but the white pillared portico and black iron railings are exactly as Coleridge must have seen them. There is no plaque, but it is another sacred site. For it was here that Coleridge arrived that April afternoon in 1816, carrying – according to Gillman himself – the proofs of 'Kubla Khan' and 'Christabel' in his pocket.

It was at this fateful interview that the despairing poet, then aged 44 and separated from his wife and children, first fully confessed the extent of his lifelong opium addiction. Dr Gillman heard him out (it took several hours), asked him to recite some poetry, and then served tea. In the kindly young doctor's opinion, if

Coleridge would come to stay as his house guest at Highgate, and submit to a medical regime of controlled opium doses, he would shortly be cured (or, alternatively, killed). I have always thought it revealing that Dr Gillman's dissertation, submitted to the Royal College of Surgeons, was *On the Bite of a Rabid Animal*.

Coleridge gratefully accepted the offer, immediately moved in, and was to remain with Dr Gillman for the rest of his life. Contrary to all expectation, this was a wonderfully extended period, in which he published several new books. It could be truly said that Coleridge came to Highgate for tea, and stayed on for 18 years. It was perhaps his finest, and wisest, digression. When his friend Charles Lamb came up to see him at Moreton House, he remarked fondly, 'Coleridge's face when he recites his verses hath its ancient glory, an Arch Angel a little damaged.'

You may soberly reflect on these golden, sunset years as you walk further down South Grove until you come to St Michael's parish church, with its dizzy spire, erected in 1832, two years before Coleridge's death. If you walk into the nave, you will find Coleridge's glossy black tombstone lying at your feet,

Coleridge got his opium in **Townsend Yard**.

inscribed with his own suspiciously pious verse epitaph: 'Stop, Christian passer-by! Stop Child of God…' It lumbers on with one of those vaguely awkward rhymes to modern ears, '…beneath this sod'; and then modestly asks you to 'lift one thought in prayer for STC'.

However, it also contains one of Coleridge's most delightfully puzzling couplets: 'Mercy for praise – to be forgiven for Fame / He ask'd through Christ. Do thou the same.' Scholars wrangle over it, but this appears to be Coleridge apologising to his Maker for being such a celebrated poet. This is a very contemporary idea, and one quails to think of Coleridge on a television chat show.

You may buy a brass rubbing of this theological conundrum from a table in the porch. Coleridge also produced a more intimate epitaph, which you will not find in the official church documentation. 'In truth he's no beauty! cried Moll, Poll and Tab; / But all of them said *he'd the gift of the Gab*.' (I'm not making this up, it's in one of his letters.) Indeed it turns out that Coleridge's remains were only interred here in the 1960s, having been moved from the graveyard of Old Highgate School Chapel, and you will have to return to the top of Highgate High Street (opposite the Gatehouse pub) to find the original site.

So this, as I warned, is just another false ending to the walk. Digress immediately back across South Grove, and into the inviting open courtyard of the Flask pub, set back behind a low hedge. Here you can linger liquidly on the wooden benches outside, or explore the labyrinth of small, dark, beamed and panelled snug rooms within, on several different levels, all dating from Coleridge's time (though heavily restored) and often used by him, as one of his favourite 'convenient little pot-houses'. It is noticeably easy to conceal yourself in one of the many shadowy corners. The odd pub sign, showing a strapped leather flask or *fiasco*, is said to advertise the excellent Highgate water from local springs. This also seems a rather pious hope.

Renewed and refreshed (Coleridge once described himself as 'obstinate in resurrection'), leave the Flask courtyard from the other (north) side and cross over the road into the aristocratic, gravel sweep of chestnut trees that forms the Grove. This beautiful, tranquil row of magnificent Georgian villas is Highgate's premier address, and used to be known as 'Quality Street'. It is the most sacred of all our sites.

To the left, or western end, of the Grove, at No.3, is Coleridge's second residence with the Gillman family, where they moved in 1823. This time it is marked by a modest square plaque, almost obscured by the branches of a splendid old magnolia grandiflora, stretching protectively across from the front garden of No.4. This cold April afternoon its waxy, tulip-shaped white blossoms burn in the air like votive flames.

No.3 is also now marked by a much flashier circular plaque, dedicated to a later literary resident, JB Priestley. But simply ignore this piece of lèse-majesté. No.3 is a grander establishment than Moreton House, as Dr Gillman's medical practice had flourished after Coleridge's arrival. It was said that fashionable clientele were attracted from all over London by his famous, poetical patient. Coleridge had a study bedroom under the eaves, on the left of the house as you face it, but on the other (hidden) side. It looks out over the sloping and charmingly terraced back garden, and far over Hampstead Heath to Lord Mansfield's house (now Kenwood House).

The house is in private hands, but once when it was occupied by builders and covered in scaffolding, I disguised myself as a plumber's mate and slipped up the fine mahogany staircase to Coleridge's erstwhile aerie. It has a sloping mansard ceiling, and from his bedroom window you can still see nothing but bright, steep grassland and dark woods, a final version of the magic landscape of 'Kubla Khan', perhaps. Coleridge wrote various late poems in the Highgate garden, including the famous springtime sonnet 'Work Without Hope'.

Between these two addresses, Moreton House and 3 The Grove, Coleridge was visited by some of the greatest intellectual figures of his day. Many of these ghosts – like the charismatic preacher Edward Irving, the German poet Tieck and the philanthropic Swedenborgian GA Tulk – have dwindled in the modern light. But some cast long shadows: Thomas Carlyle, Ralph Waldo Emerson, the young John Stuart Mill, the feminist Harriet Martineau, and Tennyson's friend Arthur Hallam.

All of them had made the same ascent of Highgate Hill. The satirical novelist TL Peacock even dramatised these intellectual pilgrimages in *Melincourt* (1817), recounting a fantastical visit to the fabled poet and philosopher 'Mr Moly Mystic' in his remote, tree-shrouded, hilltop retreat known as 'Cimmerian Lodge', situated on a small prominence on 'the Island of Pure Intelligence' (Highgate, of course).

But the finest account is surely Thomas Carlyle's, written after a visit made in

The Grove

Coleridge spent the last 18 years of his life with Dr James Gillman at **Moreton House**.

1824. 'Coleridge sat on the brow of Highgate Hill, in those years, looking down on London and its smoke-tumult, like a sage escaped from the inanity of life's battle… The practical intellects of the world did not much heed him, or carelessly reckoned him a metaphysical dreamer: but to the rising spirits of the young generation he had this dusky sublime character; and sat there as a kind of Magus, girt in mystery and enigma; his Dodona oak-grove (Mr Gillman's house at Highgate) whispering strange things, uncertain whether oracles or jargon.'

I must admit that I could walk up and down under these sacred, sighing, prophetic trees (actually they are chestnuts, not oaks) for the whole of the rest of the afternoon, reading Coleridge's verses like a monk saying his office. And perhaps I would leave you here, except that it would be just too neat, too logical, and maybe a bit too short for a full Coleridgean circuit. So lengthen your stride, and prepare finally to accompany him on his own most justly famous downhill Highgate walk, made in April 1819.

As you walk right (eastwards) along the Grove, you will suddenly notice between Nos.9 and 10 the opening of a little bush-fringed road (which you may have overlooked before) marked Fitzroy Park. Ignore the wooden barrier and 'Private' signs, as this is an ancient right of way.

Plunge firmly down the steepening hill, and you will soon find yourself miraculously transported into a country lane. This was Coleridge's favourite walk on to Hampstead Heath. It was then simply known as the lane to Fitzroy Farm (a dairy) and Lord Mansfield's estate (now Kenwood).

Today Fitzroy Park tilts and meanders downwards, descending deeper into birdsong and foliage, past a few discreet neo-Tuscan residences, some bracing vegetable allotments (spades left upright in the furrow, compost heaps steaming gently), and then (somewhat bizarrely) the North London Bowling Club. For some reason the air is warmer and more perfumed here, and I am reminded that Coleridge once informed Dr Gillman that there were over 80 species of birds on Hampstead Heath.

The road arrives without warning at the Highgate Ponds, in a sudden flash of light and opening horizons. Here at Apex Lodge you double sharply back to the right (north) along the unpaved track known rather grandly as Millfield Lane. This is the beginning of the rustic path up to Kenwood, climbing at first through trees along the eastern side of Highgate Ladies' Bathing Pond, and so up on to the open fields of the heath itself. It was along this lane that Coleridge was ambling one afternoon in April 1819 with his amanuensis, Joseph Henry Green.

A digression with Mr Coleridge

Mr Green was a surgical demonstrator at Guy's Hospital, a wonderfully gifted teacher who would later become President of the Royal College of Surgeons. It so happened that one of Green's medical students was a brilliant, but unknown, young man called John Keats. Thus it was that one of the great, unlikely, walking encounters of English poetry took place. Here is Keats's own description of it, written the same evening to his brother George in America:

'... in the lane that winds by the side of Lord Mansfield's park I met Mr Green our Demonstrator at Guy's in conversation with Coleridge. – I joined them, after enquiring by a look whether it would be agreeable. – I walked with him at his alderman-after-dinner pace for near two miles I suppose. In these two miles he broached a thousand things. – let me see if I can give you a list. – Nightingales, Poetry – on Poetical sensation – Metaphysics – Different genera and species of Dreams – Nightmare – a dream accompanied by a sense of Touch – single and double Touch – A dream related – First and Second Consciousness – the difference explained between Will and Volition – so many metaphysicians from a want of smoking – the second Consciousness – Monsters – the Kraken – Mermaids – Southey believes in them – Southey's belief too much diluted – A Ghost Story – Good morning. – I heard his voice as he came towards me – I heard it as he moved away – I heard it all the interval – if it may be called so. He was civil enough to ask me to call on him at Highgate.'

Samuel Taylor Coleridge

This is perhaps the best of all the many recorded accounts of Coleridge's entrancing and inimitable digressions. Lost in his fantastic list of subjects, and puzzling over all their possible connections, you will never get closer to the deviant Coleridgean spirit than this. It is, I now think, the proper theme and middle of our walk; and quite rightly it comes at the end. Or, since you will have read it before setting out, it is probably really the beginning, and will haunt you along the entire route. I recommend that rather than studying the map, you try memorising the list instead, and then there is no further danger of walking or even thinking in a straight line.

At all events, reflections on this should carry you right up Millfield Lane, past the splashy fountain with its carved heraldic animals, up through the trees, and on to a small gateway into the grounds fronting Kenwood House. Turn right here, up across the open meadow as far as the trim modern ironwork gazebo, with its gilded dome, perched near the entrance to Kenwood. Stand in this gazebo, and look back southwards. You will find yourself in command of the finest panorama over north London that exists. Then you will know why you did this Digression, why Dick Whittington turned back, and why Coleridge (having returned from Xanadu) became the Sage of Highgate and couldn't walk straight again.

Eating & drinking

Angel Inn
37 Highgate High Street, N6 5JT (8347 2921).
Open noon-11pm Mon-Fri; 11am-11pm Sat;
noon-10.30pm Sun. **Food served** noon-10pm
Mon-Fri, Sun; 11am-10pm Sat.

Café Rouge
6-7 South Grove, N6 6BP (8342 9797/
www.caferouge.co.uk). **Open** 9am-11pm
Mon-Sat; 9am-10.30pm Sun. French
brasserie chain.

Flask
77 Highgate West Hill, N6 6BU (8348 7346).
Open noon-11pm Mon-Sat; noon-10.30pm Sun.
Food served noon-3pm, 6-10pm Mon-Fri;
noon-10pm Sat; noon-4pm, 6-9.30pm Sun.

Gatehouse
1 North Road, N6 6BD (8340 8054/
www.jdwetherspoon.co.uk). **Open** 10am-11pm
Mon-Sat; 10am-10.30pm Sun. **Food served**
10am-10pm Mon-Sat; 10am-9.30pm Sun.

Old Crown
90 Highgate Hill, N19 5NQ (7272 3893).
Open/food served 11am-11pm Mon-Wed;
11am-1am Thur-Sat; 11.30am-midnight Sun.

Strada
4 South Grove, N6 6BS (8347 8686/
www.strada.co.uk). **Open** noon-11pm Mon-Sat;
noon-10pm Sun. Chain of Italian restaurants
specialising in pizza.

Whittington Stone Pub
53 Highgate Hill, N19 5NE (7561 8451).
Open noon-11pm Mon-Sat; noon-10.30pm
Sun. **Food served** noon-7.30pm daily.

Churches

St Joseph's Church
St Joseph's Retreat, Highgate Hill,
N19 5NE (7272 2320/www.stjosephs
highgate.org). **Open** 8am-10am Mon-Fri;
9.30am-noon, 6.30-8pm Sat; 8am-1.30pm,
6.30-8pm Sun.

St Michael's Church
South Grove, N6 6BJ (8340 7279).
Open phone for details. **Services** 8am,
9.30am, 11.15am, 6.30pm Sun.

Literature

Biographia Literaria Samuel Taylor
Coleridge (1817)
Christabel Samuel Taylor Coleridge (1816)

Highgate Ponds

Dejection: an Ode Samuel Taylor
Coleridge (1802)
Kubla Khan Samuel Taylor Coleridge (1816)
Lyrical Ballads Samuel Taylor Coleridge
with William Wordsworth (1798)

Shopping

Bailey & Saunders
*64 Highgate High Street, N6 5HX (8340 3663/
www.highgatepharmacy.co.uk).* **Open** 9am-7pm
Mon-Fri; 9am-6pm Sat; 10am-2pm Sun.

Highgate Bookshop
9 Highgate High Street, N6 5JR (8348 8202).
Open 10am-6pm Mon-Sat; noon-5pm Sun.

Highgate Village Fruiterers
3 Highgate High Street, N6 5JR (8340 0985).
Open 8am-7pm Mon-Fri; 8am-6pm Sat; 10am-
4pm Sun.

Whittington Antiquarian Bookshop
21 Highgate Hill, N19 5NL (7272 3419).
Open 10am-6pm Mon-Sat.

Others

Highgate Cemetery
*Swains Lane, N6 6PJ (8340 1834/www.highgate-
cemetery.org).* **Open** *Apr-Oct* 10am-5pm daily.
Nov-Mar 10am-4pm daily. **Admission** *East
Cemetery* £2; *West Cemetery* tours £3. Booking
essential for West.

Highgate Literary & Scientific Institution ('Lit & Sky')
*11 South Grove, N6 6BS (8340 3343/www.hlsi.
net).* **Open** 10am-5pm Tue-Fri; 10am-4pm Sat.

Kenwood House
*Hampstead Lane, NW3 7JR (8348 1286/
www.english-heritage.org.uk).* **Open** *Apr-Oct*
11am-5pm daily. *Nov-Mar* 11am-4pm daily.
Tours by appointment only. **Admission** free,
donations appreciated. *Tours* £3; £2 concessions;
£1 under-16s.

Lauderdale House
*Highgate Hill, N6 5HG (8348 8716/
www.lauderdalehouse.co.uk).* **Open** 11am-4pm
Tue-Fri; Sat, Sun subject to private bookings;
phone ahead for details. **Admission** free;
donations appreciated.

Whittington Hospital
*Highgate Hill, N19 5NH (7272 3070/
www.whittington.nhs.uk).*

Lauderdale House made the monarch merry.

Contributors

David Aaronovitch has lived in London for most of his life. Born in Hampstead, brought up in Highgate, he now works as a columnist for the *Times*. His first book – *Paddling to Jerusalem* – was an account of a journey by kayak on England's rivers and canals.

Steven Appleby was born in Northumberland in 1956 and now lives with his large and expensive family in south London. His cartoons appear weekly in the *Guardian* and the *Sunday Telegraph*. His other works include the animated television series *Captain Star*, the Radio 4 series *Steven Appleby's Normal Life*, and books such as *Jim – The Nine Lives of a Dysfunctional Cat* (2003), *Steven Appleby's ABC of Childhood* (2005) and, with writer George Mole, *Better Living Through Air Guitar* (2005).

Sue Arnold is a journalist on the *Observer*. She has lived in London since the 1960s, when she moved to Chelsea to work in Fleet Street. All her six children have been brought up in Chelsea.

Nick Barlay is the author of the three acclaimed London novels, *Curvy Lovebox*, *Crumple Zone* and *Hooky Gear*. He has written short stories and award-winning radio plays, and works as a journalist, contributing several London series to the *Times*. He was born in the Big Smoke to Hungarian refugee parents.

Lloyd Bradley is the author of *Bass Culture: When Reggae Was King*. When not contributing to *Mojo*, *ES Magazine* and sundry other publications, he will be lurking in Kentish Town with his wife and two mad children. His favourite walks are to Highbury, from his humidor to his sofa, and any that won't take him off pages 29 and 45 of the *A-Z*.

Robert Elms was born in north London in 1959. Widely published as a journalist and travel writer, he is the author of one novel, *In Search of the Crack*, and one work of non-fiction, *Spain – A Portrait After the General*. An experienced broadcaster on both radio and television, he presents BBC London Live's morning show five days a week.

Gareth Evans is a freelance writer, reviewer and film programmer. He edits the moving image journal *Vertigo*, works for the film pages of *Time Out* and writes widely on cinema, literature, performance and visual culture.

He curated the first season celebrating the work of John Berger in all media, taking place across London in April and May 2005.

Maureen Freely was born in Neptune, New Jersey, and grew up in Istanbul, Turkey. Since graduating from Harvard in 1974, she has lived mostly in England. She is the author of five novels – *Mother's Helper, The Life of the Party, The Stork Club, Under the Vulcania* and *The Other Rebecca* – and three works of non-fiction. She is a senior lecturer at the University of Warwick, where she teaches creative writing, and is a regular contributor to the *Guardian*, the *Observer*, the *Sunday Times*, the *Daily Mail* and the *Independent*.

Bonnie Greer, writer, critic and broadcaster, moved from her native America in 1986, has lived in London ever since, and is pretty sure that out of all the other contributors she is the only one to have taken an oath of allegiance to the Queen. She contributed to *Time Out*'s short story anthology *Neonlit* and was once a *Time Out* theatre critic. Her next novel, *Riding the 903*, will be published in 2006. She is a regular contributor to Radio 4 and Radio 5 as well as BBC2's *Newsnight Review*.

Simon Hoggart, who has lived in a Victorian semi in Twickenham for the past 15 years, is parliamentary sketch writer for the *Guardian*. He also chairs the *News Quiz* on Radio 4, and is wine correspondent for the *Spectator*. With your towpath picnic, he recommends a nice bottle of New Zealand Sauvignon Blanc, chilled but not iced.

Richard Holmes has lived in north London since 1967, except when wandering through France as recounted in his classic *Footsteps: Adventures of a Romantic Biographer* (1985) and *Sidetracks* (2000). His two-volume life of *Coleridge: Early Visions and Darker Reflections* (the final part of which is set in Highgate) won the Whitbread Prize and the Duff Cooper Prize.

Andrew Humphreys is a freelance writer who splits his time between London and Cairo. He's authored or co-authored guides to Egypt and other bits of the Middle East for numerous publishers. He edited the *Time Out Istanbul Guide*, which won the *Observer*/Travelex Guidebook of the Year Award (2000).

Rick Jones is a freelance writer and teacher of modern languages. He was a *Time Out* columnist and music critic for the *Evening Standard*.

Frances Morgan is the editor of *Plan B Magazine*. When not investigating underground music, she can often be found wandering the borough of Hackney, where she has lived and worked as a writer, musician and amateur local history enthusiast since 1998.

Rabbi Julia Neuberger is a Liberal Democrat member of the House of Lords and the former chief executive of the King's Fund, an independent health care charity that works to improve the health of Londoners. She became a rabbi in 1977, and served the South London Liberal Synagogue for 12 years. She has been a fellow of Harvard Medical School, is a trustee of the Imperial War Museum and is an adviser to the Sainsbury Centre for Mental Health. She is also the author of several books, on Judaism, women, health care ethics and caring for dying people. Her latest book, *The Moral State We're In* (2005), examines how we treat the most disadvantaged in our society. She also broadcasts frequently.

Courttia Newland is the author of the critically acclaimed novels *The Scholar, Society Within* and *Snakeskin*. He has contributed to the anthologies *Disco 2000, New Writing 8, Afrobeat, Rites of Spring* and *The Time Out Book of London Short Stories Volume 2*, and is co-editor of an anthology of new black writing in Britain, *IC3*. He also writes plays, scripts and essays, and lives in west London.

Liza Picard was born in 1927, and was called to the bar by Gray's Inn in 1949, but did not practise. She took up writing when she retired from the civil service. Always a keen social historian, she was frustrated that books never seemed to have the kind of detail she wanted to know, so she wrote them herself – *Restoration London* (1997), *Dr Johnson's London* (2000), *Elizabeth's London* (2003) and *Victorian London* (2005), published by Weidenfeld and Nicolson. After many years of living in the heart of London, in Gray's Inn, she has moved to Oxford.

Mark Pilkington is a writer and the editor of *Strange Attractor Journal*. While he would probably look good in a cape, he does not practise ritual magic.

Nicholas Royle was born in Manchester in 1963. He is the author of five novels – *Counterparts, Saxophone Dreams, The Matter of the Heart, The Director's Cut* and *Antwerp* – in addition to more than 100 short stories. He has edited 12 anthologies including *A Book of Two Halves* (Phoenix), *The Time Out Book of New*

York Short Stories (Penguin) and *Dreams Never End* (Tindal Street Press). He lives in Manchester with his wife and two children.

Arthur Smith is a comedian, writer and broadcaster who comes from a long line of south Londoners. He lives in Balham, frequently refers to it in his work and likes to believe he is the Mayor. He also claims never to have been to north London.

Simon Thurley is a Londoner by adoption. After university at Bedford College, London, and the Courtauld Institute, he was the curator of the Historic Royal Palaces for eight years. In 1998 he became the director of the Museum of London. He has written and broadcasted extensively on London, the royal palaces and the royal court. He lives in the East End.

Claire Tomalin was born in St Peter's Square, on the borders of Hammersmith and Chiswick, and has lived in London most of her life. She has worked in publishing, been literary editor of the *New Statesman* and the *Sunday Times*, and written books about several Londoners, including *The Life and Death of Mary Wollstonecraft* and *Mrs Jordan's Profession,* and a study of Charles Dickens and his mistress Nelly Ternan, *The Invisible Woman*. *Samuel Pepys: The Unequalled Self*, her book about the great Londoner who inspired the walk described here, was published in 2002; she is currently working on a book about Thomas Hardy.

Nigel Williams is a novelist, playwright and film-maker, whose novels include *The Wimbledon Poisoner* and *Fortysomething* (Penguin). His plays include the international hit *Class Enemy*. He lives at the top of Putney Hill with his wife and three sons. He likes mushrooms.

Joy Wotton is a non-fiction book editor. She worked with London historian EJ Burford on many of his books, and wrote *Private Vices, Public Virtues – Bawdry in London From Elizabethan Times to the Regency* with him. Co-editor of *The Encyclopedia of School Stories*, she edits a journal about Elinor Brent-Dyer's Chalet School. She has walked the Thames Path and the Grand Union Canal, and lives in Bow, where Nicholas Nickleby moved when he became respectable.

Nick Wyke is a freelance journalist for the *Times*. He has written the *Insider's Guide to Rome*, and contributed to the *City Secrets: London* guidebook and the *Time Out* guide to Athens. He lives in Battersea, between Clapham and Wandsworth Commons, and is writing a play about distant neighbour William Wilberforce for the bicentenary of the abolition of slavery in 2007.

Further reading

Fiction

Peter Ackroyd *Hawksmoor; The House of Doctor Dee; Great Fire of London.* Arcane London.

Martin Amis *London Fields.* Darts and drinking.

JG Ballard *Crash; Concrete Island; High-Rise.* Early '70s visions of London now becoming reality.

Jonathan Coe *The Dwarves of Death.* Mystery, music, malevolence and Andrew Lloyd Webber.

Wilkie Collins *The Woman in White.* A midnight encounter has dire consequences.

Joseph Conrad *The Secret Agent.* Seedy Soho.

Charles Dickens *Oliver Twist; David Copperfield; Bleak House; Our Mutual Friend.* Four of the master's most London-centric novels.

Sir Arthur Conan Doyle *The Complete Sherlock Holmes.* Sleuthing shenanigans.

Christopher Fowler *Soho Black.* Walking dead.

Graham Greene *The End of the Affair.* Adultery, Catholicism and Clapham Common.

Patrick Hamilton *20,000 Streets Under the Sky; Hangover Square.* Yearning romantic Soho trilogy; love and death in darkest Earl's Court.

M John Harrison *Travel Arrangements.* Some of these stories have superb London settings.

Oscar Moore *A Matter of Life and Sex.* Gay life in London under the shadow of AIDS.

Stewart Home *Come Before Christ and Murder Love.* Paranoia, food sex, tour-guide psycho-rap.

Maxim Jakubowski (ed) *London Noir.* Crime.

Maria Lexton (vol 1)/**Nicholas Royle** (vol 2) (eds) *Time Out Book of London Short Stories Volumes 1 & 2.* London-set short stories.

Colin MacInnes *City of Spades; Absolute Beginners.* Coffee and jazz, Soho and Notting Hill.

Derek Marlowe *A Dandy in Aspic.* Spy yarn.

Michael Moorcock *Mother London; King of the City; London Bone.* Love-letters to London.

Iris Murdoch *Under the Net.* Adventures of a talented but wastrel writer.

Courttia Newland *The Scholar.* Estate life.

Kim Newman *The Quorum.* Docklands intrigue.

George Orwell *Keep the Aspidistra Flying.* Saga of struggling writer and bookshop assistant.

Chris Petit *Robinson; The Hard Shoulder.* Soho and Kilburn, respectively, get the Petit treatment.

Derek Raymond *He Died With His Eyes Open; The Devil's Home on Leave; How the Dead Live; I Was Dora Suarez.* The darkest London *noir*.

Nicholas Royle *The Matter of the Heart; The Director's Cut.* Portraits of abandoned London.

Geoff Ryman *253.* Tube trouble.

William Sansom *Selected Short Stories.* Lyrical tales of Londoners at large.

Will Self *Grey Area; The Sweet Smell of Psychosis; Great Apes.* Metropolitan satire.

Iain Sinclair *Downriver; Radon Daughters; White Chappell, Scarlet Tracings.* The Thames's own *Heart of Darkness* by London's laureate; William Hope Hodgson via the London Hospital; Ripper murders and book dealers.

Muriel Spark *The Ballad of Peckham Rye.* The devil incarnate spreads mayhem in Peckham.

Barbara Vine *King Solomon's Carpet.* More trouble on the Tube.

Guides & reference

Ian Cunningham *A Reader's Guide to Writers' London.* Smart, yet edgy, illustrated guide.

Ed Glinert *The Literary Guide to London.* Glinert follows in the footsteps of writers.

Nick Rennison *Waterstone's Guide to London Writing; London Blue Plaque Guide.* Erudite study of capital letters; guide to who lived where.

Ben Weinreb & Christopher Hibbert (eds) *The London Encyclopaedia.* Indispensable A-Z.

History

Peter Ackroyd *London: The Biography.* Fascinating, wilfully obscurantist history.

Daniel Farson *Soho in the Fifties.* Pubs, people.

Stephen Inwood *A History of London.* Recent, readable history.

Jack London *The People of the Abyss.* Extreme poverty in the East End.

Nick Merriman (ed) *The Peopling of London.* Fascinating account of 2,000 years of settlement.

Samuel Pepys *Diaries.* Fires, plagues, bordellos.

Roy Porter *London: A Social History.* All-encompassing history of the capital.

Miscellaneous non-fiction

Felix Barker & Ralph Hyde *London As it Might Have Been.* Schemes that never made it.

Derek Hammond *London, England.* Witty, enthusiastic celebration of the capital.

George Orwell *Down and Out in Paris and London.* Autobiographical account.

Edward Platt *Leadville.* A40 – a social history.

Iain Sinclair *Lights Out For the Territory.* The time-warp visionary walks across London.

Richard Trench *London Under London.* Trench digs deep to expose the subterranean city.

Walks for...

Architecture

Nick Barlay – almost every age and type of building along the A5. Maureen Freely – protest outside some of the finest establishment buildings. Simon Hoggart – Ham and Marble Hill houses, and Georgian glories. Rick Jones – Roman ruins and modern developments. Rabbi Julia Neuberger – Victorian hospital façades, cloisters at Guy's. Courttia Newland – squares and crescents in Notting Hill. Liza Picard – cloistered peace in Temple and Lincoln's Inn. Simon Thurley – 18th-century homes in the ever-changing East End. Joy Wotton – retrace some of the City's medieval street-plan. Nick Wyke – the stuccoed elegance of Pimlico.

Film & literature

Gareth Evans – film locations and Harry Palmer remembered. Bonnie Greer – Rimbaud and other literary exiles. Richard Holmes – when Sammy met Johnny. Nicholas Royle – locate a film on the South Bank.

Gardens & parks

Sue Arnold – find peace in the pagoda of Battersea Park. Simon Hoggart – meadows, parks and gardens along the Thames. Richard Holmes – a grand conclusion on the Heath. Andrew Humphreys – Middle East bordering on Hyde Park. Frances Morgan – linger in child-friendly Clissold Park. Arthur Smith – the open spaces of Tooting and Wandsworth Commons. Nigel Williams – wooded paths and open fields in Putney, Wimbledon and Richmond.

History

Nick Barlay – from old Watling Street to the modern A5. Maureen Freely – suffragette sites across the West End. Rick Jones – Roman wall. Rabbi Julia Neuberger – south London's health provision, past and present. Liza Picard – the king and city restored. Mark Pilkington – step in the shadow of occultist Aleister Crowley. Simon Thurley – from immigrant poverty to multinational plenty. Claire Tomalin – Pepys's walk to Greenwich. Joy Wotton – Whittington's medieval city, Southwark's bawdy past. Nick Wyke – Pimlico from Cubitt to Churchill.

Nature

David Aaronovitch – birds of the waterways. Nick Barlay – there's a hide at Brent Reservoir. Lloyd Bradley – Highgate Wood hosts a feast of wildlife. Simon Hoggart – wildlife along the Thames. Frances Morgan – Clissold Park's lakes and deer. Simon Thurley – visit Stepping Stones City Farm. Claire Tomalin – pass by Surrey Docks Farm and an Ecology Park. Nigel Williams – protective does in Richmond Park.

Night-time

Steven Appleby – a South Bank story. Andrew Humphreys – the late-night neon of the Edgware Road. Nicholas Royle – start at 5pm, catch a film by 8pm.

Parents with children

Lloyd Bradley – two woods, one dark and empty… Robert Elms – short and sweet, with two playgrounds. Simon Hoggart – river, ferries, parks, gardens. Richard Holmes – after the hill, almost traffic free. Frances Morgan – graves, drinks and deer. Arthur Smith – parks, ponds and a lido. Nigel Williams – mushroom picking in Richmond Park.

Religion & death

Nick Barlay – churches, mosques, temples and synagogues. Rick Jones – City churches and churchyards. Frances Morgan – cosy Abney Park Cemetery. Nigel Williams – tangled Victorian charm in Putney Vale Cemetery.

Shopping

Sue Arnold – it may only be a short stretch, but it is the King's Road. Andrew Humphreys – sample Arabian delights and Whiteley's lights. Courttia Newland – Portobello Market, a Saturday institution.

Views

Lloyd Bradley – see all before you from Suicide Bridge. Simon Hoggart – sweeping stretches of the Thames. Richard Holmes – survey London's skyline from Hampstead's crown. Claire Tomalin – shifting sightlines through Rotherhithe and Deptford.

Water or woods

David Aaronovitch – canals, creeks and rivers. Lloyd Bradley – Highgate and Queen's, so near and yet so far. Steven Appleby – reflect on the Thames at night. Nick Barlay – the Brent Reservoir offers tranquillity and wildlife. Simon Hoggart – the Thames path from Richmond to Twickenham, and ferry rides to boot. Simon Thurley – take the Regent's Canal out of Mile End Park. Claire Tomalin – from Tower Bridge to Greenwich, riverside. Nigel Williams – woodland in the parks of south-west London.

Central London
by Area

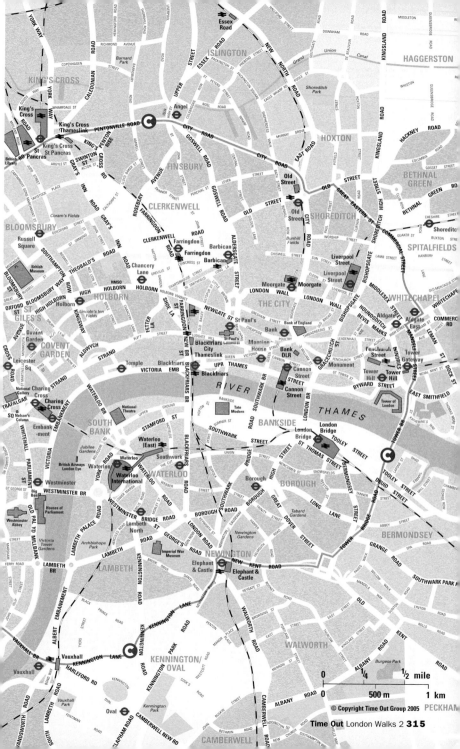

Index

Index

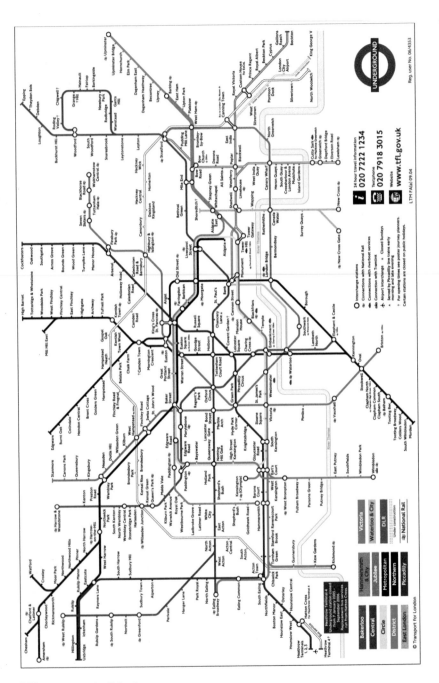